Public Knowledge in Cold War Poland

This book explores the public debates among scholars that took place in Early Cold War Poland. The author challenges the traditional narrative on the 'Sovietisation' of Central and Eastern European countries and proposes to see this process not as a spread of Marxist ideology or a Soviet institutional model, but as an attempt to force scholars to rapidly adopt new academic and civic virtues.

This book argues that this project failed to succeed in Poland and shows how the struggle against these new virtues united both Marxist and non-Marxist scholars. While covering the arc of Polish scholarly debates, the author invites the reader to go beyond Poland and to use 'virtues' as a framework for reflections on both the foundations of scholarly practice and the 'nature' of authoritarian regimes with their ambition to teach scholars how to be 'virtuous.'

Alexej Lochmatow is a Walter Benjamin Research Fellow at the University of Erfurt. He got his PhD from the University of Cologne and the Tadeusz Manteuffel Institute of History of the Polish Academy of Sciences. His research interest lies in the history of science and humanities, public knowledge, and intelligence research.

Poland: Transnational Histories

Series Editors

Maciej Górny, Polish Academy of Sciences
Catherine Gousseff, Collège de France
Maciej Janowski, Polish Academy of Sciences
Miloš Řezník, German Historical Institute Warsaw
Magdalena Saryusz-Wolska, German Historical Institute Warsaw
Keely Stauter-Halsted, University of Illinois at Chicago

The borders of Poland have shifted dynamically throughout the country's history, expanding and shrinking (or even vanishing), moving between the Baltic and the Black Seas, and the Oder and the Dnieper Rivers. Not unlike other states in the region, the spatial dynamics of Poland's history have impacted its social structure: Poland has been home to diverse religious and ethnic groups, who migrated, assimilated, resisted assimilation, persevered or suppressed others. These forces of moving populations, shifting frontiers, and mixing of peoples have resulted in a complex and dynamic set of histories in the Polish space, a phenomenon as yet poorly understood in the wider scholarly community.

The books in this series aims at presenting original research on the shifts and movements characteristic of Polish history, but that is also embedded in broader developments beyond Poland's borders. The works in the series examine the complexities and entanglements of Poland's past as a rule rather than as an exception. They consider the ways particular elements and trends in Polish history resonate globally, on the one hand, and the impact of global trends on internal Polish developments, on the other.

Public Knowledge in Cold War Poland
Scholarly Battles and the Clash of Virtues, 1945–1956
Alexej Lochmatow

For more information about this series, please visit: https://www.routledge.com/Poland-Transnational-Histories/book-series/POLSKA

Public Knowledge in Cold War Poland
Scholarly Battles and the Clash of Virtues, 1945–1956

Alexej Lochmatow

LONDON AND NEW YORK

First published 2024
by Routledge
4 Park Square, Milton Park, Abingdon, Oxon OX14 4RN

and by Routledge
605 Third Avenue, New York, NY 10158

Routledge is an imprint of the Taylor & Francis Group, an informa business

© 2024 Alexej Lochmatow

The right of Alexej Lochmatow to be identified as author of this work has been asserted in accordance with sections 77 and 78 of the Copyright, Designs and Patents Act 1988.

All rights reserved. No part of this book may be reprinted or reproduced or utilised in any form or by any electronic, mechanical, or other means, now known or hereafter invented, including photocopying and recording, or in any information storage or retrieval system, without permission in writing from the publishers.

Trademark notice: Product or corporate names may be trademarks or registered trademarks, and are used only for identification and explanation without intent to infringe.

British Library Cataloguing-in-Publication Data
A catalogue record for this book is available from the British Library

Library of Congress Cataloging-in-Publication Data
Names: Lochmatow, Alexej, author.
Title: Public knowledge in cold war Poland : scholarly battles and the clash of virtues, 1945-1956 / Alexej Lochmatow.
Description: New York : Routledge, 2024. | Series: Poland: transnational histories | Includes bibliographical references and index.
Identifiers: LCCN 2023017614 (print) | LCCN 2023017615 (ebook) | ISBN 9781032549491 (hardback) | ISBN 9781032549538 (paperback) | ISBN 9781003428251 (ebook)
Subjects: LCSH: Scholars--Poland. | Academic disputations--Poland. | Learning and scholarship--Moral and ethical aspects. | Professional ethics. | Poland--Intellectual life--1945-1989.
Classification: LCC DK4437 .L63 2024 (print) | LCC DK4437 (ebook) | DDC 943.805--dc23/eng/20230502
LC record available at https://lccn.loc.gov/2023017614
LC ebook record available at https://lccn.loc.gov/2023017615

ISBN: 9781032549491 (hbk)
ISBN: 9781032549538 (pbk)
ISBN: 9781003428251 (ebk)

DOI: 10.4324/9781003428251

Typeset in Times New Roman
by KnowledgeWorks Global Ltd.

To my parents Maxim and Marina

Contents

Acknowledgements   x

Introduction   1

What the book is about 2
How the history of post-war Poland has been written 3
How 'virtues' can open a new perspective on the history
    of public knowledge 5
What is new in this book? 7
Structure of the book 8

1   From the War to the 'Gentle Revolution'   17

Stalin's 'Polish Project' and 'Missionary-Intellectuals' 18
The 'gentle revolution' project and the virtue of
    'progressiveness' 22
Łódź as an intellectual oasis of 'new Poland' 26
'Kuźnica' and the 'radical cultural programme' 28
'Scientific' anti-authoritarianism and political ambitions of
    Polish sociology 31
Trying to avoid isolation: Catholic groups in the intellectual
    landscape of Poland 32
Bolesław Piasecki and 'progressive Catholics' 35

2   The Many Faces of the Soviet Union   48

The 'guidelines' of propaganda 51
'Discovering' Russian culture in a non-Stalinist way 53
Soviet scholarship as a foreign world 56
The 'friend' and the 'argument': The use of the 'Soviet
    Union' 60

3 The Teachers of Virtues: The French and the Early
   Post-War Project   70

   How are we seen? Representing Poland in France 73
   The French teach the Poles and vice versa 74
   French heroes of the Polish Catholic agenda 78
   Catholics 'should' adopt the French example 84

4 The Polish Intelligentsia and an Anti-Authoritarian Vision
   of Society   93

   The treason against 'progressiveness' 95
   Between nation and academia 102
   The anti-authoritarian vision of the 'new' intelligentsia 104

5 Between 'Outdated' Marxism and 'Updated' Catholicism   114

   Uncertain steps of Marxism 115
   'Quasi-religion' and 'anti-progressive' Marxism 118
   The Marxian response 121
   Unequal opponents: Catholics vs. Marxists 125
   The fragile 'compromise' on 'non-reactionary' Catholicism 131

6 The 'Failed' Quest for Unity   141

   The Cold War context and the tightening of the regime 144
   *Disciplining 'public discussions': All roads lead to the Soviet
     Union 146*
   *The Wrocław Congress and the defeat of the 'gentle
     revolution' 149*
   Reshaping the public life 151
   An unfortunate quest for 'concordia' 154

7 The School of 'New Virtues'   168

   The power and powerlessness of institutions 168
   The missionaries of new virtues 171
   Fighting the 'stubbornness' of non-Marxist scholars 177
   Can a 'non-virtuous' scholar write a textbook? 182
   The headstrong 'students' and failed teaching 185

8 '1956' as a 'Diagnosis' and 'Prognosis'   197

   Losing the control over the public sphere 198
   The quest for honesty 201

Between France and the Soviet Union, there is ... Poland 205
Polish academics and the fiasco of Stalinisation 208
Adam Schaff and his good conscience 212
Schaff's students against Stalinist virtues 214

Epilogue: The Concept of Virtues as a Lens   227

Virtuous battles in post-war Poland 227
Looking beyond Poland 230

Bibliography   235
Index   253

Acknowledgements

Boris A. Filippov was my history teacher at school, whom I, a 12-year-old boy, first told that I would like to become a historian (a very strange thought for a teenager). Of course, my interests have changed dramatically throughout my life, but I always was thankful to him for the aspiration to read books instead of textbooks and to challenge the conformist interpretations of history. Maybe it is crucial for the appearance of this book that Polish history has been Boris Filippov's research focus. He brought me to Poland and introduced me to his Polish friends, the former Solidarność fellow Krzysztof Strachalski and his wife Bożena Strachalska. Dinner conversations with them became a tradition that I miss very much if I cannot return to Warsaw for a long time. I am also very obliged to Anna Miśkiewicz and her family for their touching care of me during my first stays in Poland. My philosophy professor, Petr Riabov, also warmly supported my interest in Polish history. His outstanding commitment to scholarship and his readiness to read and discuss with me all my texts about Poland encouraged me to develop my 'Polish' interests.

I am obliged to Vsevolod E. Voronin, Mikhail V. Ponomarev, and Andrei V. Klimenko, who were my first academic supervisors, as well as to all my professors from the Moscow Pedagogical State University, the University of Cologne, the University of Warsaw, and the Higher School of Economics (Moscow). I am especially thankful to Jerzy Axer and Jan Kieniewicz from the Faculty of 'Artes Liberales' of the University of Warsaw; Ingo Eser from the University of Cologne; Elena Y. Zubkova from the Higher School of Economics; and Gennady F. Matveev from the Moscow State University for their helpful comments on my student papers on the post-war Polish–Soviet relationships. During my studies, I had the great fortune to work as a research assistant at the Poletayev Institute for Theoretical and Historical Studies in the Humanities. I always considered Irina M. Savelieva, the co-founder and then the director of the institute, an outstanding scholar. Therefore, it was a great honour and responsibility to work under her supervision. There, I firstly met Alexander N. Dmitriev, one of the most knowledgeable scholars I have ever met, who became my close supervisor. All my texts (including this book) would be much worse without his insightful comments that I appreciate very much. I also thank Aleksei Pleshkov for our long discussions about virtues ethics, Kirill A. Levinson for instructing me in some aspects of Polish–Prussian History, Sergei

Matveev for our nice scholarly conversations, as well as all other research fellows of the Poletayev Institute for the great time I had at the institute.

The idea of this book was born in Cologne, when I was studying on the MA-programme Cultural and Intellectual History between East and West (CIH). I am grateful to Ekaterina M. Boltunova, Alsu N. Biktasheva, and Yulia V. Ivanova who made my move to the University of Cologne possible. I really appreciate the support of Gasan Gusejnov with whom I had the pleasure to speak a lot during my studies here. Meanwhile, all this would not have come about without Jörg Schulte who designed, created, and supervised the CIH. My hours-long scholarly debates with Jörg will always be a part of the good memories of my study times. Thanks to the CIH, I met excellent scholars Ágnes Kriza, Dragana Grbić, Bogdana Paskaleva, Mina Đurić, Monika Rzeczycka, and many others. I am very thankful to the moderator of the CIH Inge Wanner and the librarian of the Slavonic Institute Dagmar Klingner for our wonderful discussions on various cultural topics. It is difficult to count how many hours I spend speaking to Jan Czarnecki about Polish history, poetry, and literature. It is not an exaggeration to say that the first idea of my PhD thesis was born in conversations with Jörg Schulte and Jan Czarnecki who also found time to comment on the first drafts of my project proposal. Thanks to Jan's close supervision at the early stages of my research, I could present my project to Italian academia and meet outstanding scholars Luigi Marinelli and Marcello Piacentini whose warm support and constructive feedback helped me very much in my work.

This book would not have been written without the a.r.t.e.s. Graduate School for the Humanities (Cologne). Thanks to the a.r.t.e.s., I was able to receive a unique fellowship within the Horizon 2020 project by the Marie Skłodowska-Curie Actions that allowed me to concentrate on my research without the constant search for new funding. I am very obliged to the director Andreas Speer for his support in all my bureaucratic troubles and helpful comments on my project. Andreas's academic activity inspired me to think that an engaged scholarship can make the world a bit better. I am very thankful to the a.r.t.e.s. team: Artemis Klidis-Honecker, Sabine Folger-Fonfara, Florian Petersen, Alexander van Wickeren, Laura Morris, Felix Krause, and all other team members. Nobody helped me more with my bureaucratic problems than the Vice Managing Director Aiko Wolter. I warmly thank Aiko for everything he did for me. At the a.r.t.e.s., I met excellent colleagues Lisbeth Matzer, Sophia Egbert, Merle Ingenfeld, Margarita Sardak, Guido Alt, Ina Schall, Christoph Burdich. Thanks to them and many other Artists, my time in Cologne was full of exiting intellectual experiences.

I am very thankful to Jan Surman, whose incredible energy and impressing scholarly creativity never cease to inspire me. It was Jan who introduced me to the colleagues from the Herder Institute in Marburg. There, I first presented the project of this book at the sessions of the Herder Institute Research Academy (HIRA). I am very grateful and obliged to Peter Haslinger, the director of the institute, who could always find time to help me with all my problems despite his very busy agenda. Without his advice, my academic life would be much more difficult. The co-supervision of the HIRA-colloquia by Heidi Hein-Kircher and Anna Veronika Wendland, as well as the diligent moderation by Tatsiana Astrouskaya, made

Marburg an extraordinary intellectual milieu. There I met Christoph Maisch, Svetlana Boltovska, Philipp Kröger, Friedrich Cain, Sophie Schwarzmaier, and many other excellent colleagues. Their critical feedback was crucial for my book. I am especially thankful to Friedrich, who always found time to make very helpful comments on my texts (with all his irony and wit) and to Sophie with whom we spent a lot of time when walking along Vistula and discussing our projects during our research stays in Warsaw.

When working on this book, I was closely affiliated with the Institute of History of the Polish Academy of Sciences. I warmly thank the director of the Institute, Maciej Janowski who, with his enormous academic integrity, created a wonderful intellectual milieu. I am very grateful to Marcin Wolniewicz, Mariusz Kulik, Adam Kożuchowski, Aleksander Łupienko, Joanna Nalewajko-Kulikov, Anna Nowakowska-Wierzchoś, Iwona Dadej, Paweł Lesisz, and all other colleagues from the institute for their critical feedback on my work. I am very obliged to the secretary of the Institute Elżbieta Grabarczyk for her enormous work on solving all bureaucratic problems around my enrolment as a cotutelle PhD student. I am very thankful to the director of the institute's library Aleksandra Czapelska and her team, Jolanta Epsztein and Magdalena Rege. Their kind assistance helped me to find very important materials for this book and to master the digital resources of Polish libraries.

I am very thankful to the team of the German Historical Institute in Warsaw for their support during the final stage of my work on this book. I am very grateful to the director of the institute, Miloš Řezník, who found time to give me a couple of useful words of advice on how to develop my project. I am also thankful to the vice-director Ruth Leiserowitz who supervised me during my stay at the institute. The brilliant scholarly environment of the GHI made the institute's colloquium one of the most productive discussions on my project. I am especially thankful to Magdalena Saryusz-Wolska, Felix Ackermann, Zofia Wóycicka, and Michael Zok for their comments and useful suggestions on my project. I very much appreciate my conversations with Viktoriia Serhiienko about various historical, cultural, and literary topics. My stay at the GHI would not have been so easy without the kind support of the administrative staff Grażyna Ślepowrońska, Monika Karamuz, Krzysztof Zdanowski, as well as the librarians Maciej Kordelasiński and Artur Koczara.

When working on this book, I had the pleasure to be a visiting fellow at the *Centre d'études des mondes russe, caucasien et centre-européen* at the *École des Hautes Études en Sciences Sociales* (EHESS). I warmly thank Catherine Gousseff who supervised me at the EHESS and Morgane Labbé whose expertise in the history of science in Poland helped me a lot in my work. At the scholarly events organised by the EHESS, the German Historical Institute in Paris, and the *Centre Scientifique à Paris* of the Polish Academy of Sciences, I could discuss my project with the most qualified scholars in my research field. I am very thankful to Maciej Forycki, then the director of the *Centre Scientifique*, for allowing me to work with the local archive. It was a great pleasure to work with the materials from the *Bibliothèque Polonaise de Paris* and the archive of the Literary Institute based around

Acknowledgements xiii

the journal 'Kultura' in Maisons-Laffitte. I warmly thank the colleagues from both institutions for they kind help.

In Paris, I had the fortune to speak to the philosopher and historian Krzysztof Pomian who witnessed the events described in this book and told me many exiting stories about the protagonists of my research, whom he knew personally. Two other persons whose personal stories helped me in my work, unfortunately, will not be able to read these lines. Wiktoria Śliwowska (1931–2021), a brilliant scholar with an incredible biography, and Jerzy W. Borejsza (1935–2019), a prominent historian and the son of a central figure of my research, died when I was working on this book. Their fascinating anecdotes and impressive academic integrity inspired me very much in my work. Włodzimierz Borodziej's early death in the July of 2021 was a big shock for those who knew him. His comments and suggestions as well as his help in my search for relevant sources cannot be overestimated.

I warmly thank Grzegorz Bąbiak for his kind readiness to assist me in my work not only with his deep knowledge of the subject, but also by sharing with me very important sources. When working on the book, I had the pleasure to speak to Piotr Kosicki whose comments and suggestions were very helpful for my research. I also thank Przemysław Pazik for our nice conversations on the history of Catholic social thought in Poland. I am deeply obliged to Ewa Bérard who not only readily discussed with me all my ideas but also introduced me to prominent Polish intellectuals and artists Agnieszka Holland, Adam Michnik, Marek and Anna Radziwon. Speaking to them was a very important intellectual experience that definitively helped me in my work.

When working on this book, I had the fortune to contribute to a volume edited by my friends Jade McGlynn and Lucian George. I thank them a lot for their patience with me, critical feedback on my writings, and wonderful conversations on all possible topics. I am deeply obliged to Christian Fleck whose insightful comments on my texts and enormous support made my work much easier. I warmly thank Łukasz Mikołajewski for our interesting discussions on Polish intellectual history and his helpful feedback on my papers. I really appreciate my discussions with Adela Hîncu, an outstanding specialist in the history of the social sciences and humanities under state socialism. Adela introduced me to her research group co-moderated by another brilliant colleague Isidora Grubački. Thanks to them, I could discuss my ideas with Olga Byrska, Zsófia Lóránd, Ana Lolua, Emily Steinhauer, Kristina Andělová, Raul Carstocea, and many other excellent scholars. I had the great fortune to speak to John Connelly, a leading specialist in the history of science and scholarship in Central and Eastern Europe. I am very thankful for his helpful comments on my work in general and on the proposal of this book in particular. I warmly appreciate my conversations with Fabian Link, a prominent expert in the history of the social sciences in Germany, whose deep knowledge of the subject helped me to open a new perspective on the issues discussed in this book. I am deeply obliged to Galin Tihanov who is one of a few scholars who traced the development of my ideas from the MA thesis to the final version of the manuscript of this book. I spent many hours speaking to Galin Tihanov whose enormous support and insightful comments on my writings I appreciate very much.

My special gratitude goes to Maike Lehmann who supervised my PhD thesis at the University of Cologne. Despite all difficulties, Maike was always there for me and helped me to find solutions to the biggest problems. Her patience and deep knowledge of how the academic world works helped me a lot in bringing this project to its final stage. I am very thankful to my second supervisor, Ralph Jessen whose versatile knowledge of the historical contexts around my topic and deep engagement with my work were a great inspiration for me. It is difficult to express my gratitude to Maciej Górny, my supervisor from the Polish side. Besides the fact that he is presumably the only living person (except myself) who has read all the academic texts I have ever published, Maciej did a great deal of work in making the existence of this book possible. His inimitable sense of humour and unyielding readiness to support me helped me a lot through all difficulties I faced. I am very thankful to Maciej's family – his wife Justyna, sons Mikołaj and Marceli, parents Michał and Bożenna, brother Antoni and sister-in-law Jagoda with their son Ignacy who cared of me as a family member.

I was working on the final version of this book in the welcoming environment of the University of Erfurt. I am deeply obliged and thankful to Bernhard Kleeberg for creating a unique intellectual milieu in Erfurt and his enormous engagement with me and my work. It was Bernhard who, together with Dietlind Hüchtker, Karin Reichenbach, Katrin Steffen, Jan Surman, and Friedrich Cain, founded the research group 'Political Epistemologies of Central and Eastern Europe (PECEE)' that provided me with an important theoretical framework for my work. I thank my colleagues from Erfurt Antonia Purk, Verena Lehmbrock, Sandra Janßen, Carola Oßmer, Anna Möllers, Erik Kaiser, and Meike Katzek for our interesting discussions and their critical feedback on my ideas. I especially thank Dirk Schuck for the insights into the political theory and virtuous ethics that he gave me during our long conversations. I thank the members of the administrative staff Bettina Waechter, Petra Meersteiner, Monika Leetz, Katrin Lumma, and Maximilian Kästner for their support regarding various bureaucratic issues. I am deeply obliged to Carmen Wójcik, Clara Steinbrenner, and Paul Stoll who helped me with the final preparations of the manuscripts.

This book would be definitively worse without the critical remarks and insightful suggestions of the prominent scholars Rafał Stobiecki, Eryk Krasucki, and Bartosz Kaliski. I am deeply obliged to Jim Wilson, Edward Wise, and Rebecca Shaw for making my English texts readable. I warmly thank the managing editor of the book series 'Poland: Transnational Histories' Magdalena Saryusz-Wolska and the Routledge editors Robert Langham and Kaustav Ghosh for helping me to prepare this manuscript to publication.

This book would not have been written without the constant support of my closest friends. I thank Jonas Löffler, Wiebke Rademacher, and their little daughter Rahel for their kind and warm care of me. My long and interesting discussions with Andrei Ilin were also a great support to me. I am very thankful to Johanna and Jörg Hügel for their attempts (some of which were successful) to encourage me for a trip and thus to bring me out of my routine. My sincere conversations with Dorota

Nowak were always a great joy for me. I also warmly thank Luisa Mollweide for her selfless engagement with me and our long discussions about all possible topics.

I am very thankful to my family – my grandparents Raisa and Mikhail, my sister Lisa, and my brother Nikita. My grandmother Tatiana, who spent her childhood in Erfurt where I wrote these lines, unfortunately died in 2021. This book is dedicated to my parents Maxim and Marina who have saved dozens of children's lives while I was working on this book. I was writing these lines, when my Ukrainian relatives, friends, colleagues, and the whole Ukrainian people were suffering under the aggressive and devastating war against their country. No scholarship can change what has happened.

Erfurt, 2023.

Introduction

'Mein Führer, the time is not very favourable for us. Nevertheless, from the historical point of view, it is a blessing that the Poles are doing this. We will be out of there in five or six weeks. And after that, Warsaw, the capital, the head, the intelligence of this former nation of 16–17 million Poles, this nation that has been blocking the East for 700 years and has been in our way since the first battle of Tannenberg, will be destroyed. And then, historically, the Polish question will no longer be a big problem for our children and for everyone who comes after us, and even for us.'[1] These words Reichsführer-SS Heinrich Himmler addressed to Hitler after hearing of the beginning of the Warsaw Uprising (August 1944). Even when facing the defeat of their whole campaign, the Nazi leaders found inspiration in the opportunity to destroy one more European capital. Himmler's supercilious description of such brutal acts as killing people and levelling buildings formed part of the reality in which humanity spent at least the first half of the 20th century. The division of the world into 'nations' and 'cultures,' especially in the most radical racist versions, led not only to the segregation of people due to their origin, but also to this use of language to legitimise acts of violence through reference to the struggle between 'ideals' and 'cultural phenomena.'

Meanwhile, the ruins of Warsaw, which had been destroyed by Nazi troops before their retreat from the Polish capital, were no more eloquent an illustration of the state of cultural life in Poland than the intensive discussions in cultural and academic journals, which had not stopped under the dire conditions. Even though it is difficult to picture side by side the image of a destroyed Warsaw with the reams of content produced undeterred in the cultural and academic debates of the underground press, both perspectives form the heritage of post-war Poland. The effort of the Nazi administration to remove all signs of Polish academic and cultural identity from public and personal life offered a special motivation for scholars to resist the occupants at the intellectual level. It was not only the ideological fight against Nazi occupation, but also the continuation of purely academic discussions that became the proof of the solidity of the principles upon which academic practice was based.[2]

The social conditions in which Polish academia entered the early post-war period were no less unique than those of the wartime cataclysms. The liberation of Poland from Nazi occupation made the post-war Polish state a meeting point for those who had been forcibly divided for several years and thus had experienced the

DOI: 10.4324/9781003428251-1

war very differently. This division was much deeper than it appeared at first glance. In post-war Poland, there were people who had collaborated with the Nazi authorities living alongside those who were deeply involved in the resistance movement. There were employees of the public institutions created by the Nazis who had simultaneously taken part in the underground activity and thus helped both forces. There were people who, after the war began, had left Poland for the Soviet Union, and those who emigrated through continental Europe to Great Britain, the USA, or Latin America. There were the Jews who were former prisoners of the Nazi concentration camps and those who had informed the Nazi government about the places where Jews were hiding. There were communists, former prisoners of Soviet prisons, and communist former prisoners of Soviet prisons. This list, which is far from complete, shows the scale of the problems that provide a backdrop to the issues that will be discussed in this book.

Of course, these characteristics were not exclusive to Poland. There are many respects in which the Polish experience, especially in the early post-war years, was very similar, or even identical to the general European one. The whole of continental Europe faced cruel antisemitism and witnessed the civil rights violations of Jews before and during the war and then had to coexist with those Jews who survived and returned to their homes (which were sometimes already occupied by other families). The extrajudicial punishments, clashes between the members of anti-Nazi resistance groups and those who collaborated with the Nazi regime, the return of emigrants from exile, and the mass migrations in search of a place to settle were common experiences for all 'continental' Europeans.[3]

However, the political situation in post-war Poland was, in many respects, unique. In the last years of the war, Poland not only found itself in the sphere of influence of the Soviet Union, but it also became one of the key Western military bridgeheads of Soviet troops. Even before other countries from the Soviet sphere of influence started to 'promote' socialism as the cornerstone of their political system and the Soviet Union as an 'older brother and teacher,' Poland was forced to accept the authorities formed under Soviet domination. Nevertheless, the deep roots of international affiliations and a certain autonomy in pursuing the intellectual agenda made the Polish public sphere a unique arena for clashing ideas and practices.

What the book is about

When exploring the complex intellectual landscape of post-war Europe, this book will focus on the public debates between Polish scholars, social scientists, and other intellectuals involved in the academic agenda. The period covered by the book can be described as the formative years of the socialist regime in Poland. It begins with the liberation of the Polish territories from Nazi occupation and ends with the crisis of the entire 'socialist bloc' in 1956. For convenience, the book will specify three phases in the development of the post-war public discourse: 'the early post-war years,' by which I mean the time of highly intensive and partly forgotten discussions in the cultural and academic journals immediately after World War II; 'Stalinisation' as a project, which began around 1948 and radically changed the institutions that provided the opportunities for these public discussions; and, finally, '1956' as a crisis of the regime, which started before and finished after the calendar year of 1956.

How the history of post-war Poland has been written

Of course, it would be an impracticable undertaking to describe every feature of the period between 1945 and 1956 that addresses in any way the issues discussed in this book. Therefore, my brief review will concentrate only on the facets that will help the reader to understand the place of this book in the historiographical landscape. The division of historiographies into the categories of Polish and 'other' has seen a recent decline in relevance. An increasing number of historians have been using comparative approaches to Polish sources, which make the 'national' vision of history an object of study rather than a prism through which historians see reality. Nevertheless, national history is still a very important lens through which the audience reads historical literature. For understandable reasons, the leading figures of anti-communist Polish historiography saw the period covered by this book primarily through the prism of Poland's submission to the Soviet Union.[4] Since the discourse of 'national liberation' became central to the struggle against the authoritarian regime in Poland, this context also plays a crucial role for the representation of historical knowledge in the public sphere. From this perspective, post-war history has usually been represented as a competition between 'the national' (Polish) and 'the foreign' (Russian/Soviet), while the subdivision of the post-war period usually serves to specify different stages within this competition.[5]

The main trend in English-language historiography[6] regarding this period refers to the 'Sovietisation' of the countries that found themselves in the Soviet sphere of influence after the war. This view, in which the Soviet Union played a more important role than the 'colonised countries,' was prevalent in the cold war and determined how 'Western' audiences used to perceive the establishment of socialist regimes in Central and Eastern Europe, as well as how historians used to present these issues to the public.

Even though the legacy of 'Cold War historiography' has been repeatedly criticised by new generations of historians,[7] the basic idea of 'Sovietisation' is still relevant for certain sections of the historiography. Cultural and political developments in the countries within the sphere of Soviet influence have been a source of public interest, primarily from the perspective of the spread of the Soviet ideological and institutional 'model' to other countries.[8] Outside of the field of political history (in which Soviet domination is, in any case, the central issue), this approach is typical for historians who see the post-war history of Central and Eastern Europe as imperial history. The idea that the Soviet Union represented a new form of empire, with a special approach to relationships between the centre and periphery, remains an object of intensive historiographical debate.[9]

Meanwhile, the concept of 'Sovietisation' still plays the central role for those historians who put emphasis on the plurality of paths taken by various countries within the so-called Eastern Bloc.[10] Even though it is a tendency in recent historiography to 'emancipate' the post-war histories of Central and Eastern European countries from the domination of Soviet history,[11] the concept of 'Sovietisation' serves as a bridge to the broader audience. Thus, historians continue to use the legacy of the Cold War, even when trying to paint a more complex picture of the post-war realities.[12]

At the same time, the English-speaking reader might already be familiar with transborder approaches to Polish history which challenge the traditional political narrative. Two of the most characteristic examples of this approach are the histories of Polish Marxism and social Catholicism as part of the global Marxist and Catholic movements. In recent publications, Polish Marxists and Catholics have been represented as intellectually rooted in the European (primarily French) intellectual agenda. More importantly, when seen from this perspective, the post-war realities simply provide a new context for the continuation of the previous 'stories' of Marxism and Catholicism, rather than a fundamental break in a 'national history.'[13]

This transborder approach is also visible both in historical works on various intellectual groups and in the biographies of distinguished personalities. Since the late 20th century, historians have been interested in analysing the left-wing projects that were *not* implemented in Poland due to the increase in pressure from the Soviet Union.[14] Additionally, some historians made careful attempts to detail the role of those functionaries who became the chief organisers of the post-war press in Poland, leading them to endorse the idea that this period had a unique character. It has been shown that in the early post-war period at least, it was not the aim of those who ruled Polish cultural politics to introduce a 'Soviet model' in Poland.[15]

Even though the influence of political and cultural factors on academic practice has become an increasingly important issue for the historiography, the history of science and scholarship in Poland is still a relatively closed subdiscipline. Traditionally, the institutional approach dominates Polish historical studies on academic practice.[16] However, there are many important aspects of the historical reality that are virtually ignored by the institutional history: the history of individual disciplines, which tends to describe the intellectual evolution of their key figures, fills this gap. There is, however, an obvious inequality in the historical research on various disciplines. For example, in the history of philosophy and the social sciences in Poland, the period between 1945 and 1956 is featured minimally as it did not contribute much to the development of the theory of these disciplines,[17] whereas those focused on historical writing consider this period to be formative for the history of the post-war humanities in Poland.

When writing the history of their discipline, historians have represented the variations between different phases of post-war Polish history in terms of the degree of autonomy from the authorities in public discourse.[18] Additionally, they have provided examples of scholars who maintained their opinion under the pressure of the authorities without losing their position in the professional community.[19] However, complementing the institutional history of Polish academia with insightful research on the personal strategies of scholars, historians usually consider the acceptance or denial of new methodological ideas, or Marxist–Leninist ideology, a key marker of success or failure of 'Sovietisation.' In this book, I intend to slightly change this perspective.

How 'virtues' can open a new perspective on the history of public knowledge

To see the post-war Polish history in a new light, I propose to look at the recent trends in the history of science and scholarship. In this regard, historical epistemology plays a distinguished role. Generally, the ambition of historical epistemology is not only to observe the process of how knowledge is gained historically but also to connect this perspective with research on 'scientific practice.'[20] Especially since the 1960s,[21] the question of 'how science has been made' has been the central issue for historians of science. However, historical epistemology not only explores scientific practice itself but also sees the roots of this practice in the character traits of scholars. These, in turn, are formed under the influence of global processes in the history of knowledge. The philosophical status of historical epistemology and its right to be a 'true' epistemology have been broadly discussed in recent decades.[22] Either way, the perspective offered by the authors of the historical epistemological project deeply influenced the historiographical agenda.

Among many other significant innovations, the concept of 'epistemic virtue' was one of the analytical tools developed by historical epistemology. The issue of virtues has been central to philosophy since ancient times; in many respects, Aristotle plays the key role as a theorist of virtues. In essence, the primary question that Aristotle (and many moral philosophers afterwards) wanted to answer was 'how to be a good person.' Thus, virtues were character traits that had to be cultivated to make every person capable of making the 'right decision' in every situation without having a special instruction for each individual case.[23] Virtues became a central issue not only for moral philosophy (first in the conservative agenda[24]) but also for research on epistemology in a broader sense. For example, when examining 'intellectual virtues' and 'intellectual vices,' philosophers deprived these concepts of moral connotations and made them a tool for researching 'good practice' in the 'production' of philosophy.[25] In turn, historical epistemology adopted this concept for the historical examination of epistemic practices.

Having looked at scientific routine from the perspective of 'epistemic virtues,' historians changed their way of thinking about their subject. One of the most noticeable works in this area is Lorraine Daston and Peter Galison's book on 'objectivity.' Daston and Galison not only showed that 'objectivity' had started to be considered an epistemic virtue among scientists later than had been previously supposed but also argued that it could not have happened earlier.[26] Herman Paul and his colleagues have extended this programme to a broader set of topics and showed the similarity of these processes in the sciences and humanities.[27]

Additionally, historical epistemologists have attempted to construct a collective portrait of 'good scholars/scientists' or 'scientific/scholarly personae' who have adopted the academic ethos required for their epoch and discipline.[28] The concept of 'persona' refers to the Latin persona as a mask, something one would require to play a role in ancient theatre.[29] Without adopting certain character traits, as with not wearing a mask (which, in ancient theatre, was the main sign of transformation of an actor into the 'body' of his protagonist), one ceases to be a scholar or a scientist.[30] This perspective allowed the scholars dealing with historical epistemology to examine the internal patterns of the development of academic knowledge and also to propose a nearly anthropological perspective on the 'scholarly life.'

In this book, the concept of virtues will also play a central role. Nevertheless, my usage of this concept slightly differs from the current historiographical practice. Firstly, my book is not about the theory of virtues. In contrast with publications on historical epistemology, I am not aiming to develop or improve an abstract model of 'epistemic virtues' that were typical to a long epoch in the history of science. Secondly, it is not my intention to construct any ideal types of scholarly personae gathered in Poland after the Second World War. My idea is to use the concept of virtue in its most general sense to offer a new perspective in research on scholarly practice, to view it not as a solely academic phenomenon but as part of the political realities. Echoing recent trends in political epistemology that strive to combine the perspective of historical epistemology with a vision of knowledge as a reflection of political attitudes,[31] my approach to virtues goes beyond academia. In this book, I argue that the concept of virtue can be a promising analytical tool for examining deep intersections between political and academic agendas.

Since Aristotle's time, virtues have been understood as character traits and as part of ethos, i.e. behaviour models that have been cultivated during a long period of time and are not easily changeable.[32] Therefore, a historical examination of virtues as highly stable traits under extremely changeable and fluid political conditions has the potential to be a useful and innovative approach. Of course, this approach poses some difficulties in terms of examination of the historical reality. The most obvious of these is the difference between the discourse on virtues (what was promoted as a virtue) and virtues as character traits that determined people's behaviour in a given situation. This problem is rooted in the nature of the concept of virtue. Even deprived of moral connotations, virtue remains an idealistic concept; it is always about how it should be but not about how it is.[33] Historically, we can only trace the public manifestations of virtues as certain tendencies rather than examine them as ontological categories.

There is another problematic point regarding the various visions of virtues. On the one hand, since ancient times, virtues (that are supposed to be 'cultivated') can also be seen as an instrument of education or even manipulation, which legitimises the paternalist role of the state towards its citizens.[34] On the other, from the perspective of historical epistemology, (epistemic) virtues emerge and are cultivated within academic communities (in the very concrete sense of the reference group of academic practice), which tend to overcome state and national borders, and are supposed to be resistant towards external interventions.[35] This dichotomic view of virtues is central for my approach. In this book, I will focus on the tension between the official discourse on virtues and the forms of academic practice performed publicly. Examining this practice, I will speak of the 'virtuous behaviour' of Polish scholars (who responded to the official discourse or opposed it), rather than of individual virtues that they 'possessed.'[36] In this book, virtues will appear not in isolation but in a concrete social situation as a public manifestation of conflict or agreement with the governmental discourse on this issue. This will help me to trace tendencies without making unnecessary simplifications whilst also focusing the narrative on the most essential aspects of scholarly and public life.

The history of the formative years of the post-war Polish state provides rich material for this kind of study. The extremely changeable official discourse on the virtues 'welcomed' in post-war Poland, alongside the relative autonomy of Polish scholars from the authorities, shaped the zone of conflict between the forms of 'good practice' required by the authorities and the reality of academic practice. Additionally, under the post-war conditions, Polish scholars were forced to overcome the borders between academia and politics. Since virtues are usually understood as a phenomenon formed in an (imagined) community,[37] the attempts to destroy the autonomy of academia, that is to include scholars in one 'community' with the political leadership, could not help but to sharpen the conflict between different virtues. In the field of public knowledge, by which I mean scholarly debates in the public sphere[38] and which is the main focus of the book, both support and opposition to the official discourse became a political action. Therefore, against the backdrop of state intervention in academic issues, 'academic virtues' became political, and vice versa.

What is new in this book?

In this book, the traditional narratives of the early Cold War and 'Sovietisation,' such as the spread of 'Soviet' or 'Stalinist' ideology and the reconstruction of academic institutions in accordance with the Soviet model, will lose their dominant position. Atypically, my central question is not what kind of ideology or institutional model was promoted in post-war Poland, but which virtues Polish scholars were expected to adopt under the political pressure and to what extent this project succeeded. My book will not just examine the academic practice of Polish scholars in the context of political developments, but it will also focus on the public activity of scholars and thus overcome the borders between the academic and political agendas.

Developing the most recent trends in historiography, my book will challenge more radically the homogeneity of the post-war period and revise the view of logical continuity between its different stages. I will argue that the peculiarity of the 'early post-war years,' i.e. the period from 1945 to 1948/1949, was determined not by 'softer forms' of 'Sovietisation' as it used to be represented in the historiography, but by the fact that different virtues were promoted as a basis for the early post-war project. I will show that, in this period, many Polish scholars did not see a contradiction between the virtues praised by the authorities and their own vision of 'virtuous behaviour.' They felt free to promote their own academic and political agenda, and the authorities did not prevent them from claiming publicly their ideas that stood in paradigmatic conflict both with authoritarianism in general and, more specifically, with the Soviet political practice.

The escalation of the Cold War forced the Polish authorities to radically change the character of virtues praised and promoted in Poland. I will argue that it was not Marxist–Leninist ideology and the institutional changes themselves, but the attempt to forcibly teach Polish scholars to adopt new virtues that were the cornerstone of 'Stalinisation' and a precondition for the fulfilment of this project. I will show that the 'correct' views on scientific issues that Stalinism had to offer were extremely changeable and frequently stood in contradiction to each other. One thing was stable – 'Stalinist science'[39] required its scholars and scientists to be 'virtuous' men and women with loyalty to the current political line (formally not to the state itself)[40] as the crown of these virtues. This new constellation of virtues was supposed to be adopted on Polish soil and to change the foundations of academic practice in Poland. Examining this process, I will argue that this project did not achieve these aims and, thus, failed in Poland.

This brings me to a much more general point I will make in this book. The perspective of virtue affords us a different view of the tendencies inherent in authoritarian regimes. The ideas themselves may play a secondary role in their (imaginary) structure. Even under the domination of a ruling ideology, the 'correct views' can change dramatically under the same regime. Meanwhile, authoritarian regimes tend to make scholars (much like all other citizens) 'virtuous' men and women in order to use the (quasi)moral authority of virtues for their own security and stability.[41] Loyalty to the virtues promoted by the state is an important precondition for an apparent 'unity' that would give the impression of this 'stability.' The authorities, in turn, strive not to be the creators of virtues (which should always seem 'natural') but their defenders, patrons, and teachers. Additionally, authoritarian regimes tend to represent the whole state as the only legitimate 'community' with the right to promote forms of 'good practice.' Teaching people how to be 'truly' virtuous from above can be a bloody process …[42], but can this teaching be fully 'successful'?

This book is not about virtues. Virtues are a prism through which I propose to display the history of public scholarly practice. A perspective that can refresh our view of topics which may seem very familiar and trivial but still contains much material for reflection on both the past and the present.

Structure of the book

Chapter 1 deals with the question of how the 'gentle revolution' (which was implemented in Poland in the early post-war period) made the scholarly public debates possible, despite the strict control of Soviet officials over the Polish public sphere. I will show that 'progressiveness' became the central virtue praised and welcomed by the organisers of the Polish cultural and academic press, which resulted in many scholars not feeling a conflict between their forms of 'virtuous behaviour' and the official discourse on this issue. Chapter 2 explores public discussions about the Soviet Union, Russian culture, and Soviet science in the early post-war years. I will argue that, because of the peculiarity of 'virtues politics' in the early post-war years, the images of the Soviet Union constructed in this period by the Polish academic and cultural press not only contradicted the self-image of the Stalinist regime but could have also seemed unacceptable from the 'Soviet' point of view. Chapter 3 poses the question of what 'good practice' the organisers of the early post-war project had in mind. This chapter shows that it was not the Soviet Union, but France and French intellectual culture that became the 'teacher' of virtues that those who controlled the public sphere in post-war Poland considered crucial.

Chapter 4 deals with interweaving and concealed conflicts between 'national' and 'academic' virtues in academic practice. Based on one of the biggest scholarly debates of the early post-war years – the discussion around the 'progressiveness' of the Polish intelligentsia – this chapter will show how deeply the public discourse of Polish scholars was rooted in the national agenda, a fact that made this debate a fruitful source of material for tracing noticed and unnoticed clashes among various virtues. Chapter 5 discusses how the promotion of the virtue of 'progressiveness' in conjunction with the opposition to the vice of 'reactionary attitude' affected the debates on the two central issues of the Polish agenda – Marxism and Catholicism. I will argue that, in the early post-war years, the discourse on the virtue of 'progressiveness' became a weapon against Marxism, while, due to the 'virtues politics' of 'gentle revolution,' being Catholic did not necessarily mean possessing a 'reactionary attitude.'

Chapter 6 examines the deconstruction of the early post-war project against the backdrop of the escalation of the Cold War. Examining the political mobilisation of scholars in the form of scientific congresses and conventions, I will argue that the crucial point of these events was to force scholars to rapidly adopt new forms of 'virtuous behaviour,' and that this project failed to succeed, despite the strongest political pressure. Developing upon the idea that the congresses and conventions did not achieve their desired results, Chapter 7 shows how new institutions created on the wave of Stalinisation were used for teaching Polish academics how to lead a public discussion in accordance with the new norms of 'virtuous behaviour.' In this chapter, I will argue that this part of the project of bringing new virtues to Polish soil also did not achieve its aims. The 'defeat' of Stalinisation is also the central point of Chapter 8. I will show that, during the crisis of '1956,' scholars publicly fought not Marxism itself, but the forms of academic practice promoted by the chief organisers of Stalinisation. Thus, the struggle against the virtues promoted by the authorities united both Marxist and non-Marxist scholars. This, in turn, deprived the authorities of their role as patrons and defenders of virtues and made Polish academia the central problem of the regime until its collapse.

Notes

1 Szymon Datner and Kazimierz Leszczyński, eds., *Zbrodnie okupanta w czasie powstania warszawskiego w 1944 roku (w dokumentach)* (Warszawa: Wydawnictwo MON, 1962), 306.
2 See, e.g., the description of the underground activity of those Polish social scientists who will play a central role in this book: Friedrich Cain, *Wissen im Untergrund. Praxis und Politik klandestiner Forschung im besetzten Polen, 1939–1945* (Tübingen: Mohr Siebeck, 2021), 57–71.

10 *Introduction*

3   See about this context Tony Judt, *Postwar: A History of Europe since 1945* (London: Vintage Books, 2010), 13–99.
4   Krystyna Kersten was one of a group of historians who were the pioneers of post-communist Polish historiography. Having started to publish her works with the underground publishers in the late 1970s, Kersten conducted a huge amount of work analysing the new sources from this period after the defeat of the authoritarian regime in Poland. See the translation of her book into English: Krystyna Kersten, *The Establishment of Communist Rule in Poland, 1943–1948* (Berkeley, CA: University of California Press, 1991).
5   Those who, on the Polish side, were among the organizers of the new regime or participated in establishing the public institutions in post-war Poland have sometimes been described as 'seduced intellectuals,' see, e.g., Maria Hirszowicz, *Pułapki zaangażowania: intelektualiści w służbie komunizmu* (Warszawa: Wydawnictwo Naukowe Scholar, 2001). It is noteworthy that Russian post-communist historiography tended to emphasise the specific features of the early post-war years in opposition to the period of Stalinisation. In this case, above all, the perspective of Soviet representatives and their reports on the situation in Poland played the central role. See, for example, *Sovetskij faktor v Vostochnoj Evrope 1944–1953 gg.: Dokumenty*, eds. Tatyana Volokitina, Galina Murashko, and Albina Noskova, vol. 1, *1944–1948* (Moskva: ROSSPJeN, 1999); Tatyana Volokitina et al., eds., *Moskva i Vostochnaja Evropa: Stanovlenie politicheskih rezhimov sovetskogo tipa, 1949–1953. Ocherki istorii* (Moskva: ROSSPJeN, 2002).
6   Since the book has been written in English, in this review, I will focus on the English-language historiography. It does not change the fact that there are many very important publications on post-war Polish history in German, French, Italian, Russian, and many other languages to which I will refer in my book.
7   Following this tendency, the University of North Carolina Press established a special book series 'New Cold War History' https://uncpress.org/series/new-cold-war-history/?page_number=1
8   See, for example, Michael David-Fox and György Péteri, eds., *Academia in Upheaval: Origins, Transfers, and Transformations of the Communist Academic Regime in Russia and East Central Europe* (Westport: Information Age Publishing, 2000).
9   More about the imperial perspective on Sovietisation, see Balázs Apor, "Sovietisation, imperial rule and the Stalinist Leader Cult in Central and Eastern Europe," in *The Shadow of Colonialism on Europe's Modern Past*, eds. Róisín Healy and Enrico Dal Lago (London: Palgrave Macmillan, 2014), 228–244. Generally, the imperial framework is the key for Timothy Snyder's popular book. See Timothy Snyder, *Bloodlands: Europe Between Hitler and Stalin* (New York: Basic Books, 2012). See more general theoretical works on this topic: Michael David-Fox, Peter Holquist and Alexander M. Martin, "The imperial turn," *Kritika* 7, no. 4 (2006): 705–712; Alexander Semyonov, "Empire as a context setting category," *Ab Imperio* 9, no. 1 (2008): 193–204.
10 This concept was used, for example, by John Connelly, who described the formation of the new educational systems in the countries within the Soviet sphere of influence. Connelly is, in many respects, a pioneer of comparative research in this area, who, while following the general idea of 'Sovietisation,' still very carefully examined the peculiarity of all individual cases. John Connelly, *Captive University: The Sovietization of East German, Czech, and Polish Higher Education, 1945–1956* (Chapel Hill: University of North Carolina Press, 2000). See also John Connelly, "Internal Bolshevisation? Elite social science training in Stalinist Poland," *Minerva* 34, no. 4 (1996): 323–346.
11 See Peter Haslinger, "East Central European history – Still a strategically important field of research," *Journal of Modern European History* 16, no. 3 (2018): 295–300.
12 In this regard, Patryk Babiracki's publications play an important role in the historiography of post-war Poland. Even though Babiracki's focus is Soviet 'soft power' (i.e. Soviet cultural propaganda), he pays a lot of attention to the issue of 'cultural resistance' to

Soviet influences in cultural issues, see Patryk Babiracki, *Soviet Soft Power in Poland: Culture and the Making of Stalin's New Empire, 1943–1957* (Chapel Hill: University of North Carolina Press, 2015).

13 The key publications in this area are the works of Marci Shore and Piotr Kosicki. Shore traces the fate of Polish Marxists who had been formed by the European socialist movements of the interwar period, as well as by the unpleasant experiences in Soviet concentration camps. Shore's approach to the history of Marxism in Poland emphasised those people who identified as Marxists, with their aspirations, hopes, and frustrations, thus helping the reader to see another perspective on Polish history in the 20th century that is not determined by the history of Soviet domination (see Marci Shore, *Caviar and Ashes: A Warsaw Generation's Life and Death in Marxism, 1918–1968* [New Haven/London: Yale University Press, 2006]). Piotr Kosicki's research on the different directions in social Catholicism put the emphasis on the international intellectual agenda of Polish Catholics; Kosicki invites the reader to see the post-war realities as only one more episode in a bigger story of Polish French intellectual relationships, which had been influenced by Soviet domination only in a limited way (Piotr H. Kosicki, *Catholics on the Barricades: Poland, France, and "Revolution", 1891–1956* [New Haven/London: Yale University Press, 2018]). See more on the 'period borders' in writing post-war Polish history: Aleksei Lokhmatov, "'Periodisations' in intellectual history: On the plurality of continuities in the post-war public debates of Poland," in *Rethinking Period Boundaries: New Approaches to Continuity and Discontinuity in Modern European History and Culture,* eds., Jade McGlynn and Lucian George (Berlin: De Gruyter, 2022), 149–174.

14 See, e.g., Zbigniew Żabicki, *"Kuźnica" i jej program literacki* (Warszawa: Wydawnictwo Literackie, 1966); Stefan Żółkiewski, "Sur l'exemple de l'hebdomadaire 'Kuźnica'," *Acta Poloniae Historica* 31 (1975): 188–189; Hanna Gosk, *W kręgu "Kuźnicy": dyskusje krytycznoliterackie lat 1945–1948* (Łódź: Państwowe Wydawnictwo Naukowe, 1985); the journals 'Odrodzenie' and 'Twórczość' also became the topics of a book: Wiesław Szymański, *"Odrodzenie" i "Twórczość" w Krakowie, 1945–1950* (Wrocław: Zakład Narodowy im. Ossolińskich 1981).

15 See, for example, Eryk Krasucki's book about one of the central figures in the history of the Polish press industry in the early post-war years, Jerzy Borejsza. See Eryk Krasucki, *Międzynarodowy komunista. Jerzy Borejsza: Biografia polityczna* (Warszawa: Wydawnictwo naukowe PWN, 2009). Krasucki argued against the view that Borejsza's activity was a part of the 'Stalinisation' process, a perspective which had dominated Polish historiography previously (Barbara Fijałkowska, *Borejsza i Różański: Przyczynek do dziejów stalinizmu w Polsce* [Olsztyn: Wyższa Szkoła Pedagogiczna, 1995]); see Krasucki's criticism against this approach: Krasucki, *Międzynarodowy komunista*, 15. Besides Eryk Krasucki's book on Jerzy Borejsza, see Grzegorz P. Bąbiak's publications on Borejsza's activity: Grzegorz P. Bąbiak, ed., *Na rogu Stalina i trzech krzyży: Listy do Jerzego Borejszy, 1944–1952* (Warszawa: Czytelnik 2014); Grzegorz P. Bąbiak, *"Odrodzenie" (1944–1950): Bibliografia zawartości* (Warszawa: Wydział Polonistyki Uniwersytetu Warszawskiego, 2017). Additionally, research on the personal strategies of scholars in post-war Poland showed, among other things, how the Polish context transformed the ideas of those young intellectuals whose professional formation happened parallel to the construction of the new regime. See, for example, the newly published English biography of Zygmunt Bauman written by Izabela Wagner: Izabela Wagner, *Bauman: A Biography* (Cambridge, UK: Polity Press, 2020).

16 See recent research on this topic: Christian Fleck, Matthias Duller and Victor Karády, eds., *Shaping Human Science Disciplines: Institutional Developments in Europe and Beyond* (London: Palgrave Macmillan, 2019). In the Polish context, besides the works of John Connelly mentioned above, Piotr Hübner plays, without a doubt, the central role in historiographical pantheon. Hübner's publications cover very different aspects of the development of scientific institutions in post-war Poland. Based on a huge number of

archival materials, Hübner depicts the reorganisation of Polish academia through the prism of institutions and represents this as a consistent and logical programme, see Piotr Hübner, *I Kongres Nauki Polskiej jako forma realizacji założeń polityki naukowej państwa ludowego* (Wrocław: Zakład Narodowy im. Ossolińskich, 1983); Piotr Hübner, *Nauka polska po II wojnie światowej: idee i instytucje* (Warszawa: Centralny Ośrodek Metodyczny Studiów Nauk Politycznych, 1987); Piotr Hübner, *Polityka naukowa w Polsce w latach 1944–1953: geneza systemu*, 2 vols. (Wrocław: Zakład Narodowy im. Ossolińskich, 1992).

17 Marta Bucholc, one of the leading historians of Polish sociology, defines this period as a 'survival': Marta Bucholc, *Sociology in Poland: To Be Continued?* (London: Palgrave Macmillan, 2016), 15–28. See also a very important publication by Joanna Bielecka-Prus in which this period plays a minor role: Joanna Bielecka-Prus, "The social roles of Polish sociologists after 1945," *Comparative Sociology* 10 (2011): 735–765. The important exception is the book by the sociologist Agata Zysiak, who conducted extremely important research on the theory of the new type of university that was to be constructed in post-war Poland. However, as a sociologist, Zysiak is not focused on tracing the changes in the discourse of the main actors in the debates on the new model of university, but on representing these discussions as a competition between different models of a 'people's university.' See Agata Zysiak, *Punkty za pochodzenie: Powojenna modernizacja i uniwersytet w robotniczym mieście* (Kraków: Nomos, 2016). Zysiak formulated the key point of her insightful research in an English language article: Agata Zysiak, "Modernizing science: Between a liberal, social, and socialistic university; the case of Poland and the University of Łódź, 1945–1953," *Science in Context* 28, no. 2 (2015): 215–236; the newest research on the history of Polish 'language sciences' in the 19th and 20th century was conducted by Tomasz Zarycki: Tomasz Zarycki, *The Polish Elite and Language Sciences: A Perspective of Global Historical Sociology* (London: Palgrave Macmillan, 2022). Based on the methodology of Pierre Bourdieu, Zarycki examines the discourses of Polish academic debates, primarily, in Polish linguistics and literary studies as a field of struggle between various global narratives of dominance. See, e.g., Tomasz Zarycki, *The Polish Elite and Language Sciences*, 361–376.

18 Rafał Stobiecki was among the first historians who convincingly showed that the early post-war years represented a continuity from the interwar academic agenda. Additionally, he argued that the period of Stalinism led, among other things, to the internationalisation and 'scientification' of Polish historiography in this period, see Rafał Stobiecki, *Historia pod nadzorem: Spory o nowy model historii w Polsce – druga połowa lat czterdziestych – początek lat pięćdziesiątych* (Łódź: Wydawnictwo Uniwersytetu Łódzkiego, 1993); Rafał Stobiecki, *Historiografia PRL: Ani dobra, ani mądra, ani piękna ..., ale skomplikowana; Studia i szkice* (Warszawa: Wydawnictwo TRIO, 2007). Besides Rafał Stobiecki's works, Tadeusz Rutkowski's publications on the institutional history of historical writing and Zbigniew Romek's works on the role of (self)censorship in Polish historiography significantly changed this research field. See, for example, Tadeusz Rutkowski, *Nauki historyczne w Polsce 1944–1970: Zagadnienia polityczne i organizacyjne* (Warszawa: Wydawnictwa Uniwersytetu Warszawskiego, 2007); Zbigniew Romek, *Cenzura a nauka historyczna w Polsce 1944–1970* (Warszawa: Wydawnictwo Neriton – Instytut Historii PAN, 2010). In the English-language historiography, Anna Sosnowska's book presents an overview of the post-war history of historical writing in Poland. Even though Sosnowska concentrated on economic history, the book also shows how the historical community existed under the authoritarian regime in Poland: Anna Sosnowska, *Explaining Economic Backwardness: Post-1945 Polish Historians on Eastern Europe* (Budapest/New York: Central European University Press, 2019). Additionally, the comparative approach in research on the 'Sovietisation' of historiographies in various socialist countries testified that local historians rather than advisers from Moscow were the leading forces in this process: Maciej Górny is one of the key

Introduction 13

figures in this research area, see Maciej Górny, *The Nation Should Come First: Marxism and Historiography in East Central Europe* (Frankfurt am Main: Peter Lang, 2013); see also Jan Szumski's book, which specifies the role of Soviet historians in the Stalinisation of Polish historiography: Jan Szumski, *Historia a polityka: ZSRR wobec nauki historycznej w Polsce 1945–1964* (Warszawa: ASPRA, 2016). See also a sociological view of historiographical practice in post-war Poland: Valentin Behr, *Powojenna historiografia polska jako pole walki: Studium z socjologii wiedzy i polityki* (Warszawa: Wydawnictwo Uniwersytetu Warszawskiego, 2021).

19 See, for example, Marcin Wolniewicz's publications on the academic biography of one of the leading Polish historians, Stefan Kieniewicz: Marcin Wolniewicz, "W stronę *origines de la Pologne contemporaine* – poszukiwania metodologiczne Stefana Kieniewicza w latach 1946–1948," *KLIO POLSKA: Studia i Materiały z Dziejów Historiografi i Polskiej* 9 (2017): 87–88; Marcin Wolniewicz, "On the process of de-Stalinization of Polish historiography: Stefan Kieniewicz (1907–1992) and the insurgent tradition," *Acta Poloniae Historica* 115 (2017): 235–266; see also Elżbieta Orman's article on the biography of two 'rebellious' historians – Kieniewicz and Henryk Wereszycki: Elżbieta Orman, "O paradoksach historiografii w czasach PRL-u na przykładzie korespondencji Stefana Kieniewicza i Henryka Wereszyckiego," in *Stefan Kieniewicz – Henryk Wereszycki. Korespondencja z lat 1947–1990*, ed. Elżbieta Orman (Kraków: Instytut Historii PAN, 2013).

20 By research on 'scientific practice,' I mean a sociological perspective on methods of doing science. Lorraine Daston, "Historical Epistemology," in *Questions of Evidence: Proof, Practice, and Persuasion Across the Disciplines,* eds. James Chandler, Arnold Davidson and Harry Harootunian (Chicago: University of Chicago Press, 1994), 282–289.

21 The popularity of Thomas Kuhn's concept of 'scientific revolution' has played an important role in turning the focus of many historians of science towards studying the 'scientific practice': Thomas Kuhn, *The Structure of Scientific Revolutions* (Chicago: University of Chicago Press, 1962). The rediscovery in English language literature of Ludwik Fleck's publications on the constructive nature of scientific facts and his idea of '*Denkkollektiv*' (Ludwik Fleck, *Entstehung und Entwicklung einer wissenschaftlichen Tatsache* [Basel: Schwabe Verlag, 1935]) also played an important role in intensifying the debate on the social conditions of 'knowledge production.' Of course, Fleck's ideas had been influenced by the sociology of knowledge (see, e.g., K. Mannheim, *Ideologie und Utopie* [Frankfurt am Main: Vittorio Klostermann, 1985]).

22 See the overview of this debate: Uljana Feest and Thomas Sturm, "What (good) is historical epistemology? Editors' introduction," *Erkenntnis* 75 (2011): 285–302.

23 See Aristotle, *The Nicomachean Ethics* (New York and London: Penguin, 2020).

24 See, for example, Alasdair C. MacIntyre's famous book in which he formulates the key ideas of the conservative programme on the philosophy of virtues: Alasdair C. MacIntyre, *After Virtue: A Study in Moral Theory* (Notre Dame, Ind.: Univ. Notre Dame Press, 1984).

25 See, for example, Jason Baehr, *The Inquiring Mind: On Intellectual Virtues and Virtue Epistemology* (Oxford: Oxford UP, 2011); Jason Baehr, *Intellectual Virtues and Education: Essays in Applied Virtue Epistemology* (New York: Routledge, 2015).

26 Lorraine Daston and Peter Galison, *Objectivity* (New York: Zone Books, 2007), 39–42.

27 Herman Paul and his colleagues play the central role in this historiographical trend. See Herman Paul, "Distance and self-distanciation: Intellectual virtue and historical method around 1900," *History and Theory* 50, no. 4 (2011): 104–116; Herman Paul, "Weak historicism: On hierarchies of intellectual virtues and goods," *Journal of the Philosophy of History* 6 (2012): 369–388. For a general review of this approach, see Herman Paul, *Historians' Virtues: From Antiquity to the Twenty-First Century* (Cambridge, UK: Cambridge University Press, 2022).

28 Herman Paul, "What is a scholarly persona? Ten theses on virtues, skills, and desires," *History and Theory* 53 (2014): 348–371; Herman Paul, *How to Be a Historian: Scholarly Personae in Historical Studies, 1800–2000* (Manchester: Manchester University Press, 2019). See also research on 'good' and 'bad' habits (read virtues and vices), according to which, the social sciences appeared as a 'disciplining' science: Bernhard Kleeberg, "Bad habits and the origins of sociology," in *Rethinking Order: Idioms of Stability and Destabilization*, eds. Nicole Falkenhayner, et al. (Bielefeld: Transcript, 2015), 47–62.

29 The authors of this metaphor emphasise that, in ancient theatre, putting on a mask implied a real transformation of a person. See Lorraine Daston and Heinz O. Sibum, "Introduction: Scientific personae and their histories," *Science in Context* 16, no. 1–2 (2003): 1–8. Of course, this interest of historical epistemology to the constructive nature of the scholarly 'self' had been strongly influenced by Michel Foucault. His works on the hidden mechanisms of power had a huge impact on how historians analyse the power relations that stay behind the academic practice. See first of all his famous book: Michel Foucault, *Discipline and Punish: The Birth of the Prison* (New York: Pantheon Books, 1977). Even though, many of the issues discussed in this book could be examined from the Foucauldian perspective, my research goes beyond his paradigm of power. Therefore, Foucault remains a relevant author for this book, but his research programme does not determine my research procedure.

30 Of course, there are scholars dealing with the scientific practice who understand virtues as part of the moral agenda. See, for example, Steven Shapin, *The Scientific Life: A Moral History of a Late Modern Vocation* (Chicago: University of Chicago Press, 2008).

31 The recent research on historical and political epistemology with a special emphasis on Central and Eastern Europe is also a noteworthy tendency in historiography. The programme initiated by Dietlind Hüchtker, Jan Surman, Bernhard Kleeberg, and Friedrich Cain will hopefully result in ground-breaking research based on sources from the Eastern and Central European region: Jan Surman, Bernhard Kleeberg and Friedrich Cain, "The past and present of political epistemologies of (Eastern) Europe," *Historyka Studia Metodologiczne* 49 (2019): 7–13; Jan Surman, Bernhard Kleeberg, Dietlind Hüchtker, and Friedrich Cain, "A new culture of truth? On the transformation of political epistemologies since the 1960s in Central Europe and Eastern Europe," *Stan Rzeczy* 17, no. 2 (2019): 9–21; see also Volker Roelcke, "Auf der Suche nach der Politik in der Wissensproduktion: Plädoyer für eine historisch-politische Epistemologie," *Berichte zur Wissenschaftsgeschichte* 33 (2010): 176–192. Among recent publications on the theory of virtues, the research programme on book reviews as a form of academic practice plays a distinguished role. The authors of this project made the concept of virtues a central category in the analysis of forms of 'good scientific practice' reflected in book reviews. See Aleksei Pleshkov and Jan Surman, "Book reviews in the history of knowledge," *Studia Historiae Scientiarum* 20 (2021): 629–650.

32 This differentiates virtues from values which not supposed to be character traits. The topic of values has already been thematised in the historiography of post-war Poland: John Connelly, "Polish universities and state socialism: 1944–1968," in *Universities Under Dictatorship*, eds. John Connelly and Michael Grüttner (University Park: Pennsylvania State University Press, 2005), 185–212. See also insightful research on the moral aspects of producing a 'new man' conducted by Mariusz Mazur: Mariusz Mazur, *O człowieku tendencyjnym ... Obraz nowego człowieka w propagandzie komunistycznej w okresie Polski Ludowej i PRL 1944–1956* (Lublin: Wydawnictwo Uniwersytetu Marii Curie-Skłodowskiej w Lublinie, 2009), 318–400.

33 Especially in its holistic version, virtue is an unreachable destination of a striving (see Julia Annas, *Intelligent Virtue* (Oxford: Oxford University Press, 2011), 1–8.

34 See, e.g., Douglas J. Crawford-Brown, "Virtue as the basis of engineering ethics," *Science and Engineering Ethics* 3 (1997): 481–489.

35 Lorraine Daston and Peter Galison, *Objectivity* (New York: Zone Books, 2007), 39–42.
36 To some extent, my idea of 'virtuous behaviour' corresponds with Bernhard Kleeberg's research on the praxeology of truth in that, as a whole, it makes sense only in a concrete social situation. See Bernhard Kleeberg, "Post post-truth: Epistemologies of disintegration and the praxeology of truth," *Stan Rzeczy* 17, no. 2 (2019): 25–52.
37 See more in the article of MacIntyre's followers: Daniel J. Hicks and Thomas A. Stapleford, "The virtues of scientific practice: MacIntyre, virtue ethics, and the historiography of science," *Isis* 107, no. 3 (2016): 449–472.
38 Of course, both elements of the concept 'public knowledge' require a clarification. There is a considerable debate on the limits of the concept of knowledge and its relation to other phenomena (see Lorraine Daston, "The history of science and the history of knowledge," *KNOW* 1, no. 1 (2017): 131–154; Martin Mulsow, "History of knowledge," in *Debating Two Approaches to History*, eds. Marek Tamm and Peter Burke (London: Bloomsbury, 2019), 159–187). In this book, the concept of knowledge will refer primarily to the discourses of scholars that overcame the disciplinary and academic borders but still required the mobilisation of their professional training. As it was said, 'public knowledge' refers to the intellectual practice performed in the public sphere. It is noteworthy that, in this book, this term is a technical one and does not have any normative connotations. The fact that Jürgen Habermas's Öffentlichkeit was translated (not very accurately) into English as 'public sphere' deeply influenced the perception of this term among the reading public. Even though some of the issues discussed in the book are concerned with Habermas's Öffentlichkeit, this is not my focus here. Public sphere simply means a set of practices performed publicly. About the Polish public sphere during the Cold War, see the newest publication: Kyrill Kunakhovich, *Communism's Public Sphere: Culture as Politics in Cold War Poland and East Germany* (New York: Cornell University Press, 2023).
39 Regarding the debates on the concept of 'Stalinist science,' to which I will refer in this book, see the review of publications on this topic: Michael Gordin, "Was there ever a 'Stalinist science'?," *Kritika: Explorations in Russian and Eurasian History* 9, no. 3 (2008): 625–639.
40 The matter concerns loyalty not as an opportunism, but conscious loyalty, in other words, loyalty as an epistemic virtue. I will argue that making loyalty a virtue contradicted the forms of forced confession described, e.g., by Foucault (see Michel Foucault, *Wrong-Doing, Truth-Tellin: The Function of Avowal in Justice* [The University of Chicago Press, 2004], 11–26). On the concept of loyalty in the Central and Eastern European context see M. Schulze Wessel, "Loyalität" als geschichtlicher Grundbegriff und Forschungskonzept: Zur Einleitung, in *Loyalitäten in der Tschechoslowakischen Republik, 1918–1938: Politische, nationale und kulturelle Zugehörigkeiten*, ed. Martin Schulze Wessel (München: Oldenbourg, 2004) 1–22.
41 Of course, this kind of virtue fundamentally differs from virtues in the sense of – to take one example – republicanism (see, e.g., Richard Dagger, *Civic Virtues: Rights, Citizenship, and Republican Liberalism* [Oxford: Oxford University Press, 1997]). Even though the lens of political theory is not my perspective, one can briefly refer to the Confucian approach to virtues, which also makes the loyalty a central virtue (see, e.g., Steven Angle and Michael Slote, *Virtue Ethics and Confucianism* [New York/London: Routledge, 2013]). The paternalist nature of the Soviet state has also been intensively discussed in historiography although not exclusively from the perspective of virtues (see, for example, George Avis, *The Making of the Soviet Citizen: Character Formation and Civic Training in Soviet Education* [New York/London: Routledge 1987]). The concept of stability plays the central role in most utopian ideas of the state as a marker of the 'successfulness' of a political system (the literature on this topic is enormous, see, for example, an essay on the adoption of the concept of homeostasis as a sign of 'internal stability' in the political theory of the Scottish idealists: Steve Sturdy, "Biology as social

theory: John Scott Haldane and physiological regulation," *The British Journal for the History of Science* 21 (1988): 315–340).
42 Of course, the literature on the forms of subjection and re-education by various authoritarian regimes is enormous. See, e.g., Peter Fritzsche and Jochen Hellbeck, "The New Man in Stalinist Russia and Nazi Germany," in *Beyond Totalitarianism: Stalinism and Nazism Compared*, eds. Michael Geyer and Sheila Fitzpatrick (Cambridge: Cambridge University Press, 2010).

1 From the War to the 'Gentle Revolution'

'Today, we are moving towards a new era – the era of peace ... this is the time to write a new history of free, democratic, and united Poland.'[1] With these words, Bolesław Bierut (1892–1956), who had been 'elected' to the head of the State National Council (a quasi-parliament created under Soviet supervision), appealed to Polish people who faced the new political realities with strong feelings of uncertainty and suspicion. The Second World War had been the main reorganiser of both the geographical and political landscape of the world. Following the pattern of the previous war, the fate of the world was decided by the leaders of the countries on the winning side. Nevertheless, since the Grand Alliance was the first experience of political collaboration (at such a global level) between the 'Western' countries and the Soviet Union as a bastion of communism, the new conditions required new principles for resolving controversial issues. Thus, the division of the world into 'spheres of influence' became a new political reality. It was not referendums and votes but the 'percentages agreement' between Stalin and Churchill, as well as decisions taken at the Yalta and Potsdam Conferences, that determined the shape of the world after the war.[2]

The necessity of finding a compromise regarding the political future of the world was especially relevant in the case of Poland. At the beginning of the war, the territory of the Polish Republic was occupied by Nazi troops and the Red Army in accordance with the so-called Molotov–Ribbentrop Pact (1939). On the 'Soviet side,' several thousand Polish officers, soldiers, and civilians were captured by the Red Army and treated as war prisoners. Meanwhile, the members of the Polish political leadership fled through continental Europe to London, where they established a government in exile. For understandable reasons, the relationships between the Soviet Union and the Polish government in London were difficult even after the Nazi Germany entreated the Soviet territories and the Soviet state started to play a key role in the Grand Alliance.[3] However, the 1943 disclosure of the mass graves of Polish officers in the village of Katyn (not far from Smolensk) was a turning point in 'new' Polish history. Of course, the Nazi leadership was very inspired by the discovery of the fact that, in 1940, the Soviet security services executed thousands of Polish war prisoners[4] and actively used this issue to disintegrate the alliance of their enemies. Nevertheless, the role of the Soviet Union in the war, as well as the importance of the Eastern front for the anti-Nazi coalition, allowed Stalin to take

18 *From the War to the 'Gentle Revolution'*

over the initiative in this situation. Thus, the conflict with the Polish government in exile (which demanded official explanations from the Soviet side regarding the mass graves) became a catalyst for starting a new 'Soviet Polish project.'

Stalin's 'Polish Project' and 'Missionary-Intellectuals'

Stalin, an unfortunate Soviet commander during the Polish–Soviet War (1919–1921) and an organiser of repressions against Poles as 'hostile elements' during the early war period, fully understood the antipathy towards communism and Soviet Russia that was prevalent amongst Polish people. Moreover, anti-communist sentiment among the Polish population was not the only 'Polish' problem in Stalin's agenda. The establishment of Soviet control over the International, during Stalin's dictatorship, led to an attack on the Polish communists and the disbanding of the Communist Party of Poland in 1938. This made not only most of the Polish population but also most Polish communists 'hostile elements' from the perspective of the Stalinist ideology. Thus, Poland represented the most unpleasant soil for the creation of a 'friendship' with the people living there.

It was Stalin's idea to choose a broader ideological framework for the 'Union of Polish Patriots,' which became the first Polish political institution in Soviet territory, to attract Poles to his non-alternative political programme.[5] Though immediately following the beginning of the Second World War, being of Polish descent was reason enough for arrest followed at the very least by deportation, the changes in the political agenda during the war necessitated bringing together people who could help to convey the impression of 'Polishness.' Polish officers, soldiers, and even political staff were asked to highlight their Polish identity, which had earlier been a reason for prosecuting most of them.[6] The 1st Tadeusz Kościuszko Infantry Division, a Polish military unit created in the Soviet Union in 1943 'on the initiative' of the Union of Polish Patriots, became a laboratory for the artificial formation of Polish national identity: Polish children were allowed to take religious classes in schools,[7] while military officers and soldiers participated in common Church services and collectively sang Polish national songs during official ceremonies.[8]

Scholars, writers, and journalists who were recruited for the implementation of the 'Soviet Polish project' had faced a difficult journey to fulfil this mission. For many of them, participation in this project was the only way to save their lives.[9] The Polish–Soviet writer Wanda Wasilewska (1905–1964) (who had a close relationship with Stalin[10]) was chosen as the face of the campaign for the mobilisation of Polish intellectual resources under Soviet patronage. According to her recollections, Stalin told Wasilewska's husband, the Ukrainian writer Oleksandr Korniychuk, in 1943: 'the situation seems like the final break [in the relationship] between the Polish émigré government and the Soviet Union will take place … [and] in this case, Wanda could do a lot of [useful] things.'[11]

Wasilewska's activity is a good illustration of the Stalinist vision of the task of scholars and writers. After the beginning of the war, Wasilewska came to Lviv (former Lwów), which was occupied by Soviet troops, and soon became a member of the National Writers' Union of Ukraine. At this stage, Wasilewska was an ardent supporter of the Sovietisation and de-Polonisation of the eastern regions of the former Polish Republic. Among other things, she worked on the editorial board of the newspaper 'For the Soviet Ukraine'[12] and became a consultant on the propagandist film 'Wind from the East (*Veter s vostoka*, 1940).' This film promoted the idea that the coming of Soviet troops brought the liberation of Ukrainian peasants from the domination of Polish landowners.[13] The idea legitimised repressions against Poles who lived in the territory by depicting them as the exploiters of Ukrainian trade in these territories and suggesting that Sovietisation was the only fair decision for resolving this centuries-long conflict.[14] However, as disciplined Communists, Wasilewska and her group fulfilled the party tasks.

When the party line changed, Wanda L'vovna (as she was respectfully called among Russian speakers) turned to the Polish traditions and implemented Stalin's design of an alternative Poland. After consultations with Wasilewska, Stalin agreed to release many Polish writers and scholars from Soviet concentration camps. Being able to both gain Stalin's satisfaction with the project and skilfully imitate 'Polish traditional elements' were the key measures of the success of the mission. Characteristically, the Soviet participants in the 'Polish Project' under Wasilewska's supervision would ironically be called a 'pop (*pełniący obowiązki Polaka – an acting Pole*),' provoking an association with the Russian word '*pop*' which means 'priest.' The tolerance of the public display of religious beliefs and national customs was also a part of the programme designed by the Soviet leader and was understood by the 'Soviet Poles' as necessary concessions.[15]

After a series of defeats of Nazi Germany and the offensive of the Red Army on the Eastern front, the outcome of the war became clear. The character of the tasks that the 'Soviet Poles' faced became more extensive. With the approach of Soviet troops to the Polish territories, they had to find a method to reduce the resistance of the local population to the Red Army. Wasilewska's group played a central role in the preparation of the ideological programme of the Polish Committee of National Liberation, which was also called 'Lublin Committee.'[16] The Manifesto of the committee invited all sections of the country's population to take part in constructing a 'free,' 'independent,' and 'peaceful' Polish state. It was promised that 'fair' agrarian reforms would be implemented and that the property taken away by the Nazi regime would be returned. No communist mottos were included in the Manifesto. On the contrary, the promises to compensate the losses caused by the war to 'ordinary citizens, peasants, merchants, artisans, small and medium enterprises, institutions and the Church'[17] were supposed to convince readers of non-communist character of the reforms that the new government intended to implement in Poland. Additionally, the restarting of the Catholic University of Lublin (which was famous for his radically conservative agenda in the interwar period) was a sign of the readiness to allow a level of plurality both in religion and in the academic area of the Polish territories to which the Red Army would come.[18]

Nevertheless, the task of the pro-Soviet propaganda was still highly problematic. The interwar images of Soviet Russia, the fear of collectivisation and repressions against the Catholic Church were all strong obstacles in the path of establishing the new regime. Moreover, the arrival of the government supported by Communist Russia was strongly associated in popular opinion with the interwar idea of *Żydokomuna* (Polish for 'Judeo-Communism').[19] All these stereotypes had been mobilised by the leaders of the underground resistance movement that was controlled by the London government. The so-called Home Army, which coordinated the underground struggle against Nazi occupants during the war, was among the most important forces that were opposed to the establishment of the new government supported by the Soviet Union. For them, the coming of a pro-Communist government would mean not only defeat in the war, but also the collapse of the interwar ideas of Polish statehood. Therefore, their press propaganda actively used the anti-Soviet sentiment among the population to prevent the Soviets establishing their rule in Polish territory.[20]

One of the key events that influenced the balance of forces in this competition was the Warsaw Uprising in August–October of 1944. Having received the orders from London, the Home Army initiated the greatest anti-Nazi uprising of the last years of the war. The aim of the uprising was to liberate Warsaw from the Nazi occupation before the Soviet troops that were on their way to Warsaw. The idea of the Red Army arriving at Warsaw, which was under Polish rule, was the last chance to salvage an alternative political future for Poland. The leaders of the Home Army were able to mobilise the population of Warsaw for the struggle against the enemy, which still was superior in strength and military power. Nevertheless, Nazi troops fought against rebellious Warsaw in a cruel way. Mass executions, the devastation of the city, and huge human losses were events faced by all the residents of Warsaw in the last months of the war.[21] Thus, the Warsaw Uprising framed, in many respects, the end of the war and its results for most of the Poles who spent this time in Warsaw.

The inaction of Soviet troops, which was most likely caused by the fact that Soviet leaders knew about the 'anti-Soviet character' of the uprising, played an ambiguous role in post-war history. On the one hand, the propaganda of the leaders of the Home Army emphasised, during the final stages of the uprising, that the Soviet Union did not provide help to the Poles because it strove to destroy the patriotic movement in Poland. On the other, the tragic consequences of the entire campaign had negative consequences for the influence of the Home Army's ideology among the Polish population. Besides huge human losses, the defeat of the Warsaw Uprising resulted in a decrease in the authority of the organisers of the uprising and increased frustration regarding the abilities of the Polish Underground State.[22]

The advance of Soviet troops and the inability of the Home Army to oppose the establishment of the regime of the Lublin Committee forced the exiled Polish government into a dialogue with the Soviet government. The Prime Minister of 'British Poland' Stanisław Mikołajczyk (1901–1966) decided to make compromises with the Soviet Union in order to participate in the formation of the new Polish state. The fact that Stalin agreed to Mikołajczyk's participation in his 'Polish project' showed that the Soviet leader was still not convinced that the regime could be stable without building a sense of continuity with the exiled government.

During his meetings with Mikołajczyk, Stalin repeatedly emphasised the 'independence' of the Lublin Committee and argued that the Soviet government can only 'recommend' their 'Polish comrades' to take any given decision.[23] Countries from the Soviet sphere of influence being ruled via 'fraternal recommendations' became an important feature of late Stalinism.[24] This kind of management made it possible to follow various patterns in different countries and, at the same time, to keep the general political agenda under the control of Moscow. Thus, the Lublin Committee proposing Mikołajczyk for the office of Deputy Prime Minister was, of course, Stalin's 'fraternal recommendation' aimed at reducing the resistance to the Red Army on its way to the West.

Seeing himself both as a great geopolitician and as a theorist of political economy,[25] Stalin repeatedly mentioned that Poland had 'its own path.' The theoretical framework that made this possible was simple: the Red Army helped Poland 'to force capitalists out,' which made the dictatorship of the proletariat unnecessary. Stalin argued that Poland had 'a lighter, less bloody path, the path of socio-economic reforms.'[26] During one of the meetings with Stanisław Mikołajczyk, Stalin said: 'Polish people should not follow the Soviet Union. They should go together with the Soviet Union. The Polish nation has its path while the Soviet Union has its path.'[27]

Moreover, Stalin told Polish communists that a legal opposition was necessary to lure people out of the underground military units,[28] which were about to be violently destroyed by the Soviet security services.[29] Having understood the role of the Church in winning the loyalty of rural people, Stalin (who had, in 1943, re-started the Moscow Patriarchate destroyed by the Bolsheviks after the revolution) paid special attention to the role of the Catholic Church in the new Polish state. He assured Polish communists that the Church, 'under certain conditions, though not because of its love for the regime, could go together with the government.'[30] Thus, Stalin himself formulated the thesis of a 'special path' for Poland. The meaning and degree of the peculiarity of this path was open for wide interpretation.

Of course, there were areas that were directly ruled by the young Polish security services acting under the supervision of 'Soviet comrades.' Along with the activity of the remnants of the Home Army units, the popularity of Mikołajczyk in Polish society became a problem that could be resolved only violently. Thus, the security services started to play an increasingly important role in 'stabilising' the regime. They provoked a decline in the parties that were not under the direct control of communists and socialists.[31] In search of legitimisation for the regime, the security services falsified the referendum of 1946 in which, by all appearance, most voters showed their support for Mikołajczyk's political programme.[32] A large-scale falsification was also 'required' for faking the defeat of Mikołajczyk in the election of January 1947. Finally, facing the threat to be arrested, Mikołajczyk left the country. Thus, by the end of 1947, the security services had already destroyed the main forces of political opposition in Poland.[33]

Even though the early post-war years were a time of intensive struggle against the forces classified by the security services as enemies, there were sections of social life that were only indirectly affected by this struggle. The model proposed by Stalin implied a level of plurality in the public sphere of the new Polish state and, at the same time, presented certain opportunities for some 'anomalies' in its development. On the one hand, the Polish authorities were precepted by a large part of their population as agents of Moscow and collaborators with the occupant. The possibility of large-scale military resistance to the regime was always an issue in the authorities' agenda. On the other, Soviet 'advisors' never tired of bombarding Moscow with complaints about the trespasses of the Poles.[34] From the perspective of Soviet officials working in Poland, the concessions that 'Polish comrades' made with the 'reactionary elements' were unacceptable. Nevertheless, the criticism of individual Soviet officials did not provoke a large-scale reaction from Moscow. This ambiguity and the possibility to broadly interpret Stalin's suggestions allowed Polish functionaries to organise the areas of their activity in a special way. While the security services were dealing with the destruction of the political opposition, those sections of public life in Poland that were not directly associated with the forces marked as 'hostile' by the authorities developed differently. The cultural and academic life of Poland was the area of the public sphere that eloquently illustrated the peculiarity of the 'Polish path' in the early post-war period.

The 'gentle revolution' project and the virtue of 'progressiveness'

The prominent Polish poet Antoni Słonimski wrote about the roots of the project that determined the 'intellectual profile' of Poland in the early post-war years: 'When light was not yet separated from darkness, when there was no Union of Writers and no trams, the spirit of [Jerzy] Borejsza was hovering over the face of the waters.'[35] Indeed, the person who became the face of the Polish press in the early post-war period was Jerzy Borejsza (1905–1952). Borejsza had a rich biography. He came from a Polish Jewish family (his real name was Beniamin Goldberg) and grew up in the Zionist milieu of his father, Abraham Goldberg, who was among the founders of the Jewish journal '*Hajnt.*'[36] As a teenager, Borejsza participated in the activity of the '*Ha-Szomer Ha-Cair*,' which was a part of the Zionist movement, but later joined the left-wing section of the Polish Scouting and Guiding Association. The radicalisation of his activity resulted in a short spell in jail, after which his father sent young Beniamin Goldberg to France. This trip started the page of Goldberg's personal history that would later give the prominent Polish writer and Nobel Prize winner Czesław Miłosz the right to call Borejsza 'the most international of Polish communists.'[37] Paris (he studied Spanish studies at Sorbonne), Berlin, and Barcelona (as a centre of the 'anti-fascist' movement) became points on the map of Goldberg's intellectual experiences. There was a period when Borejsza was engaged in the anarcho-syndicalist movement, but later he turned to the most radical forms of communism.[38] After his return to the Polish Republic, he joined the Communist Party of Poland and was a member of this party until its disbandment by the Comintern in 1938.[39]

After the war began, Borejsza came to Lviv, which was occupied by Soviet troops, and joined the group of Wanda Wasilewska. In November 1939, he attained the position of director of the cultural and research institution 'Ossolineum.' In this position, Borejsza started his activity as an organiser of Polish cultural and scholarly life. The specific feature of Borejsza's style was to unite very different scholars and writers under the banners of 'progressiveness' and 'Polish culture.' Even though some members of the research staff characterised Borejsza as an 'ambitious Jewish dilettante who uses communism to make a career,'[40] his colleagues recognised his aspiration to find a platform for dialogue between scholars who represented different views. The prominent Polish sociologist Stanisław Ossowski, who worked for 'Ossolineum' as a research fellow, wrote about his impression of Borejsza's activity as a director:

> Borejsza is very tactful – no ostentation [in his behaviour], [he proposed the programme of] protection of culture, [he showed a] skilful attitude to former employees. [He delivered an] announcement of the opening of the Marx-Engels [research] Department and a large exhibition dedicated to Mickiewicz.[41]

In this brief remark, Ossowski highlighted the feature of Borejsza's administrative work that would determine his programme after the war had ended: the protection of peaceful collaboration between 'old' scholars and 'new' (Marxist) fellows.

Borejsza's skills in compromisation helped him to make a career when this competence started to play a central role in the new regime. Striving, according to the Polish writer and communist activist Jerzy Putrament, to be an *éminence grise* in the field of state-run publishing institutions, Borejsza soon became the 'Pope of the Press,' playing a significant role in censorship and propaganda.[42] With the creation of the Lublin Committee, Borejsza became the editor-in-chief of its official newspaper 'Rzeczpospolita (The Republic).' Later, he co-founded the publishing corporation 'Czytelnik (The Reader)' which, in the situation of the paper shortage, held large resource for the construction of post-war Polish journalism.[43] Contrasting the disciplined Soviet communist Wanda Wasilewska, who decided to stay in the Soviet Union after her 'patriotic Polish part' had been finished, Borejsza reached the peak of his career only after the war. Along with the organisation of the post-war press industry, Borejsza served as a cultural ambassador for the new Polish state. He took a journey to the USA and to Britain with a mission to promote the new image of Poland as a land of enormous cultural possibilities.[44]

Understandably, the emigrant newspapers were not inspired by the mission of Borejsza. The Polish press in exile was filled with claims such as 'the mass raid of Warsaw Communists against American Polonia – be careful!' and 'Now, the red press-Tsar of the Polish Communists Borejsza has again arrived in the USA to make a breakthrough in the Polish-American press and to inveigle some people from American Polonia to the Red Court with books and other lures.'[45] Nevertheless, Borejsza was able to establish personal contact with many famous Polish emigrant writers and scholars and to attract some of them into collaboration with the publishing institutions that he headed after the war. The idea that the new stage in Polish history and the certain autonomy of Poland from the Soviet Union opened up the opportunity to implement the most 'progressive' tendencies in Polish history was the main argument that Borejsza used in his negotiations.[46]

The concept of 'gentle revolution' (which Borejsza used as a title for an article explaining his political programme) is central to the early post-war project. It is noteworthy that this concept had its history in the Polish intellectual agenda. During the early stages of historical reflection on the Constitution of May 3, 1791, which played one of the central roles in Polish émigré historiography of the 19th century, the prominent Polish historian Joachim Lelewel (1786–1861) described this event as a 'gentle revolution.' The introduction of the Constitution of 3 May was one of the last significant reforms of the Polish state before the second (1793) and third (1795) partitions of Poland among Prussia, the Habsburg Monarchy, and the Russian Empire. Then, Polish king Stanisław August Poniatowski, with his followers, who were the most prominent representatives of the Polish Enlightenment, attempted to strengthen Royal power to make Poland more resistant to external threats. Along with attempts to maintain the sovereignty of the Polish state, the authors of the reforms associated with the Constitution of 3 May strove to use the centralised power to spread the ideas of the Enlightenment among the Polish population. The separatism of the nobility (whose rights were violated by the Constitution) was seen as a resistance of obscure landlords to the group of educated people united around the King for implementing progressive reforms. More importantly, Lelewel's 'gentle revolution' was a non-violent alternative to the French Revolution that dominated the intellectual agenda of the 19th century.[47]

All these allusions were important to Borejsza.[48] With his programme, he invited scholars and writers to become not the implementers of a programme prescribed from above but the main creators of the post-war reality. A non-authoritarian vision of culture and scholarship was central to Borejsza's ideology. The aim of the new regime was, according to him, not to govern culture but to create a milieu in which it would flourish. Arguing so, he wrote:

> If statism in the field of literature were not [nothing but] the most powerful idea of officials-illiterates, it would be necessary to create a department of training and education of writers, and begin training with the Jacobin literature of the late 18th century. But the revived and renewed Polish literature, no doubt, will do without statism and without coercion in the field of culture. The course of events and the social system compel the writer to abandon false opinions and return to a leading role in creating great changes.[49]

Developing this programme, Borejsza, in fact, argued that the 'gentle revolution' did not denote the introduction in Poland of the cultural and scholarly model established and made routine in the Soviet Union.

Implementing this project, Borejsza created a branch of journals that were meant to become a platform for the discussions between scholars and writers who were invited to conduct the 'gentle revolution.' The plurality in the public sphere was an important issue for Borejsza. The favourite child of his, the journal 'Odrodzenie (The Revival),' became an embodiment of his design. So, on the pages of this journal, one could find the essays of scholars and writers associated with the different intellectual movements of the interwar period, including Catholic activists.[50] In one of his articles published in 1947, he wrote: 'according to our deep conviction, the conviction of the Lublin men, it was the crucial task for us to call to gather everything that was alive and well.'[51] Making 'the old' a basis for 'the new' became a *leitmotif* of Borejsza's cultural politics[52] and his recipe of 'progressiveness' that started to be praised as a central virtue in the new Polish state.

From Borejsza's perspective, 'progressiveness' meant taking 'all the best' from both national and world culture and eliminating the elements that had lost their relevance. The call 'to be progressive' addressed to Polish scholars and writers meant primarily the necessity to critically reflect on their own intellectual background and to update their knowledge through the removal of 'reactionary elements.' In this sense, 'progressiveness' was supposed to become a self-improvement technique that scholars and writers were asked to adopt. It is not unimportant that Borejsza did not see 'progressiveness' in isolation from the idea of spreading knowledge among the broad masses.[53] Based on the Polish tradition of social criticism and, especially, the legacy of the prominent writer Stefan Żeromski (1864–1925), who among plenty of other novels wrote a small book with a characteristic title 'Snobbism and Progress (*Snobizm i postęp*),'[54] Borejsza saw the virtue of 'progressiveness' in opposition to the vice of snobbism.[55] Being sunk in the purely academic agenda or literary self-reflections, one could not be truly 'progressive.' Scholars and writers were supposed to be engaged in current politics and to take part in sharing their knowledge with the social groups that had not had access to the same cultural goods. This became the core of the 'virtues' politics' conducted by the 'Pope of the Press' and also the setting for the development of the Polish public sphere in the early post-war period.

Of course, the whole project of 'gentle revolution' was integral to establishing the new political regime in Poland. However, Borejsza was among those functionaries who could risk his own career for achieving the aims he had set. This line was not unproblematic for himself. His perseverance in constant competition with 'Soviet comrades,' who repeatedly threatened to replace Borejsza with 'a Pole from Voronezh'[56] because of 'anti-Soviet elements' in his press politics,[57] became a very important sign of his conviction that the project could be implemented in post-war Poland. The peculiarities of the staff of the censorship departments (who were under the direct influence of Borejsza[58] and frequently failed to be diligent in their work[59]) together with the fact that many of the Soviet advisors did not speak Polish were among the factors that allowed Borejsza to run his project. Moreover, the authority of Borejsza, who referred to the principles outlined by Stalin, resulted in the support that he had among other Polish communist leaders. High-ranking Polish officials, who personally discussed with Stalin the 'Polish project,' helped him to resolve the conflicts with Soviet officials.[60]

Borejsza's project was not isolated from the academic agenda. For Polish academics, the creation of the cultural and science-popular press in post-war Poland was not only a way of earning money under the conditions of post-war devastation, but also a reconstruction of a habitual platform for their public activism. Additionally, the restarted academic journals (many of them were also supported by Borejsza's 'publishing empire') addressed not only the academic community but also a broader audience. Most disciplinary journals started their first issues with claims of continuity from the 'most progressive' traditions of their professional communities and striving to make their scholarly achievements public domain.[61] Additionally, the government propaganda on fighting the legacy of the 'reactionary' regime of Józef Piłsudski (1867–1935)[62] (who had seized power in the Polish republic in 1926 and conducted the so-called sanation of Poland by introducing authoritarian methods of ruling) could meet some understanding in the academic circles. In combination with the ideas of 'gentle revolution,' it could be seen as a reference to the role that scholars played in the Polish republic before Piłsudski's *Coup d'État*, when academics could determine government politics.[63] Moreover, the formal destruction of the right-wing discourse in the post-war public sphere[64] and the limitation of the role of the Church in Poland could be seen as positive tendencies from the perspective of many Polish academics. Either way, the settings proposed by the 'gentle revolution' could not help but lead to the plurality permitted in the Polish public sphere that became an important marker of the early post-war period.

Łódź as an intellectual oasis of 'new Poland'

'I still cannot get used to the role of an important person who has to make daily decisions on issues that are important to other people. I am engaged in dancing among swords, wishing to give the University of Łódź a liberal face.'[65] With these words, the prominent Polish philosopher–logician Tadeusz Kotarbiński (1886–1981) described his first steps as a rector at the newly established University of Łódź in September 1945. Kotarbiński, a representative of the world-famous Lvov–Warsaw School of logics,[66] was chosen to preside over the construction of the infrastructure of Polish academic institutions. Kotarbiński, who spent the war in Poland and was one of the key figures of underground teaching under the Nazi occupation, was himself a symbol of continuity with the interwar intellectual tradition.

The devastation of Warsaw made Łódź, at least for a short period, the academic and intellectual capital of Poland.[67] It would not be an exaggeration to say that Łódź played a decisive role in the post-war history of Polish academia. Many of the key actors in the post-war academic debates had been involved in the creation of the new-style university in Łódź or were students at this university.[68] Łódź had not been as badly destroyed during the war as Warsaw. Therefore, this city possessed not only the infrastructure required for starting academic activity but also the industry that could make it the symbol of the reconstruction of the Polish state.[69] The University of Łódź became a laboratory for creating an academic milieu that could serve as an intellectual profile of the new regime. It is not an accident that the biologist Teodor Vieweger (1888–1945) was initially chosen to become the first rector of the new university. Vieweger's intention was to continue the tradition of the Free Polish University (*Wolna Wszechnica Polska*), which had been a 'people's university' in interwar Poland and had aimed at bringing the most progressive ideas to the broad masses. The tragic death of Vieweger in an accident did not allow him to head the university,[70] and the prominent non-Marxist philosopher Kotarbiński was chosen to replace him in this position.

Kotarbiński's idea was to create a 'liberal university' that would allow the masses to access university education. At the same time, his strategy to make the university affordable for the 'broader masses' was not based on 'class principles' in conducting the entrance examination to the university. Kotarbiński organised free access courses aimed at helping entrants from peasant and worker families prepare for their studies at the university. Meanwhile, he opposed the idea to make origin a criterion for university enrolment. The liberalism proclaimed by Kotarbiński meant, first of all, the university as a platform for academic dialogue. The freedom from any political or religious agenda that Kotarbiński promoted meant, on the one hand, the possibility of equal discussions between the representatives of different attitudes, and on the other, the idea that scientific/academic discourse should be purged of ideological elements.[71]

In one of his interviews for the press, Kotarbiński said:

> The University of Łódź wants to be accessible mainly to the children from working families; it wants to be truly progressive (the fact that it is [a] new [university] makes it easier [for us] to free [ourself] from the medieval ballast inherent in the tradition of old universes), it wants to be decidedly secular, it wants to have a free hand against any rigid ideological, worldview, historiosophical and other systems. It wants to serve the truth according to the best understanding of each individual researcher and teacher. Let the truth emerge from honest and free factual discussion.[72]

These ideas were rooted in Kotarbiński's philosophical attitude. In the interwar period, he had published his articles (among others) in the journal 'Racjonalista (The Rationalist)' and was among the active fighters against metaphysics and irrationalism both in academic and in public debates. More importantly, he had been deeply involved (together with other Polish logicians) in the methodological debates on logic and phenomenology which had, among other things, the aim of finding a purely scientific and non-ideological language for academic debates.[73] For him, the implementation of these principles to the academic practice[74] did not contradict the requirement of 'progressiveness' but instead embodied it.

His remark on the freedom from 'any rigid ideological systems,' which Kotarbiński mentioned in his interview, suggested that the University of Łódź was not supposed to become a 'Marxist' university. Among the professors who taught at this university under Kotarbiński's rectorship, there were many prominent scholars such as the philosopher Maria Ossowska, sociologist Stanisław Ossowski, and the theorist of pedagogical studies Sergei Hessen, who had emigrated from Soviet Russia to Prague and later came to Poland.[75] None of them were Marxists and the diversity of their intellectual attitudes demonstrated the plurality of approaches to 'progressive views' promoted by Kotarbiński. Of course, Marxists also found their place in the intellectual landscape of the University of Łódź. Nevertheless, the names of the departments, which dealt with Marxism, still contained their 'non-ideological' character,[76] and being a rector, Kotarbiński defended this principle when developing the structure of the new university. Either way, based on his philosophical attitude, Kotarbiński created, in Łódź, a milieu which was supposed to cultivate 'progressiveness' through the constant and critical discussion between representatives of various disciplines and various methodological and ideological attitudes.

Of course, the university was not the only centre of intellectual life in Łódź after the war. For example, the Scientific Society of Łódź (*Łódzkie Towarzystwo Naukowe*), which was restarted after the war, provided a platform for debates between scholars and the broader audience. Continuing the long tradition of scientific societies,[77] the Łódź Society hosted many public discussions between scholars representing different views. During these events, the broader public got the opportunity to discuss scientific issues with prominent Polish professors and learn about the recent achievements in the fields of their specialisation.[78] Additionally, many academic and popular science journals that would determine the intellectual profile of post-war Poland started their activity in Łódź.[79] During the early post-war period, the popular and scientific press, controlled and supervised by Borejsza, became the main sign of governmental support for the scholars who were ready to participate in the 'reconstruction of the Polish state.'

'Kuźnica' and the 'radical cultural programme'

One of the key actors in the post-war debates, the journal 'Kuźnica (The Forge),' first appeared in the summer of 1945, in the 'alternative capital' of the destroyed Poland.[80] This journal became a symbol of the 'radical cultural programme' for the post-war Polish state that was rising from the war ruins.[81] Although the leading figures of the journal described themselves as Marxists, 'Kuźnica' also became a platform for discussions between the representatives of very different methodological and ideological attitudes, which were classified by the editors as 'progressive.' The people who would constitute the core group around 'Kuźnica' took their first steps in public discussions under the patronage of Jerzy Borejsza. The intellectuals attracted by the appeals of the Lublin government joined the journal 'Odrodzenie.' Marxist philologists Stefan Żółkiewski and Jan Kott, as well as writers Zofia Nałkowska and Mieczysław Jastrun, were among the most notable people on the first editorial board of the journal.[82]

All of them belonged to the socialist milieus of interwar Poland, which had strong French sympathies and deep engagement with the cultural life of Paris and Warsaw. Before the war, they acted more as 'café intellectuals,' interested in critical social theory with very non-dogmatic Marxist sympathies. So, for example, on the eve of the war, Żółkiewski wrote from Warsaw to Kott, who was staying in Paris at the time: 'I am almost a Thomist. I am reading the "Summa [Theologiae]" the whole time and getting angry. This is perfectly done. Has no holes. Like a sphere of Parmenides. But there is no Marxian humour in this.'[83] This ironic tone demonstrates the character of the discussions that were led by intellectuals who, at that time, had no access to power and stood in radical opposition to the authoritarian regime created in Poland by Józef Piłsudski.[84]

The experience of the war, which most of the organisers of 'Kuźnica' spent in the General Governorate (i.e. the part of Poland occupied by the Nazis from 1939), increased their engagement with communism. Meanwhile, their knowledge of Soviet Marxism was limited. Unlike many of his colleagues, Jan Kott received training in the Stalinist version of Marxism–Leninism, under the supervision of Wanda Wasilewska in Lviv. Nevertheless, Kott did not leave Lviv alongside the retreating Soviet troops and instead came back to Warsaw, where Stefan Żółkiewski, along with other left-wing intellectuals, was already 'deeply stuck in the Communist underground.'[85] Since they both understood themselves as philologists, Polish studies became their subject within underground academic circles.[86] Thus, the 'circle of Polonists (Koło polonistów),' which was organised in Warsaw under the Nazi occupation, became a platform for discussions on Marxism and the Polish 'rationalist tradition,' forming a community that would shape the core of the editorial staff of the Łódź journal. The year 1944, in which they joined 'Odrodzenie,' saw a radical change in their status in the public sphere; the former 'café intellectuals' and underground combatants became the creators of a pro-government cultural programme for the whole country.[87]

The ideological agenda promoted by 'Kuźnica' was based on the idea of the essential differences among the political, cultural, and educational conditions of the interwar Polish state and the new post-war realities. According to this programme, the changes that happened after the war were an opportunity to move from 'eclectic stagnation, mystical, pessimistic or elitist escape from the reality' to positive and progressive cultural development. The issue that the editorial board viewed as a key task for 'new Poland' was 'to raise the new strata of the intelligentsia' from the working class and peasantry and to 'splice them with the progressive and radical achievements of our centuries-old culture.'[88] This statement illustrates an ambition to revise the vision of literature, science, and scholarship as self-contained entities and make them serve current social needs.

The most famous figures in Polish intellectual history were invoked to justify the 'progressiveness' of the programme promoted by 'Kuźnica.' The most prominent Polish poet Adam Mickiewicz played the central role in the pantheon of 'progressive thinkers,' as an intellectual who had a 'radical attitude' towards the social reality.[89] Besides the world-famous name of Mickiewicz, the Enlightenment thinkers started to dominate the public discourse of the left-wing press and serve as legitimisers of the radical social programme in Poland. Stanisław Konarski, Hugo Kołłątaj, Stanisław Staszic,[90] and other Polish Enlightenment thinkers were characterised as the 'realists' of the 18th century, while 'realism,' which in a broader sense meant 'social utility,' became an important criterion for demarcating 'progressive' and 'reactionary' ideas.[91]

Remarkably, even the Polish Romantics joined the ranks of Polish 'realists' in this understanding of the word. Thus, Mieczysław Jastrun, the vice-editor 'Kuźnica', wrote in one of his articles:

In occupied Warsaw, one could read, with trepidation, Mickiewicz, Homer, the Psalms of Kochanowski, Norwid, and some works of Słowacki, but the poems of most symbolists and late stylists could not be read. It was possible to find help in the works of the first [group of poets]; the others did not convince. They did not pass the hardest exam. They were useless.[92]

The Renaissance poet Jan Kochanowski (1530–1584), the father of Polish messianism Adam Mickiewicz (1798–1855), the mystic Juliusz Słowacki (1809–1849), and Cyprian Norwid (1821–1883) with his romantic motifs[93] were well accepted in the new realities, formally, because of their 'usefulness.' From this perspective, the post-war period brought not only hope for the implementation of the socialist ideals but also the socio-political conditions for the second birth of the most 'progressive' and 'useful' ideas of earlier Polish history.

In some respects, 'Kuźnica's vision of 'progressiveness' was even more radical than that of Borejsza. The legacy of the key thinkers of the Polish Enlightenment received, in their interpretation, certain Bolshevik traits. The editors of the journal claimed that progressive scholars and writers had to become the leading force of cultural reforms, which did not contradict Borejsza's programme. Meanwhile, unlike Borejsza, 'Kuźnica' had the ambition to rule and govern the cultural process. Developing this idea, Stefan Żółkiewski wrote in one of his publications:

> [under the old regime] the fact that the material means of literary production were owned by the private capitalist shaped literature and subjected it to the class interests of reaction. Our principal task is not only to obtain these means of production for the writer .... The reconstruction of our culture must have a planned character.[94]

Even though the 'capitalist regime' had been broken in Poland, the 'Kuźnica' group still strove to make culture a part of industrial planning. Later, Żółkiewski developed this idea in a more general and theoretical article discussing, among other things, the issue of artificial freedom:

> The postulate of the creative freedom of the artist introduces a lot of ambiguity in the practice of contemporary cultural policy .... First of all, the freedom of the artist is not a sociological fact .... The changeable historical conditions of the artist are the only sociological fact which is available for examination.[95]

On the one hand, this could be understood as a promotion of Borejsza's idea of the uniqueness of the post-war conditions that did not require any supervision over scholars and writers. On the other, Żółkiewski understood artists only as reflections of the socio-political conditions and put much more emphasis on the necessity of manipulative character in ruling the cultural process.[96] Although not a political party, but 'progressive' scholars and writers were supposed to run the 'radical cultural project,' and this programme had more obvious authoritarian tendencies. In this regard, 'Kuźnica's 'progressiveness' manifested itself differently than, for example, that of Borejsza[97] and Kotarbiński.

'Scientific' anti-authoritarianism and political ambitions of Polish sociology

The sociological group that emerged in Łódź also actively participated in the public debates and promoted their own vision of society. More so than representatives of other disciplines, sociologists considered the issues related to the 'construction' of a new society their sphere of expertise. So, the prominent sociologist Józef Chałasiński became not only the main organiser of a sociological institute in Łódź but also one of the central figures in the post-war Polish scientific journalism. Chałasiński came from a peasant family and made his career in the Polish interwar academic institutions. Being involved in various international research projects, Chałasiński was very familiar with the legacy of the Chicago school of sociology and even felt himself in agreement with their agenda. During the war, Chałasiński, much like Kotarbiński and many other colleagues, tried to continue his academic practice and give unofficial seminars, which had to be held in the strictest confidence.[98] So, by the end of the war, Chałasiński was already an established scholar with rich international experiences in his research field.

Chałasiński understood the early post-war years as a huge opportunity to develop sociology at a new level, as a discipline that would play a significant role in society. The first issue of 'Przegląd Socjologiczny (*The Sociological Review*)' represented the review of the most 'progressive' tendencies in Polish sociology. According to Chałasiński, these tendencies only increased in relevance in 'new Poland.'[99] Chałasiński's teacher, one of the founders of Polish sociology, Florian Znaniecki, played the central role in this genealogy of the social sciences in Poland. Znaniecki was the founder of the first Polish sociological institute in Posen (1921) and the first sociological journal 'Przegląd Socjologiczny' (1930) that Chałasiński restarted in Łódź after the war. Znaniecki argued that sociology belonged to the humanities and dealt with 'social facts' that appeared in interactions between people. Under the obvious influence of the Neo-Kantian programme, Znaniecki developed the concept of the 'humanistic coefficient (*współczynnik humanistyczny*),' which meant that the scholar should be capable of a psychological understanding of the 'sociological facts' that he examines.[100] According to Chałasiński, the 'progressiveness' of Znaniecki's legacy was, among other things, in his readiness to revise outdated sociological views based on a universalistic vision of social development (and Marxism was, of course, one of such 'outdated sociological views').[101]

In the early post-war years, Chałasiński did not hesitate to emphasise the importance of international communication for the most significant achievements of Polish social sciences.[102] It is noteworthy that the chief figure of the most important sociological projects of the interwar period, Znaniecki, left Poland for the USA in the interwar period and, by the end of the war, had become an American citizen and professor at the University of Illinois at Chicago. This was not an obstacle to listing his name among the members of the editorial board of the post-war issue of 'Przegląd Socjologiczny.'[103] On the contrary, Chałasiński considered the international reputation of the sociological projects originated and implemented in Poland the main measure of their academic relevance.

Of course, Łódź became a centre of attraction not only for Znaniecki's students orientated to the sociological agenda of the Chicago school. There were also specialists in French and German sociological traditions who developed their own research agenda under the banner of the sociological institute created by Chałasiński.[104] The seminars of sociologists at the newly established university were always a scientific event. In the early post-war years, all of the classics of world and Polish sociology could be freely discussed within research seminars. These discussions established the continuity of Polish sociology not only with the legacy of Polish sociologists but also with the classics of the German, French, and North American sociological traditions.[105]

Striving 'to be progressive,' the sociological journal reviewed the recent relevant publications in Polish, English, French, German, Russian, and other languages. This concerned not only the newest books but also recent articles in the leading sociological periodicals of Europe and the USA.[106] The list of books reviewed in the journal was also a good illustration of the agenda of 'Przegląd Socjologiczny.' For example, the authors put special emphasis on the relevance of the prominent book 'Ideology and Utopia' by Karl Mannheim with his criticism against ideology. Moreover, the liberal manifesto 'The Open Society and Its Enemies' by Karl Popper, who cruelly criticised totalitarianism in both fascist and communist versions, was warmly welcomed by Polish sociologists.[107]

Social scientists publicly argued that professional sociology should play a leading role in organising society under the post-war conditions.[108] Developing Karl Popper's agenda, Józef Chałasiński promoted the concept of 'public opinion,' which he claimed would become the main principle of 'democratisation' in Poland. Developing this argument, he wrote in 1947:

> Without public opinion, there is no democracy. Without public opinion, democracy is not possible at all. And public opinion does not arise in a vacuum. It is always based on social associations, independent of the state. This is a condition of democracy that applies everywhere, regardless of the changing system of class relations.[109]

Thus, Chałasiński, based on the newest sociological agenda, promoted the programme, which implied non-governmental forms of self-organisation as the cornerstone of his idea of democracy. Generally, this programme did not contradict the guidelines prescribed by the 'gentle revolution' project, though it stood in conflict with the idea of ruling the state promoted, and partly conducted, by the authorities. Either way, responding to the call for 'progressiveness,' the sociological group considered it their duty to publicly condemn the authoritarian tendencies in the development of the state and society.[110]

Trying to avoid isolation: Catholic groups in the intellectual landscape of Poland

Even a brief review of the developments in the intellectual landscape of post-war Poland would not be complete without mentioning Catholic journals.

For understandable reason, the Catholic press played a very special role in the post-war public debates. Even though the official status of Catholicism was not clarified in this period, it was obvious that affiliation with Catholic groups was not the best way to show loyalty to the new regime. So, publishing in Catholic journals was not the safest strategy for scholars who wanted to participate in the public debates. Nevertheless, the Catholic journals were always able to find authors for their issues. For the editors of the Catholic press, the idea of plurality in the public sphere promoted under the close supervision of Borejsza was vital. This guaranteed their right to publicly promote their views under the new political conditions. Without it, the public debates in the early post-war years would have been different.

There were two significant groups of Catholic scholars and writers that were directly financed by the Catholic Church and actively participated in the public debates. The first group was gathered around the priest Zygmunt Kaczyński who headed the Warsaw journal 'Tygodnik Warszawski (The Warsaw Weekly)'; the second one founded their cultural bastion in Kraków around the journal 'Tygodnik Powszechny (The Catholic Weekly).' Immediately after the war, the collaboration between these groups was very close. Most of the scholars involved in their activity could publish their articles in both journals. Nevertheless, the strategies of these groups were very different.

The Catholic journal 'Tygodnik Warszawski' became one of the most noticeable actors in the early post-war public discussions due to its radical attitude towards the role of Catholicism in the future of Poland. The journal started to adopt this attitude after the priest Zygmunt Kaczyński (1894–1953) returned from exile and headed the Warsaw Catholic group.[111] Kaczyński was born in Warsaw and, as a young man, entered the seminary. Since Warsaw was then a part of the Russian empire, Kaczyński continued his education in Petrograd at the Catholic Spiritual Academy. In the imperial capital, he had witnessed the decline of the Russian Empire and came back to Poland to celebrate the independence of the country. In Poland, the young priest Kaczyński had been deeply involved in politics: he became a member of the Christian Democratic Party, and later was among the founders of the Labour Party (Stronnictwo Pracy), based on the ideology of Christian Democracy. In 1919, Kaczyński became one of the youngest members of the Sejm and, several years later, was appointed to rule the Catholic Press Agency (Katolicka Agencja Prasowa, KAP). When the Second World War began, Kaczyński joined the Civil Defence Committee and was wounded in a fight. In autumn 1939, he left Poland, escaping from the persecution of the Gestapo, and visited the Vatican with the intention of informing the Pope about the situation in Poland. After his arrival in London, Kaczyński became a Minister of Religions and Public Enlightenment in the Polish government in exile.[112]

Thus, Kaczyński returned to Poland as a seasoned politician with extensive administrative experience in the field of 'enlightenment' and saw himself, much like Mikołajczyk, as a figure of Polish political and historical continuity. Immediately after his arrival in Warsaw, Kaczyński attracted many scholars and writers to both publishing and Catholic activism. He organised public lectures in history, politics, economics, and theology given by Catholic scholars who shared his political values.[113] The political and cultural programme of the Warsaw Catholic group was based on the conviction that 'The Catholic Church is a serious force and cannot help but fight for the right to participate in the political life of the country.'[114] One of the young authors from Kaczyński's group wrote in his article that compromises on issues of worldview 'can be understood by the opponents as a sign of weakness, therefore the Catholics have no right to retreat in this battle.'[115]

At the same time, it was the key issue in the agenda of Kaczyński's group to prove that their political and intellectual programme did not contradict the principle of 'progressiveness' in terms of their social programme.[116] They strove to show that the encyclicals *Rerum Novarum* (1891)[117] and *Quadragesimo anno* (1931),[118] which represented the response of the Holy See to the challenges of socialism, did not stay in conflict with the ideology proclaimed by the Lublin Committee. More importantly, according to Kaczyński, the social doctrine of the Catholic Church should be interpreted in an anti-authoritarian way. He argued that a true democratisation was not possible without the massive participation of Catholics in ruling the country in which they represent a majority.[119]

In general terms, the Warsaw group just mobilised the 'most progressive' ideas of the social part of their interwar programme. Promoting the traditional agenda of Polish Christian Democracy, the prominent economist and Kaczyński's associate Kazimierz Studentowicz (1903–1992) prepared an economic programme that proposed organising the Polish economic system 'from below' to avoid the concentration of power in 'the hands of the bureaucracy.' Developing his anti-authoritarian model, Studentowicz published a detailed analysis of the self-governing bodies that should take away management of the state economy from governmental institutions. Studentowicz's programme implied the decentralisation not only in the field of politics but also in the distribution of common goods.[120] It is noteworthy that the Warsaw group promoted this programme after the falsified victory of the anti-Mikołajczyk 'Democratic Block.' Then, they still hoped that their anti-authoritarian programme and the argument of majority could help to improve the situation of Catholics in the Polish state.

Another Catholic journal 'Tygodnik Powszechny' was founded on the initiative of the famous Kraków Cardinal Adam Sapieha, who spent the war in Poland and was deeply involved in the underground activity of the Church under the Nazi occupation.[121] The prominent theologian and priest Jan Piwowarczyk, who had been called a 'Red Prelate' for his radical social views in the interwar period,[122] was chosen to be the leader and supervisor of the Kraków group. Like Kaczyński and his colleagues, Piwowarczyk claimed his readiness to actively participate in the current politics. Developing this idea, he argued that 'the intelligentsia [in the postwar Polish state] became Catholic and thus the Poland that they will build will be Catholic.'[123]

Nevertheless, not all the members of the Kraków group were ready to actively engage in the current politics. Therefore, unlike their Warsaw colleagues, the Kraków Catholic group gained the reputation of a self-isolationist collective in terms of political issues.[124] Of course, many of the scholars and writers associated with the Kraków group also took part in the discussions that went beyond exclusively theological issues. Nevertheless, the younger members of the editorial board saw the destination of the journal differently than their supervisor Piwowarczyk. If Piwowarczyk came from a very radical (in terms of social reforms) 'right-wing' milieu,[125] then the people who would shape the post-war agenda of the journal had a different background. So, for example, the philosopher and journalist Jerzy Turowicz (1912–1999) (who would later become the long-term editor-in-chief of the journal) came from the non-antisemitic branch of the youth movement within interwar Catholicism.[126] Despite his unquestionable loyalty to Piwowarczyk as a Church supervisor,[127] Turowicz represented a different approach to many worldview issues. Like many other Catholics, he claimed that the war was a sign of the defeat of liberal values, which had been based on the 'wrong conception of the human nature' and criticised 'bourgeois culture' as a bearer of a wrong ideology. Meanwhile, echoing the influential trends within Catholicism, he argued that the ideology of the Enlightenment and scientism were the reason for the catastrophe of the Second World War. Nevertheless, Turowicz did not have any ambition to make Poland an 'island of salvation.' He was not much involved in the social agenda and the issues related to the agrarian reform. In contrast to Kaczyński's group and Piwowarczyk, Turowicz did not think that the crisis that Europe faced could be overcome by the political activism of Catholics.[128]

Another key member of the Kraków group, the theorist of law and philosopher Stanisław Stomma, developed this idea in one of the most prominent articles of the early post-war Catholic agenda. He argued that the Church had to be ready to survive the unpleasant times even 'in catacombs.' Responding to the accusations of opportunism,[129] Stomma warned Catholics against the 'primitive feeling of [their] own strength,' which could lead to a catastrophic clash between the new realities and Catholicism.[130] With this idea in mind, the young leaders of the Kraków group promoted the idea of not contradicting the official agenda without supporting it. The label of a non-political journal, which the editors themselves actively promoted, reflected their attempt to exist in the socialist period without striving to prove their 'progressiveness' in front of the coming social changes. This strategy allowed the Kraków collective to avoid being labelled as a 'dangerous group' in the secret reports of the security services.[131] Meanwhile, 'Tygodnik Powszechny' still provided a platform for those scholars, who were deeply involved in the public agenda of post-war Poland.

Bolesław Piasecki and 'progressive Catholics'

There was another group of Catholic activists that represented a special phenomenon in the post-war intellectual landscape. This group gathered around the charismatic figure of Bolesław Piasecki (1915–1979) and did not have a direct link to the Church hierarchy. Piasecki was born in 1915 in Łódź. From his youth, according to his friends' accounts, he organised different school clubs and underground communities while believing in his 'special destination.'[132] During the early interwar period, Piasecki was an active member of the national-democratic institutions headed by the nationalist Roman Dmowski and soon became one of the leaders within the group 'ONR-Falanga,' which represented the most radical wing of the nationalist movement.

Despite severe conflicts among nationalist leaders, Piasecki was able to maintain his prominent position among the radical right-wing fellows.[133] During the war, Piasecki prepared the project of collaboration with the Nazi authorities against the Soviet Union[134] but was soon arrested by the Gestapo. According to one version of events, he was released from prison after the personal intercession of Mussolini, because of Piasecki's contact with Italian fascists.[135]

With the arrival of Soviet troops, he was arrested by the NKVD but was able to get an opportunity to speak personally to the Soviet general Ivan A. Serov. In his talk with the general, Piasecki blamed the Polish Committee of National Liberation for its faulty propaganda strategy and asserted that nobody explained the real aims of the Red Army to Polish society. According to Piasecki, the new government should have emphasised the fact that Poland was an independent state and would not be included in the Soviet Union, nor would rebellious persons be deported to Siberia, thereby destroying the political diversity of the Polish state.[136] This act of political art was successful. Piasecki represented himself as an ardent patriot who was striving to act in favour both of 'his nation' and friendship with the Soviet Union, as well as being able to interest General Serov in his project (and in his personality).[137] There was a lot of showmanship to this: he repeated with his own tongue the slogans of Soviet propaganda on 'the Polish question,' and the director of the 5th Department of the Ministry of Public Security, Julia Brystiger, who was responsible for struggling against 'Catholic reactionaries,' wittily remarked later that Piasecki 'has sold to the Soviet comrades what he did not have.'[138]

Thanks to his charm and charisma, Piasecki got the opportunity not only to survive and to be released from prison but also to create a political organisation that allowed for the meeting of like-minded intellectuals and the creation of a publishing house for producing philosophical and historical books. Despite the fact that the previous activity of Piasecki in the fascist organisation ONR-Falanga was reason enough for his execution or, at least, for another arrest,[139] he was able to take a particular position in the socio-political landscape of post-war Poland. The Soviet general released him from prison, and there is evidence that Piasecki continued contact with the Soviet embassy[140] that protected him, by all appearances, against the Polish authorities. At the same time, he established direct contact with some chiefs of the security services that allowed him to continue his activity, even though the secret reports defined his activity as reactionary.[141] In any case, it was Jerzy Borejsza who played a decisive role in establishing the journal 'Dziś i Jutro (Today and Tomorrow)' as a press organ and, later, organisation 'PAX' for representing the views of 'progressive Catholics' lead by Piasecki.[142]

Piasecki and his colleagues from the interwar milieu understood the necessity of adapting their ideology to the new realities. It was not possible, in a state with the 'progressive' ideology, to keep calling democracy 'the Jewish bastard of the 19th century (żydowski bękart XIX wieku)'[143] as they did before the war. Under the new conditions, Piasecki did not deny his intellectual biography (it would be senseless since he was famous for his interwar activism) but started 'repenting' for his previous 'misbelief.' He wrote: 'We believed in the strength of a nation united from above, in one universal organisation. We did not recognise the elections and denied their meaning. We were overt supporters of a mono-party.'[144] Obviously, his 'repentance' was intended to refer to the propagandist promises of the communists not to destroy the political pluralism that had allowed him to continue his political activity under the banner of 'progressiveness' (even though in a very specific form).

Developing his 'pluralistic' vision of post-war Poland, he argued: 'We are currently opposed to a mono-party and all related systems,' mentioning that 'the opportunity to choose between good and evil without any mechanical pressure is the condition for the full development of the individual citizen. We have recognised this opportunity not only for ourselves but also for others. Hence, democratisation is a challenge for us.'[145] Thus, under the new conditions, democracy guaranteed the coexistence of 'materialistic and Catholic attitudes' in the public sphere. Of course, Piasecki understood that he could not dictate the rules of the game, and his new scheme was a protective one. Democracy served as an argument to prevent the monopolisation of the public space by communists and socialists. He blamed himself for the ideas that he now understood as dangerous for his own post-war activity.

At the same time, Piasecki maintained his monolithic image of the nation. The 'Program Declaration' of the group contained the idea that 'Poland is a nationally monolithic state.' This meant that the axiological hierarchy remained unchangeable in its most essential points; the highest aim of a person was, according to him, 'the service of the Polish nation.'[146] Immediately after the war, Piasecki had to formulate a new interpretative pattern for the Jewish question that was closely connected with his understanding of 'nation.' He declared a change in his pre-war attitude towards this issue.[147] The 'Program Declaration' contains this statement: 'Any manifestation of racial hatred against Jews should be condemned.'[148] At the same time, Piasecki remarked: 'Nevertheless, it should be noted that the new source of antisemitism is too much participation of Jews in the ruling apparatus ... disproportionate to their total number in the country.'[149] This statement demonstrates that the very idea of Jews as representatives of 'Jewish' but not 'Polish' interests was not only not rejected at the theoretical level but also promoted publicly. This ontological understanding of the Polish nation having its own special interests was very important for Piasecki's self-representation under the new conditions.[150]

Most importantly, Piasecki's group chose the closest collaboration with the security services as a survival strategy. When developing the idea of a national path to socialism (which was quite typical to Stalinist idea of nation),[151] Piasecki represented himself as a theorist of both socialism and Catholicism. The concepts of 'national historical aims' and 'national interests' remained in his writings and were, later, laid down on the basis of the sophisticated concept of the 'socialist-patriotic formation' (*formacja patriotyczno-socjalistyczna*).[152] His relationship with the security services and his international contacts[153] helped him not only to convince the authorities that his activity was necessary for the state, but also to make his publishing house (under the brand of 'PAX')[154] an alternative, non-governmental, and non-Church institution for spreading both philosophical and religious literature.

Close collaboration with the regime and participation in the provocations organised by the security services against the official Church[155] broke Piasecki's relationships with the official Church, which considered him an agent of the state.[156] Meanwhile, Piasecki's ambition to represent 'progressive' Catholics in Poland is one of the telling examples of how different 'progressiveness' could manifest itself under the 'gentle revolution.' Strengthening his positions in the intellectual landscape of post-war Poland, he strove to create a parallel intellectual world and put special emphasis on attracting university students and scholars who wanted to play an active part in politics beyond the state-run institutions. The realities of post-war Poland made it possible.

*

The idea of the particularity of the 'Polish path' became an issue in the Polish agenda from the beginning of the 'Polish Soviet Project.' With the establishment of the new regime in Poland, this idea opened a broad field for interpretation. The project of 'gentle revolution' was one of the results of this uncertainty of the limits of what was permittable under the new conditions. The fact that the organiser of this project, Jerzy Borejsza, played a key role in managing the biggest publishing corporation in the country made the public debates in the early post-war years possible. 'Progressiveness' became an umbrella under which Borejsza intended to gather 'everything that was alive and well' and became the central virtue that was praised in 'new Poland.' Meanwhile, the official discourse on 'progressiveness' received very different responses from the scholars who agreed to participate in the public debates of post-war Poland. For many of them, 'to be progressive' did not mean any significant change in their previous academic practice. On the contrary, they could continue to publicly promote the best forms of 'good scientific practice' typical to their disciplines and intellectual milieus. The censorship did not prevent them from publicly opposing the authoritarian model of society and academia. The idea that scholars and writers had to determine the intellectual agenda of post-war Poland became a cornerstone of 'gentle revolution' and a factor that resulted in the considerable plurality of the Polish public sphere. This made the state not a teacher and supervisor of scholars, but a helper in spreading the 'progressive' agenda among the Polish population. At the same time, Catholic participation in the Polish public sphere showed how far the visions of 'progressiveness' could go beyond the government's logic and to what extent they could openly contradict the authoritarian ambition of the regime.

Notes

1 *Rzeczpospolita*, no. 123, May 10, 1945.
2 Rudolf Pikhoja, *Moskva. Kreml'. Vlast'. Sorok let posle vojny. 1945–1985* (Moskva: AST, 2007), 110–115. Even though 'democratic election' was a precondition for the agreement with the Soviet Union, the control over the process was passed to the Polish authorities created under Soviet domination which made this 'preconditions' a fictive issue.
3 On the Polish–Soviet War 19191920, see: Norman Davies, *White Eagle, Red Star: the Polish-Soviet War, 1919-20* (London: Macdonald and Company, 1972); about the conflicts of national narratives in the region between the Soviet Union and Poland, see: Timothy Snyder, *The Reconstruction of Nations: Poland, Ukraine, Lithuania, Belarus, 1569–1999* (New Haven & London: Yale University Press, 2003); see more about

the preconditions and consequences of Katyn story: Inessa Jazhborovskaja, Anatolij Jablokov and Valentina Parsadanova, *Katynskij sindrom v sovetsko-pol'skih i rossijsko-pol'skih otnoshenijah* (Moskva: ROSSPJeN, 2014).

4 Usually, the concept of 'Katyn massacre' describes the execution of nearly 22,000 Poles not only in Katyn but also in other concentration camps like Kozelsk, Starobelsk, Ostashkov, as well as Kharkov and Mednoe. See more Natal'ja S. Lebedeva, *Katyn': Prestuplenie protiv chelovechestva* (Moskva: Progress Kul'tura, 1994).

5 Patryk Babiracki, *Soviet Soft Power in Poland Culture and the Making of Stalin's New Empire, 1943–1957* (Chapel Hill: The University of North Carolina Press, 2015), 20–30.

6 Many of them experienced difficulties with speaking Polish, see: Babiracki, *Soviet Soft Power in Poland*, 20–30.

7 About religion lessons, see the memories of Karol Modzelewski, a leader of the opposition, who stared his education in Moscow: Karol Modzelewski, *Zajeździmy kobyłę historii. Wyznania poobijanego jeźdźca* (Warszawa: Iskry, 2013).

8 Babiracki, *Soviet Soft Power in Poland*, 20–30.

9 About the experiences of Polish Marxists and socialists in Soviet concentration camps see: Marci Shore, *Caviar and Ashes: A Warsaw Generation's Life and Death in Marxism, 1918–1968* (New Haven/London: Yale University Press, 2006), 90–152; so, for example, Zygmunt Bauman was one of those young intellectuals for whom the participation in the 'Soviet Polish project' was the only chance to return to a public activity (see: Izabela Wagner, *Bauman: A Biography* (Cambridge: Polity Press, 2020), 74–85).

10 For example, Sławomir Koper argues that Wasilewska had Stalin's private telephone number, see: Sławomir Koper, *Kobiety władzy PRL* (Warszawa: Czerwone i Czarne, 2012), 58–59.

11 Wanda Wasilewska, "Wspomnienia Wandy Wasilewskiej 1939–1944," *Archiwum Ruchu Robotniczego* 7 (1980): 383.

12 Natal'ja A. Groznova, "Vasilevskaja Vanda L'vovna," in *Russkaja literatura 20 veka: prozaiki, pojety, dramaturgi. Biobibliograficheskij slovar' v 3 tomah*,1, ed. Nikolaj N. Skatov (Moskva: OLMA-PRESS Invest, 2005), 337–339.

13 Veter s vostoka, 1940 [Film], URL: https://youtu.be/k2v3ou8eFAo

14 See more: Jan T. Gross, *Revolution from Abroad: The Soviet Conquest of Poland's Western Ukraine and Western Belorussia* (Princeton: Princeton University Press, 1988).

15 Babiracki, *Soviet Soft Power in Poland*, 29.

16 All the most important documents were prepared in Moscow, and the first seat of the Committee was a small town, Chełm. Lublin became the seat of the Committee on August 1, 1944. Formally, the provisional government would be formed several months later. See about the formation of the regime: Krystyna Kersten, *The Establishment of Communist Rule in Poland, 1943–1948* (Berkeley: University of California Press, 1991).

17 See the text of the Manifesto: "Manifest Polskiego Komitetu Wyzwolenia Narodowego," *Rocznik Lubelski* 2 (1958): 7–14.

18 See: *Katolicki Uniwersytet Lubelski "Deo et Patriae"* (Lublin: Towarzystwo Przyjaciół KUL, 1947).

19 Marcin Zaremba, *Wielka trwoga: Polska, 1944–1947: ludowa reakcja na kryzys* (Kraków: Wydawnictwo Znak, 2012), 53–85.

20 See, about the propaganda of the Home Army: Grzegorz Mazur, "Walcząc bez broni: Propaganda i prasa Armii Krajowej," in *Wielka Księga Armii Krajowej*, ed. Ewelina Olaszek (Kraków: Znak Horyzont, 2016).

21 For the narrative of the Uprising, see: Norman Davies, *Rising '44: the battle for Warsaw* (New York: Macmillan, 2003).

22 Andrzej Friszke, *Opozycja polityczna w PRL. 1945–1980* (Londyn: "AN EKS", 1994), 8–9; Krystyna Kersten, *Narodziny systemu władzy. Polska 1943–1948* (Lublin: Wydawnictwo Lubelskie, 1989), 241.

23 Tatyana Volokitina, ed., *Vostochnaja Evropa v dokumentah rossijskih arhivov: 1944–1953 gg.*, vol. 1 (Novosibirsk: Sibirskij hronograf, 1997), 48–52.
24 See more about it: Nikita Petrov, *Po scenariju Stalina: rol' organov NKVD-MGB SSSR v sovetizacii stran Central'noj i Vostochnoj Evropy, 1945-1953 gg.* (Moskva: ROSSPJeN, 2011).
25 One of the concepts that Stalin used as a theory was the concept of 'people's democracy.' Coined during the Civil War in Spain, this concept provided a theoretical framework for the description of the post-war processes in the countries from the Soviet sphere of influence: Tatyana V. Volokitina, Galina P. Murashko, Albina F. Noskova, *Narodnaja demokratija: mif ili real'nost'? Obshhestvenno-politicheskie processy v Vostochnoj Evrope 1944-1948 gg.* (Moskva: Nauka, 1993).
26 Aleksandr Nekipelov, ed., *Central'no-Vostochnaja Evropa vo vtoroj polovine XX veka* 1 (Moskva: Nauka, 2000), 33.
27 See: "Zapis' besedy I.V.Stalina s chlenami pol'skoj pravitel'stvennoj delegacii vo glave s S.Mikolajchikom o vozvrashhenii prem'er-ministra v stranu, pomoshhi vosstavshej Varshave, poslevoennoj politike po otnosheniju k Germanii," in *Sovetskij faktor v Vostochnoj Evrope: 1944–1953 gg.: Dokumenty.* Vol 1: 1944–1948, ed. Tatyana Volokitina et al. (Moskva: ROSSPJeN, 1999), 86. See more about the role of Stalin in Chapter 1.
28 Tatyana Volokitina, ed., *Vostochnaja Evropa v dokumentah rossijskih arhivov: 1944-1953 gg.*, vol. 1 (Novosibirsk: Sibirskij hronograf, 1997), 457–459.
29 See more; Waldemar Strzałkowski, Andrzej Krzysztof Kunert and Andrzej Chmielarz, *Proces Szesnastu. Dokumenty NKWD* (Warszawa: Oficyna Wydawnicza RYTM, 1995).
30 Rudolf Pikhoja, *Moskva. Kreml'. Vlast'. Sorok let posle vojny.1945–1985,* 133.
31 Besides the Peasant Party, the Labour Party (*Stronnictwo Pracy* – which was a Christian-Democratic party with a 'progressive' ideology) became the main opposition for the representatives of the Polish Workers Party (in fact, communists) and Polish Socialist Party, which ruled the crucial ministries including that of Public Security, i.e. the repressive apparatus.
32 The first one concerned the abolition of the Senate as an upper house of parliament (the authorities wanted to make the Sejm the only house of the parliament to simplify the way of taking decisions); the second question dealt with a vague term of 'agricultural reform' and the proposition to nationalise only the 'big industry'; the third question referred to the integration of the former Eastern regions of Germany (occupied by Soviet and Polish troops) into the Polish state. Mikołajczyk opposed the discourse of communists and socialists who propagated the motto "Three Times Yes" and asked his followers to answer only the second and third questions positively. Even though, due to the mechanisms of falsification, it is difficult to estimate the exact results of the referendum, historians argued that the majority of Polish population answered the first question negatively. See: Andrzej Paczkowski, *Od sfałszowanego zwycięstwa do prawdziwej klęski. Szkice do portretu PRL* (Warszawa: Wydawnictwo Literackie 1999), http://www.kedyw. info/wiki/Andrzej_Paczkowski,_Referendum_z_30_czerwca_1946_r._Pr%C3%B3ba_ wst%C4%99pnego_bilansu
33 Of course, the 'alliance' with the Catholic Church mentioned by Stalin could not be unproblematic. Immediately after the war, no anti-religious propaganda was allowed in the official propaganda of the new authorities. Big Church ceremonies were tolerated even though they attracted many more people than political demonstrations organised by communists and socialists. Nevertheless, the Church had an ambition to actively participate in the political life of the country. Since the difference in the Church's vision of the political reality and that of the authorities were obvious, the Church became the key enemy of the security services. An enemy that they were not able to entirely defeat or to bring under full control. See about this competition in the early post-war years (see: Antoni Dudek and Ryszard Gryz, *Komuniści i Kościół w Polsce (1945–1989)* [Kraków: Znak, 2003]).

34 Kamila Kamińska-Chełminiak, *Cenzura w Polsce 1944–1960: Organizacja. Kadry. Metody pracy* (Warszawa: Oficyna Wydawnicza ASPRA, 2009), 48.
35 Eryk Krasucki, *Międzynarodowy komunista. Jerzy Borejsza. Biografia polityczna* (Warszawa: Wydawnictwo naukowe PWN, 2009), 9.
36 Krasucki, *Międzynarodowy komunista,* 23–37.
37 Krasucki, *Międzynarodowy komunista,* 9.
38 The son of Jerzy Borejsza, the prominent Polish historian Jerzy Wojciech Borejsza, told me in a private conversation that his father spoke openly about his former fascination with anarchism because it was a 'venial sin' of his youth that could help him to avoid conversation on the less pleasant sins of his biography. The matter obviously concerned first of all his Zionist activism.
39 Krasucki, *Międzynarodowy komunista,* 38–65.
40 Tadeusz Mańkowski, "Ossolineum pod rządami sowieckimi," *Czasopismo Zakładu Narodowego im. Ossolińskich* 1 (1992): 144–145.
41 Maria i Stanisław Ossowscy, *Intymny portret uczonych. Korespondencja Marii i Stanisława Ossowskich*, ed. Elżbieta Neyman (Warszawa: Wydawnictwo Sic!, 2002), 759.
42 Krasucki, *Międzynarodowy komunista,* 107.
43 See the structure of this publishing corporation: AAN, Ministerstwo informacji i propagandy, Sygn. 180. Sprawozdanie z działalności Spółdzielni "Czytelnik". K. 1–2. More about the foundation of the Corporation of "Czytelnik," see more about the corporation: Eryk Krasucki, "*Spółdzielnia Wydawnicza 'Czytelnik'—fenomen kulturalny lat 1944–1948*," in *Zaraz po wojnie*, ed. Joanna Kordjak and Agnieszka Szewczyk (Warszawa: Zachęta—Narodowa Galeria Sztuki, 2020), 114–117.
44 Grzegorz P. Bąbiak, "'Czytelnik' od Warszawy po Nowy Jork," in *Na rogu Stalina i trzech krzyży. Listy do Jerzego Borejszy, 1944–1952*, ed. Grzegorz P. Bąbiak (Warszawa: Czytelnik, 2014), 23–25.
45 "Jerzy Borejsza," *Gwiazda Polarna*, no. 28 (1947): 1 (Cit. ex: Bąbiak, "'Czytelnik' od Warszawy po Nowy Jork," 24.)
46 See his correspondence with the writers: Grzegorz P. Bąbiak, ed., N*a rogu Stalina i trzech krzyży. Listy do Jerzego Borejszy, 1944–1952* (Warszawa: Czytelnik, 2014).
47 Andrzej Wierzbicki, *Konstytucja 3 Maja w historiografii polskiej* (Warszawa: Wydawnictwo Sejmowe, 1993), 10, 17.
48 These historical allusions could be found in publications from the early post-war period. See, e.g.: Adam Ostrowski, "Hugo Kołłątaj i łagodna rewolucja 1791," *Kuźnica* 1945, no. 4–5 (1945): 11–13.
49 Jerzy Borejsza, "Rewolucja łagodna," *Odrodzenie*, no. 10–12 (1945): 1.
50 See: Hanna Gosk, *W kręgu "Kuźnicy": dyskusje krytycznoliterackie lat 1945-1948* (Łódź: Państwowe Wydawnictwo Naukowe, 1985), 59–60.
51 Jerzy Borejsza, "Ludzi i klimaty," *Odrodzenie*, no. 11 (1945): 1.
52 See more: Krasucki, *Międzynarodowy komunista,*. 113.
53 See more in Chapter 4.
54 Stefan Żeromski, Snobizm i postęp, in *Pisma Stefana Żeromskiego. Pierwsze Wydanie Zbiorowe, Utwory Publicystyczne* (Warszawa, Kraków: Wydawnictwo J. Mortkowicz 1926), https://literat.ug.edu.pl/snobizm/index.htm#spis.
55 Jerzy Borejsza, *Na rogatkach kultury polskiej* (Warszawa: Spółdzielnia Wydawnicza "Czytelnik", 1947), 14–15.
56 It referred to the principles of the recruitment of the staff for the Kościuszko Division. It meant a 'Soviet (quasi)Pole,' see: Kamila Kamińska-Chełminiak, *Cenzura w Polsce 1944–1960, Organizacja. Kadry. Metody pracy* (Warszawa: Oficyna Wydawnicza ASPRA, 2009), 48.
57 For example, Borejsza wanted to make Polish citizenship a criterion of access to the public sphere which, of course, was directed against Soviet dominance in the Polish press, see: Kamińska-Chełminiak, *Cenzura w Polsce 1944–1960*, 47.

58 Krasucki, *Międzynarodowy komunista*, 108–111.
59 Many of them were not party members and just followed the general guidelines prescribed by Borejsza. See e.g.: Kamińska-Chełminiak, *Cenzura w Polsce 1944–1960*, 66, 67; more about the staff of censorship, Ibidem, 57–75.
60 In such a way, Jakub Berman attempted to prevent all possible conflicts between Borejsza and the Soviet advisors, see e.g.: Kamińska-Chełminiak, *Cenzura w Polsce 1944–1960*, 42–43.
61 On the example of historiography, see: Tadeusz Rutkowski, *Nauki historyczne w Polsce 1944–1970. Zagadnienia polityczne i organizacyjne* (Warszawa: Wydawnictwa Uniwersytetu Warszawskiego, 2007), 129–135.
62 Józef Piłsudski became a central figure in the post-war propaganda. In the official press, Piłsudski was represented as an ally of Germans who helped Hitlerism and 'sold' Poles to Nazi-Germany: See e.g. "Człowiek, który nie powinien powrócić," *Głos Ludu*, no. 10, 13 January 1945; "Utworzenie Rządu Tymczasowego to cios dla Niemiec hitlerowskich," *Głos Ludu*, no. 11, 14 January 1945.
63 See about the role of scholars and scientists in the determining the borders of the independent Polish state: Maciej Górny, *Drawing Fatherlands: Geographers and Borders in Inter-war Europe* (Leiden: Brill, 2022). About the role of the scientists and scholars in the political agenda of the Polish Republic in the interwar period: Katrin Steffen, *Blut und Metall: Die transnationalen Wissensräume von Ludwik Hirszfeld und Jan Czochralski im 20. Jahrhundert* (Göttingen: Wallstein, 2021), 218–338.
64 Of course, the representatives of the right-wing movement remained in the public sphere not only in the form of 'nationalist ideology,' which was a part of legitimation of the regime (see: Marcin Zaremba, *Komunizm, legitymizacja, nacjonalizm. Nacjonalistyczna legitymizacja władzy komunistycznej w Polsce* [Warszawa: Trio, 2005]), but also in the direct continuity to the nationalist movement. One of the examples, Bolesław Piasecki, will be discussed below.
65 Maria Kuźnicka and Tadeusz Kotarbiński, *Poczta do Karmelu. Korespondencja Tadeusza Kotarbińskiego i Marii Kuźnickiej z lat 1945–1973* (Warszawa: Instytut Filozofii i Socjologii PAN, 2006), 26.
66 It is noteworthy that Tadeusz Kotarbiński self-criticised this term and made a division between the Lvov School and the Warsaw schools of logic, see more in Chapter 7. Nevertheless, this stereotypical name of the school was broadly used by both within and outside Poland.
67 See more about the complex contexts of the social and cultural processes in the city Łódź: Agata Zysiak, "People Will Enter the Downtown – the Postwar Ruralization of the Proletarian City. Łódź 1945-1955," *Rural History* 30, no. 1 (2019): 71–86.
68 When the University of Warsaw started its post-war work, many professors taught at two universities at the same time. The students who studied at the University of Łódź will contain the core of the group of young scholars who would be asked by the regime to lead Stalinisation in Poland and, later, became the leading figures in the protest movement of 1956. See more in Chapters 7 and 8.
69 Even though the situation with accommodation for students and professors was not unproblematic (see: "Uniwersytet dumą roboczej Łodzi," *Dziennik Łódzki* 13 [1946], 1), the rapid development of the city shaped, compared to Warsaw, unique opportunities for resolving these problems (Agata Zysiak, *Punkty za pochodzenie. Powojenna modernizacja i uniwersytet w robotniczym mieście* [Kraków: Nomos, 2017], 53).
70 Zysiak, *Punkty za pochodzenie*, 52.
71 See more: Agata Zysiak, "Modernizing Science: Between a Liberal, Social, and Socialistic University–The Case of Poland and the University of Łódź (1945–1953)," *Science in Context* 28, no. 2 (2015): 221–222.
72 *Dziennik Ludowy*, no. 38, 7 Febraury 1946).
73 See, the review of the interwar agenda of the milieu in which Kotarbiński was one of the central figures: Zbigniew Jordan, "Rozwój logiki matematycznej i pozytywizmu

logicznego w Polsce w okresie międzywojennym (fragmenty)," in *Fenomen Szkoły Lwowsko-Warszawskiej*, ed. Anna Brożek and Alicja Chybińska (Lublin: Academicon 2016), 223–232.
74 Zysiak, *Punkty za pochodzienie,* 63–66. It is important not to reduce the project of the University of Łódź to a communist project. The 'progressiveness' of this university was based primarily on very general idea of struggle against 'obscurantism' and the protection of the university from the influences of the Church. Most of the people who taught at the university were not Marxists. See, e.g. the syllabus of Leszek Kołakowski who was then among Łódź students in: Wiesław Chudoba, *Leszek Kołakowski. Kronika życia i dzieła* (Warszaw: Wydawnictwo IFIS PAN, 2014), 39.
75 Marek Styczyński, "Sergei Hessen, Neo-Kantian," *Studies in East European Thought* 56 (2004): 55–71.
76 Thus, the Department of Contemporary Social and Political Doctrines and the Department of the History and System of Soviet Law became the bastions of academic Marxism at the University. The Department of Contemporary Social and Political Doctrines was created for the Marxist philosopher Adam Schaff, who would play the key role in the process of Stalinisation of Polish academia, see more about his activity in the following chapters.
77 See more: Zbigniew Kruszewski, ed., *Towarzystwa Naukowe w Polsce. Dziedzictwo, kultura, nauka, trwanie* (Warszawa: Rada Towarzystw Naukowych przy Prezydium PAN, 2013).
78 Julian Kuciński, *Łódzkie Towarzystwo Naukowe w latach 1936-1996*, Część 1, 2: materiały (Łódź: ŁTN, 1996); Jerzy Mikucki and Sławomir Gala, *Kalendarium Towarzystwa Przyjaciół Nauk w Łodzi w latach 1936–1946 i Łódzkiego Towarzystwa Naukowego w latach 1946–2005* (Łódź: ŁTN, 2006).
79 For example, the journals like 'Kuźnica,' 'Myśl Współczesna,' and 'Wieś' that play a central role in this book were firstly published in Łódź. More about the cultural milieu of the city: Agata Zysiak, "Modernizing Science", 220–221.
80 Hanna Gosk, *W kręgu 'Kuźnicy,'* 50.
81 Zbigniew Żabicki, *"Kuźnica" i jej program literacki* (Warszawa: Wydawnictwo Literackie, 1966).
82 Gosk, *W kręgu 'Kuźnicy,'* 30–32.
83 Jan Kott, *Przyczynek do biografii. Zawał serca* (Kraków: Wydawnictwo Literackie, 1995), 29.
84 About the atmosphere of the cultural debates among the 'café intellectuals,' see the book of Marci Shore who, among other things, describes in detail the experiences of the intellectuals who were arrested for their communist convictions in the interwar period: Shore, *Caviar and Ashes,* 10–51.
85 Kott, *Przyczynek do biografii*, 103.
86 About the underground activity of Polish scholars, see: Friedrich Cain, *Wissen im Untergrund Praxis und Politik klandestiner Forschung im besetzten Polen (1939–1945)* (Tübingen: Mohr Siebeck, 2020).
87 See more: Aleksei Lokhmatov, "'Periodisations' in Intellectual History: On the Plurality of Continuities in the post-war Public Debates of Poland," in *Rethinking Period Boundaries: New Approaches to Continuity and Discontinuity in Modern European History and Culture,* ed. Jade McGlynn and Lucian George (Oldenburg: De Gruyter, 2022), 155–162.
88 See the manifesto of the journal: *Kuźnica*, no. 1 (1945): 1.
89 Mieczysław Jastrun, "W strefach ulewy i grzmotu," *Kuźnica*, no. 15 (1946): 1, 2.
90 Stanisław Konarski (1700–1773), Hugo Kołłątaj (1750–1812), and Stanisław Staszic (1755–1826) were key figures in the Polish Enlightenment. Besides occupying important positions in the Church hierarchy (Konarski was a monk, whilst Kołłątaj and Staszic were priests), each of them was central to educational reforms in Poland. What is more, they all advocated the centralisation of the Polish state at the late 18th century and fought against the privileges of the nobility (*szlachta*).

91 Jan Kott, "Droga do realizmu," *Kuźnica*, no. 8 (1946): 8, 9.
92 Mieczysław Jastrun, "Poza rzeczywistością historyczną," *Kuźnica*, no. 1 (1945): 16.
93 See on the cruel debates on the relations between Norwid and romanticism: Mieczysław Inglot, ""Norwid a romantyzm polski", Wiesław Rzońca, indeks oprac. Urszula Krzysiak, Warszawa 2005: [recenzja]," *Pamiętnik Literacki*, no. 3 (2009): 246–254.
94 Stefan Żółkiewski, "W sprawie organizacji życia literackiego," *Odrodzenie*, no. 4–5 (1944): 8.
95 Stefan Żółkiewski, "Uwagi o polityce kulturalnej," *Kuźnica*, no. 27 (1947): 1.
96 See more about Żółkiewski's cultural programme: Maryla Hopfinger, "Commemorative essay. Stefan Żółkiewski: 9 December 1911–4 January 1991," *Semiotica* 93, no. 3–4 (1993): 201–206.
97 The son of Jerzy Borejsza, Jerzy W. Borejsza, told me that his father took a distance to the activity of '*Kuźnica*' and attempted to make '*Odrodzenie*' more liberal the Łódź journal.
98 After being outside of Warsaw in the first years of the war, Chałasiński came back in 1942 and joined the academic community that continued the underground teaching under the Nazi occupation (Friedrich Cain, *Wissen im Untergrund. Praxis und Politik klandestiner Forschung im besetzten Polen, 1939–1945* (Tübingen: Mohr Siebeck 2021), 257.
99 Józef Chałasiński, "Wznowienie 'Przeglądu Socjologicznego'," *Przegląd Socjologiczny*, no. 1 (1946): 1–3.
100 There was an obvious influence of Wilhelm Dilthey's research programme that specified the fundamental difference between the natural sciences and the humanities. See: Wilhelm Dilthey, *Introduction to the Human Sciences* (Princeton: Princeton University Press, 1989). Max Weber's concept of *Verstehen* as a methodological tool also played a central role for Znaniecki, see: William T. Tucker, "Max Weber's 'Verstehen'," *The Sociological Quarterly* 6, no. 2 (1965): 157–165; about the research programme of Znaniecki, see: Elżbieta Hałas, *Towards the World Culture Society: Florian Znaniecki's Culturalism* (Frankfurt am Main: Peter Lang, 2010).
101 Aleksei Lokhmatov, "Auf dem Weg zur 'Einheit': Józef Chałasiński und die Suche nach einer 'erlaubten' Genealogie der Soziologie im Nachkriegspolen (1945–1951)," *NTM Zeitschrift für Geschichte der Wissenschaften, Technik und Medizin* 28, no. 4 (2020): 524–528. See more in Chapter 5.
102 The projects that Chałasiński conducted under Znaniecki's supervision, in close collaboration with the American sociologist William Isaac Thomas (1863–1948), constituted the core of Chałasiński's concept of continuity. This project, which implied the gathering of interviews with Polish peasants and Polish people who emigrated to the USA, was represented by Chałasiński as a valuable legacy of the Polish sociological school. See: Józef Chałasiński, "Zasadnicze stanowiska we współczesnej socjologii Polskiej," *Przegląd Socjologiczny*, no. 1 (1946): 33–36.
103 Lokhmatov, "Auf dem Weg zur 'Einheit'," 526.
104 The students of the other famous Polish sociologists, Stefan Czarnowski (1879–1937), Nina Assorodobraj-Kula (1908–1999) and Stanisław Ossowski also found a space for promoting the legacy of their teacher. During the early post-war years, Czarnowski was an important figure in the genealogy of Polish sociology, not least because of his interest in Marxism. Even though Czarnowski's programme had little to do with Soviet Marxism, for the early post-war years, Czarnowski seemed to be a good reference person for emphasising the 'progressive nature' of Polish sociology. See, for example: Stanisław Ossowski, "Stefan Czarnowski," *Kuźnica*, no. 6 (1947): 2.
105 The personal archive of Nina Assorodobraj-Kula contains her notes from these seminars, from which we can learn about discussions on Emile Durkheim, Max Weber, Georg Simmel, and many other sociologies whose works were not accessible to the public (and students) in the Soviet Union, see: Rps BUW nr aks 4228, I Kongres Nauki Polskiej.

106 See the section 'reviews' in 'Przegląd Socjologiczny' from 1946, 1947, and 1948(9).
107 See: Review on the book of Karl Popper, *Przegląd Socjologiczny*, no. 9 (1947): 477–483; The legacy of Karl Popper was intensively discussed among Polish sociologists after the war. See about the reception of Popper's works the diaries of the prominent sociologist Jan Szczepański: Jan Szczepański, *Dzienniki z lat 1945–1968* (Ustroń: Offsetdruk i media, 2013), 19. Regarding the influence of Karl Manheim, see Chałasiński's anti-Marxist programme in Chapter 4.
108 See, for example, Stanisław Ossowski's popular article about the importance of the social sciences in the post-war realities: Stanisław Ossowski, "Socjologia w świecie powojennym," *Kuźnica*, no. 25 (1946): 1–2.
109 Józef Chałasiński, "O społeczny sens reformy uniwersytetów," *Kuźnica*, no. 24 (1947): 3. This research programme was the cornerstone of Chałasiński's idea of formation of new intellectuals. See more in Chapter 3.
110 See about this period in the activity of Chałasiński: Leszek Wojtczak, ed., *Bunty i służebności uczonego: Profesor Józef Chałasiński* (Łódź: Wydawnictwo Uniwersytetu Łódzkiego, 1992); Andrzej Kaleta, ed., *Chałasiński dzisiaj: Materiały z konferencji naukowej* (Toruń: Wydawnictwo Uniwersytetu Mikołaja Kopernika, 1996).
111 The first issue of the journal was published at the end of 1945 when the chancellor of the metropolitan curia Zygmunt Choromański was asked to create a forum for representing 'Catholic views' in post-war Poland. Initially, the newly created 'Catholic Publisher's Committee' included primarily eparchial church scholars. Mirosław Biełaszko "'Tygodnik Warszawski' i jego środowisko (1945–1948)," *Biuletyn IPN*, 75, no. 4 (2007): 77.
112 Katarzyna Śliwak, "Activities of priest Zygmunt Kaczynski–Minister of Religious Affairs and Public Education in the government in-exile (1943-1945)," *Przegląd Historyczno- Oświatowy*, no. 3–4 (2016): 196–208.
113 Andrzej Friszke, *Między wojną a więzieniem. 1945–1953. Młoda inteligencja katolicka* (Warszawa: Instytut Studiów Politycznych PAN, 2015), 126.
114 "Katolicyzm społeczny a polityczny," *Tygodnik Warszawski*, no. 25 (1946): 5.
115 [A. Żur], "Neopozytywizm na tle rzeczywistości," *Tygodnik Warszawski*, no. 25 (1946): 5.
116 See, for example: Stefan Kisielewski, "Krytykom Kościoła," *Tygodnik Warszawski*, no. 30 (1946): 2.; T.N. Grabowski, "U źródła nowożytnej demokracji," *Tygodnik Warszawski* 41, no. 34 (1946): 1; Konstanty Turowski, "O pracy i ustroju społecznym," *Tygodnik Warszawski*, no. 44 (1946): 3.; Józef Maria Święcicki, "Demokracja a obyczaje," *Tygodnik Warszawski*, no. 128 (1946): 2. This issue will also be discussed in Chapter 5.
117 Leo XIII, *Rerum Novarum* (URL): http://www.vatican.va/content/leo-xiii/en/encyclicals/documents/hf_l-xiii_enc_15051891_rerum-novarum.html
118 Pius XI, *Quadragesimo anno* (URL): http://www.vatican.va/content/pius-xi/en/encyclicals/documents/hf_p-xi_enc_19310515_quadragesimo-anno.html
119 Zygmunt Kaczyński, "Kościoł, naród, państwo," *Tygodnik Warszawski*, no. 49 (1946): 3.
120 dr. Kazimierz Studentowicz, "Samorząd społeczno-gospodarczy," *Tygodnik Warszawski*, no. 26 (1947): 5.
121 See: Jacek Czajowski, *Kardynał Adam Stefan Sapieha* (Wrocław: Zakład Narodowy im. Ossolińskich, 1997).
122 See: Paweł Strachnik, "Ksiądz Jan Piwowarczyk, ojciec 'Tygodnika Powszechnego'," *Dziennik Polski* 24, January 18, 2016, http://www.dziennikpolski24.pl/artykul/3232284,ksiadz-jan-piwowarczyk-ojciec-tygodnika- powszechnego,1,id,t,sa.html
123 Ks. Jan Piwowarczyk, "Ku katolickiej Polsce," *Tygodnik Powszechny*, no. 1 (1945): 1.
124 See more about this 'escape to culture': Michał Jagiełło, *Tygodnik Powszechny i komunizm 1945–1953* (Warszawa: Niezależna Oficyna Wydawnicza, 1988).

125 See about his interwar discourse on the Jewish question: Jacek Leociak, *Młyny Boże. Zapiski o Kościele i Zagładzie* (Wołowiec: Czarne, 2018), 59–63.
126 Turowicz started to study at Lwów Polytechnic but soon changed his subject and, in 1939, completed a course in philosophical studies (though without receiving a diploma) at the University of Kraków. He spent the war in a village outside of Kraków but continued to take part in the activity of the underground Catholic press, see: Anna Mateja, ed., *Ludzie Znaku* (Kraków: Wydawnictwo Znak, 2015), 27–40.
127 See, an interview given by Turowicz in which he told about their relationships with Piwowarczyk: Tadeusz Kraśko, *Wierność. Rozmowy z Jerzym Turowiczem* (Poznań: SAWW, 1995), 20, 21.
128 Jerzy Turowicz, "Drogi do Europy," *Tygodnik Powszechny*, no. 3 (1945): 1–2.
129 More about this discussion, see: Przemysław Pazik, *Spory i wybory ideowe katolików świeckich w okresie narodzin komunistycznego systemu władzy w Polsce (1945-1948)* (PhD thesis, Warsaw: University of Warsaw, 2019), 22–25.
130 See about Stomma's strategy: Radosław Ptaszyński, *Stommizm. Biografia polityczna Stanisława Stommy* (Kraków: Społeczny Instytut Wydawniczy "Znak", 2018), 85–124.
131 See the characteristics of the Kraków group in the secret reports of the security services: Friszke, *Między wojną a więzieniem,* 218. It is noteworthy that the Soviet information bureau just repeated the official propaganda on the activita of the Catholic journals and, among others, the 'Tygodnik Powszechny,' see: GA RF F. P4459. Op. 6. D. 4382. L. 84–85.
132 About his belief in his special mission, see: Antoni Dudek and Grzegorz Pytel, *Bolesław Piasecki. Próba biografii politycznej* (London: ANEKS, 1990), 12.
133 See, for instance, his struggle in the national-democratic camp of interwar Poland: Dudek and Pytel, *Bolesław Piasecki. Próba biografii politycznej*, 100–102.
134 He did not sympathise with the Third Reich: he hated Germany and Germans. According to several records, he strove to create a public institution for protecting his underground activity. See.: Dudek and Pytel, *Bolesław Piasecki. Próba biografii politycznej*, 108–109.
135 Dudek and Pytel, *Bolesław Piasecki. Próba biografii politycznej*, 111–112.
136 See: Nikita Pietrow, *Stalinowski kat Polski Iwan Sierow* (Warszawa: Demart, 2013), 51. Piasecki skillfully played with the Polish 'progressive' tradition and expressed his ambition to participate in building 'houses of glass (*szklane domy*)' in Poland, which was a reference of the novel 'The Coming Spring (*Przedwiośnie*)' by the celebrated left-wing writer Stefan Żeromski and meant a fair and independent Polish state. Meanwhile, a 'house of glass' did not contradict the Soviet idea of Poland and was mentioned in the Tadeusz Kościuszko Infantry Division's song 'The March of I Corps.' I thank Bartosz Kaliski for drawing my attention to this fact.
137 It was commonly believed that the Soviet military named him 'a genius boy' in his personal conversations with the Soviet comrades. This story circulated through the different narratives. It was said, for instance, by one of the leaders of PPR Jakub Berman during the interview with Teresa Torańska (see: Teresa Torańska, *Oni* [London: Agencja Omnipress, 1989], 88).
138 This story was mentioned in the interview with a prominent Polish publicist Stefan Kisielewski ("Stefan Kisielewski o Bolesławie Piaseckim i jego rozmowach z Sierowem," in *Archiwum Stowarzyszenia PAX*, vol. 1, ed. Ryszard Reiff [Warszawa: Wydawnictwo Komandor, 2006], 76).
139 There was a special department that dealt with 'endecja elements' (The word Endecja is formed from the abbreviation for ND – National Democracy) within the Ministry of Public Security, see: Zbigniew Nawrocki, "Struktura aparatu bezpieczeństwa," in *Aparat bezpieczeństwa w Polsce. Kadra kierownicza.1944-1956*, vol. 1., ed. Krzysztof Szwagrzyk (Warszawa: Instytut pamięci narodowej, 2005), 27.

140 Mikołaj S. Kunicki, *Between the Brown and the Red. Nationalism, Catholicism, and Communism in 20th-Century Poland – The Politics of Bolesław Piasecki* (Athens: Ohio University Press, 2012), 77–180.
141 Andrzej Friszke, *Między wojną a więzieniem. 1945–1953. Młoda inteligencja katolicka* (Warszawa: Instytut Studiów Politycznych PAN, 2015), 243–263.; Dudek and Pytel, *Bolesław Piasecki. Próba biografii politycznej*, 151–189.; Kunicki, *Between the Brown and the Red*, 77–110.
142 The son of Jerzy Borejsza, Jerzy W. Borejsza told me an anecdote that circulated in the circles of the Workers Party. According to this story, when Piasecki came to meet the first secretary of the Central Committee of the Polish Workers' Party Władysław Gomułka, his secretary reported: 'Comrade Gomułka! Borejsza's Catholics have come to see you!' Of course, Borejsza was harshly criticised for his contacts with Piasecki. For example, the writer Julian Tuwim directly accused Borejsza of 'flirting' with a fascist, see more: Krasucki, *Międzynarodowy komunista*, 128–130.
143 Jacek Srokosz, "Model państwa totalnego w myśli Bolesława Piaseckiego," *Studia Erasmiana Wratislaviensia* 4 (2008): 74.
144 "Po prostu," *Dziś i Jutro*, no. 1 (1945): 2.
145 "Po prostu," *Dziś i Jutro*, no. 1 (1945): 2.
146 The formulations of the principles of the group seemed very similar to Piasecki's program from the interwar period in their key points, see: Bolesław Piasecki, *Kierunki, 1945–1960* (Warszawa: Wydawnictwo PAX, 1981), 7.; *Zasady programu Narodowo Radykalnego* (Warszawa: [no publisher] 1937), 1.
147 Bolesław Piasecki, "Po prostu," *Dziś i Jutro*, no. 1 (1945): 2.
148 Piasecki, *Kierunki*, 8.
149 Piasecki, *Kierunki*, 8–9.
150 See about the development of the discourse of Piasecki on the issue of Polish nation: Kunicki, *Between the Brown and the Red*, 77–180.
151 See more on this topic in Chapters 6 and 7.
152 See, for instance: Bolesław Piasecki, *O rozwój formacji patriotyczno-socjalistycznej*, in *Siły rozwoju*, ed. Bolesław Piasecki (Warszawa: Wydawnictwo PAX 1971), 5–16.
153 To take one example, with the French journal 'Esprit': Piotr H. Kosicki, *Catholics on the Barricades: Poland, France, and "Revolution," 1891–1956*. (New Haven/London: Yale University Press, 2018), 135, 142–143, 164–165; and with other Catholic institutions from different countries: Kunicki, *Between the Brown and the Red*, 77–180.
154 The security services allowed Piasecki to earn money through by private transportation, see: Andrzej Friszke, *Między wojną a więzieniem. 1945–1953. Młoda inteligencja katolicka* (Warszawa: Instytut Studiów Politycznych PAN, 2015), 246, 261.
155 In such a way, Piasecki took part in the project of the authorities that was called 'Priests-patriots.' The security services attempted to split the Church and the rural masses, see e.g.: Mikołaj Rostworowski, *Słowo o Paxie 1945–1956* (Warszawa: Wydawnictwo PAX, 1968), 48.
156 Friszke, *Między wojną a więzieniem. 1945–1953*, 257.

2 The Many Faces of the Soviet Union

Wiktoria Śliwowska (1931–2021), one of the most prominent Polish experts in Russian history,[1] had a favourite anecdote about her experience in communication with a 'comrade' from the Institute for Slavic Studies of the Academy of Sciences of the Soviet Union, Alexander Manusevich (1913–1997). In her story, Manusevich arrives in a Warsaw hotel and starts rebuking Śliwowska – who was responsible for meeting Soviet guests – for unacceptable working conditions in his hotel room, specifically the absence of a writing-desk. The young Śliwowska responded by saying that, though there are no writing-desks in Warsaw hotels, Soviet historians have access to all the archives, while in the Soviet Union, Polish historians receive a writing-desk without any access to the archival inventories. Following this conversation, Śliwowska was asked to visit the director of the institute of history, Tadeusz Manteuffel, who was famous for his harshness in communication. According to later retellings, Manteuffel told Śliwowska: 'there is a denunciation against you … from the international office of the Academy of Sciences …. Manusevich complained about you and asked not to allow you to meet Soviet historians …. I want to say sorry about that …. I have no influence on who has been sent to us … [and] no guarantee that it will not happen again.'[2]

This story, which happened several years after the period discussed in this chapter, properly illustrates the complex context of forced Polish–Soviet friendship, which became a central topos of post-war propaganda. The very figure of Manteuffel, who became the first director of the Institute of History of the Polish Academy of Sciences (after it was created on the back of the wave of 'Stalinisation' with the purpose of inscribing Polish historiography into the Six-Year Plan), is perhaps good evidence of this complicity. Manteuffel's hand was injured during the Polish–Soviet War (1919–1921) and this frequently caused awkward pauses in conversation with 'Soviet comrades,' who thought their Polish colleague had been wounded in battle against the Third Reich.[3]

This fact was not an individual case. One of the research fellows associated with Chałasiński's sociological institute (Chałasiński himself also participated in the war), Stanisław Ossowski, wrote in the autumn of 1920 to his wife, philosopher, Maria Ossowska:

> We are now driving the Bolsheviks out of what used to be Eastern Galicia. You would admit that it was nicely done: a victory under the walls of the

DOI: 10.4324/9781003428251-3

capital! Although we have huge losses, the country is devastated, everything will end in our favour ... my leg [was] hurt pretty bad .... Additionally, there are plenty of morally disgusting things that happen. Now, I understand that, in certain situations, Stoic philosophy is the last resort. Though I prefer our Polish 'somehow it will be (*jakoś to będzie*).'[4]

Thus, Ossowski, much like many other Polish scholars who took an active part in the post-war public debates, not only was among the courageous fighters against Bolshevist Russia but also developed his scholarly agenda under the impression of the Polish–Soviet War.

Of course, participation in the war against the young Soviet state was not the only possible 'misconduct' against the 'elder brother' that could have happened in the recent past. The interwar activities in Zionist organisations and the fascination with anarchism of the communist functionary Jerzy Borejsza did not make for the ideal intellectual biography in the view of the Soviet bureaucracy, which characteristically looked for discrediting relationships in the past.[5] Moreover, the 'Stalinisation' of the Communist Party of Poland in the late 1920s, the cruel struggle against the social-democratic parties as 'fascists,' and at last the disbandment of the party by the International in 1938 for their 'harmful (*vreditel'skaja*)' activity, left most of the people whose opinions will make up the core of this book 'in the same boat' regarding their 'problematic past' in the face of 'close friendship' with the Soviet Union. Immediately after the war, the absence of clear instructions on how Soviet Russia had to be represented[6] resulted in the appearance of various 'Soviet Unions' in the Polish public sphere. Therefore, the public debates on the Soviet Union are a good source for tracing the readiness of Polish scholars to defend their own academic agenda.

The surface image of the Soviet Union in the Polish public sphere came to Poland through the propaganda of the Red Army. In accordance with the logic of reducing resistance to the establishment of the new regime, not academics but the abstract 'popular masses' were the voiceless target audience for a propagandistic campaign that was aimed at 'revising anti-Soviet stereotypes.' During the Polish–Soviet War, the Polish streets were filled with such posters as 'Again the Jewish hands? No, never!'[7] or 'Who believes in God – let's defend [the icon of] Ostrobramska,[8]' while the Polish Episcopate characterised the Bolsheviks in their epistles as enemies who 'combine cruelty and the desire for destruction with the hatred of the entire culture, especially Christianity and the Church,' and who were led by the 'spirit of the antichrist.'[9] Besides the religious and antisemitic aspects of the 'popular image' of the Soviet Union, of course, the stories regarding the Bolsheviks' methods of collectivisation became a challenge for pro-Soviet propaganda following the war. The active role of the peasants in the Polish–Soviet War was mostly determined by conviction that the arrival of the Bolsheviks would mean the loss of their land holdings.[10] The combination of these factors was reason enough for constant emphasis of the independence of the new Polish state from the Soviet Union in the propaganda of the new government.

Major K. I. Orlov, a representative of the Soviet Information Bureau (Sovinformbiuro) in Poland, had many troubles with 'Polish comrades,' who led the 'information policy,' to the Soviet eye, 'in a very unacceptable way, with the excuse being the peculiarity of the Polish context.'[11] Nevertheless, accepting the peculiarity of the Polish context, he wrote to Moscow asking them not to send articles written by authors with Jewish names, and to avoid any references to collectivisation.[12] Besides this, Orlov reported to Moscow, 'the Polish intelligentsia considers us, Russians, to be Asians and themselves to be the bearers of high Western culture.'[13] This remark reflected the fact that the Soviet advisers not only failed to enjoy much respect in the Polish intellectual circles but also were well aware of it. The self-image of the Soviet Union, which had usually shaped the core propaganda on this issue, did not seem to be working in postwar Poland.

Of course, this did not make Soviet officials more modest in promoting the 'correct view' of Soviet Russia. On the contrary, the Soviet adviser Iakovlev repeatedly attempted to teach Jerzy Borejsza how to represent the image of the Soviet Union in the Polish public sphere and complained about his mistaken understanding of the information policy.[14] Nevertheless, the author of the 'gentle revolution' project did not seem to follow Iakovlev's guidelines and continued to promote his own ideological programme, which did not imply a deep admiration of the achievements of Stalinist Russia. The Polish publishing institutions led by Borejsza repeatedly refused to publish the materials proposed by the Sovinformbiuro[15] and thus insisted on the independence of their public agenda.

The ability to resist the pressure of Soviet advisors regarding one of the most 'unsafe' issues is only one more illustration of the peculiarity of the early postwar period under the 'gentle revolution.' The 'delicate character' of this issue and the possible consequences of imprudence regarding this matter were the central arguments in the agenda of Borejsza and his colleagues, which encouraged them to contradict Soviet officials. Of course, the Polish government fully understood that the reports of the Sovinformbiuro, the Soviet Embassy, and the Telegraph Agency of the Soviet Union (TASS)[16] ended up on Moscow tables and could cause at least a few difficulties in their communication with the Soviet government. Therefore, the treatment of the image of the Soviet Union still was very careful. However, the authors of the 'gentle revolution' project did not want to establish total control over the use of the image of the Soviet Union in the public sphere, nor did they want to destroy the certain autonomy of the participants in the public debates. All the participants in the public agenda of Poland understood that the Soviet Union was a dangerous topic. The public statements that concerned the Soviet Union could only be 'positive.' Nevertheless, they could be coloured by different shades of this 'positiveness.' Playing with these colours was a way of delivering various messages not only regarding the Soviet Union itself but also regarding the current political and academic agenda. The official propaganda provided the participants in public discussions only with very general guidelines in this regard.

The 'guidelines' of propaganda

It is noteworthy that Borejsza strove for independence from 'Soviet comrades' even in defining the basics of post-war propaganda. Due to this, the issues related to the Soviet Union took only 11th and 17th place in the list of relevant topics for the training of propaganda staff.[17] Usually, the propagandistic image of the Soviet Union appeared in relation to the issues that were supposed to win the sympathies of the Polish population. The official newspaper of the Polish Workers' Party 'Głos Ludu (The Voice of People)' became one of the leading forces in delivering the 'official point of view' on the current issues. This newspaper was headed by communist Ostap Dłuski, who left Poland for the Soviet Union in 1929 while escaping from the persecution of the Polish authorities. Later, Dłuski became an activist of the Slavic Committee, which promoted 'All-Slavic Unity' in the struggle against Nazi Germany. 'Głos Ludu' was especially active in delivering the idea that the 'reactionary Sanation regime' of Józef Piłsudski – sympathies to which had to be vanished from Polish minds – intentionally distorted the 'true image of the Soviet Union,'[18] playing right into the hands of 'his German friends.'[19] So, the 'Sanation' was reactionary because of the 'pro-German sympathies' of Piłsudski, who 'had sold Poland to the Germans,'[20] and the Soviet Union was a friend, first of all, because it liberated Poland from Germany.[21]

Since the 'German question' was, in a sense, a precondition of a positive image of the Soviet Union, this aspect played a central role in the official discourse on this matter. The 'usefulness' of the friendship with the Soviet Union was determined by references to the threat of a 'German revival.' The new territory image of the post-war Polish state also played an important role in the pro-Soviet agenda. Under the supervision of the Soviet Union, the Polish government established administrative institutions in the former eastern territories of the German state. Additionally, at the international level, Soviet diplomacy promoted the idea of putting these territories officially under Polish rule, and such a decision had been taken at the Potsdam conference (1945).[22] Among other things, Polish rule over the new, well-industrialised territories was commonly regarded as 'compensation' delivered by the Soviet Union to Poland 'instead' of the eastern regions of the Polish Republic, which had been annexed by the Soviet Union in 1939. In the official propaganda, the new western regions of Poland were described as 'Recovered Territories' with references to the history of the Polish medieval 'Piast dynasty' that had possessed part of these lands, while the Soviet Union was represented as the only defender of the new western Polish borders.[23]

This aspect shaped a space for the promotion of 'Slavic Unity,' which was hardly applicable to the Polish intellectual tradition. At the institutional level, this ideology was propagated primarily by the All-Slavic Committee.[24] Nevertheless, it still seemed highly unnatural in the Polish political discourse and even Major Orlov from the Sovinformbiuro predicted a problematic future for this ideology in Poland.[25] Either way, even though the emphasis on the All-Slavic ideology was orientated more to 'the readers in Moscow,' the idea of the German threat allowed the creators of this discourse to bring a certain 'logic' to the concept of the 'brotherly friendship' between the Polish and 'Soviet' nations. Since the image of the Soviet Union referred, in the popular view, to the image of Russia, there was no essential contradiction in depicting the historical competition with Germany as an opposition between the German and 'Slavic' nations.[26] Developing this idea, the communist ideologist and disciplined broadcaster of the workers' party line Roman Werfel (1906–2003) succeeded in glorifying the leading role of the Soviet Union in the Slavic movement, as well as promoting the idea of the 'Slavic dam' on the western borders as the most vital argument for orientating towards the Soviet Union in foreign policy.[27]

Another significant aspect of the image of the Soviet state promoted by propaganda can also serve as evidence of the ambiguity of the task faced by the propagandists. While the regime of Józef Piłsudski was accused of intentionally distorting the Soviet project in the eyes of the Poles, the October Revolution was represented as the key event in Russian history that had changed the nature of the Russian state. The negative image of the Russian empire rooted in both traditional Polish historical narratives and in the personal experience of many Poles was considered in the 'revision of national stereotypes.' The Soviet state was described as an antipode to the Russian empire, and thus the Red Army as an antithesis to the imperial one. According to this logic, if the czarist regime was based on oppression of the people and 'czarist soldiers' served the authorities without knowing the aim of their service, Soviet Russia had become a 'people's state' and Soviet soldiers were fully conscious of their high mission.[28] Of course, there was no place for the Polish–Soviet War in this picture of the official propaganda. Moreover, the references to friendship with the Red Army could also be seen as a warning. It was repeatedly emphasised that the main source of legitimacy for the new regime was the alliance of the Polish governmental institutions with Soviet troops, which made them the only possible power in the Polish territories.[29] Thus, the opponents of the new authorities would become the enemies of the Red Army.

Meanwhile, continuing the strategy proposed by Stalin, the early post-war propaganda emphasised the fundamental differences between the Soviet Union and Poland. Stalin's idea of the 'special path' for Poland was also used in propaganda to convince Poles of the 'safety' of this friendship. The liberation of the Polish territories was represented as a common achievement of Soviet and Polish troops, with the Soviet Union as the only protector of Polish independence.[30] Additionally, reacting to the fears of the rural population regarding the possible collectivisation of their lands, the propaganda claimed that there was no need for such radical agrarian politics in Poland. Continuing the line of the Lublin Committee, the official propaganda claimed that the agrarian reform planned for Poland was a manifestation of the Polish 'special path' and evidence of the possibility of not following the model of the Soviet state.[31]

The 'revision of anti-Soviet stereotypes' was not a programme prepared in Soviet cabinets[32] but a task for Polish propagandists who, in turn, had to consider plenty of factors. The opinion of Moscow, the stereotypes of the Polish population, and the possibility of civil war were among the key factors that formed the basic framework for the public discourse on this issue in the early post-war years. In this regard, propaganda served as a guideline but not a set of clichés that were to be repeated without deep reflections on their content. The lack of a strong idea (also among the censorship staff) on what the limits of the permissible were could not help but lead to a plurality of approaches to the image of the Soviet Union. In the combination of basic principles of the 'gentle revolution,' the debates on the Soviet Union became a reflection of the peculiarity of the 'virtues' politics' conducted in the early post-war years.

'Discovering' Russian culture in a non-Stalinist way

One of the most prominent specialists in Russian history, Andrzej Walicki (1930–2020), wrote in his memoirs that the key reason why he decided to choose Russian studies was the 'unreliability' of studying Polish literature.[33] Since the ban on the study of Polish language and culture was one of the main sanctions that had been used by the czarist government against rebellious Poles in the 19th century, the obstacles faced by Walicki on his way to Polish studies were, in a sense, a lesson on the subject of his future specialisation. Nevertheless, the realities of the early post-war years were different. The story, which Walicki told the reader, can illustrate the difference between the realities of the early post-war period and the time of Stalinism, the point at which Walicki entered Polish academia. In the early post-war years, 'Russian culture' was still not an instrument of repressions, despite all the attempts of Soviet officials to make it an instrument in winning the sympathies of the Polish population.[34]

The writer and Nobel prize winner Czesław Miłosz (who emigrated from Poland in 1951) wrote in his prominent book 'The Captive Mind' about the interwar period:

> We lived less than a hundred miles from the borders of the Soviet Union, yet we had no more knowledge of it than did the inhabitants of Brazil. The border was hermetically sealed. We were situated on the peripheries of a world that differed from the East as much as if it were another planet.[35]

Miłosz's statement was not an exaggeration. The knowledge of the Soviet realities among most Polish scholars and writers was not as deep as it may appear at first glance. In a sense, the early post-war years were, for them, a time of 'learning' how to speak about the Soviet state that could represent a direct military threat to people living in Poland. Since the direct supervision of Soviet advisers over the Polish public sphere was very limited by the barriers constructed by Borejsza, the search for a 'Soviet Union' that would not threaten the principles of 'gentle revolution' became an important feature of the early post-war period.

It would be an overstatement to say that the Soviet Union played a crucial role in the public sphere of Poland immediately after the war. Of course, all cultural periodicals in post-war Poland contained reviews of Soviet current events and articles reporting on the scientific and cultural achievements of the Soviet state. The professional journals of individual disciplines, in turn, provided reviews of Russian language publications. Nevertheless, the Soviet Union did not dominate either the public or academic agenda in Poland. The fact that most academic journals continued to present their tables of contents in Polish, English, and, in some cases, French was one of many signs of the intellectual orientation of Polish academia.[36]

The leading cultural and popular science journals provided the reader only with very general information regarding the Soviet cultural and academic life. Such titles as 'the Soviet Academy of Sciences,'[37] 'the Cultural Chronicles of the USSR,'[38] and the 'Organisation of Science in the Soviet Union'[39] preceded rather brief reviews of general ideological attitudes and celebrated the Soviet Union without having any significant impact on the agenda of the current public debates. Understandably, the general ideological claims of current propaganda were repeated in the introductory articles of the key state-run journals,[40] but the core publications avoided deep affiliation with the Soviet Union.

Meanwhile, 'Russian culture' still played a noticeable role in the public discourse of the state-run press. Traditionally, literature was a favourite instrument of Soviet 'cultural propaganda,'[41] and the Polish public got the opportunity to read famous pieces of Russian literary canon in Polish translation. Of course, this 'interest' towards 'Russian culture' in the state-run press reflected the necessity to publish the results of the official institutional collaboration within the 'Polish-Soviet cultural friendship,' rather than the aspirations of the editors of the Polish journals.[42] Either way, the promotion of Russian literature was a good compromise regarding the fundamental principles the 'gentle revolution' project was based on. On the one hand, the publication of Russian literature could be seen as a sign of loyalty towards the Soviet Union and a kind of 'consolation' for Soviet officials. On the other, the legacy of Russian culture could be used for propagating forms of 'progressiveness' that became the cornerstone of 'gentle revolution.'

The collection of authors selected to represent Soviet culture was diverse. Not surprisingly, the prominent Russian poet Alexander Pushkin (1799–1837) started to play the central role in the campaign for familiarising the Polish audience with Russian culture. Posthumously, Pushkin became the central figure in Russian literary canon. After a brief period of revolutionary rebellion against the classics of Russian culture, Pushkin returned to his leading position in the cultural pantheon of Stalinist Russia. During the new wave of Stalinist terror in the Soviet Union, the 100-year anniversary of Pushkin's death in 1937 became a symbol of acceptance of the Russian intellectual tradition by Stalin's command. The main propaganda newspaper 'Pravda (the Truth)' wrote in its publication on this occasion: 'Pushkin is entirely ours, Soviet, because the Soviet government inherited everything that is best in our nation. Ultimately, Pushkin's work merged with the October socialist revolution, as a river flows into the ocean.'[43] This 'our Soviet' Pushkin played the central role in the self-presentation of the Soviet Union, and his appearance in the Polish public sphere was, in a sense, a reflection of this role of the Russian poet.[44]

The image of Pushkin was also represented in his constant dialogue with the Polish cultural icon of the 19th century, Adam Mickiewicz. Their 'friendship' was to become a symbol of the friendship between Polish and Soviet cultures.[45] Of course, these references to the figure of Pushkin and his 'friendship' with Mickiewicz were historically problematic. The radical break in the relationship between the two poets was determined by the Polish Uprising of 1830–1831 that was violently suppressed by the Russian empire and provoked huge indignation in many European countries. Then, Pushkin wrote verses like 'To the Slanderers of Russia'[46] and 'Borodino Anniversary,'[47] in which he accused Western Europe of 'intersection' in the internal 'Slavic issues' and threatened them with a 'repetition' of the Russian triumph in Europe after the Napoleonic wars.[48] Naturally, this attitude was irreconcilable with Mickiewicz's perception of the uprising. Not only the cruelty of Russian troops itself but also the 'slavish' devotion of Russian people to the Czar, as well as their inability to stop the violence became a topic for many literary works of Mickiewicz.[49] Nevertheless, these historical contexts were not an issue for the state-run press. Pushkin had been cleared of 'reactionary elements' and became a Soviet cultural ambassador in post-war Poland.

At the same time, Vladimir Mayakovsky (1893–1930), a revolutionary poet and member of a literary group who had proposed in their programme to throw 'Pushkin, Dostoevsky, Tolstoy ... from the steamer of modernity,'[50] also became a hero of publications in the Polish cultural press. During the interwar period, an excursion into the poetry of Mayakovsky was, for many left-wing intellectuals in Poland, an insight into the revolutionary art, and, at the same time, a living example of global changes in modern art. In 1927, Mayakovsky visited Warsaw on his way to Paris but only spent a day there. During this visit, the Soviet revolutionary poet met some of those Polish left-wing literary scholars and writers who would constitute the editorial boards of 'Kuźnica' and 'Odrodzenie' after the Second World War.[51] So, for Adam Ważyk, a leading Polish vanguard poet, who translated Mayakovsky's poetry into Polish after the war, the revolutionary poet and his poetry were not just a historical phenomenon but a part of his personal experience in the interwar period.[52]

Another figure from the Soviet cultural pantheon whose works were presented to the Polish publics was the poet Boris Pasternak (1890–1960).[53] Later a Nobel Prize winner and the subject of the most known smear campaign in the post-Stalinist period, Pasternak not only survived the Stalinist purges but also became a kind of Stalin's protégé. It was Stalin who allowed him, a poet with obvious roots in the prohibited Silver Age literature, to play one of the central roles in the representation of the Soviet Union on the international scene.[54] His key role in the activity of the Sovinformburo and the All-Slavic committee made him an obvious candidate to represent Russian poetry in post-war Poland. The non-revolutionary character of most of Pasternak's works translated to Polish was, in turn, an occasion to celebrate the plurality of 'progressiveness' promoted in post-war Poland.[55]

However, the limits of the 'permissible' when interpreting the 'progressiveness' of Russian culture, which was developed under the 'gentle revolution,' and that of the Soviet government was still completely different. Following the method of 'Kuźnica' to make all 'good' poets, who were capable of being 'useful' 'progressive,'[56] Polish literary scholars went far beyond the framework of Soviet scholarship in their selection of pieces of Russian culture. If the publication of semi-disgraced Anna Akhmatova (1889–1966) before a government smear campaign against her in 1946 could be seen as somehow acceptable, then the poetry of Marina Tsvetaeva (1892–1941) would seem at least unusual for the 'readers' in Moscow. Tsvetaeva spent the last years of her life without any opportunity to publish and finally hanged herself in the provincial town of Yelabuga.[57] The fact that Tsvetaeva's poetry was selected by Polish philologists to represent Russian culture was evidence that their idea of the subject was not determined by the self-image of the Soviet Union.

This discrepancy became much more obvious with the publication of works by the repressed poet Osip Mandelstam (1891–1938). There were no doubts about Mandelstam being beyond the official vision of 'Russian culture.'[58] Mandelstam was firstly arrested in 1934, not least because of his verse 'We live without feeling the country beneath us' which contained lines calling Stalin a 'Kremlin mountaineer' for whom 'executions are like raspberry.' After the series of arrests, Mandelstam died, in 1938, in one of the Soviet concentration camps and was fully rehabilitated only in 1987.[59] Nevertheless, Polish philologists selected his works for celebrating Russian poetry. Not only the literarily journal 'Twórczość,'[60] but also leading journals such as 'Kuźnica'[61] and Borejsza's 'Odrodzenie'[62] made the Polish reader familiar with Mandelstam's works, which were not accessible in the Soviet Union.[63]

The discussions on Russian culture in the state-run press showed the complexity of the context that surrounded the project of 'gentle revolution.' Even though the publication of Russian literature did not significantly influence the agenda of the public debates themselves, it transmitted an important message regarding the realities of the early post-war period. Even demonstrating the loyalty to 'friendship' with the Soviet Union, Polish scholars insisted on pursuing their own agenda. In the early post-war years, it was not necessary to take example from the Soviet Union and adopt its vision of 'progressiveness.'

Soviet scholarship as a foreign world

Discussions on Soviet scholarship under the 'gentle revolution' also reflected the tendency of Polish scholars to keep a distance from the Soviet academic agenda. The leader of the 'Kuźnica' group, Stefan Żółkiewski, started his positive literary programme with a detailed review of the 'progressive approaches' to literature. For Żółkiewski, Soviet literary studies represented only one of many interesting intellectual tendencies in the European intellectual landscape. Moreover, if the 1920s were, according to him, the years of dominating Soviet literary theory, 'between 1935 and 1939, there appeared many interesting [ideas] ... in Czech[oslovakia] and Austria [as well as in] France and the Scandinavian countries, which were even more interesting than [ideas on literary theory] in the Soviet Union.'[64]

When writing about Soviet literary studies from the 1920s, Żółkiewski obviously referred to the Russian Formalists, who are considered among the founders of literary theory in general.[65] However, the way in which he deals with the legacy of Russian Formalism seems especially noticeable. Developing his programme, Żółkiewski wrote:

> In the Soviet Union, literary studies, for all their ingenuity, concreteness, and credible honesty, were rather one-sided. I am referring primarily to the works of the so-called Formalists [...] The activity of the most prominent Formalists (Shklovsky, Tynyanov, Zhirmunsky, Eikhenbaum) falls in a relatively short period [...] However, their students remain in the Soviet Union.[66]

This fragment is noticeable for many reasons: firstly, the very concept of Formalism became a fighting word during the Stalinisation of the cultural field in the Soviet Union in the 1930s and was not only an officially banned approach but also held stigma that meant 'reactionism' in a broader sense[67]; secondly, if Yury Tynyanov (1894–1943) died in Moscow during the war, Viktor Shklovsky (1893–1984), Viktor Zhirmunsky (1891–1971), and Boris Eikhenbaum (1886–1959) were not only living at the moment of the publication of Żółkiewski's review but also (having experienced several arrests) had continued their professional activity in one form or another.[68] More importantly for Marxist orthodoxy, all of them 'had overcome Formalism,' and, of course, none of their students could be labelled as 'Formalist' in Stalinist Russia.[69]

Nevertheless, Shklovsky, Tynyanov, Zhirmunsky, and Eichenbaum became for Żółkiewski, 'old Formalists' who, among others, played a very progressive role in the development of literary thought:

> I cannot imagine a reliable literary studies in Poland without digesting the achievements of the old Formalists and without constantly tracking the work of their students, although they provide only schematic, one-sided, technical-literary analyses.[70]

It is difficult to say who the students of the 'old Formalists' were, whose works Żółkiewski was 'constantly tracking' after the war, but, from his perspective, Formalism was still an important stage in the development of literary theory, even though Żółkiewski, like many other Marxists,[71] criticised them for schematism and ignoring political contexts.

Moreover, the 'right orienteers' for the progress of literary studies were also to be found in the Russian academic tradition. Żółkiewski referred to the figures of the 'most genius of Formalists' Roman Jakobson (1896–1982) and the Soviet linguist Viktor Vinogradov (1895–1869). He wrote:

> [Thanks to Jakobson and Vinogradov] literary studies became a branch of linguistics, and only through [linguistics it became a branch of] sociology, which is the normal hierarchy of the humanities (*dyscyplin humanistycznych*).'[72]

In such a way, Żółkiewski highlighted that, thanks to these Russian scholars, literary studies became a strict and progressive science.[73]

Though Vinogradov (despite having experienced several arrests) could return from exile after the war and become a professor at Moscow State University,[74] the figure of Roman Jakobson would seem much more problematic from the Soviet perspective. Having participated in the foundation of the first formalist group 'OPOJAZ' (the Russian abbreviation of Society for the Study of Poetic Language), Jakobson was involved in espionage activities in the interwar period. Being initially a representative of Soviet governmental organisations in Czechoslovakia, he had been playing a complex game and became later a citizen of the Czechoslovak Republic. There, Jakobson was among the founders of the prominent 'Prague linguistic circle,' which allowed Żółkiewski to argue that 'the foreign activity of Jakobson in Czechoslovakia possessed the highest value.' In such a way, Jakobson, who was, by then, already an American professor[75] was, for Żółkiewski, the most valuable example of Russian literary scholarship in his role as a creator of the school whose main achievement was 'the logical correctness of their theory, which was able to meet the most stringent requirements of modern methodology developed in the logistics environments of Vienna and Warsaw.'[76]

In such a way, Żółkiewski created a very specific picture of Soviet scholarship. Firstly, the most relevant tendencies in the Russian academic tradition, which he specified in his publications, were ones that were banned in the Soviet Union. Secondly, his approach to Russian Formalism shows that he did not care much about the self-representation of Soviet academia and its own vision of 'progressive' science. Even though he also criticised Formalism, his discourse on this matter testifies that he did not feel obliged to take the fate of Formalists in the Soviet Union into account. Żółkiewski's approach shows that Soviet scholarship (in his interpretation) was only one of the European intellectual traditions that could be of relevance in creating the agenda of literary studies in post-war Poland, but not the root and symbol of 'progressiveness' in itself.

Of course, this approach was not unique to Żółkiewski. So, for example, Tadeusz Kotarbiński also publicly reviewed Soviet academic realities with a critical eye. In March 1946, Kotarbiński wrote a report on his business trip to Moscow and published it in 'Kuźnica.' Kotarbiński came to the Soviet capital to celebrate the anniversary of the Russian/Soviet Academy of Sciences. Having praised the high level of Soviet natural sciences, Kotarbiński expressed his preoccupation concerning the fate of his discipline, logic, in the Soviet academic landscape. He wrote:

> It would be a lie to say that I saw a bloom of logic in Moscow and Leningrad <...> here [in the Soviet Union], for a long time, they did not trust logic in its new Western European form, because they were afraid of it as a tool for justifying a reactionary worldview ....[77]

Kotarbiński did not hesitate to disagree with this approach to logic and with the Soviet understanding of 'reactionary worldview.' Logic had, according to him, a 'very instrumental utility' and could help in resolving very practical problems. Moreover, Kotarbiński expressed his hope that the Soviet Union would reconsider its attitude towards logical studies and restart logic as an academic discipline. In his view, 'Russian science and culture in general returns to early national patterns' in terms of the rehabilitation of the scientific approaches that had vanished from the academic agenda on the wave of the revolutionary radicalism. Kotarbiński argued that this change in the official line was a good occasion for a reconstruction of logical studies in the Soviet Union.[78] Thus, Kotarbiński not only distanced himself from the Soviet academic tradition with which he disagreed but also proposed certain improvements of the Soviet academic agenda through the development of logical studies.

However, there were more 'professional' statements regarding Soviet academic realities in the Polish public sphere under the 'gentle revolution.' One of the providers of such statements was the Marxist philosopher Adam Schaff. It is noteworthy that Schaff took part in the public debates remotely, from Moscow, where he was based until 1948.[79] Therefore, Schaff saw his task as clarifying the Soviet academic principles of which his Polish colleagues had a limited idea. In his publications, Schaff not only explained to the Polish audience the 'great achievements' of Soviet academia but also referred to the typical argument that all Poles had to be thankful to the Soviet Union and to the Russian Revolutionaries who enabled the independency of Poland and thus the development of Polish science.[80]

More importantly, Schaff attempted to familiarise the Polish audience with the recent 'achievements' of Stalinist science. One of the leading 'Russian scholars' (he used the adjective 'Russian' rather than 'Soviet') whose ideas Schaff wanted to promote in Poland was a prominent linguist of Scottish and Georgian origins, Nicholas Marr (1865–1934).[81] Marr had become one of the most charismatic academic figures of the early 20th century and, after the October Revolution, found a strong Marxist feeling within himself, which was not typical for him before the coming of the Bolsheviks to the power.[82] Marr's 'Japhetic theory'[83] challenged the traditional classification of languages and claimed that so-called Japhetic languages[84] were much older than the Indo-European languages. With the Stalinisation of Russian academia, Marr reoriented his programme and became a theorist of the 'class nature of languages.'[85] Since Stalin positively characterised Marr's work, the main theorist of the Stalinist repressions, then the rector of the Moscow State University, Andrey Vyshinsky (1883–1954) ordered the inclusion of Marr's theories in the syllabus of philology students.[86] Thus, Marr became one of the leading figures in 'Stalinist science' and the protagonist of Schaff's writings.

Since Marr's programme was, at that time, officially established in Soviet academia, Schaff could not know that several years later (in 1950) Stalin would write in his famous article 'Marxism and Problems of Linguistics' that 'Marr introduced into linguistics the incorrect, non-Marxist formula ... got himself into a muddle and put linguistics into a muddle.'[87] So, in 1946, Schaff explained to the Polish audience the deep Marxian roots of Marr's theory, who 'started out as a proponent of the theory of Indo-Europeanism, but in the course of his long-standing work ... came directly to Marxism.'[88] It is difficult to say to which stage in Marr's theory Schaff was referring when mentioning his fascination with 'Indo-Europeanism,'[89] but Marr's references to Engels, which appeared in his publications during Stalinisation,[90] helped Schaff to present Marr as a scholar who, thanks to his loyalty to

Soviet ideology, followed a path from a misconception to the true progressiveness, thus becoming a Marxist.[91]

Nevertheless, this attempt to represent a research programme, which had been considered 'pseudo-science' by most scholars, as a relevant point in the current academic agenda due to its governmental support in the Soviet Union did not represent a mainstream tendency of the early post-war years. Schaff's contributions, much like publications of some other scholars experienced in the Soviet academic realities,[92] were 'islets' of Soviet scholarship in the Polish cultural and academic press, rather than characteristic traits of its agenda. Following the call 'to be progressive,' most Polish scholars still felt free from the Soviet understanding of 'progressiveness' and distanced from Soviet academic tradition.

The 'friend' and the 'argument': The use of the 'Soviet Union'

In a noticeable way, the Soviet Union played a more important role in the discourse of Catholic scholars and writers during the early post-war years. Since the general declaration of friendship with the Soviet Union was among the key preconditions for participation in public debates, this topic became, for them, an act of loyalty to the 'new reality,' which was not required in the case of the state-run press. More importantly, the image of the Soviet Union was obviously taken into service by the representatives of various Catholic groups for the defence of their position in the public sphere of post-war Poland. Despite the differences in strategies undertaken by Piasecki's group, 'Tygodnik Warszawski,' and 'Tygodnik Powszechny,' the discussion on the Soviet Union united them into a single camp, not least in their intellectual fight against the authorities that were going to reduce the role of Catholics in the public sphere. For example, Bolesław Piasecki, who was an expert in adapting to the changeable political realities, repeatedly claimed that the task of Polish intellectuals was to 'break with the typical approach of Polish journalism to the Soviet Union.'[93] He publicly 'regretted' the 'negative tradition' that had been established in the relationships between Poland and the Soviet Union.[94] More intensively than the government propaganda, Piasecki emphasised the fundamental difference between 'old' and 'new' Russia. Echoing the settings of the official discourse on this matter, the October Revolution had created a new reality and made Russia a world leader of social and political changes, a 'representative' and 'instrument' of the 'revolution of the new epoch,' which would be inevitably spread across the countries under Soviet influence.[95]

In a similar way,[96] the prominent historian and professor of the Jagiellonian University Stanisław Kutrzeba wrote in his article for 'Tygodnik Powszechny': 'with doubts, we were watching the struggle between the Soviets and Germany, especially when the first war years brought a catastrophe for the Russian army.' According to Kutrzeba, the reason for such a 'miscalculation' was confusion regarding the 'spirit' of the 'imperial' army and that of the 'Soviet' army: 'We were thinking that it was a former czarist soldier, who used to obey the orders but not understand the aims of his struggle. The significance of the psychological turn which took place in the huge territories of Russia after 1917 was underestimated.'[97] In this way, Stanisław Kutrzeba, who was not only a prominent historian of law but also, as a diplomat, fully aware of the circumstances of the Polish–Soviet War (1919–1921),[98] used the guidelines of propaganda to claim the loyalty of his intellectual milieu to the official version of a 'historical agreement' with Soviet Russia.[99]

Developing this idea, the historian Paweł Jasienica praised the Soviet state, claiming that 'unfortunately, we are not orientated enough towards the Soviet Union in its national politics.' Jasienica asserted that, while before the October Revolution, the Russian empire was 'split by the national question,' the new Soviet Russia had found a *modus vivendi* for many different nationalities within the same state, thus ending the violence against the minor nations.[100] The same article by Jasienica illustrates another significant aspect of the 'Catholic approach' to the image of the Soviet Union. For understandable reasons, Catholics were active in emphasising the idea that Poland had a 'special path' and should not follow the path of the Soviet Union. Developing this idea, Jasienica argued that such a 'successful' coexistence of different nationalities within the same state was possible only because the countries of the Soviet Union did not have a 'cultural tradition [which would be] independent from Moscow.' Thus, Jasienica represented the Soviet Union as an empire founded on the domination of Russian or even Muscovite culture.[101] Meanwhile, Poland, according to him, had an 'independent culture' that made it impossible to adopt the experience of the Soviet Union.[102] Thus, the relationship between Poland and the Soviet Union after the war was, for him, a new stage in the relationship between Polish culture and Russian culture. Maintaining the distance between these two cultures was a key issue for the safety of this 'friendship.'

Moreover, in the public discourse of Catholics, the Soviet Union was not only a 'friend' but also an 'opponent.' Bolesław Piasecki even spoke of possible disputes with the Soviet Union regarding the models of socialist revolution: 'We regard the ideological achievements of Russia (sic! – A.L.) as a point of view on revolution. We represent another point of view. We want to have an ideological competition [with the Soviet Union].'[103] In this case, Piasecki meant, of course, the programme of 'progressive Catholics' and 'public competition between idealism and materialism' as an alternative version of socialism. Either way, Piasecki, who not only saw himself as a theorist but also closely collaborated with the security services, publicly expressed the readiness of his group to lead a dispute with the Soviet Union on the theory of revolution. According to his programme, the presence of Catholics in the Polish public sphere was an alternative to the socialist model of the Soviet Union.

Frequently, Catholic authors went beyond the frameworks prescribed by propaganda. Doing so, they repeatedly used the authority of the Soviet Union in their criticism against communists and socialists. So, for example, Zygmunt Kaczyński, who headed the Warsaw group that led the toughest ideological fight against Polish communists and socialists, made the Soviet Union one of the key arguments in his public discourse. Interestingly, Kaczyński referred to the example of the Soviet Union when promoting the conservative aspects of his social programme. In doing so, the priest criticised the simplification of divorce proceedings that were conducted by the authorities and argued that 'even the Soviet Union tightened the rules of divorce in 1933.'[104] It is highly striking that Kaczyński (by all appearance) believed in the pact with Stalin. During a conversation with his colleagues, Kaczyński said: 'We [Catholics] are ardent supporters of friendship with Russia.... Russia is obviously helping. The Communists do not destroy the Church, because Russia does not allow it.'[105] Thus, Poland, according to Kaczyński, was to take the example of the Soviet Union ('Russia') in combining 'progressive' social reforms with a conservative moral agenda.

Not surprisingly, Catholics also referred to the example of the Soviet Union when writing about the necessity of tolerating religion. For example, Jan Piwowarczyk referred to the Soviet Union in his debate regarding religious freedom. According to Piwowarczyk, the recreation of the Moscow patriarchate in the Soviet Union was a good sign that Soviet Russia had revised revolutionary ideology towards religion.[106] Kaczyński, in turn, went even further and represented revolutionary Russia as opposed to the injustice of czarist politics regarding religious issues. According to Kaczyński (who witnessed the revolution in Petrograd), it was absolutely clear that 'czarism will not survive this war [World War I]' and Lenin with his comrades had become the 'only political force' that was able to bring Russia out of the revolutionary chaos. Developing this argument, Kaczyński claimed that he had spoken in person to Lenin to discuss the fate of the Catholic Church and the Catholic Academy in Petrograd. According to him, Lenin assured the priest that the 'Catholic Church received full freedom and, now, there are no obstacles to continuing teaching.'[107] Thus, the Soviet Union 'invented' by Catholic authors after the war became not only an ideological 'opponent' of Catholicism but also a 'defender' of Catholics in front of Polish communists, under the fluid political situation of the early post-war years.[108]

*

Nearly all images of the Soviet Union constructed during the public discussions in the early post-war years had one feature in common – they had little to do with the self-image of the Soviet Union. This feature testifies to the fact that the construction of a 'Soviet Union' was a task for Polish scholars and writers themselves. It is noteworthy that the 'Soviet Union' in public discourse nearly always meant 'Russia.' The disputants referred to Russian history, Russian scholarship, and the transfiguration of Russia after the October Revolution. Of course, the dominance of the Russian national narrative was a characteristic trait of late Stalinism. Nevertheless, the Polish historical tradition through which the participants in the debate saw the new realities played a more important role in this. The level of autonomy that Polish scholars and writers had in their post-war activity resulted in national stereotypes becoming the only common denominator in this discussion. The Soviet Union was seen as a new reincarnation of Russia.

More importantly, discussions on the image of the Soviet Union (the most unsafe issue in the post-war public agenda) showed how the 'gentle revolution' worked. Despite the constant pressure of Soviet advisors (whose propositions had been frequently rejected by Polish editors), the participants in the discussion had enough independence not only to develop their own vision of Russian culture but also to do so in a highly provocative way. The Polish audience could read not only the works of Russian authors who had been inducted into the canon of Soviet 'culturedness (*kulturnost'*)' but also the authors whose works were banned in the Soviet Union. Thus, to some extent, it was not the public discourse of Polish scholars that was adapted to fit the Soviet realities, but the Soviet realities that were adapted to the needs of the 'gentle revolution.'

The same applied to the image of Soviet (Russian) scholarship, which noticeably differed from the self-representation of Soviet academia. The authority of the Soviet Union was not a consideration in itself for most of those scholars who told the Polish reader about Soviet scholarship. Soviet (Russian) academia was not the unique bearer of 'progressiveness.' It had its merits and its disadvantages. Without having any special instructions on this matter, scholars could praise those tendencies in Soviet science that they thought positive and criticise (though very carefully) the shortcomings in Soviet academic practice. Even though the space for criticism was very limited, Polish scholars were not forced to radically change the form of 'good scientific practice' to publicly write about Soviet academia in the early post-war years.

The situation seemed different in the case of the scholars and writers associated with the Catholic press. For them, the discussions on the Soviet Union were much more important than for other participants in the public debates. The governmental pressure on the Catholic Church could not go unnoticed by Catholic journalism. The important role of the Soviet Union in the public agenda of Catholics reflected their survival strategy. Their idea that the instrumentalisation of the Soviet Union could help Catholics to maintain their position in the public sphere determined this tendency in the Catholic press. Nevertheless, even for them, the Soviet Union was a foreign country and Soviet ideology was foreign ideology that should not be followed. The necessity of becoming Soviet scholars was not an issue in their agenda. This was commonplace for all participants in the debates of the early post-war years.

Notes

1 Unfortunately, Wiktoria Śliwowska died on December 27, 2021, at the age of 90.
2 Wiktoria Śliwowska wrote about this episode in her memoirs, which were called 'Russia – Our Love.' This title was not an ironic one. Śliwowska wrote about her most important intellectual experiences, which she and her husband had in the Soviet Union: Wiktoria Śliwowska and René Śliwowski, *Rosja, nasza miłość* (Warszawa: Iskry, 2008), 160–161.
3 This story has been circulating, in an oral form, in the Institute of History of the Polish Academy of Sciences from the times of the directorship of Manteuffel.
4 Stanisław Ossowski and Maria Ossowska, *Intymny portret uczonych. Korespondencja Marii i Stanisława Ossowskich* (Warszawa: Sic!, 2002), 87.
5 The son of Jerzy Borejsza, the prominent Polish historian Jerzy Wojciech Borejsza, told me in a private conversation that his father spoke openly about his former fascination with anarchism because it was a 'venial sin' of his youth which could help him to avoid conversation on the less pleasant sins of his biography.
6 It is highly likely that the 'clear instruction' from 'Soviet comrades' which had been rejected by Borejsza (see Chapter 1) did not reach the participants in the public debates.

7 Sylwia Szczotka, "Wizerunek bolszewika w polskich plakatach propagandowych wojny polsko-rosyjskiej 1919-1920 ze zbiorów Muzeum Niepodległości w Warszawie," *Niepodległość i Pamięć* 19, no.1–4 (37–40) (2012): 211.
8 Matka Boska Ostrobramska – Our Lady of the Gate of Dawn – the icon from Vilnius, then the Polish city Wilno.
9 Marian M. Drozdowski, Hanna Eychhorn-Szwankowska and Jerzy Wiechowski, eds., *Zwycięstwo 1920. Warszawa wobec agresji bolszewickiej* (Paryż: Editions Dembinski, 1990), 45.
10 About the others aspects of the Bolsheviks' image, see Marcin Zaremba, *Wielka trwoga: Polska, 1944-1947: ludowa reakcja na kryzys* (Kraków: Wydawnictwo Znak, 2012), 49–86.
11 Patryk Babiracki, *Soviet Soft Power in Poland Culture and the Making of Stalin's New Empire, 1943–1957* (Chapel Hill: The University of North Carolina Press, 2015), 64.
12 GA RF F. R-8581, op. 1, d. 207, L. 29.
13 Cit ex.: Babiracki, *Soviet Soft Power in Poland*, 62.
14 Babiracki, *Soviet Soft Power in Poland*, 66.
15 Ibid., 59–67.
16 See reports with the reviews of Polish press, GA RF. F. P4459 Op. 6.
17 See the education plan for the propaganda staff: AAN, Ministerstwo Informacji i Propagandy, Sygn. 625, K. 1,2; the two issues which concerned the Soviet Union were 'the sources of the force of the Red Army (Nr 11)' and 'Russian Democracy and the Polish Question (Nr 17).'
18 "Przyjaźń polsko-radziecka – polityka narodu," *Głos Ludu*, no. 4, January 4, 1945.
19 "Człowiek, który nie powinien powrócić,"*Głos Ludu*, no. 10, January 13, 1945.
20 The idea that Piłsudski sold Poland to the Germans was intensively indoctrinated by the propaganda; see, for instance, "Człowiek, który nie powinien powrócić," *Głos Ludu*, no. 10, January 13, 1945.
21 "Utworzenie Rządu Tymczasowego to cios dla Niemiec hitlerowskich, "*Głos Ludu*, no. 11, January 14, 1945.
22 About the Polish perspective on this issue (with an accent on the Yalta agreements between the leaders of the anti-Nazi alliance), see Krystyna Kersten, *Jałta w polskiej perspektywie* (Londyn-Warszawa: Wydawnictwo ANEKS & NOWa, 1989); about the decisions on the 'Polish question' in Potsdam, see Alfons Klafkowski, *Umowa Poczdamska a sprawy polskie 1945–1970* (Poznań: Wydawnictwo Poznańskie, 1970).
23 See "Naród Rosyjski – przyjaciel Polski," *Głos Ludu*, no. 27, February 2, 1945; "Nad Odrą i Bałtykiem," *Głos Ludu*, no. 20, January 25, 1945.
24 The All-Slavic Committee (1941–1962) was a political institution that was created as an 'anti-fascist organisation' and aimed at the unification of the Slavic peoples in their struggle against 'fascism' and first of all Nazi Germany. Stalin intensively supported this ideology immediately after the war, but with time, the necessity of integrating many non-Slavic countries into the Socialist bloc resulted in drop in the interest of the Soviet government to this organisation and it was routinized at the level of different academic and public organisations. See Nikolai I. Kikeshev, *Slavjanskoe dvizhenie v SSSR: 1941-1948 gody*. (PhD thesis, Moscow: The Institute of Russian History of the Russian Academy of Sciences, 2008).
25 Babiracki, *Soviet Soft Power in Poland*, 62.
26 Of course, in fact, there were many contradictions in this, first of all regarding the Polish traditional narrative on Germany, though, as it was said, the creators of the propaganda discourse found themselves between two fires and the 'certain logic' referred, in this case, to the relative internal coherence of the ideological discourse on 'German – Slavic' competition.
27 Roman Werfel, "Na Piastowskie tory wraca polityka zagraniczna nowej Polski," *Głos Ludu* July 17, 1945; see also "Przyjaźń polsko-radziecka – polityka narodu," *Głos Ludu*, no. 4, January 4, 1945; "Solidarność słowiańska,"*Głos Ludu*, no. 65, March 25, 1945;

"Odra i Nisa – puklerzem pokoju całej Słowiańszczyzny. Zw. Radziecki popera stanowisko Polski w sprawie granic zachodnich," *Głos Ludu*, no. 247, September 8, 1946.
28 "Jak Związek Radziecki przygotował swe zwycięstwo," *Głos Ludu*, no. 7, January 9, 1945; It is noteworthy that this is, in fact, the reformulation of Lenin's idea that he expressed when he spoke about the necessity of the war against the Polish bourgeoisie during the Polish-Soviet War, see "Rech' na shirokoj raboche-krest'janskoj konferencii v Rogozhsko-Simonovskom rajone 13 maja 1920," *Kommunisticheskij Trud*, no. 44, May 14, 1920.
29 This idea was emphasised in the Manifesto of the Polish Committee of National Liberation (see "Manifest Polskiego Komitetu Wyzwolenia Narodowego," *Rocznik Lubelski*, no. 2 [1959]: 7–14.) Of course, it was, at the same time, a signal to the underground groups of the Home Army, whose resistance threatened to lead to a new civil war, see "W Polsce nie będzie wojny domowej," *Głos Ludu*, no. 8, January 10, 1945.
30 See, e.g., "Manifest Polskiego Komitetu Wyzwolenia Narodowego," 7; "Przyjaźń polsko-radziecka – polityka narodu," *Głos Ludu*, no. 4, January 4, 1945.
31 Henryk Słabek, *Dzieje polskiej reformy rolnej 1944-48* (Warszawa: Wiedza Powszechna, 1972), 17.
32 The reactions of the representatives of the Sovinforbiuro and Soviet Embassy are good evidence for that.
33 His father, Michał Walicki, was arrested in 1949 which made it impossible for his son to study such an ideologically dangerous subject as Polish literature. See more about Andrzej Walicki, *Idee i ludzie. Próba autobiografii* (Warszawa: Oficyna Wydawnicza Aspra-Jr, 2010).
34 That is basically the central point of Patryk Babiracki's book: Babiracki, *Soviet Soft Power in Poland*.
35 Czesław Miłosz, *The Captive Mind* (New York: Vintage Books, 1955).
36 See, e.g., the contents of *Przegląd Filozoficzny, Przegląd Socjologiczny* and other academic journals from these years.
37 "Akademia nauk w ZSRR," *Kuźnica*, no. 10 (1945): 6.
38 "Kronika kulturalna Z.S.R.R.," *Kuźnica*, no. 10 (1945): 6.
39 Ludwik Sawicki, "Organizacja nauki w Związku Radzieckim," *Odrodzenie*, no. 16–17 (1946): 15.
40 See *Odrodzenie*, no. 1 (1944): 1; *Kuźnica*, no. 1 (1945): 1.
41 See, for example, Michael David-Fox, *Showcasing the Great Experiment: Cultural Diplomacy and Western Visitors to the Soviet Union, 1921–1941* (Oxford: Oxford University Press, 2011).
42 About the institutional aspects of the forced 'friendship' with the Soviet Union, see Maciej Chłopek, *"Zdumiewający świat". ZSRR i ludzie radzieccy w propagandzie Polski Ludowej lat 1944–1956,"* (Radzymin: wyd. von Borowiecky, 2014), 91–121.
43 *Pravda*, 7. 02. 1937. About the cult of Pushkin under Stalinism, see Jonathan Brooks Platt, *Greetings, Pushkin! Stalinist Cultural Politics and the Russian National Bard* (Pittsburgh: University of Pittsburgh Press, 2016).
44 During the early post-war years, the Polish poet Julian Tuwim, who spent most of the wartime in the USA and was one of the most inspired supporters of 'gentle revolution,' presented the Russian classic in the pages of 'Odrodzenie' with the translation of 'Eugene Onegin,' the most celebrated verse novel of Pushkin. "Eugeniusz Oniegin," *Odrodzenie*, no. 14, no. 27 (1946): 1, 2.
45 See, e.g., about the friendship between Mickiewicz and Pushkin as a factor of education: Piotr Zwierzchowski, "Spór o wychowanie patriotyczne na podstawie "Nowej Szkoły" z lat 1948–1953," *Biuletyn Studenckich Kół Naukowych* 3 (1995): 207–212.
46 See the text of 'To the Slanderers of Russia' in English: https://aleksandr-pushkin.su/klevetnikam-rossii/?lang=en
47 See the text of 'Borodino Anniversary' in English: https://aleksandr-pushkin.su/borodinskaya-godovshhina/?lang=en

48 In his letters, Pushkin wrote: 'The news regarding the Polish uprising shocked me entirely. So, our primordial enemies will be finally exterminated.... The war that is beginning will be a war until the extermination [of Poles] – or at least it should be so,' Cit ex. Leonid Frizman, "Pushkin i pol'skoe vosstanie 1830–1831 godov," *Voprosy literatury* 3 (1992): 213.
49 See only one of many examples – the verse 'To the friends Moskals (*Do przyjaciół Moskali*)' from the third part of one of his main works '*Dziady*': https://wolnelektury.pl/media/book/pdf/dziady-dziadow-czesci-iii-ustep-do-przyjaciol-moskali.pdf that was published in Paris in 1832.
50 The matter concerns the group of Cubo-Futurists who published, in 1912, their manifesto in the volume under the title 'A Slap in the Face of Public Taste,' and Mayakovski was among the key figures in this movement.
51 Though not all Polish socialists were inspired by the figure of Mayakovsky, see Marci Shore, *Caviar and Ashes. A Warsaw Generation's Life and Death in Marxism, 1918–1968* (New Haven: Yale University Press, 2006), 52–69. About an ambiguous opinion of Mayakovsky, to take one example, the communist poet Władysław Broniewski, see Shore, *Caviar and Ashes*, 59. Of course, some of the Polish socialist writers and poets met Mayakovsky before in Moscow, see Marci Shore, *Caviar and Ashes*, 58.
52 See, for example, "Poezja Rosyjska," *Kuźnica*, no. 21 (1946): 1.
53 See, e.g., [b/a], "Rzeź niewiniątek," *Kuźnica*, no. 20 (1946): 10.
54 See Lazar Fleishman, *Boris Pasternak: The Poet and His Politics* (Cambridge, MA: Harvard University Press, 2013).
55 Despite the official fight against idealism, Pasternak played an important part in the Stalinist project of 'culturedness (kulturnost).' See about the concept: Vadim Volkov, "The Concept of Kul'turnost': Notes on the Stalinist Civilizing Process," in *Stalinism: New Directions*, ed. Sheila Fitzpatrick (London: Routledge, 1999), 210–230.
56 See Chapter 1.
57 Among others, 'Twórczość' published the poetry of Fyodor Tyutchev, Vladimir Benediktov, Fyodor Sologub, Mikhail Kuzmin, Alexander Blok, Pavel Antokolsky, Nikolai Tikhonov, Stepan Schipachev, see "*Kolumna Poezji Rosyjskiej*," *Twórczość* 3 (1945): 74–99.
58 A collection of Mandelstam's verses was firstly published in 1973: Osip Mandelstam, *Stihotvorenija*, Leningrad: Sovetskij pisatel', 1973. See an extremely interesting interview in English with his wife, Nadezhda Mandelstam on her husband: https://www.youtube.com/watch?v=pMTcMOlGQyQ
59 See more about this verse, Oleg Lekmanov, *Mandelstam* (Boston: Academic Studies Press, 2010).
60 Kolumna Poezji Rosyjskiej, *Twórczość* 3 (1945): 90–91.
61 "Poezja Rosyjska," *Kuźnica*, no. 21 (1946): 1.
62 "Z poezji Rosyjskiej," *Odrodzenie*, no. 24 (1946): 5.
63 It is noteworthy that the translator of the poetry of Mandelstam, Jerzy Pomianowski, spent most of the war years in Tajikistan and, between 1944 and 1946, worked as a representative of the Polish Press Agency (Polpress) in Moscow. There are some other less noticeable examples of the 'wrong' usage of Russian literature in the Polish public sphere. Thus, among the poems translated for the Polish audience, there was the Russian philosopher-mystic Vladimir Solovyov (1853–1900) whose works were, to put it mildly, not among the most readable in the Soviet Union. Solovyov with his purely religious philosophy did not fit in the canon of the official Soviet 'Russian culture.' At the same time, Solovyov played the central role in the agenda of those philosophers who were forced to leave the country after the October Revolution; see the section about Solovyov in the book written by Russian emigrant philosopher Nikolay Lossky: Nikolay Lossky, *History Of Russian Philosophy* (London: George Allen and Unwin Ltd), 81–133.

64 Stefan Żółkiewski, "O pozytywny program literacki," *Odrodzenie*, no. 37 (1945): 1.
65 Galin Tihanov, *The Birth and Death of Literary Theory. Regimes of Relevance in Russia and Beyond* (Stanford: Stanford University Press, 2019), 27.
66 Stefan Żółkiewski, "O pozytywny program literacki," *Odrodzenie*, no. 37 (1945): 1.
67 The first official criticism against Formalism was conducted by Leon Trotsky, who called the Formalist group an 'extremely arrogant bastard (*nedonosok*),' though his criticism was rather an unequal discussion (Lev D. Trockij *Literatura i revoljucija* (Moskva: Politizdat, 1991), 130–145). The governmental smear campaign against Formalism was conducted ten years later, when Formalism became a fighting word (see, for example, the article of Maxim Gorky: Maksim Gor'kij, "O formalizme," *Pravda*, no. 99, April 9, 1936.
68 About the fate of Formalists and Formalism in Soviet academia and various forms of survival, see Aleksandr Dmitriev and Jan Levchenko, "Nauka kak priem: eshhe raz o metodologicheskom nasledii russkogo formalizma," *Novoe literaturnoe obozrenie* 50, no. 4 (2001) (URL): https://magazines.gorky.media/nlo/2001/4/nauka-kak-priem-eshhe-raz-o-metodologicheskom-nasledii-russkogo-formalizma.html
69 Now, it is difficult to say what Żółkiewski meant by 'a relatively short period [of the activity of the Formalists]' – the first formalist literary group OPOJAZ was founded in 1916, and various formalist groups existed until the repressions against them in the 1930s.
70 Żółkiewski, "O pozytywny program literacki," 1.
71 See Tony Bennett, *Formalism and Marxism* (London & New York: Routledge, 2004).
72 As was shown in the chapter about the genealogy of Polish sociology constructed by Józef Chałasiński, sociology in the Polish tradition was not opposed to the humanities but, in some of the sociological programmes, even belonged to the humanities. Of course, such an idea of the 'normal hierarchy' of sciences seems a reference to Positivism.
73 'co ślina na język przyniesie mniej czy więcej naiwnie "czytającemu sobie" (Żółkiewski, "O pozytywny program literacki," 1.)
74 In 1951, Vinogradov even became a Stalin Prize winner.
75 See more about Jakobson's exiting biography: Peter Steiner, "Which Side Are You on? Roman Jakobson in Interwar Prague," in *Roman Jakobson, linguistica e poetica*, ed. Edoardo Esposito, Stefania Sini and Marina Castagneto (Milano: Ledizioni, 2019), 75–86; Tomáš Glanc, "Razvedyvatel'nyj kurs Jakobsona," in *Roman Jakobson: Teksty, dokumenty, issledovanija*, ed. Henryk Baran and Sergeej I. Gindin (Moskva: RGGU, 1999), 359–360.
76 Żółkiewski, "O pozytywny program literacki," 1; The fact that the affiliation with logic was, for Marxist Żółkiewski, a progressive aspect in the activity of Russian Scholars is an important marker in itself. I will clarify this point in Chapter 4.
77 Tadeusz Kotarbiński, "Garstka wspomnień z pobytu w Moskwie," *Kuźnica*, no. 10 (1946): 5.
78 Kotarbiński referred, among others, to the name of Russian mathematician and logician Platon Poretsky (1846–1907). Tadeusz Kotarbiński, "Garstka wspomnień z pobytu w Moskwie," *Kuźnica*, no. 10 (1946): 5; It is noteworthy that, indeed, logic was rehabilitated in the Soviet Union. Even though it obviously did not have something to do with the visit of Kotarbiński, the decision on the rehabilitation logic was taken during the meetings of the Politburo in 1946 and, in 1947, a new Soviet textbook was published, see Sergej N. Vinogradov, *Logika* (Moskva: Gosudarstvennoe izdatel'stvo politicheskoj literatury, 1947).
79 See more about Schaff in the following chapters.
80 In his publications, Schaff meant both the formation of an independent Polish state in 1918 and the liberation from the Nazi occupation. See, for example, Adam Schaff, "Rewolucja Październikowa a Polska," *Kuźnica*, no. 18 (1945): 3–4.

81 His father spoke English and French and his mother spoke only Georgian, see Vladimir M. Alpatov, *Istoriya odnogo mifa. Marr i Marrizm* (Moskva: URSS, 2004), 6.
82 Alpatov, *Istoriya odnogo mifa*, 79–111.
83 From the name of the biblical character Japheth, one of the sons of Noah.
84 The content of the research programme changed with time, but his native Caucasian languages always belonged to the Japhetic languages.
85 See about the political context of the establishment of Marr's theory: Vladimir M. Alpatov, *Istoriya odnogo mifa*, 107–111.
86 Vladimir M. Alpatov, *Istoriya odnogo mifa*, 83.
87 Joseph V. Stalin, *Marxism and Problems of Linguistics,* in Stalin Reference Archive (marxists.org) 2000 (URL): https://www.marxists.org/reference/archive/stalin/works/1950/jun/20.htm
88 Adam Schaff, "Nowa teoria języka profesora Marra," *Kuźnica*, no. 13 (1946): 6.
89 Before the Revolution, Marr also opposed the 'Europocentric' approach in the classification of languages.
90 Though these references seemed very unnatural and were not brought into accordance with the Orthodox Marxism: Alpatov, *Istoriya odnogo mifa. Marr i Marrizm*, 99.
91 Adam Schaff, "Nowa teoria języka profesora Marra," 7. See more about this topic in Chapter 5.
92 Another example of a 'Soviet scholar' in the Polish public sphere was the historian Celina Bobińska. Following her mother, Bobińska had emigrated to Russia in 1918 and studied there, then returned to Poland having received a Soviet PhD degree in History. In her publication in cultural and academic press, Bobińska wrote articles on the glorious story of true Russian patriots who joined the progressive movement for fighting czarism. See, for example, her article about 'Russian patriots' – the Decembrists: Celina Bobińska, "Dekabryści," *Kuźnica*, no. 18 (1945): 3–4.; see also her publication glorifying the Soviet Union: Celina Bobińska, "Prawdziwy obraz ZSRR," *Kuźnica*, no. 45 (1947): 9–10.
93 Bolesław Piasecki, "Kierunki," *Dziś i Jutro*, no. 5 (1946): 2.
94 Bolesław Piasecki, "Ogólne zasady światopoglądowe (deklaracja programowa. lipiec 1945 r.)," in Bolesław Piasecki, *Kierunki 1945-1960* (Warszawa: PAX, 1981), 24.
95 Piasecki, "Kierunki," 2. It is highly likely that Piasecki strove to emphasise that this was an inevitable scenario for Poland.
96 Of course, not in terms of Piasecki's claim of the inevitability of the social revolution; in this case, I mean the repetition of the general idea – prescribed by propaganda – that the October Revolution changed Russia which was known to Poles before the war.
97 Stanisław Kutrzeba, "Siły dziejów," *Tygodnik Powszechny*, no. 1 (1945): 1–2.
98 He took part in the formation of the image of Europe during the peace conference in Paris in 1919; under the Nazi occupation, he was arrested and sent to a concentration camp and, later, took part in underground teaching; see Andrzej Śródka and Paweł Szczawiński, eds., *Biogramy uczonych polskich. Nauki społeczne* (Wrocław: Zakład Narodowy im. Ossolińskich, 1984), 279–285.
99 Of course, it was, to some extent, a strategic statement, but the fact that this statement was delivered by such a prominent historian gained authority for this idea.
100 Paweł Jasienica, "Z prądem historii," *Tygodnik Powszechny*, no. 18 (1946): 2.
101 'Moscow culture' in this context is, of course, not an accident. The lands between Poland and Russia were historically under different rulers. For the Polish historian, the 'imperialism' of Russia was associated, first of all, with the spread of 'Muscovite Rus,' which started in the late 13th century and, with time, included, among others, the territories which were the part of the Grand Duchy of Lithuania and belonged to the Polish Republic. Thus, Moscow became the symbol of Russian imperialism.
102 Jasienica, "Z prądem historii," 2.

103 Piasecki, "Kierunki," 2. Presumably, Piasecki thought it possible to make such statements because he assured the security services of his 'mission' to get young people from the underground movement, which allowed him to have a certain 'radicalism' in defending 'Polish interests' in the ace of the Soviet Union.
104 Zygmunt Kaczyński, "Kościoł, naród, państwo," *Tygodnik Warszawski*, no. 49 (1946): 3.
105 "Soobshhenie korrespondenta TASS v Varshave o planah sozdanija katolicheskoj partii v Pol'she. Sent. 1947 g.," in *SSSR – Pol'sha. Mehanizmy podchinenija. 1944–1949*, ed. Gennadi Matveev et al. (Moskva: AIRO-HH, 1995), 218–222.
106 Ks. Jan Piwowarczyk, "Teologia marksizmu," *Tygodnik Powszechny*, no. 32 (1945): 2.
107 Zygmunt Kaczyński, "Rewolucja Październikowa," *Tygodnik Warszawski*, no. 46 (1947): 3.
108 More importantly, the idea of orientation to Russia in foreign policy legitimised the return of the nationalist thinker Roman Dmowski as a relevant thinker in the public discourse of Catholics. Dmowski was an opponent of Pilsudski and thought that Poland should use the support of Russia to prevent Germanisation. This fact legitimised the presence of the nationalist in the public sphere of the state which was 'on the way to socialism.' See, e.g., Bolesław Szczepkowski, "To i owo o R. Dmowskim," *Tygodnik Warszawski*, no. 5 (1945): 3. See more about the reflections of Catholics on the image of the Soviet Union: Aleksei M. Lokhmatov, "Obraz SSSR v refleksii Pol'skoi katolicheskoi intelligentsii (1945–1948)," in *Rossiia i mir glazami drug druga*, ed. Alexander V. Golubev (Moskva: Institut rossijskoj istorii Rossijskoj akademii nauk, 2017), 201–214.

3 The Teachers of Virtues
The French and the Early Post-War Project

'We are glad to greet you, gentlemen! Everyone will be praised in accordance with his contribution. Everything has been elaborated very well. There is just an absent guillotine for the bourgeoisie. Please accept our highest respect.'[1] With these words, the French revolutionaries Robespierre, Marat, Danton, and Desmoulins saluted the readers of the journal 'Odrodzenie' following the liberation of Polish territories from the Nazi occupation. The author of this historical allusion, Jerzy Borejsza, presenting an attractive image of the 'new Polish realities,' repeatedly referred to the French Revolution to illustrate the extent of intellectual 'freedom' in Poland after the war. Promoting the 'gentle revolution' project, Borejsza chose France as a reference point deliberately. Besides the obvious fact that French Enlightenment thinkers and the heroes of the French Revolution were the icons of the communist movement, the historical ties with France made its role in Polish intellectual life a unique one. For people involved in the cultural and academic debates in Poland, France played a more important role than any other country. Since Poland went through the most essential stage in the forming of European nationalisms, having lost its statehood, the tradition of the 'Great Emigration' that settled in Paris shaped the romantic image of Polish history and culture and established the basic categories for the perception of world history.[2]

More importantly, France became a meeting point for the two opposing ideological camps that shaped the agenda of post-war Poland. Both for socialists and Catholics, France was the centre of intellectual culture and a window to the global perspective on their agenda. Of course, from the perspective of purely scholarly issues, the domination of the French tradition was not so obvious. The interwar milieu around the Sociological Institute in Posen was much more oriented to contact with US social scientists, while, for philosophers, German phenomenology, as well as Austrian and British logical studies, were the key guidelines in their research.[3] Either way, the French academic agenda was still crucial for many Polish historians, philologists, and scholars who dealt with historical sociology.[4] More importantly, French culture was an integral part of the public agenda in all Polish territories. French language, and thus literature written in French, was not only a part of education for noble families but also a basic competency for educated people from non-noble or poor noble families.[5]

DOI: 10.4324/9781003428251-4

Thus, France, as a cultural topos, became a route through which to find a common language between people involved in the intellectual and academic debates of various ideological camps. It was not accidental that the programme promoted by Borejsza under the banner of 'gentle revolution' did not contain any references to the Soviet Union as a prototype of the near future of the Polish state. The image of France became an object of temptation that was to help in gaining the confidence of Polish scholars and writers. This was an example of leftist culture that could be attractive to a broader audience than a few sympathisers of the Soviet Union, some of whom already had the experience of the Stalinist camps behind them.[6] Since Paris was a metropolis of European art and literary experiments, the knowledge of socialist ideals as well as the forms of political and academic debates came to Poland from France rather than from the Soviet Union. The isolation of Soviet Russia, especially after the Polish–Soviet War (1919–1921), made France the main source of knowledge about new trends in socialism.[7]

The Parisian research institution *Centre Scientifique de l'Académie Polonaise des Sciences*, with its history rooted in the second half of the 19th century,[8] became an important symbol in the Polish struggle for French sympathies. Their historical ties with the Polish Academy of Arts and Sciences (*Polska Akademia Umiejętności*) made this centre a symbol of Polish–French academic collaboration. After the Second World War, this centre started to reconstruct its scholarly contacts with French academic institutions and supported Polish studies at French universities.[9] More importantly, after the war, this research centre promoted books written by Polish scholars in 'new Poland,' and thus, the regime established in the Polish state. From the reports of the *Centre Scientifique*, one learns about the interest of French academic institutions in developing collaborations with scholars from the newly established Polish state. For example, the French academic institutions offered their assistance in writing reviews of books published in Poland.[10] It is noteworthy that Polish émigré organisations based in Paris[11] attempted to start a legal process that would take the *Centre Scientifique* away from the control of the new Polish regime and make it an émigré scholarly institution.[12] However, this initiative was not successful. The new Polish regime struggled for the attention and interest of French society and the ideological image of the new state was not foreign to the French authorities.[13]

The opinion of French intellectuals was extremely important in promoting the project of the 'gentle revolution.' From the perspective of this project, France provided an example of 'true progressiveness' in terms of public engagement of academics in the political struggle. Meanwhile, since the ideology of 'gentle revolution' referred to the key role of scholars in creating the new realities, Polish academics seemed to be in a privileged position. Unlike French left-wing scholars and writers who, 'together with French people,' led the struggle against the authorities, their Polish colleagues, according to the official programme, were the creators of the new realities. This shaped a space for a new chapter in the relations with their French colleagues.

The state-run journals that were created under the supervision of Borejsza devoted special issues to French cultural and academic events. Additionally, numerous translations of French authors ensured the Polish cultural press was involved in the intellectual agenda of France. The constant references to the legacy of the French Enlightenment became a central feature of the 'gentle revolution' and formed a natural link between the new Polish realities and the intellectual image of France. The satirical and political texts of Voltaire, Diderot, and other French Enlightenment icons were to convince the reader of the similarities between the changes that happened in Poland after the war and the ideals of the French political philosophers. Realism, which was the cornerstone of the leftist literary programme,[14] found its patrons in the figures of Gustave Flaubert and Guy de Maupassant, while the realist paintings of Gustav Courbet and Honoré Daumier, published in the pages of the cultural journals, visualised the presence of the 'French spirit' in the post-war Polish political project. This connection between images and the 'world of words' reached the apex of its apparent fulfilment of French prophecy (which took place in Poland) after the war. The possibility of promoting the 'progressive' agenda at the national level was to become a sign that the new regime was opposed to *l'ancien regime* of Józef Piłsudski.[15]

Special attention to the new political agenda of France was also a significant aspect of pro-French orientation in the post-war Polish cultural press. The observations of French political events constituted an integral part of self-comparison with the French 'teachers' and friends. The description of the difficulties faced by French socialists and communists in winning the majority in the French Parliament was, at the same time, a reference to the fact that Poland had already passed this stage; the power was already under the control of 'people's authority.' France had to overtake Poland, and the Polish leftist press was 'rooting' for the 'team' of French socialists at the general election.[16] The collaboration with French academic institutions and cultural journals was described as the most vital issue of the new agenda, and the interest of French scholars in the Polish project was seen as a sign of their recognition of the promising future of 'new Poland.'[17]

Of course, it was not less important that the community of Polish émigré fellows, which would be the main centre of opposition to communism during the second half of the 20th century, was also formed in Paris and felt the continuity of the tradition of the 'Great Emigration.'[18] Even though, before the 1950s, the Parisian group around the journalist Jerzy Giedroyc did not play yet the role that would make the journal 'Kultura (Culture)' famous as the European centre of anti-communism,[19] the movement of the group from their initial location in Italy to France was seen as a symbolic act. Since Paris hosted many academic events, and a business trip to France was slightly less problematic[20] than trips to other 'capitalist countries,' the position of 'Kultura' allowed Giedroyc's colleagues not only to receive all periodicals published in Poland but also to obtain first-hand some non-official and unpublished reports on the situation in Poland at the time. Even though 'Kultura' was very active in developing their contacts with research institutions in the USA,[21] French became the language of the promotion of the Polish agenda in the European academic and intellectual circles.[22] France, in turn, would become the meeting place of the 'exiled' Poland and the 'socialist' Poland.

How are we seen? Representing Poland in France

The perception of the new Polish realities in French intellectual circles was one of the most vital issues for those Polish 'cultural delegates' whose trips to France were supposed to promote the post-war Polish political project.[23] The prominent Polish writer and one of the leading 'cultural ambassadors' of the new regime, Jarosław Iwaszkiewicz, repeatedly expressed his admiration of the interest of French society in Poland. According to his impression, relations with the French people had changed since the interwar period; the French were extremely thankful 'for the love to France that Poles demonstrated at the moment when France needed to strengthen the faith in its own value.' Additionally, French intellectuals saw in Poland a 'significant market' for spreading its scholarly and fictional literature. In 1946, Iwaszkiewicz assured the reader that the ease of communication with French colleagues and lightness of establishing new contacts among Western scholars were the most visible changes compared with the interwar period (a statement which would seem a bitter irony several years later). Iwaszkiewicz enjoyed the attention that the Polish delegation attracted among French academics and writers and told the reader about the 'queues' of people who wanted to speak to the Polish cultural delegates at Sorbonne and College de France.[24]

Meanwhile, the most practical task of the Polish delegation in Paris was to establish the exchange of cultural and academic press with French scholarly institutions. According to the author, key cultural journals, such as 'Kuźnica,' 'Odrodzenie,' 'Twórczość (Creativity),' and the literary magazine 'Życie Literackie (The Literary Life),' edited by Iwaszkiewicz himself, found such a broad audience in France that he complained about the shortage of copies taken from Poland. Moreover, it was important for Iwaszkiewicz to emphasise that the theoretical and cultural articles that had been published in the Polish journals after the war reached a broader audience than exclusively professors and students of Slavic studies at the leading French universities. According to him, the essays of Polish scholars also were well accepted in the French academic and cultural press. He wrote:

> Interest in Polish affairs is really great. Our articles appear on the front pages of [French] journals, and everything that we brought with us [from the Polish publications], is already translated into French and has found its place in weekly and monthly magazines; there is already a preliminary agreement on contracts for publishing books.[25]

The positive relation of the French people to the new realities of post-war Poland was a vital argument 'testifying' to the rightness of the path taken by Poles. The fact that the intellectual metropolis paid attention to its Polish 'students' and rejoiced at their success was the best reward for the organisers of post-war Polish academic and cultural life.[26]

Nevertheless, the effectiveness of the response to the French audience's fascination with Polish realities was not unquestionable for the creators of the new cultural image of post-war Poland. Enjoying the opportunity to spend a lot of time in Paris, the philologist Jan Kott argued that the propaganda of new Polish culture in France did not work at the required level. Kott shared Iwaszkiewicz's conviction that the new Polish realities would find a considerable audience in France. 'The French people are currently much more interested in Polish affairs than they were before the war,' wrote Kott, '[they] know more about us and their interest in what is happening with us is more vital and broader [than in the interwar period].'[27] Meanwhile, Kott argued that the measures that were implemented in France by the Polish authorities were insufficient. Despite the activity of the Polish institutions in France, it was nearly impossible to find a Polish book or journal in French bookshops, though other countries and languages were represented there very well. He wrote: 'We inform about Poland too little and badly; the press that sympathises with us or is indifferent to us still publish articles which harm us or just [contain] nonsense.'[28]

The fact that Kott publicly criticised the Polish governmental institutions for the failure of the propaganda work illustrated, among other things, how he understood his role in the new realities. The engagement with the current politics under the 'gentle revolution' implied the public criticism of the government politics. Kott understood the creation of the intellectual image of Poland in the French public sphere as a common task for Polish scholars and writers. Responding the call to be 'progressive' in terms of social and political engagement, Kott publicly promoted a concrete plan for the improvement of the image of the new Polish state in France. According to him, the organisation of the 'uninterrupted supply' of cultural and academic journals to the French capital was to become the most important challenge for the Polish government in this regard. Kott was outraged that French literature and journals could be bought both in Warsaw and in Łódź, while it was a huge problem to find a Polish newspaper in Paris.[29]

Another important point in Kott's programme concerned translations. According to him, the *Bureau d'Informations Polonaises* had to invest more resources into the translation of Polish literature and journal papers into French. Additionally, Kott was convinced that the cultural and academic relationship with French universities needed special legal and financial support from government institutions. Besides the organisation of academic and cultural conferences, wrote Kott, French students would be attracted to Poland by fellowships for studying at Polish universities. This form of academic exchange would serve the development of mutual understanding between French and Polish intellectuals.[30]

Thus, the danger of not using the interest of the French public in the new Polish realities was one of the essential issues for the 'gentle revolution' project. The postwar conditions shaped, for them, a new opportunity to secure Poland's place in the French intellectual agenda, and the task of Polish intellectuals was to not lose the chance for visibility on the horizon of their 'teachers.'

The French teach the Poles and vice versa

Another significant aspect of the French presence in post-war Poland directly addressed the issue of intellectual discussions and Borejsza's idea of the inseparability of 'progressiveness' and political engagement. It was much more convenient for the Polish reader in the early post-war period to hear about the responsibility of intellectuals in the struggle against 'rotting capitalism' from the French philosopher and politician Roger Garaudy (1913–2012) than from a Soviet scholar. In the article translated for the Polish reader, Garaudy assured the audience that the most beautiful and creative masterpieces of world history were not the creation of individuals but the result of the self-expression of whole nations. The Bible, the Iliad and Odyssey, as well as the Song of Roland were the result of collective work, while the greatest prophets always expressed the 'anxiety and anger of the whole nation.' The most productive epochs of Ancient history were those that implied the mobilisation of the creative sources of the broad mass of mankind. Garaudy opposed collective creativity with the Hitlerian cult of 'great individuals' and argued that only those artists who were able to serve their nations could become the co-creators of the new world.[31] In such a way, Garaudy 'called' for Polish scholars not to isolate themselves from the grassroots but to be the expressors of their culture.

The sublime style of Garaudy was a very important element in legitimising the project of the 'gentle revolution.' His discourse on the role of scholars in the new political realities would provide a relevant example of the model of scholarly activity that was to become a Polish reality in the early post-war period. The idea that all scholars should be mobilised for serving their nation, expressed by the prominent French philosopher Garaudy, was an important argument that Poland was implementing the most progressive project possible. The fragment of Garaudy's writings that had been translated as a separate book[32] was chosen to illustrate the actual moment, and to mobilise the reader to see himself not as an active participant in the historical process.

Interestingly, the classic works of Marxism frequently appeared to the Polish audience in the interpretations of authors associated with the French socialist movement. So, none other than Roger Garaudy explained to the Polish audience the ethical teaching of Marx and Engels, in the pages of the official journal of the Polish Workers' Party 'Nowe Drogi (The New Paths).' Moreover, the Polish reader could learn, from Garaudy's writings, not only about the ethical attitude of the classics of Marxism but also about the ethical principles formulated by Lenin and the Soviet writer Maxim Gorky.[33] Thus, while, in the early post-war years, it was hard to find any theoretical texts on Marxism written by Soviet scholars,[34] French socialists and communists introduced the Marxian teaching to the Poles.

The fact that Lenin's legacy was introduced to the Polish public by the French philosopher Garaudy was not an isolated case. The French communist historian Jean Fréville[35] became the main expert in Leninism in the Polish cultural and academic press. Fréville was born in Kharkov, then part of the Russian empire, but, after the October Revolution, his family emigrated to France, where he came of age. Fréville joined the French communist party and became a historian with a special interest in Russian revolutionary thought. Thus, it was Fréville, not a Soviet author, who familiarised the Polish audience with the realities of revolutionary Russia and the cultural programme of the Bolsheviks. In Fréville's representation, Lenin was 'very Russian, but, at the same time, very international; [Lenin] was the leader of the [Working] class that continued the whole [European] culture of the past.'[36]

The very idea that the Soviet version of Marxism was the highest point in the development of the best European traditions was Leninist.[37] Nevertheless, Fréville's Lenin was much closer to the ideology of the 'gentle revolution' than the Lenin of the Bolsheviks. Fréville's text told the Polish reader that Lenin's main ideal was just to overcome the split between educated people and the working masses. From this perspective, the task of scholars was to familiarise the working class with the achievements of European culture.[38] It was not the uncompromising struggle against the class enemies in the cultural field (which was the key point in the ideology of the Bolsheviks),[39] but the development of European culture that formed the main 'Leninist idea' in Fréville's representation. This could be read as a direct reference to the programme implemented by Jerzy Borejsza.

The Polish slogans of the early post-war years could be seen in the translation of the sublime article written by the French literary critic and philologist, Léon Pierre-Quint (1895–1958). His reflections on the role of intellectuals in society could be regarded as an echo[40] and, thus, justification of the key principles of 'gentle revolution.' Pierre-Quint argued that the post-war generation of scholars and writers had to play a distinguished role in reconstructing the world destroyed by fascism. The engagement of intellectuals in the struggle between the 'progressive culture' and 'reactionary attitude' was the central idea of Pierre-Quint's publication. His literary metaphors depicting this struggle referred to the competitions between Zeus and Prometheus, Titans and gods, and Jacob and Jehovah and were supposed to inspire the reader about fulfilling this sublime mission in Poland.[41]

The idea of public discussions as a form of political engagement (without which 'true progressiveness' was not possible) also benefitted from the activities of French left-wing academics. The Polish cultural press published the transcripts of public debates between French intellectuals. The contradictions between the representatives of various opinions were presented as the principles that should help the disputants to find the best solution in the future.[42] It was French philosophers, not the Soviets, who explained to Polish readers that it was necessary to establish certain limits of the acceptable in art and scholarship to ensure they served the social needs of the nation.[43] Thus, French scholars became authority figures in spreading the idea that the service of the social needs of the nation was the key task of both academic work and art.

Moreover, the interpretation of current Soviet cultural realities also came not from the Soviets but from the French side. It was the philosopher Pierre Hervé who familiarised the Polish reader with the ideological campaign, organised by the leading ideologist of late Stalinism Andrei Zhdanov,[44] against prominent Russian poet Anna Akhmatova in 1946.[45] Of course, Hervé supported Zhdanov and explained to his opponents that the poetry of Akhmatova was an example of the isolation of the artist from the social needs of her nation, as well as an escape from reality into the world of illusions. Hervé even argued that 'many French artists and writers would recognise themselves in the characteristics given by Zhdanov' and that the only excuse for this is that France (unlike the Soviet Union) still lived in a bourgeois society.[46] In this way, Hervé just repeated Soviet propaganda. Nevertheless, the fact that the commentary on the new smear campaign organised by the Soviet authorities came to Poland through France in the form of an 'open discussion' on different forms of knowledge is telling.

Of course, the French communist party was, to put it mildly, under the 'influence' of the Soviet government or, to be more precise, had accepted the Stalinist line in post-war politics. The texts on Marxism and Russian revolutionary culture written by French authors could hardly be considered heretical, even from the 'Soviet point of view' (in contrast to the texts written by the Poles themselves[47]). Even though the plurality of views represented among French communists was broader than that of the Soviet Union, the general slogans of Stalinism were well accepted among the key figures of the French communist Party.[48]

Nevertheless, the fact that the basic principles of Marxism, the theoretical heritage of Russian revolutionaries, and the comments on the Soviet cultural realities came to Poland from France was an important feature of the early post-war years. The Polish intellectual habit of learning about the newest intellectual tendencies from French journals was one of the most important resources that the organisers of the 'gentle revolution' project wanted to use. It was important to propose to the Polish audience to compare themselves not with the Soviet Union but with France.

Even though the superiority of socialist regimes over the realities of 'capitalist' countries was one of the key propagandist slogans during the second half of the 20th century, the idea that Poland got a unique opportunity to fulfil the prophecy of the French philosophers had, in the early post-war years, special connotations. The general idea that the Bolsheviks had adapted the key ideas of French utopian socialism but then, having destroyed capitalism after the October Revolution, had overtaken France, was formulated during the discussions of the Third International.[49] Nevertheless, this argument seemed different from the mouth of Polish intellectuals after more than 25 years of Soviet regime. France was still the source of progressive thought, and the post-war realities were reflected and interpreted from the perspective of the interwar relations between Polish and French scholars and writers.

The idea that post-war Poland could overcome its teachers in their aim for 'progressiveness' found its public expression in the Polish public sphere. For example, the Polish representative in Paris, Mieczysław Bibrowski, concluding his examination of the intellectual heritage of the French thinkers, wrote:

Beloved France! You have been and remain a country of freedom and reason. And if, as [Jules] Michelet predicted,[50] Poland will overtake you by one step in the work on social progress, you will support us in this work by giving us and the whole world countless bones of your great, beautiful, immortal culture.[51]

Thus, the French post-war political realities gave the participants in the 'gentle revolution' project the impression that their opportunities to cultivate 'progressiveness' on various levels were much broader in comparison with their French colleagues.

Developing the idea of the superiority of the Polish state on the way to 'progressiveness,' the writer and translator Paweł Hertz reflected on his fascination with French culture in the interwar period and the conviction of young Polish socialists that Poland has the same 'civilisational path' as France. The spirit of France, the masterpieces of Picasso, and the landscapes of Seine, all made France, according to Hertz, the centre of European intellectual culture. Nevertheless, the collaboration of many French intellectuals with the pro-Nazi regime divided, in his view, French society into two opposing camps. Both were fighting for France, but their ideas of France were different. The war, wrote Hertz, became the moment of truth that showed that many French people defended the bourgeois values but not the country of great humanists and enlighteners.[52] In this regard, post-war Poland, in which most intellectuals claimed their 'progressiveness,' appeared to be a more loyal student of the great French thinkers. Developing this idea, he wrote:

> Polish intellectuals, perhaps not without surprise, should discover that the group of intellectuals and writers in Poland who promote the 'gentle revolution' has the same cultural program and a similar attitude to fundamental issues of culture and art [as it was understood by French socialists].[53]

So, not France but Poland first received the opportunity to promote 'the scientific logical thinking based on the best traditions of European culture' at the level supported by the authorities.[54] In this regard, it was France's turn to take an example from the young Polish state.

French heroes of the Polish Catholic agenda[55]

The unique role of France in Polish cultural life was determined not only by the Francophile attitude of left-wing intellectuals but also by the historical roots of the close relationship between Polish and French Catholics. Both the ideological struggle of some French Catholics against socialists and the attempts of other Catholic scholars to find a compromise with socialist ideologies were a part of the Polish intellectual agenda of the interwar period. The cultural authority of France had its implications in the special interest of Polish Catholics in the social thought of their French coreligionists. The exchange of seminary students, the rise and internationalisation of Catholic philosophy in Poland, and the aggravation of the political struggle in both countries were the factors that determined intensive intellectual exchange between Polish and French Catholics.[56]

French personalism became one of the most notable intellectual movements that dealt with the problem of coexistence of Marxism and Christianity. Even though the term 'personalism' had been used for various directions in the Catholic thought that dealt with the value of human personality, in the history of political thought, this term usually refers to the Catholic group that took the most radical position regarding the collaboration between Catholicism and the socialist movement. The journal '*Esprit*,' soon after its foundation in 1934, began to be considered among the most significant centres in attracting those Catholics interested in debating the current social processes. The founder of the periodical, Emmanuel Mounier (1905–1950), became the face of this group. Being influenced and supported by the well-known Thomistic philosopher Jacques Maritain, Mounier discussed the reconciliation of the Catholic doctrine with the socialist ideology in a considerable number of his essays.[57]

One of the most prominent of Mounier's works, '*A Personalist Manifesto*' (1936),[58] seemed to be a summary of the crucial ideas of *Esprit*'s movement. The Manifesto included many significant interpretations of the opposition between the person and the collective, the ideas concerning the nature of the social processes, and a critical review of Marxism. However, it is more important to highlight that the promotion of the idea of *engagement* as an integral part of 'progressiveness' was a guiding spirit in Mounier's programme. The idea that Catholics should engage with and not ignore social changes was crucial for all of Mounier's writings. More importantly, this programme implied not only participation in the current political events but also the adaption of the social teaching of Christianity to the Marxist ideology. Taking into account the decisively negative position of the official Church towards Marxism, such ideas were doomed to provoke an ambiguous reaction among the Catholics who had to choose between their loyalty to the Holy See and their feeling of necessity to renew the Catholic idea of global social processes.[59]

Often harshly criticised by the conservative Pope Pius XI, Mounier promoted the idea that the social changes about which Marx spoke were inevitable, and that the Catholics' aim was to spiritualise these social changes and fill them with Christian values. The experience of the Second World War strengthened Mounier's conviction that radical changes in the social structure of the 'Western society' were necessary. He developed his programme at the new level and wrote: 'Communism and Christianity reinforce each other as Jacob and the Angel, with a rigour and brotherhood-in-arms that infinitely surpass the struggle for power,'[60] arguing: 'It is not we who have invented socialism. It was born from man's suffering and his reflections on the disorders that oppressed him.'[61] These statements distinctly illustrate the aspects of Mounier's programme that seemed so relevant for the post-war Polish reality.

The post-war debates on French personalism in Poland were, in many respects, a sign of continuity with the previous tradition of the Polish Catholic thought.[62] So, for example, the leaders of the post-war Kraków group, Jerzy Turowicz and Stanisław Stomma, had repeatedly visited Paris to speak to French Catholics after the First World War. Moreover, they regularly read '*Esprit*' and considered personalism to be one of the most promising socio-political ideas within social Catholic thought.[63] After the war, the Kraków Catholics translated many texts written by French philosophers and theologians to prove the correctness of this conviction. Thus, for example, the Kraków group published an article written by the Catholic philosopher Jean Daniélou (1905–1974). In this essay, Daniélou characterised both liberalism and Marxism as movements that had lost their philosophical and political relevance,[64] while arguing that Mounier's personalism, Maritain's personalistic Thomism, and existentialism[65] represented the mainstream in contemporary philosophy.⁶⁶ All of these philosophical approaches meant the concept of personhood played the central role in the scholarly agenda.

From the perspective of the Kraków group, the idea of personhood should be in the centre of any political ideology as well. In one of his articles, Turowicz considered personalism a middle path between the extremes of Fascism and Communism. He wrote:

> The only correct solution to the problem [of collectivist ideologies] is personalism. Personalism is seeing a person against the background of the complete natural and supernatural reality of the human condition, knowing that a human being is either good or bad not by nature, but through culture, education, and above all, grace.⁶⁷

Developing this idea, Turowicz proposed a model of a 'personalist democracy':

> A personalist democracy, an organic, strong state, organising and managing the planned economic life and material well-being of society and everything that is within its scope, as well as leaving maximum freedom in the field of culture, and thus education, and especially the highest vocation of the human person.⁶⁸

Of course, Turowicz did not call for the creation of a 'personalist party,' or any other political organisation, since it was nearly impossible under the post-war political conditions.⁶⁹ Turowicz's reflections on a 'personalist state' were a new occasion to discuss the political realities of the early post-war years. For good reasons, maintaining 'maximum freedom' was key for the Kraków group to keep its position in the socio-political landscape of the Polish state after the Second World War. Therefore, discussion on personalism became, for the Kraków group, not a theory of *engagement* but a part of a defensive strategy against the invasion of the state into the 'personal' issues.

Another leader of the Kraków group, Stanisław Stomma, made this point clearer. He provoked an intense debate⁷⁰ on the limits of what was acceptable when applying the ideas of the French theorists on Polish soil. Stomma argued that Mounier's main argument, that the fulfilment of Marx's prophecy was inevitable, was based on his criticism against the social structure of western societies. Developing this argument, Stomma referred to Oswald Spengler (who was highly popular in conservative circles) to illustrate the difference between French and Polish contexts. According to Stomma, the European nations, about which Spengler spoke in his writings, are old ones. Therefore, French and Polish Catholics are situated in entirely different contexts. The Slavic countries belong to the 'young nations' and do not have such an established social system as those of 'old Europe.' Therefore, the 'opportunism' of French Catholics in front of Marxism and the belief in the inevitability of the fulfilment of the Marxian prophecy were not suitable for Poland.⁷¹ From Stomma's perspective, the radical engagement with Marxism that had been proposed by Mounier could threaten Catholic social principles. Moreover, it would be a contribution to the project that could not be implemented in Poland due to its social structure.

Thus, the Kraków group, proclaiming personalism to be their central philosophical theory (with references primarily to the French thinkers), interpreted it as a defence of the value of personhood in front of the collectivist ideology rather than a theory of political action. This interpretation of the French philosophers helped them to 'adapt' the ideas coined in the open public debates of 'bourgeois' France to the political situation of post-war Poland. Thus, French personalism, being, first of all, a programme of *engagement* in current social and political processes, became the cornerstone of the strategy of self-isolation under the unpleasant political conditions.

The Catholic group associated with the charismatic figure Bolesław Piasecki proposed an opposite interpretation of French personalism. Even though the works of the French personalists did not play any significant role in the interwar activity of Piasecki, the search for a survival strategy led him to a deep interest in the theories of French Catholics. Immediately after the war, Piasecki and his following adopted a considerable proportion of the arguments that had been used by the French personalists. In this case, the most radical idea of collaboration between Catholics and communists was the central point in developing the Catholic agenda under the new conditions. Unlike the Kraków group, Piasecki's followers were not particularly interested in the concept of personhood formulated by the French thinkers. Meanwhile, the concept of *engagement* became crucial for them. Developing their programme of collaboration with Marxists for 'reconstructing the Polish state,'[72] Piasecki's group used the authority of France to secure their place in the intellectual landscape of post-war Poland.

Much like Mounier, Piasecki had the ambition to 'spiritualise' the social changes that had been conducted by socialists. He wrote: 'At the same time, it is true that the revolutionary spiritualist forces exist in Poland. It is also true that these forces, while accepting the socio-economic changes, at the same time profess the Catholic worldview.'[73] Additionally, like Mounier's group, Piasecki made the idea of the inevitability of the 'great social changes' propagated by Marxism the central point in his programme. In one of the publications, Piasecki wrote: 'The process of forming a new era can be seen as an inevitable phenomenon that will occur, despite our desire or opposition.'[74] Piasecki argued that Catholics could not help but engage in the socialist reforms conducted by Marxists since '<...> In the current historical period, there is no possibility of the isolated existence of large communities.'[75]

The references to French theory were important for Piasecki, not only to legitimise his collaboration with the authorities. The positive reputation of France in the leftist circles, and the idea of the collaboration between Catholicism and Marxism that had been developed by the French Catholic philosophers, were important resources for making his programme relevant at an international level.[76] After the war, Piasecki continued to develop a highly nationalist programme with a strong emphasis on the service of the 'Polish nation.' Nevertheless, this was an internal, Polish issue that could help him to use his former ideology to establish his position among the nationalist and 'patriotic' wings of communists and socialists.

Meanwhile, French personalism provided the opportunity to prove his 'usefulness' in the creation of the political image of Poland on the international stage.[77] Thus, the positive image of his group in the French intellectual agenda become one more component in his survival strategy.[78]

It was not accidental that Piasecki's group played a key role in establishing the 'diplomatic' relationship with French Catholic thinkers. The visit of Mounier to post-war Poland became a significant challenge for Piasecki's group, for whom it was a chance to familiarise the philosopher with their active line regarding collaboration with Marxism and the socialist authorities. During his trip to Poland in 1946, Mounier visited Łódź, Kraków, and Warsaw, and all these cities attracted (though for various reasons) his interest. Even though Mounier's trip to Kraków was organised with the support of the local Church hierarchy, headed by Cardinal Adam Sapieha, and the Kraków Catholics were among the key initiators of his visit to Poland, Mounier got the impression that it was desired by Piasecki's group. The 'progressive Catholics' were able to present themselves as the vanguard of Catholic thought in Poland and convince him of the promising future of their activity.

After his return to France, Mounier published a detailed article regarding the social, political, and economic situation in post-war Poland. Considering the position that France took in the Polish intellectual landscape, this publication is extremely important for understanding the role that Poland played for the French audience in general and for French Catholics in particular. Mounier started with typical 'compliments' for Poland and its post-war realities and said that 'new Poland represents an interest that is underestimated in the epoch when eyes are riveted on the massive prototypes of the developing world.'[79] Moreover, the plurality of contexts including Soviet influences, the huge role of the Catholic Church, and the mix between 'Eastern' and 'Western' cultural elements had been preparing, according to Mounier, 'a new chemistry' that might be of 'great importance' for Europe. Nevertheless, Mounier's article did not contain any idealisation of the regime established in Poland. On the contrary, he depicted a destroyed country with huge human losses caused by the war and emphasised the significant reduction of the number of educated people.[80]

Describing his Polish experiences, Mounier paid much more attention to the political and economic issues than to Polish intellectual life. Among other things, he wrote a special section on the 'anti-Russian' sentiments among the Polish population which were, according to his impression, very strong. Mounier wittily remarked that 'the Pole needs passion as the Englishman needs phlegm' and claimed that 'the current passion of Poles is an anti-Russian passion.'[81] Mounier was well informed regarding the roots of the anti-Russian mood and referred to the defeat of the Warsaw Uprising in autumn 1944, the arrest of the leaders of the Home Army and the Moscow trial against them, as well as the idea of the 'new occupation' by Soviet troops. The fact that Mounier could see the anti-Russian 'passion' with his own eyes during his trip to Poland is very notable. He recognised that the political landscape of Poland did not have anything to do with that of the Soviet Union (with which he did not sympathise).[82] At the same time, it is difficult to say that Mounier was deeply inspired by the situation in which Poland found itself after the Second World War. The notability of the Polish case was, for him, not in the 'unique' conditions for further cultural development that Poland had, about which 'bourgeois' France could not even dream, but in the combination of such elements as anti-Russian sentiments and the necessity to claim loyalty to the Soviet Union, which stood in contradiction to each other.

Mounier, whose name played the central role in the theoretical reflections of Catholic intellectuals, devoted only a small piece of his paper to the public activity of the Catholic theologians, philosophers, and journalists in post-war Poland. Moreover, when characterising Polish religiosity, Mounier referred to its 'non-intellectual' character. According to Mounier's impression, 'both right- and left[-wing people] are Catholic [in Poland] except for a small minority,' but 'it would probably be fairer to highlight the role of a historical habit [in this] and, above all, the absence of intellectual tradition, which is cruelly felt [here].'[83] Developing this argument, Mounier emphasised that Polish Catholicism was closely connected to a kind of 'national sentiment'; he referred to his conversations with a Catholic who was, at the same time, a member of the Polish Workers' Party and told the French reader about a Polish military fellow with the banner 'God save us!'[84]

The 'depth' of his interest in the intellectual agenda of his Polish followers was reflected in the fact that only two paragraphs in his 35-page long essay were devoted to the groups of Catholic intellectuals. According to his 'analytics,' the group of the weekly 'Tygornik Warsewski [Tygodnik Warszawski]' headed by the priest 'Kaczypski [Kaczyński]' was 'very moderate (*très modéré*)' in responding to the 'modern times,' while the group of 'Tygordnik Powsredny [Tygodnik Powszechny]' were much better at this than their Warsaw colleagues. More importantly, it was only Piasecki's group that attracted some empathy from the side of Mounier. He was obviously informed in Poland about Piasecki's 'nationalist past' and had heard such characteristics of his activity as 'he sold out himself to the Marxists.' Nevertheless, it was not an obstacle for Mounier to devote to Piasecki's group more than one sentence and to write, among other things that 'the team of *Dris i Jutro* [Dziś i Jutro] seems to us to be starting a good job, in which we must wish [them] success.'[85]

It is striking that Mounier was much better informed about the differences between Polish Democratic, Socialist, and Workers' parties than he was about the intellectual agenda of Polish Catholic scholars. The role that the Catholic groups played in Mounier's article could hardly gladden his Polish followers, who regularly read '*Esprit*,' and the superior tone regarding the 'non-intellectual' and 'nationalist' character of Polish Catholicism did not seem to be the best reward for the Catholic groups. It is not surprising that Jerzy Turowicz, after a new round of exchanged letters, painfully related his misunderstanding with the French philosopher.[86] Meanwhile, Piasecki reached his main aim and, thanks to his young representative Wojciech Kętrzyński, not only was praised by Mounier but also established a long-term relationship with the journal '*Esprit*,' which became a link in the network of his post-war international relations.[87]

Catholics 'should' adopt the French example

French Catholicism appeared as an important reference point not only in internal discussions between Catholics but also in the state-run press. Such a reference to the French experience of collaboration between Marxists and Catholics under the banner of 'progressiveness' and 'engagement' was a relevant example for the organisers of the 'gentle revolution' project. The state-run press repeatedly attempted to convince the Catholics to consider the French case as a possible example of loyalty to 'true progressiveness.' Blaming those Catholics who hesitated to accept Mounier's radical social programme, Paweł Hertz wrote in one of his essays:

> There were Communists and Catholics who fought [together] for the France of Jeanne d'Arc and the Great Encyclopaedia. For our Catholics, who have lived in Vatican Quietism[88] for years, this [collaboration between Catholics and Marxists] would seem impossible.[89]

On the one hand, this was one of many attempts to attack Polish Catholics for opposing the Enlightenment and thus the 'correct' version of 'progressiveness.' On the other, this formulation demonstrated that the organisers of the 'gentle revolution' still saw the Catholics as participants in the Polish public sphere. The French example was an opportunity to encourage them to join the 'camp of the Enlightenment' under the post-war conditions.[90] Thus, in the early post-war period, the 'French myth' exemplified the ideal form of collaboration between Catholics and Marxists in post-war Poland.

The idea that the authority of France could be used to attract Polish Catholics to the governmental programme was openly claimed by left-wing scholars. So, for example, Jan Kott argued that the main resource for the promotion of the 'gentle revolution' was 'both the traditional bonds of sympathy between French Catholics and Poland ... and the true respect of the left-wing French [intellectuals] to our social reforms.'[91] Therefore, the intellectual and academic relationship of Polish Catholics with their French coreligionists could, from the perspective of the early post-war project, become a valuable resource for implementing the 'French ideal' in the post-war Polish state, as well as a very important trait of self-representation of the new Polish state in France.

This point was very important for Polish cultural diplomacy. The idea that Poland, at the governmental level, will find a compromise between religion and 'progressiveness' played an important role in the early post-war cultural diplomacy. So, for example, during his visit to Paris, Iwaszkiewicz reported with inspiration that the representatives of '*Esprit*' were among the editors of the French journals who wanted to meet him during his trip to France.[92] So, Mounier's programme was the prism through which the organisers of cultural politics saw possible coexistence in post-war Poland.

Of course, the 'French example' was constructed by the organisers of the 'gentle revolution' from the perspective of their project's needs. Mounier's ideas and his difficult relationships with the official church made him a good candidate for 'teaching' Polish Catholics how to prefer 'progressiveness' regarding the social issues in loyalty to the Church hierarchy. It is remarkable that the communist theoretical journal 'Nowe Drogi (The New Paths)' published an article on the activity of the '*Esprit*' group. The author of this contribution, Julia Hartwig, was a prominent translator of French literature into Polish and one of those Polish intellectuals who was engaged in the activity of both the Catholic and left-wing groups.[93] On the pages of the communist journal, Hartwig made the reader familiar with the 'positive fruits' of the collaboration between Mounier and French communists.[94]

In accordance with the idea of teaching Catholics how to be 'progressive' in social issues, Hartwig lamented the passivity of Polish Catholics in following the example of the '*Esprit*' group. Characterising Mounier's activity, Hartwig wrote:

> At the present time, '*Esprit*' gives us an occasion for a discussion [on the relationships between Catholics and Marxists which is an issue] of an extremely deep political nature, because this is the only way to estimate the discussion between the Marxist and Catholic camps under our conditions.[95]

Hartwig could only lament the fact that not all Polish Catholics were ready to accept the form of political activism prescribed by the '*Esprit*' group:

> '*Esprit*,' which is the mainstay of the left-wing social progressive movement of Catholics in France, is more often quoted in 'Kuźnica' than in 'Tygodnik Powszechny'[96] ... the intellectual activity of Mounier's group and its main desire to participate in the broad movement of social reforms may have the value of a model for the Catholic camp in Poland, [which is] not comparable with [their] comrades from the banks of the Seine either in independence [from the Vatican] or in finding [new] paths.[97]

Hartwig concluded her essay with the statement as follows:

> The activities of the '*Esprit*' group are proof of how a truly Patriotic attitude and a correctly understood public interest can be used to create a common platform for the activities of various ideological branches, for the benefit of the nation and social progress.[98]

This remark seemed to be a call to Polish Catholics to adapt the example of the '*Esprit*' group and thus to fulfil the mission proclaimed by the organisers of the 'gentle revolution.'

Since Piasecki's group actively used the reputation of Mounier in their public activity, the call of the organisers of the 'gentle revolution' was addressed, first of all, to the Kraków Catholic group. Nevertheless, several months after the visit of Mounier to Poland, the Kraków Catholics were more decisive in questioning the opportunity to apply the French experience on Polish soil. According to the Marxist historian of literature Kazimierz Wyka, the Kraków Catholics replied to the proposition to follow Mounier, during one of the public debates between Marxists and Catholics,[99] as follows:

> The left wing of the French Catholics, led by Mounier and the group of *'Esprit,'* does not represent the entirety of French Catholicism; this is just an attempt to create a common platform [for dialogue between Catholics and Marxists] that does not affect politically, in any significant way, French Catholicism.[100]

Thus, the Kraków group opposed the attempts of their Marxist opponents to force Polish Catholics to follow Mounier's example. Moreover, the argument that was, according to Wyka, used by the Catholic side of the discussion, concerned the differences in the roles that Catholicism played in Polish and French societies. During this debate, Jerzy Turowicz argued that the French used to defend their positions in French society in front of the increasing influence of materialism, while Polish Catholics did not find this strategy necessary for the Polish context.[101] The Kraków Catholics still believed that the domination of religion in Polish society allowed them not to cross their line of *non possumus* in following the social doctrine of the Catholic Church.

The debates on France in the early post-war years showed another aspect of this issue. While the left-wing intellectuals saw their advantage over France in the destruction of the 'bourgeois' and 'capitalist' system in Poland, Polish Catholics argued that Catholicism had much broader support in Polish society than in France. 'Rural' Catholicism, which had been superciliously characterised by Mounier as 'non-intellectual,' was for them an argument not to give up in their ideological competition with the new political realities.[102] So, like their left-wing opponents, Catholics had their own 'advantage' over their 'teachers.' Being in a country that declared itself a socialist regime, Catholics thought that they could defend their ideology better than their French coreligionists in republican France.

Thus, the Warsaw group of Bolesław Piasecki was the only Catholic group that readily accepted the form of 'progressiveness' promoted by the authorities. While more conservative Catholic fellows like Zygmunt Kaczyński's colleagues were not particularly interested in applying the ideas of the French philosophers on Polish soil, the Kraków group attempted to 'synthesise' a non-political personalism that would not stay in contradiction to the official attitude of the Catholic Church. So, Piasecki's group got the opportunity to use the personalist programme to legitimise his post-war activity. Other Catholic groups did not accept the image of France promoted by the state-run press. Their ideal image of France was different.

*

It would not be entirely wrong to say that the project of the 'gentle revolution' aimed to make Poland 'a France but better.' French culture played a much more important role in the public debates of the early post-war years than any other 'national' culture. Unlike the Soviet Union and its intellectual tradition, French thought was the source of many positive examples, even though there was no coherent image of 'good France' under the 'gentle revolution.' For the organisers of the early post-war project, France (not the Soviet Union) was the homeland of the virtue of 'progressiveness' based on engagement with the current political process. The idea that, in post-war Poland, scholars and writers determined the 'progressive' agenda and received support from the authorities was represented as the advantage of Poland over the French teachers. Additionally, the French example was useful for finding an 'ideal' form of collaboration between Catholics and the left-wing intellectuals in the Polish public sphere after the war.

However, the main problem with the French as 'teachers' of virtues was that significant parts of Polish Catholicism had a very different idea of France than that promoted by the state-run press. Most of the heroes of the publications in the cultural press were French communists whose pro-Soviet sympathies were obvious. Of course, it was not the same to be a sympathiser of the Soviet Union in France and to propagate the Stalinist ideology in the Soviet state. In any case, the attractive image of 'progressive' France propagated by the state-run press was supposed to force Catholics to prefer 'progressiveness' over the loyalty to the hierarchy of the Catholic Church. The concreteness of this question led to a split among the Catholics into those who accepted the priority of 'progressiveness' over the Church discipline and those who did not.

Either way, it was not the purely scientific agenda, but the questions related to the public activism of scholars and the forms of 'progressiveness' promoted under the 'gentle revolution' that became central in the debates around French culture. The role of France in the post-war public debates was determined by the 'national' intellectual tradition. The virtues that had to be learned in France were to become 'national' virtues in terms of 'academic service' of the nation. Scholars were asked to bring the 'progressiveness' to the broader public and thus become 'good members' of the nation. But what if the national virtues were in conflict with those gained in the professional community?

Notes

1 Jerzy Borejsza, "Rewolucja łagodna," *Odrodzenie*, no. 10–12 (1945): 1.
2 See e.g.: Halina Stankowska, *Literatura i krytyka w czasopismach Wielkiej Emigracji (1832-1848)* (Wrocław: Zakład Narodowy im. Ossolińskich, 1973).
3 It does not mean that Polish philosophers developed exclusively the ideas of their German (Austrian) and British colleagues. On the contrary, for example, Polish logicians were full participants in the development of this philosophical field, though the language of publications that made their works available for the international community was, usually, German. See more about the genesis and the international influence of the Lvov-Warsaw School: Anna Brożek, Friedrich Stadler, Jan Woleński, ed., *The Significance of the Lvov-Warsaw School in the European Culture* (Cham: Springer, 2017).
4 The matter concerns, for example, the students of Stefan Czarnowski, who was one of the key figures in cultural sociology and significantly influenced philosophical studies. See, a special issue of the journal 'Kuźnica' that was devoted to the heritage of Czarnowski: Stanisław Ossowski, "Stefan Czarnowski," *Kuźnica*, no. 6 (1947): 2; Tadeusz Kotarbiński, "Wspominki o Stefanie Czarnowskim," *Kuźnica*, no. 6 (1947): 4; Witold Kula, "'Kultura' Czarnowskiego," *Kuźnica*, no. 6 (1947): 5.
5 See e.g.: Adam Massalski, "Nauczyciele języka francuskiego męskich szkół średnich rządowych Królestwa Polskiego w latach 1833-1862, Studia Pedagogiczne," *Problemy*

Społeczne, Edukacyjne i Artystyczne, no. 14 (2003) 55–81; Grażyna Karłowska, "Edukacja domowa dziewcząt w rodzinie polskiej XIX i na początku XX wieku w świetle pamiętników," *Biuletyn Historii Wychowania*, no. 1–2 (2004): 23–38.

6   Marci Shore, *Caviar and Ashes: A Warsaw Generation's Life and Death in Marxism, 1918-1968* (New Haven/London: Yale University Press, 2006), 90–152.

7   See below the examples of examination of Lenin's publications through the prism of their French interpretations. About French experiences of Polish socialists: Shore, *Caviar and Ashes*, 10–51.

8   See about the history of the foundation of the *Centre Scientifique*: Danuta Rederowa, Bohdan Jaczewski, and Waldemar Rolbiecki, *Polska Stacja Naukowa w Paryżu w latach 1893–1978* (Wrocław: Zakład Narodowy im. Ossolińskich, 1982), 45–84.

9   See, the reports on the activity of the institution: Centre Scientifique de l'Académie Polonaise des Sciences (Archive): Sprawozdanie z działalności stacji PAN w Paryżu (mat. arch.): *Sprawozdanie Kierownika Działu Humanistycznego Stacji Naukowej PAN w Paryżu*. K 1–8.

10 One of the reports of the *Centre Scientifique* contains the information regarding the initiative of French sociologists who were interested in Polish social sciences to review all of the recent publications of Polish sociologists in the French academic and cultural press, see: Centre Scientifique de l'Académie Polonaise des Sciences (Archive): *Stacja Naukowa Polskiej Akademii Umiejętności w Paryżu [Sprawozdanie], 1947*, K. 5.

11 Of course, Giedroyc's group was not the only one in France that took an active part in public life. About the French émigré fellows, see: Leon Turajczyk, *Społeczno–polityczne organizacje polskie we Francji 1944–1948* (Warszawa: Książka i Wiedza, 1978).

12 The legal process against the Polish Academy of Arts and Sciences was initiated by the *Société Historique et Littéraire Polonaise*, which played the role of the Polish exiled cultural institution in Paris, see: Société Historique et Littéraire Polonaise (Archive) sygn. 389 1/2, Notatki do procesu THL przeciwko PAU, K. 1–5.

13 For information about the relations between the Polish exiles in France and the French government, see: Paweł Sękowski, "Francja wobec polskich uchodźców wojennych i dipisów w pierwszych latach po drugiej wojnie światowej," *Dzieje Najnowsze* 2 (2014): 71–83.

14 See Chapter 1.

15 See more about this tendency: Grzegorz P. Bąbiak, "'Czerwona Marianna' o polsko-francuskich związkach literackich na łamach 'Odrodzenia' (1945–1950)," *Prace Polonistyczne* 70 (2015): 9–29.

16 See, for example: Zbigniew Mitzner, "Sprawy wewnętrzne Francji," *Kuźnica*, no. 9 (1945): 7; "Kronika Francuska," *Kuźnica*, no. 6 (1946): 11.

17 "Z Towarzystwa Przyjaźni Polsko-Francuskiej," *Kuźnica*, no. 9 (1945): 7.

18 The idea of continuity between two emigrations was reflected in historiography, which describes the political exile of the 20th century as 'The Second Great Emigration,' see: Andrzej Friszke, *Druga Wielka Emigracja: Życie polityczne emigracji 1945–1990* (Warszawa: Więź, 1999); Rafał Habielski, *Druga Wielka Emigracja: Emigracja w polityce międzynarodowej* (Warszawa: Więź, 1999); Paweł Machcewicz, *Druga Wielka Emigracja: Życie społeczne i kulturalne emigracji* (Warszawa: Więź, 1999).

19 The weakness of the exile press in the years immediately after the war was described by the specialist of the exile press, Rafał Habielski. Habielski showed that, until the middle of the 1950s, the Paris journal 'Kultura' (which shaped the image of the emigration in the 1960s) played a secondary role in the press of the exile, while the London journal 'Wiadomości' was the leader of the émigré press (see: Rafał Habielski, *Życie społeczne i kulturalne emigracji* [Warszawa: Biblioteka Więzi, 1999], 145). Nevertheless, the journal 'Wiadomości' did not develop an influential cultural programme in this period. The financial difficulties forced the émigré fellows, first of all, to fight for survival under the difficult conditions. Regarding the level of the cultural and academic press published in

the exile, even some émigré fellows claimed the 'degradation' of the culture of public debates. The literary critic and writer Jan Bielatowicz wrote in his paper entitled 'The Decline of Great Journalism': 'Emigrant journalism is a thing of the past in its subject matter, methods, and reactions to historical events' (Jan Bielatowicz, "Upadek wielkiej publicystyki," in *Literatura na emigracji*, ed. Jan Bielatowicz [London: Nakład Polskiej Fundacji Kulturalnej, 1970], 37). The intellectual activity was determined, first of all, by such individual scholars.

20 Not counting several years of Stalinisation. Stalinisation changed the plans of many scholars regarding their trips to Paris. In such a way, Witold Kula lamented the lack of opportunity to visit the Historical Congress in Paris in 1951, see: Maciej Górny, *The Nation Should Come First. Marxism and Historiography in East Central Europe* (Frankfurt am Main: Peter Lang Edition, 2013), 50–52.

21 Józef Czapski and Jerzy Giedroyc, who were the key figures of the group in the journal culture, had a very intensive correspondence with James Burnham (1905–1987), an extremely conservative philosopher and the hardliner towards communist influence in Europe. The idea that was propagated by Czapski and Giedroyc was the creation of 'Central European Studies' at American Universities to promote the idea of the principal difference in the history and culture of the Soviet Union and the countries that found themselves in the zone of Soviet Influence. See: Archiwum 'Kultura,' Korespondencja Burnham. Sygn. 75, T. 1, e.g. K. 6, 7.; Archiwum 'Kultura,' Korespondencja Burnham. Sygn. 76, T. 2, e.g. K. 17–20.

22 See below reflection on how to make Poland a central issue in the francophone agenda.

23 For more general aspects of the Polish–French intellectual exchange: Jarosz Dariusz and Maria Pasztor, *Polish-French relations, 1944–1989* (Frankfurt am Main: Peter Lang, 2015), 34–45.

24 Jarosław Iwaszkiewicz, "Wizyta w Paryżu," *Kuźnica*, no. 10 (1946): 3, 4.

25 Ibid., 3.

26 See about the 'socialist period' in the activity of Iwaszkiewicz: Marek Radziwon, *Iwaszkiewicz. Pisarz po katastrofie* (Warszawa: Wydawnictwo wab, 2010), 181–364.

27 Jan Kott, "Stosunki kulturalne Polsko-Francuskie," *Kuźnica*, no. 47 (1946): 8.

28 Ibid., 8.

29 Ibid., 8.

30 Ibid., 8. See more about fellowships for French students: Dariusz and Pasztor, *Polish-French relations*, 43–45.

31 Roger Garaudy, "Intelektualiści w ślepym zaułku," *Kuźnica*, no. 9 (1945): 3.

32 See: Roger Garaudy, *Komunizm i odrodzenie kultury francuskiej* (Łódź: Spółdzielnia Wydawnicza "Książka", 1945).

33 Roger Garaudy, "Komunizm a etyka," *Nowe Drogi*, no. 4 (1947): 135–153. Additionally, Garaudy's publications and the works of another prominent communist philosopher, René Maublanc (1891–1960), which had been translated for 'Nowe Drogi,' explained to the Polish reader such basic concepts of the communist teaching as freedom and humanism Roger Garaudy, "Komunizm a wolność," *Nowe Drogi*, no. 1 (1947): 130–139; René Maublanc, "Marksizm a wolność," *Nowe Drogi*, no. 3 (1947): 151–161.

34 Except for such 'Polish Soviets' as Celina Bobińska and Adam Schaff and the classics of Russian revolutionary thought, whose works were translated as a part of 'Soviet-Polish friendship.'

35 His article was published under the name 'Jacques Freville,' but taking into account the content of this contribution, it is more than likely that the author was Jean Fréville (1895–1971), whose real name was Eugène Schkaff.

36 [Jacques] Freville, "Lenin i Kultura," *Kuźnica*, no. 13 (1946): 5–6.

37 See: Vladimir Lenin, "The Three Sources and Three Component Parts of Marxism," accessed September 9, 2020, https://www.marxists.org/archive/lenin/works/1913/mar/x01.htm

38 Freville, "Lenin i Kultura," 6.
39 See, the official version of the Russian Revolution in 'The History of the Communist Party of the Soviet Union (Bolsheviks)' which was prepared as an academic course under the Stalinist rule: *The History of the Communist Party of the Soviet Union (Bolsheviks)*, New York: International Publisher, 2006 [1939]: http://www.marx2mao.com/Other/HCPSU39NB.html
40 Borejsza's article on the 'gentle revolution' was published several months earlier.
41 Léon Pierre-Quint, "Pisarze wobec społeczeństwa," *Kuźnica*, no. 9 (1945): 4.
42 See, for example, the transcript of the discussions led by such prominent cultural figures of France as Roger Garaudy, the communist philosopher Pierre Hervé (1913–1993), the surrealist poet Louis Aragon (1897–1982): "Spór o estetykę komunistyczną," *Kuźnica*, no. 6 (1947): 9–10.
43 "Spór o estetykę komunistyczną," *Kuźnica*, no. 6 (1947): 9–10.
44 See biography of Zhdanov: Kees Boterbloem, *The Life and Times of Andrei Zhdanov, 1896-1948* (Montreal: McGill-Queen's University Press, 2004).
45 This campaign (against Akhmatova and the writer Mikhail Zoshchenko) was a part of Stalin's measures for disciplining Soviet writers after the war, see: Vladislav Kutuzov, "A.A. Zhdanov i postanovlenie CK VKP(b) o zhurnalah 'Zvezda' i 'Leningrad'," *Novejshaja istorija Rossii* 1 (2011): 146–152. As I wrote in Chapter 2, the poetry of Anna Akhmatova was translated into Polish and published in the cultural press.
46 "Spór o estetykę komunistyczną," *Kuźnica*, no. 6 (1947): 9.
47 See Chapter 2.
48 See more: David Scott Bell and Byron Criddle, *The French Communist Party in the Fifth Republic* (Oxford: Clarendon Press, 1994), 149–165.
49 About the implementation of this ideology in early Soviet Academia, see: Michael David-Fox, *Revolution of the Mind: Higher Learning Among the Bolsheviks, 1918-1929* (Ithaca & London: Cornell University Press, 1997), 133–191.
50 Jules Michelet (1798–1874) – a French historian who wrote, among other things, about Russia and Poland as nations that would play a significant role in history, see: Jules Michelet, *Pologne et Russie* (Paris: La Librairie Nouvelle, 1852); and his book about the Polish uprising 1863: Jules Michelet, *La Pologne martyre* (Paris: Dentu, 1863).
51 Bibrowski, "O Francji żywej," 1.
52 Paweł Hertz, "Partia inteligencji francuskiej," *Kuźnica*, no. 5 (1946): 6.
53 In this sentence, Hertz meant the book of Roger Garaudy, which had been translated into Polish. Nevertheless, since Garaudy represented the 'most progressive' tendencies in French thought, this idea implied the entire French socialist tradition. See: Hertz, "Partia inteligencji francuskiej," 6.
54 Hertz, "Partia inteligencji francuskiej," 6.
55 Some of the arguments used in this subchapter had been thematised in my article: Aleksei Lokhmatov, "Theory in Action: French Personalism in the Public Debates of Post-war Poland," *Religiski-filozofiski raksti*, no. 1(2019): 277–293.
56 See about this period: Piotr H. Kosicki, *Catholics on the Barricades. Poland, France, and "Revolution", 1891–1956* (New Haven and London: Yale university press, 2018), 21–61.
57 See, for example, his writings that have been published in book form: Emmanuel Mounier, *Révolution personnaliste et communautaire* (Paris: Éd. Montaigne, 1934); Emmanuel Mounier, *De la propriété capitaliste à la propriété humaine* (Paris: Desclée de Brouwer, 1936).
58 Emmanuel Mounier, *Manifeste au service du personnalisme* (Paris: Éd. Montaigne, 1936).
59 Kosicki describes the attempts of some Catholic theologians to teach Marx at Spiritual Seminaries; the practice that was stopped by the Church hierarchy, see: Kosicki, *Catholics on the Barricades*, 78–80.

60 Emmanuel Mounier, *Feu la Chrétienté*, in Emmanuel Mounier, *Œuvres: 1944-1950* (Paris: Le Seuil, 1962), 614.
61 Emmanuel Mounier, *Be Not Afraid: Studies in Personalist Sociology* (New York: Harper, 1954), 195.
62 However, in the interwar period, the figure of Jacques Maritain played in the Polish reception of French Personalism a more important role than that of Mounier. One of the most influential figures of inter-war Polish Catholicism, the priest and philosopher Władysław Korniłowicz (1884–1946) was, in a sense, a mediator between the broader Catholic audience and the French Catholic thinkers. The group of Catholics gathered around Korniłowicz developed the so called 'Laski's Thomism (From the name of the village "Laski" not far from Warsaw),' and Jacques Maritain was among the key authors for the fellows of this circle. Moreover, not only did Korniłowicz's students visit Paris to see the French philosopher, but Maritain himself visited Warsaw by the invitation of 'Laski's Thomists.' See: Kosicki, *Catholics on the Barricades*, 40–49, 60–76.
63 Turowicz spoke once to Mounier in person, see: Kosicki, *Catholics on the Barricades*, 53–54; It is noteworthy that Mounier's texts were broadly discussed, not only among Catholics, but also in the circles of Polish sociologists who proposed them as readings for students before and during the war at the underground universities that acted under the Nazi-occupation, see: Kosicki, *Catholics on the Barricades*, 78–80. Meanwhile, there is no evidence of Bolesław Piasecki contacting French personalists during the interwar period, even though, in the post-war period, Piasecki's group were the main propagators of Mounier's theory.
64 The argument regarding the outdated character of Marxism was not an exclusively Catholic argument in the post-war debates, see Chapter 5.
65 In this case, existentialism referred to Jean-Paul Sartre with his famous article published in 1946 that had been earlier given as a lecture, see: Jean-Paul Sartre, *L'existentialisme est un humanisme* (Paris: Nagel 1946)
66 Jean Daniélou, "Życie umysłowe we Francji (Komunizm, Egzystencjalizm, Chrześcijaństwo)," *Znak*, no. 1 (1946): 93–109.
67 Jerzy Turowicz, "W stronę uspołecznienia," 89.
68 Ibid., 90. This article is one more evidence that the Kraków group took part in the discussions on political issues, even though they cared of maintaining the image of a non-political journal. See more in Chapter 1.
69 About the discussions around the opportunity to create a Catholic party, see Chapter 1.
70 See more about the contexts of the discussion: Przemysław Pazik, *Spory i wybory ideowe katolików świeckich w okresie narodzin komunistycznego systemu władzy w Polsce (1945-1948)* (PhD thesis, Warszawa: University of Warsaw, 2019), 22–25.
71 Stanisław Stomma, "Maksymalne i minimalne tendencje społeczne katolików," *Znak*, no. 3 (1946): 266–270.
72 See more in Chapter 5.
73 Bolesław Piasecki, "Zagadnienia istotne," *Dziś i Jutro*, no. 1 (1945): 2.
74 Bolesław Piasecki, "Kierunki," in Bolesław Piasecki, *Kierunki 1945–1960* (Warszawa: Instytut wydawniczy PAX, 1981), 22.
75 Bolesław Piasecki, "Walka o odpowiedzialność," in Bolesław Piasecki, *Kierunki 1945–1960* (Warszawa: Instytut wydawniczy PAX, 1981), 37.
76 Of course, Piasecki's group published the translations of the theological texts written by the French authors (see, e.g.: Jacques Maritain, "Nieśmiertelność naszego 'Ja'," *Dziś i Jutro*, no. 47 [1947]: 1–2). Piasecki understood that the number of his followers and readers was also a resource in his struggle for post-war political survival. That is why the journal published many purely theological texts that could help them to represent the journal as a platform both for theological and political debates.

77 See more about the international engagements of nationalists, which David Motadel calls 'a reactionary cosmopolitanism': David Motadel, "The global authoritarian moment and the revolt against empire," *American Historical Review* 124, no. 3 (2019): 843–877, especially p. 848.
78 About the development of international networking, see Mikołaj S. Kunicki, *Between the Brown and the Red. Nationalism, Catholicism, and Communism in 20th-Century Poland – The Politics of Bolesław Piasecki* (Athens: Ohio University Press, 2012), 77–180.
79 Emmanuel Mounier, "L'ordre règne-t-il à Varsovie?," *Esprit* 123, no. 6 (1946): 970.
80 Ibid., 971.
81 Ibid., 973.
82 About the anti-Russian moods among Poles, see: Mounier, "L'ordre règne-t-il à Varsovie?," 975–979.
83 Mounier, "L'ordre règne-t-il à Varsovie?," 995.
84 Ibid., 995–997.
85 Ibid., 998.
86 Kosicki, *Catholics on the Barricades*, 114–116.
87 Ibid., 135, 142–143, 164–165.
88 Quietism was a mystical movement in the Catholic Church that was especially popular in the 17th and 18th centuries. Even though this movement had been condemned by the Holy See, Hertz meant in this case a meditative but not rational approach to religion.
89 Paweł Hertz, "Partia inteligencji francuskiej," *Kuźnica*, no. 5 (1946): 6.
90 See more about this issue in Chapter 5.
91 Jan Kott, "Stosunki kulturalne Polsko-Francuskie," *Kuźnica*, no. 47 (1946): 8.
92 Jarosław Iwaszkiewicz, "Wizyta w Paryżu," *Kuźnica*, no. 10 (1946): 3, 4.
93 See about Julia Hartwig: Janusz R. Kowalczyk, "Julia Hartwig," *Culture.PL* July 23, 2020, https://culture.pl/pl/tworca/julia-hartwig
94 Julia Hartwig, "'Esprit'," *Nowe Drogi*, no. 1 (1947): 173.
95 Ibid.
96 Ironically, Adam Schaff said that Marxism was more often discussed in the Catholic press than in the left-wing journals; see Chapter 4.
97 Julia Hartwig, "'Esprit'," *Nowe Drogi*, no. 1 (1947): 173.
98 Ibid., 175.
99 See more about this debate in Chapter 5.
100 Kazimierz Wyka, "Socjalizm, komunizm i katolicyzm," *Odrodzenie*, no. 27 (1946): 9.
101 Ibid.
102 See more in Chapter 5.

4 The Polish Intelligentsia and an Anti-Authoritarian Vision of Society

'Our intelligentsia faces the big challenge of forming the cultural image of the new Poland. Inevitably, a new intelligentsia will grow, which will replace the ranks which had been cut down by the occupant, and, if necessary, replace those reactionary representatives of the professional intelligentsia who do not want to roll up their sleeves in order to work on building a democratic Poland.'[1] With these words, Jerzy Borejsza specified the role of the intelligentsia in the project of 'gentle revolution.' The issue of the intelligentsia belonged to the topics which, on the one hand, had shaped the agenda of Polish public debates since the 19th century and, on the other, had gained a new political meaning after the Second World War. The idea that the 'progressive intelligentsia' would be the main organiser of the 'gentle revolution' made discussions on this matter one of the central issues during the early post-war years.

Promoting his project, Borejsza put a special emphasis on the continuity between the 'old' and 'new' intelligentsia. Developing this argument, he wrote:

> The question of merging the older generation of our intelligentsia with the great wave of the new intelligentsia, which must be prepared soon, is undoubtedly in the interests of our culture and its development… Undoubtedly, the older generation of our intelligentsia can and should pass on their extensive professional and cultural experience [to the new intelligentsia]. There is no doubt that, at every stage of our cultural life, we must refer to the progressive national heritage.[2]

Thus, in the early post-war years, the discourse on the intelligentsia was closely related to the general call 'to be progressive' that was promoted by the authors of the 'gentle revolution' project. The members of the intelligentsia were supposed not only to purify themselves from the 'reactionary elements' but also to take part in cultivating the new intelligentsia. Most importantly, the concept of intelligentsia did not make sense beyond the paradigm of the Polish nation. The Polish intelligentsia was a national issue by definition. Therefore, during the scholarly debates on the intelligentsia, scholars were expected to combine three perspectives on the subject of their discussion: for them, the intelligentsia was a political project oriented to the future; a national issue, that is, an issue of national tradition rooted in the past; and a research question that should be treated 'scientifically.'

Stereotypically, the concept of 'intelligentsia' is often considered a unique Russian social phenomenon,[3] which is more than unfair. This concept started to play a significant role in the Russian public sphere only after the Polish Uprising in 1863–1864. Then, the Polish *inteligencja* was accused in the conservative press of deceiving rural people and forcing them to rebel against the Russian rule.[4] In any case, the Russian debates on the nature and role of the intelligentsia at the turn of the 19th and 20th centuries poorly influenced the Polish agenda on this issue. The concept of 'intelligentsia' had rapidly developed in different parts of the former Polish state partitioned by Russian, Prussian, and Austro-Hungarian empires even before it became a central issue in the agenda of Russian journalism.[5]

Meanwhile, the Russian context was important for making 'intelligentsia' an analytical and sociological concept at the international level. The writings of Russian revolutionaries (Lenin was a key figure in this regard[6]) influenced the formation of the vocabulary of 'scientific socialism.' By the end of the Second World War, the intelligentsia became one of the key concepts in the self-image of the Soviet Union. The ideal member of the Soviet intelligentsia was one who embodied the Stalinist vision of 'culturedness,' which determined the cultural and academic project of the late Stalinism.[7] Either way, in Soviet Marxism, the concept of 'intelligentsia' became an analytical tool of social analysis and received the legitimisation of this status at the highest political level.

If for the public debates in the cultural and academic press the communist concept of intelligentsia played a small role, the governmental discourse frequently referred to the Soviet rhetoric on this issue. For example, the Workers' Party functionary Włodzimierz Sokorski claimed that the process of 'democratisation' in post-war Poland would result in the merger of the intelligentsia with the rural people. In fact, Sokorski (a Polish communist with considerable Soviet experience) attempted to apply Lenin's discourse on the intelligentsia on Polish soil. During one of his public speeches delivered to Polish writers in 1946, Sokorski claimed:

> The intelligentsia is not able to create its own ideology and culture, because it is neither a class nor [a representative of its own] social function, and any attempts in this area, such as [Herbert] Wells's fantasy on a dictatorship of specialists,[8] have met with failure and did not cause any social consequences. The intelligentsia belongs to the world of labour. Paraphrasing with gross historical inaccuracy, we can compare the role of the intelligentsia in the era of capitalism with the role of the freedmen of the last era of the Roman Empire.[9]

From this perspective, it was not the intelligentsia but the proletariat that was the bearer of 'its own ideology and culture' that should succeed in Poland. In fact, Sokorski argued that the intelligentsia had to disappear as a social stratum after its mission in post-war Poland would be fulfilled.

There were some theoretical difficulties with this programme for those who claimed that the proletariat and not the intelligentsia was the bearer of 'true culture.'[10]

The communist scholar and the theorist of culture Jadwiga Siekierska attempted to resolve this contradiction. She wrote:

> The social advantage of the worker over the member of the intelligentsia is that, being excluded from the sources of spiritual culture, he is aware of his inferiority and fights for the right to [have access to] culture and [to] participate in its creation [while the intelligentsia] protects the world of their ideas from the hustle and bustle of life and struggle. [Nevertheless, organising a] closer contact of the intelligentsia with the workers and peasants within cultural and educational institutions <...> is, at the same time, the method to change the image of the intelligentsia itself.[11]

Thus, the special destination of the proletariat lost its prophetic character and became a field of work for the intelligentsia. As a group of educated people, its members were supposed to change the intellectual image of the post-war Polish state. So, Siekierska could only repeat the general idea from the government that 'a proper solution for the problem [i.e. the split between the intelligentsia and the working class] lies in the planned and careful formation of the intelligentsia by the rural people.'[12] In any case, none other than scholars themselves were expected to become the educators of the proletariat.[13]

The treason against 'progressiveness'[14]

The official discourse on the Polish intelligentsia still was very vague. Since the intelligentsia was understood as a 'problematic' social stratum, sociologists could not stay away in this discussion. It was Józef Chałasiński's research programme on the 'social genealogy of Polish intelligentsia' that provoked one of the most noticeable public debates of the early post-war years. The peculiarity of this discussion was that all its participants responded (as a rule) directly to Chałasiński's programme and thus exchanged arguments having in mind the same theoretical approach that they criticised or supported. More importantly, the representatives of various disciplines attempted to apply their professional knowledge in this debate. This showed the plurality of perspectives on the same issue.[15]

The public debate on this topic started with the publication, in the cultural journal 'Kuźnica,' of the lecture given by Józef Chałasiński at the newly established University of Łódź. Greeting the students at the beginning of the academic year in 1946, Chałasiński talked about the sociological approach to analysing the 'genealogy of the Polish intelligentsia.'[16] The very situation of this lecture was a particular one. Chałasiński stood in front of those who were expected to become the 'new intelligentsia' and critically reviewed the history of 'their' predecessors. In this way, Chałasiński obviously intended to make his contribution to the national project of the 'production' of the 'new intelligentsia.'

Chałasiński argued that the intelligentsia historically had the ambition of being a 'true representative' of Polish culture after the partition of Poland by the great empires in the late 18th century. He stressed that the intelligentsia strove to adopt the role of a 'moral authority for Polish people (*moralny rząd narodu polskiego*)' after the decline of the nobility (*szlachta*), which had traditionally played this role in the established canon of Polish culture. Thus, according to Chałasiński, the intelligentsia inherited both the nobility's conviction of being 'truly cultural' and their arrogant attitude towards rural people.

Sociologically, the intelligentsia was, for Chałasiński, both 'a kind of social stratum (*swoista warstwa społeczna*)' and a 'political force.'[17] Developing this idea, he strove to question the 'progressiveness' of the intelligentsia in the context of the social and economic processes of the 19th century. Doing so, he remarked upon the fact that Poland was a marginal European country in terms of economic development;[18] the nobility was in turn in opposition to the economic changes provoked by capitalism. Arguing so, Chałasiński regarded the intelligentsia to be a by-product (*uboczny produkt*) of capitalism's invasion of the nobility's economy. According to this view, the intelligentsia had become a 'resident of foreign capitalism in Poland' without any participation in the economic processes taking place in the Polish territories. Developing this argument, Chałasiński asserted:

> The resident [the intelligentsia] did not think anywhere in accordance with economic categories. The resident did not participate anywhere in creating the economic reality of the country and did not feel responsible for that – the economic issues were not the issues of their honour.[19]

Thus, the intelligentsia, according to Chałasiński, had been born by capitalism but did not influence the economic life of the Polish territories as had happened with the Bourgeoisie in Europe.

This led the author to the conclusion that there was no period in Polish history when the intelligentsia was truly 'progressive' and working in conformity with the people's interests. Obviously referring to the previous journalistic tradition of 'social criticism,'[20] Chałasiński formulated a very radical judgment:

> The Polish intelligentsia, being closed in its socio-cultural ghetto, grew its culture not as a vanguard and an elite of the lowest stratum, but as the satellites of the ancestral aristocracy and landowners' nobility.[21]

Aiming to describe the 'social type' of a 'member of the intelligentsia (*inteligent*),'[22] Chałasiński highlighted the most essential aspects of this phenomenon, that is, belonging to the upper stratum of society (*warstwa wyższa*) and representing 'amateurish but not professional'[23] intellectual culture.

Chałasiński's idea of 'amateurish culture' is a noteworthy concept in itself; according to this view, the intelligentsia's culture was amateurish because it had been determined by the 'old aristocratic style' rather than the 'current social necessity,' i.e. the 'progressiveness' that should distinguish, in his view, a 'professional' culture. Thus, the intelligentsia, in Chałasiński's view, acquired a special ethos, considering themselves to be 'Polish Europeans – Polish Londoners and Parisians – in the land of indigenous peasants.'[24] So, Chałasiński differentiated between the

'European culture' that had been promoted by the intelligentsia and the 'Polish rural culture' that determined the life of rural people. However, this opposition did not contain a negative message regarding 'European culture' in itself. Chałasiński's point was that the Polish intelligentsia imitated 'Western culture (which was national for European cultures)' instead of working on the formation of their own national culture. Thus, for him, 'being progressive' was only possible through being a part of nation.

Another important characteristic of Chałasiński's programme was rooted in his approach to the historical analysis. Looking for sources to prove his vision of the 'member of the Polish intelligentsia,' Chałasiński referred to literary fiction as a fount of relevant social types, from which he could draw the 'social type of the intelligentsia.' According to him, the identity of the intelligentsia who saw themselves to be 'civilisers' was very similar to the British colonialism shown in the books of Rudyard Kipling and Joseph Conrad. Attempting to give evidence for the 'fact' that the Polish intelligentsia regarded their own country through the prism of the 'colonialist paradigm,' Chałasiński took examples from Polish fiction. Thus, he referred to the novels of Henryk Sienkiewicz,[25] with his 'gospel of the Trilogy [the collection of his most famous books]'[26] and the writings of another prominent Polish writer, Stefan Żeromski, with his 'gospel of Prometheism.'[27] According to Chałasiński, the books of these two classical authors constructed an image of the members of the intelligentsia as the 'civilisers' of rural people. Thus, based on the literary characters created at the turn of the 19th and 20th centuries, Chałasiński argued that colonial logic was an integral part of the ethos of a member of the intelligentsia, which had been formed during the 19th century.

In his sociological analysis, Chałasiński also addressed a very sensitive issue – the role of the intelligentsia as the 'defenders of the Polish spirit' under the rule of the great empires. Chałasiński argued that 'this defence [of the Polish spirit against the occupants] was stigmatised with a social pathology and had been deeply influenced by the mentality of Polish captivity.' According to him, 'Poland' became for the Polish intelligentsia a kind of religious belief rather than a real subject. Chałasiński stressed that, for the intelligentsia, the 'Polish interests' were situated in the spiritual, rather than in the material plane, while 'the collective life of the nation is neither a church service nor a theatrical performance ... it is not only the heart of a patriot and churches but also factories, mines, railways which are the nation.' In this way, the whole romantic agenda of the 19th century could be seen and an escape from 'true progressiveness' in terms of reforming the core of the economic life of the nation. Thus, facing the audience of the 'new intelligentsia' from the University of Łódź, Chałasiński represented the old Polish intelligentsia as 'Europeans without Europe' and 'Poles without any responsibility for the social fate of Poland'[28] whose problematic heritage was to be resolved by the new political realities.

The publication of Chałasiński's lecture in one of the central cultural journals provoked considerable debate. His criticism corresponded neither with the Marxist vision of the intelligentsia nor with the Polish traditional discourse on this matter. Since the issue of the intelligentsia was closely related to the idea of the service of a nation, it was important to many scholars to defend the 'progressiveness' of the Polish intelligentsia. The philologist and literary critic Karol Wiktor Zawodziński published a long and sophisticated article examining Chałasiński's arguments. From Zawodziński's perspective, there was one particular point in Chałasiński's research programme that had led to his misconception. This point concerned the 'myth' that the intelligentsia had originated from the nobility and that this origin determined its ethos as a social stratum.

Zawodziński started with an examination of 'The Golden Age' of Polish literature, namely the 16th century, as an 'epoch of Jan Kochanowski' (1530–1584), who was one of the most prominent Polish renaissance poets. Zawodziński remarked upon the fact that Kochanowski formally belonged to the nobility. Nevertheless, his education, travelling experience, and service at the King's court did not permit regarding him as part of the land-owning aristocracy. The social milieu in which Kochanowski lived had nothing to do with the nobility's domination about which Chałasiński was talking in his lecture. Developing his idea, Zawodziński argued that the nobility as a social stratum was not able to determine the intellectual activity of the 'working intelligentsia (*inteligencja pracująca*)' of the 16th century as he characterised Kochanowski's milieu. [29]

Promoting his idea, Zawodziński referred to the research and fiction of Józef Ignacy Kraszewski, one of the most prolific writers, ethnologists, and literary critics of the late 19th century. In Zawodziński's view, the characters of Kraszewski's fictional stories, representing the people of the late 18th century, could testify to the non-noble genealogy of the intelligentsia. Zawodziński wrote:

> [Kraszewski,] not without reason, makes the son of a peasant (*Sfinks*)[30] or of a petty bourgeois (*Król i Bondarywna*) a representative of national painting in the epoch of Stanisław [August Poniatowski],[31] and shows the unbelievable career of a scribbler who had risen from lower social strata to the nobility in the same epoch (*Kawał literata*).[32]

Thus, Zawodziński, referring to the Polish literary tradition, showed that the Polish intelligentsia had nothing to do with the nobility as a social category and had its origins primarily in specialised intellectual practice. According to Zawodziński, becoming a member of the intelligentsia increased the social status of an individual, it was not a demotion. Generally, Zawodziński did not see a reason for speaking either of a degradation of the nobility as a factor in the intelligentsia's rise or of the intelligentsia's 'reactionary character' due to their isolation from the nation.[33] Thus, still not going 'to excuse the sin of nobleness (*szlachectwo*)' as an arrogance towards rural people, Zawodziński defended with his literary analysis the good name of the Polish intelligentsia in front of Chałasiński's sociological criticism.

The next author whose essay contributed to the debate was the communist historian Aleksander Litwin. Referring to the Marxist vision of history, Litwin attempted to analyse the genealogy of the intelligentsia through the prism of Lenin's idea of Prussian and American paths of capitalism. Joining the criticism against Chałasiński's attitude, Litwin proposed a completely different perspective in which the Polish literary tradition did not play any significant role. He argued that Poland, 'unfortunately,' had chosen the Prussian capitalism, leading to the '*Verjunkerung* of the bourgeoisie, its mentality, and thus its intelligentsia.'[34] According to Lenin, the Prussian path implied a soft change from the feudal dependence of rural people on landowners to the dependence of rural people on capitalists,[35] and Poland took, in his view, exactly this path. From Litwin's perspective, the processes that had been described by Chałasiński testified to the fact that the Polish case represented not the 'outskirts of capitalism' but one of the main paths towards capitalism. Thus, Litwin argued that Chałasiński's argument was incorrect because it ignored the 'objective' and 'universal' character of the economic processes.[36]

Continuing his criticism, Litwin argued that the Polish Uprising (1863–1864) became a crucial moment in the history of the 'Polish intelligentsia.' The social movement against czarism shaped, in his view, the situation in which 'the Polish petty bourgeoisie and its intelligentsia (*mieszczaństwo polskie i jego inteligencja*)'[37] shifted towards radicalism[38] and 'progressiveness,' when breaking their ties with the nobility. Since the petty bourgeoisie could play a 'progressive role' and unite with the 'working people,' as it had done in other European countries, there was nothing that prevented Litwin from recognising the 'progressiveness' of the Polish intelligentsia. Thus, even though 'liberal mimicry' was always a typical trait of this social group, 'the main <...> factions of the intelligentsia,' wrote Litwin, 'started to tend towards progress,' and thus played a positive role in Polish history.[39]

Most importantly, Litwin's references to the universal laws of social development did not prevent him from references to the concept of nation. He understood Chałasiński's lecture as an attempt to break both the continuity of Polish history and the objective rules that determine the historical development of the Polish nation. Opposing this tendency, Litwin wrote:

> The Polish intelligentsia has grown on the soil of the previous history of the nation and of the history of its classes and strata... [the new Polish culture was to be formed] not by breaking with history but just the opposite, on the basis of the history of the nation, based on its best traditions.[40]

Thus, Chałasiński's historical and sociological criticism of the tendencies, which were not welcomed in 'new Poland,' still provoked accusations that it broke the coherency of the national history.

The non-Marxist historian Stefan Kieniewicz was the first to propose clarifying the key concept of the debate. Publishing his articles in the Catholic journal 'Tygodnik Powszechny,'[41] Kieniewicz specified several social groups that could be defined as the intelligentsia:

1. the functionaries of the public services (officials, teachers, and clergymen);
2. the technicians working in agriculture, industry, trade, communication, banking, etc.;
3. the so-called liberal professions – meaning medicine, the legal profession, the press, science, art.[42]

Thus, the definition of the intelligentsia through formal professional training became a starting point of Kieniewicz's approach to this issue.

Additionally, Kieniewicz argued that there had been no intelligentsia except for the clergy before the centralised state system was created in Poland. Arguing so, the historian emphasised the fact that influential figures of the Polish Enlightenment, such as Ignacy Krasicki, Stanisław Staszic, Hugo Kołłątaj, and Franciszek Bohomolec[43] 'all wore a soutane' and took up significant positions in the Church hierarchy.[44] According to Kieniewicz, the rapid development of the intelligentsia became possible only after the creation of an extensive bureaucratic apparatus. In this regard, the creation of Congress Poland (*Królestwo Polskie, Kongresówka*) in 1815 as a part of the Russian empire played a central role in the history of the intelligentsia. This institutional approach led the author to assert that bureaucracy, i.e. a social group that was loyal to each regime established in the Polish territories, shaped the core of the Polish intelligentsia.[45]

Most importantly, Kieniewicz argued that the intelligentsia was not a coherent phenomenon in terms of ideology. He wrote: 'We can find among the intelligentsia of the time the classics and romantics, progressives and obscurantists, royalists and conspirators. A social stratum is neither a political camp nor an ideological one.'[46] This statement seems to be an endorsement of the impossibility of examining the intelligentsia as an entity possessing a unified ideology. The historian also stressed the fact that the differences in the social and political conditions of the empires that owned the Polish territories inevitably influenced the different strategies undertaken by the members of the intelligentsia:

> In each of the partitioned regions the development went in a different way. In the Kingdom [the part of Poland under the Russian rule], the intelligentsia lost the government offices but gained a profitable field of work [in industry, building etc.] ...[and] were ready to collaborate with Russia... In Galicia, the intelligentsia kept the administration of the region ... the scholarly life flourished around the universities... at last, in Prussia, the intelligentsia was in the forefront of the struggle against Germanisation.[47]

This approach led Kieniewicz to the statement that there was no historically coherent social group like 'the intelligentsia' that had an ideology that would be typical for all the members of this social group. Nevertheless, concluding his article, Kieniewicz still argued that there was a commonality between all groups of the Polish intelligentsia, namely 'a sense of superiority to other social strata.'[48] Thus, feeling his duty to make a political statement on the nationally relevant issue, Kieniewicz, in fact, contradicted the logic of his 'professional' examination of this question and joined the discussion on the intelligentsia as a historically coherent group with its ideology.

At the end, Kieniewicz's disagreement with Chałasiński concerned the relationships between the intelligentsia and the nobility, but not the fact that the intelligentsia had an ideology. He wrote:

> The ideology of the intelligentsia was coined in the struggle against the primacy of the nobility. The intelligentsia wrote on its flags the mottos of equality, loyalty to the nation and working for it <...> the average *inteligent* formed his worldview, at least in theory, on the principles coined for him by [the writers Bolesław] Prus, [Stefan] Żeromski and [Maria] Konopnicka.[49]

Thus, having failed to find an ideology of the intelligentsia in the historical sources, Kieniewicz, based on the national literary tradition of the late 19th and early 20th century, joined Zawodziński and Litwin in arguing that the Polish intelligentsia possessed and cultivated the virtue of 'progressiveness.'

Responding to his opponents' criticisms, Józef Chałasiński later published a lengthy article with his counterarguments. This response demonstrates in a very characteristic way the difference between the basic ideas of research that the participants in the debate had been referring to. Chałasiński started by quoting the well-known interwar Polish sociologist Stefan Czarnowski[50]:

> A historian is capable of recognising the facts of the general process as far as he can classify them as the changes of types... he should know the norm ... so, it is a necessary condition of him carrying out his tasks that he should be a sociologist.[51]

The ignorance of the sociological approach was, according to Chałasiński, the main reason for his opponent's misconceptions. He wrote: 'History of culture that is based just on individual facts but not on a sociological typology does not have a scientific basis for the systematisation of facts.'[52] Thus, the rejection by some of his opponents of his image of the ideal member of the intelligentsia meant, in his view, the rejection of the 'scientific approach' to the issue.

Developing this idea, Chałasiński remarked upon the sociological inconsistency of the many points of Zawodziński's criticism. He wrote:

> Interpretation of the 'intelligentsia' of the 16th century as a synonym for the intelligentsia of the 19th or 20th century leads to conceptual 'anarchy' [while] the interpretation of Jan Kochanowski as a member of the intelligentsia is situated at the same level of sociological correctness as the interpretation of a lord's peasant as a synonym for a modern hired agricultural worker.[53]

Chałasiński asserted that Kieniewicz's approach was much closer to his own, since, in this version, the intelligentsia 'is not eternal, [and existed] neither in the time of the Piasts [Dynasty 9th–14th century], nor in the time of the Jagiellons [Dynasty 14th–16th century].' However, Chałasiński still criticised Kieniewicz's descriptive style as an attempt to avoid the discussion on the 'social type of a member of the intelligentsia and the genesis of this type.' In his view, no 'exact facts' can explain 'where their [the intelligentsia's] sense of superiority, or the conviction that they represent the whole nation, or the myth about its noble origin come from.'[54]

At the same time, Chałasiński decisively declined the accusation of breaking the coherency of the national history. On the contrary, he wrote:

> Had the continuity between the intelligentsia as a leading stratum of the nation and the nobility been completely broken, we would not be a historical nation, we would not be a nation at all, because the nation exists only through its historical continuity. This fact cannot be ignored by scientific analysis.[55]

The peculiarity of Polish national history was a key argument in Chałasiński's criticism of Litwin's Marxist approach. For Chałasiński, the intelligentsia was a specific feature of the Polish nation and its history and, in this case, no universal 'laws' of social development were applicable. Arguing so, he wrote:

> This is the heart of the matter, that, in Poland, the nobility as a dominating stratum was replaced not by the petty bourgeoisie as it was in the West but by the intelligentsia – the social stratum derived from the nobility but not from the petty bourgeoisie <...> uncritical transfer of the generalisations of Western European history to Poland does not meet the Polish realities.[56]

The 'reactionary attitude' of the intelligentsia was, for him, a 'national issue' that could be resolved only at the national level. Chałasiński's intelligentsia was born in the 19th century and continued to exist in post-war Poland. He repeatedly argued that the actual task of researching the genealogy of the intelligentsia was to understand 'the essence and dimensions of the historical process that is now underway.' The intelligentsia, according to Chałasiński, 'has a huge task in playing a new historical role' in the post-war realities, namely 'being an intellectual elite of the peasants and working people' but not the 'separate aristocratic social strata.'[57] In this regard, Chałasiński's research programme could be seen as a very radical response to the call of the 'gentle revolution' to make 'progressiveness' a technic of self-purification from 'reactionary elements.' According to Chałasiński, the whole of the Polish intelligentsia had to find reactionary traits in their character.

Between nation and academia

Chałasiński's approach was rooted in his idea of sociology. Combining very different methodological ideas, Chałasiński followed his teacher Znaniecki in understanding sociology as a part of the humanities.[58] From his perspective, there was nothing problematic in defining the 'sense of superiority' as a 'sociological fact' and thus a historical and sociological research question. His intention to 'scientifically' resolve existing 'social deviations' was the starting point of his research programme.

It is notable that Chałasiński's critics understood his approach as an attempt to question the 'progressiveness' of the entire Polish culture.[59] Regardless of the discipline the disputants represented, they understood Chałasiński's message as a blow against the Polish national tradition to which they all belonged.

At the same time, the language, categories, and conventions to which the participants in the debate referred were manifestly different. For the philologist Zawodziński, the intelligentsia manifested itself not so much as a social stratum, but as the progressive force of Polish culture or, to be more precise, the creators of Polish literature. Therefore, for him, there was no considerable difference between the Renaissance poet Kochanowski and a Polish writer or artist of the 19th century. Kieniewicz's perspective was more historicist in terms of a *wie es eigentlich gewesen [ist]* (how it really was)[60] approach. His educational and scholarly background led Kieniewicz to the necessity of clarifying the key concept of his examination. He was looking for 'a truly existing' institution such as, in this case, imperial bureaucracy, to 'objectively' examine and base his argument on. It is no less noteworthy that the highly cautious attempt of Litwin to refer to the 'international' and 'universal' reading of Marxism–Leninism (even in a highly specialised way) was not supported by the other disputants.[61] All other voices (and at times Litwin himself) portrayed a very holistic vision of the 'nation and its history.'

It is especially remarkable that no disputant thematised the obviously normative character of the issue that was broached by Chałasiński. Even Kieniewicz, whose academic training should lead him to questioning the very possibility of a 'scientific' debate in the categories proposed by Chałasiński did not rebel against the 'national agenda.' There are no sources to prove the alleged 'sense of superiority' or 'self-perception as representatives of the whole nation,'[62] of the intelligentsia, either as a 'social entity,' or as the totality of 'educated people.' However, this point was not part of the criticisms directed against Chałasiński. His opponents started to defend the 'progressiveness' of the intelligentsia, which, according to them, had 'another ideology' in opposition to that described by Chałasiński. The only source that was used to find out the 'ideal type' of a member of the intelligentsia, and to examine their 'ideology,' was fictional stories, which can be defined as the totality of the texts written by 'educated people.' This fact encouraged a closed circle of literary stereotypes, which started to become axiomatic in the 'scientific' discourse.

Having appeared in the discourse of romanticism, which saw the nation as a body and educated people as its brain or its 'intelligence,' the concept of the intelligentsia became a self-marker of the people involved in the literary and journalistic life of their countries in the 19th century.[63] More importantly, the concept of the intelligentsia became a national issue, since literary traditions (due to their connection with canonised forms of written language) played a key role in defining the 'borders' of national cultures. Public debates on this issue made the intelligentsia more and more 'real' and, primarily in the late 19th century, proposed the ideal types of members of the intelligentsia, which were created and reproduced by people involved in the public debates in literary and cultural journals.[64] For them, belonging to this discourse was a part of their service to the 'nation,' and thus a form of being a 'good Pole.'

Since the late 19th century, scholars and journalists publicly blamed the intelligentsia (themselves?) for its carelessness and disregard towards rural and common people.[65] This issue became an act of self-criticism among the 'educated people' who promoted responsibility for 'the fate of nation.'[66] In other words, it was an emotion made objective in the texts written by the intellectuals taking part in the public discussion on this issue. The post-war discussion on the intelligentsia was also a debate between scholars educated within this (widely understood) literary tradition of responsibility for 'national issues.' The public dispute in the cultural journals represented a familiar form of 'public service.' The concept of the intelligentsia, much like the concept of the nation, became the category that had received a new status with the rise of journalism and its invasion of the field of politics, in which they had been 'naturalised' and thus justified.

Of course, the rise of nationalism deeply influenced the scientific practice at least from the 19th century. Loyalty to a nation became one of the central virtues that influenced the image of 'good scientific practice' in many countries and disciplines. The post-war discussion on the intelligentsia showed the strong influence of the authority of the national canon shaped by literary and journalist tradition. Scholars whose 'academic' virtues stood in conflict to the national virtues preferred the second ones.[67] Nevertheless, the fact that the authorities actively used the nationalist discourse in their propaganda[68] was not the key factor in this case. The discussion on the intelligentsia showed the readiness of the scholars to defend their own vision of 'national' culture and 'progressiveness' that also stood in conflict to the authoritarian agenda of the government. The development of the public discourse on the intelligentsia in the early post-war years was yet more evidence for that.

The anti-authoritarian vision of the 'new' intelligentsia

Of course, the discussion on the intelligentsia was not reduced to the historical and sociological aspects of this issue. The discourse on the 'formation of the new intelligentsia' was closely related to the issue of the reform of post-war higher education. Along with the industrial rhetoric of the 'production' of 'new intellectuals,' there was another context in which the recreation of universities was closely connected to the issue of the intelligentsia. The Nazi administration established in Polish territories during the war openly claimed that its aim was the destruction of the 'Polish intelligentsia.'[69] Many professors and research fellows, who represented the core of the academic staff during the interwar period, had been killed during the Nazi occupation. At the same time, the opportunity to recreate universities in a completely new way made this issue a matter of considerable debate.[70]

Writing about 'renewing the Polish intelligentsia,' the famous physician and biologist Zygmunt Szymanowski argued that the success of the post-war project would be determined by the sympathies of the young people. Developing this argument, Szymanowski wrote: 'during the last years before the war we [had seen enough things which made us] convinced that repression will not achieve anything.' The most unacceptable feature of Polish academia in the interwar period was, in his view, the segregation that did not allow everyone to get access to higher education and share in its intellectual benefits. Szymanowski referred to the antisemitism and anti-communism of the interwar universities, which could not be tolerated under the new conditions. Developing this idea, Szymanowski especially emphasised that the revolutionary experiences of Soviet Russia were exactly the example of what should not happen in post-war Poland. He warned about the danger of 'the ostracism that was used in Soviet Russia when the children of previously privileged classes did not have access to higher education.'[71] Thus, an ideal Polish university that would correct the mistakes of the past was to represent equal access to education regardless of the origin and, to some extent, the political views of the young people who would come to study.[72]

The idea of the common accessibility of higher education was the central topic for the authorities as well. The communist functionary Włodzimierz Sokorski, who was one of the key figures in the educational politics of the authorities, constantly reported on his programme in the cultural press. Sokorski assured the reader that there was no threat to the freedom of science in post-war Poland and repeated the motto of the 'gentle revolution' to make Polish scholars the creators of the academic agenda. At the same time, Sokorski saw the future of Polish education in the governmentalisation of the whole educational system, from schools to universities. According to Sokorski, the domination of the state in the field of education was to contribute to the unification and mobilisation of all human resources for the formation of the new intelligentsia.[73]

Moreover, Sokorski thought it necessary to destroy the autonomy of universities in order to cultivate 'progressiveness' at the governmental level. This, according to him, would break the separatism of different intellectual centres with various ideas of the cultural and academic agenda. Developing this argument, he wrote:

> Lagging behind European trends has always been the tragedy of Polish science... [this was a sign of] backwardness covered by the toga of University autonomy. This was the case in the 15th and 16th centuries, when, after the great progress of Polish science, we were closed in the circle of scholastic science.[74]

So, Sokorski claimed that the autonomy and the traditionalism of the universities were the main reasons for the backwardness of Polish science. The governmentalisation of higher education was supposed to help to overcome the backwardness of Polish academia and thus create a national 'progressive' intelligentsia, but not a local one.

Referring to the example of post-revolutionary France, Sokorski argued that the universalisation and governmentalisation of the appointment of professors would make scholars responsible in face of the whole nation, but not within their local communities. Developing this argument, Sokorski wrote:

> People's Democracy has the right to demand that universities penetrate deeper into our current state system; that they open the doors to the currents

and ideas by which the whole country is inspired; that they [universities/ scholars] turn their faces to these events, which are happening before our eyes; and then we do not have to worry about the result.[75]

In such a way, during the early post-war period, Sokorski did not promote governmental control over the intellectual practice of scholars. He claimed that the only task of the governmental institutions was the reorientation of scholars from their own agenda to the agenda of the whole 'nation.' So, the role of the state was not to teach scholars how to do their job but to create an institutional situation in which they would be aware of the issues that were relevant for the whole nation.

Nevertheless, the idea of the governmentalisation of all academic institutions could not be accepted by all scholars positively. Sokorski's project faced a strong criticism from the 'main' post-war expert in the intelligentsia, Józef Chałasiński. Developing his research programme formulated in his Łódź lecture, Chałasiński himself opposed the formation of a 'ghetto' of the intelligentsia in Polish universities. He agreed that it was necessary to avoid the isolation of Polish academia from the current social realities. The separatism of Polish universities was a personal issue for Chałasiński. From the beginning of his career, he faced the arrogance of old Polish universities towards the new academic institutions (like sociology) he was associated with. So, Chałasiński did not miss the opportunity to critically remark on the scepticism of old Polish academia towards the new university in Łódź as a sign of the continuation of this negative tradition. He did not oppose Sokorski's idea that the conservativeness of the Polish academic tradition required a revision of the principles on which the old Polish universities had been based. He wrote:

> The old Polish social concept of the university as a great 'factory' producing the intelligentsia as a kind of social aristocracy isolated from the broad masses of society no longer corresponds to our times. The university should find ways to make a spiritual contact with the movement of the workers and peasants, so that the whole educational atmosphere of the university should change radically [... and should be based on] the cultural forms of coexistence and cooperation between intellectuals and workers and peasants within a common national culture.[76]

Thus, Chałasiński welcomed the general idea to create a 'national' intelligentsia and to break the separatism of old Polish universities.

Nevertheless, his idea of democratisation went in another direction than that of Sokorski and thus of the Polish government. In his view, the governmentalisation of academia contradicted the democratic character of the formation of the 'new intelligentsia.'[77] Chałasiński argued that it was necessary to create a national independent institution which, through the procedures of self-government, would determine the image of Polish academia. In 1947, Chałasiński still insisted that universities had to become a milieu that would be a breeding ground for the formation of the new intelligentsia, but not a bureaucratic organisation for the implementation of a party or governmental programme. He wrote:

> Reducing bureaucracy to a minimum, limiting to a minimum the role of state and party-political agents in this field, which is colloquially called 'culture, art and science,' is not only necessary from the point of view of the ultimate democratic perspective of economic and political reform; it is also necessary from the point of view of the process of democratisation itself.[78]

Due to his professional background, Chałasiński saw 'culture, art and science' not as independent institutions but as the space of social practices that should be organised through the shaping of special conditions. The general ideas that shaped Chałasiński's project were freedom of discussion, self-governance, and the independence of academia, not within a selected university but at the national level as a parallel institution to the governmental hierarchy. In his view, it was the only way to produce a 'truly progressive' intelligentsia.[79]

In general terms, Chałasiński appealed (though based on a developed sociological programme) to the principles that had been proclaimed by the 'gentle revolution.' Of course, his anti-authoritarian understanding of this project could seem too broad and too democratic from the perspective of the authorities. Nevertheless, the realities of the early post-war years did not provide any visible obstacles for Chałasiński's programme. Attempting to apply his professional competencies to the current politics, Chałasiński dreamed in his publications about a 'republic of scholars' that was united under the banner of 'nation' but was independent from the state. This project was his 'academic' contribution to the discussion on the nationally relevant issue.[80]

Of course, there were several contexts that stood behind Chałasiński's public activism. During the early post-war years, Chałasiński was looking for an opportunity both to secure the position of his discipline and to make space for the activity beyond Marxism, which he treated critically.[81] Taking into account the post-war political developments, Chałasiński was suspicious of the rise of the role of the government and thus the people with Marxist views in post-war Polish academia. This tendency threatened both his discipline and his ambition to influence the current agenda of the public debates. His programme of a 'national' approach to governing Polish academia and 'producing' a new intelligentsia was, on the one hand, a blow to the conservative features of the old Polish universities; on the other, it was an attempt to protect himself and his discipline from the growth of governmental instruments with the capacity to destroy his post-war project. In any case, the 'national' and 'democratic' format of the unification of scholars was, in his view, the only way to create a 'national' and 'truly progressive' intelligentsia.

*

The discussion on the intelligentsia helps us to record several crucial traits of the Polish academic discourse in the early post-war years. Loyalty to the nation as a virtue was firmly established in Polish academia. For many scholars, there was no contradiction between the 'national' and 'academic' virtues, since the 'good scientific practice' was seen through the prism of the service of the nation. If professional training led scholars to a conflict with the coherent vision of the nation, the national virtues started to play a dominate role. Of course, this was not unique to Poland. Nevertheless, the discussions about the intelligentsia became more evidence for the independence of the Polish scholars in defining their own agenda. The idea that the intelligentsia was a 'national' issue developed in the Polish public sphere as an opportunity to promote an anti-authoritarian model of Polish society in general. Even though the project of the 'gentle revolution' implied certain autonomy of scholars, the debate on the intelligentsia opened the opportunity to question the role of the authorities as a mediator in conducting the 'progressive' changes.

The analysis of discussions on the 'production' of a 'new intelligentsia' also shows to what extent the Polish discourse on this issue differed from the Soviet one. All the participants in the debate (including the authorities) understood the 'democratisation' of Polish academia as an opportunity to make universities free of charge and non-elitist institutions. In fact, it represented an opposition to what happened to Soviet academia under Stalinism. After 1940, Soviet universities were to become, on the contrary, spaces of the formation of the 'intellectual elites' of the regime. The obligation of Soviet students to pay for their studies made the universities inaccessible for many people.[82] Thus, the debate on the intelligentsia became a new stage not only for the criticism against the authoritarian tendencies in general but also against Soviet academic realities to this issue in particular. Characteristically, even the authorities, when promoting the governmentalisation and centralisation of Polish academia, referred to the French example but not to the Soviet one. Nevertheless, this model of authoritarianism faced public criticism under the 'gentle revolution.' In a sense, this opposition to the authoritarian vision of 'progressiveness' was a part of anti-Marxist agenda promoted by many Polish scholars in the early post-war years.

Notes

1 Jerzy Borejsza, "Rewolucja łagodna," *Odrodzenie*, no. 10–12 (1945): 1.
2 Ibid.
3 See, for example, Vitalij Kurennoj, "Osnovnye social'nye ponjatija," in *Mysljashhaja Rossija. Intellektual'no aktivnaja gruppa*, ed. Vitalij Kurennoj (Moskva: Fond "Nasledie Evrazii," 2008), 23–48.
4 See Nathaniel Knight, "Was the intelligentsia part of the nation? Visions of society in post-emancipation Russia," *Kritika: Explorations in Russian and Eurasian History* 7, no. 4 (2006): 733–758.
5 Maciej Janowski, *Birth of the Intelligentsia – 1750–1831* (Frankfurt am Main/Berlin/Bern/Bruxelles/New York/Oxford/Wien: Peter Lang, 2014).
6 Though Lenin's discourse on the intelligentsia was also not homogenous and was frequently instrumental, see the classical version of the interpretation of Lenin's concept of the intelligentsia: Lev Erman, *V. I. Lenin o roli intelligencii v demokraticheskoj i socialisticheskoj revoljucijah, v stroitel'stve socializma i kommunizma* (Moskva: Znanie, 1970).
7 Benjamin Tromley, *Making the Soviet Intelligentsia. Universities and Intellectual Life under Stalin and Khrushchev* (Cambridge, UK: Cambridge University Press, 2014), 6–7.

8 The matter concerns Herbert George Wells and his journalistic publications and science fiction.
9 Włodzimierz Sokorski, "O demokratyczną kulturą narodową," *Kuźnica*, no. 45 (1946): 2.
10 For example, Celina Bobińska (who was trained as a historian in the Soviet Union) argued in her publications that the Polish intelligentsia had to learn from the proletariat the correct ideology and thus 'true culture,' not the other way around. See, for example, Celina Bobińska, "Komisja edukacyjna' klasy robotniczej," *Kuźnica*, no. 12 (1947): 1–2.
11 Jadwiga Siekierska, "Drogi kultury," *Kuźnica*, no. 12 (1947): 4.
12 Ibid., 4.
13 See brief remark on this problem in the context of the formation of the new university in Łódź.
14 Some of the arguments used in this section were discussed in my article: Aleksei Lokhmatov, "The 'scientific view' of the intelligentsia: The literary roots of scholarly public debates in post-war Poland (1946–1948)," *Historyka. Studia Metodologiczne*, 49 (2019): 77–100.
15 Interestingly, this discussion that took place in the cultural press became a historiographical fact and influenced many later historical and sociological works on the Polish intelligentsia. The opinions coined in this debate remained relevant both for historians and sociologists dealing with this issue a long time after it took place. It is remarkable that the authors of the multivolume project of the Institute of History of the Polish Academy of Sciences entitled *'Inteligencja polska XIX i XX wieku. Studia'* repeatedly referred to the approach of Józef Chałasiński and his opponents (see, for example, Ryszarda Czepulis-Rastenis (ed.), *Inteligencja polska pod zaborami* [Warszawa: PWN, 1978], 13, 47, 170). The debate was also relevant for sociologists writing about the intelligentsia (see, for example, Jan Szczepański, *Inteligencja i społeczeństwo* [Warszawa: Książka i Wiedza, 1957]). Based on this debate, Józef Chałasiński also developed his arguments (Józef Chałasiński, *Przeszłość i przyszłość. inteligencji polskiej* [Warszawa: Świat książki, 1997 [1958]]).
16 It should be remarked that, in this article, I will refer, first of all, to the version of Chałasiński's approach that was published and discussed in the cultural press, even though the book produced after the public debate contains several essential changes and requires a special examination. See Józef Chałasiński, *Społeczna genealogia inteligencji polskiej* (Warszawa: Czytelnik, 1946).
17 Józef Chałasiński, "Inteligencja polska w świetle swojej genealogii społecznej," *Kuźnica*, no. 4 (1946): 1.
18 Regarding the concepts of economic backwardness, see Anna Sosnowska, *Explaining Economic Backwardness. Post-1945 Polish Historians on Eastern Europe* (Budapest and New York: Central European University Press, 2019).
19 Józef Chałasiński, "Inteligencja polska w świetle swojej genealogii społeczne," 1. See more on discussions about economic 'backwardness' in Polish historiography and sociology: Anna Sosnowska, *Explaining Economic Backwardness*.
20 The references to the writings of Stanisław Brzozowski testify to the truth of this statement. This fact has been remarked upon by Lewandowski, see Czesław Lewandowski, "Dyskusja prasowa nad koncepcją inteligencji," *Kwartalnik Historii Prasy Polskiej* 29, no. 3–4 (1990): 100–101.
21 Józef Chałasiński, "Inteligencja polska w świetle swojej genealogii społecznej," 1–2.
22 For describing a member of the intelligentsia, I will use the word '*inteligent*' as derived from the word '*Inteligencja*' in its Polish spelling so as not to confuse it with 'intelligent' in English.
23 Józef Chałasiński, "Inteligencja polska w świetle swojej genealogii społeczne," 1.
24 Ibid., 2.
25 It was Sienkiewicz who had helped Polish scholars to describe the 'spirit' of the famous battle in Grunwald (1410) during the debates on the 'German question.' See Chapter 2.

26 The Trilogy (Trylogia) was a series of three novels by Henryk Sienkiewicz (With Fire and Sword [1884], The Deluge [1886], and Fire in the Steppe [1888]), which became the popular and influential narrative of Polish national idea.
27 In this case, Chałasiński refers to the 'mentality of the intelligentsia' described in the book *Ludzie bezdomni* by Stefan Żeromski, but not to an imperialist project initiated by Józef Piłsudski which was also called 'Prometheism,' see Jan Bruski, *Between Prometheism and Realpolitik: Poland and Soviet Ukraine, 1921–1926* (Krakow: Jagiellonian University Press, 2016).
28 Józef Chałasiński, "Inteligencja polska w świetle swojej genealogii społecznej," 2.
29 Karol W. Zawodziński, "W sprawie genealogii inteligencji polskiej," *Kuźnica*, no. 12 (1946): 3.
30 '*Sfinks*,' '*Król i Bondarywna*,' '*Kawał literata*' are the titles of Kraszewski's novels.
31 Stanisław August Poniatowski (1732–1798) was the last monarch of the Polish Republic before the last partition of Poland resulted in the disappearance of the Polish state.
32 Zawodziński, "W sprawie genealogii inteligencji polskiej," 3.
33 Zawodziński, "W sprawie genealogii inteligencji polskiej," 4. The phrase seems a bit confusing, but Zawodziński attempted to prove that the intelligentsia became a metastratum, including both the nobility and another social strata.
34 In the original: "'zjunkeryzowanie' narodu, jego psychiki, a więc i jego inteligencji." See Aleksander Litwin, "O społecznej genealogii polskiej inteligencji," *Kuźnica*, no. 14 (1948): 2.
35 See about the Prussian path: Vladimir I. Lenin, *Polnoe Sobranie Sochinenij V.I. Lenina 5-e izd.*, vol. 16 (Moskva: Izdatel'stvo politicheskoj literatury, 1967), 216; and about the American one: Vladimir I. Lenin, *Polnoe Sobranie Sochinenij*, vol. 17 (Moskva: Izdatel'stvo politicheskoj literatury, 1967), 137.
36 Aleksander Litwin, "O społecznej genealogii polskiej inteligencji," 2.
37 There is nothing unique about the idea that each class has 'its intelligentsia.' The more elaborated theory of this idea of the intelligentsia, within the Marxist approach, can be found in the writings of Antonio Gramsci (see, for example, Charles Kurzman and Lynn Owens, "The sociology of intellectuals," *Annual Review of Sociology*, 28 [2002]: 64).
38 Of course, for the author, the word "radicalism" had a strong positive connotation.
39 Aleksander Litwin, "O społecznej genealogii polskiej inteligencji," 3.
40 Ibid.
41 Another opinion published in the Catholic press was the essay of the publicist Stefan Kisielewski (Stefan Kisielewski, "Inteligencja," *Tygodnik Warszawski*, no. 20 [1946]: 6). The references to the Catholic press can also be found in the book by Chałasiński which was published after this debate, see Józef Chałasiński, *Społeczna genealogia inteligencji polskiej* (Warszawa: Czytelnik, 1946), 79–81, as well as in the sociological and historical periodicals such as *Przegląd Socjologiczny* (see, for example, the issues of *Przegląd Socjologiczny* for 1946 and 1947).
42 Stefan Kieniewicz, "Rodowód inteligencji polskiej," *Tygodnik Powszechny* 56, no. 15 (1946): 1.
43 Franciszek Bohomolec (1720–1784), Ignacy Krasicki (1735–1801), Hugo Kołłątaj (1750–1812), and Stanisław Staszic (1755–1826) were key figures in the Polish Enlightenment. Besides occupying important positions in the Church hierarchy (Krasicki was a bishop and the primate of Poland; Bohomolec was a Jesuit monk, whilst Kołłątaj and Staszic were priests), each of them was central to educational reforms in Poland. What is more, they all advocated the centralisation of the Polish state at the late 18th century and fought against the privileges of the nobility (szlachta).
44 See about Kieniewicz's approach to the history of the Church: Marcin Wolniewicz, "W stronę *origines de la Pologne contemporaine* – poszukiwania metodologiczne Stefana Kieniewicza w latach 1946–1948," in *KLIO POLSKA. Studia i Materiały z Dziejów Historiografi i Polskiej*, vol. 9 (2017): 87–88.

45 Kieniewicz, "Rodowód inteligencji polskiej," 1.
46 Ibid., 1.
47 Ibid.
48 Ibid.
49 Ibid., 2.
50 Stefan Czarnowski (1879–1937) was a Polish sociologist and art historian. Many Polish sociologists and historians such as Stanisław Arnold, Nina Assorodobraj-Kula, Henryk Jabłoński, and Irena Nowakowska were his students.
51 Chałasiński referred to the book: Stefan Czarnowski, *Społeczeństwo – Kultura* (Warszawa & Poznań: Polski Instytut Socjologiczny, 1939), 26–29.
52 Józef Chałasiński, "Socjologia i historia inteligencji polskiej," *Kuźnica*, no. 20 (1946): 1.
53 Ibid.
54 Ibid.
55 Ibid.
56 Ibid., 3.
57 Ibid.
58 See Chapter 1.
59 This is noteworthy that Chałasiński's research programme provoked a similar reaction in the émigré journals. His ideas were understood as an attempt to question the coherency of Polish cultural history, see, e.g., Marek Święcicki, "Sąd i próba wyroku na inteligencję polską," *Dziennik Polski i Dziennik Żołnierza*, no. 88 (1947): 1; Zbigniew Jordan, "Społeczna funkcja inteligencji," *Kultura*, no. 7 (1948): 31–38; even though most of the publications on Chałasiński's programme were primarily political manifests, which were supposed to 'protect Polish cultural tradition,' but not academic texts, the review on Chałasiński's book published by the Polish historian based in London Marian Kukiel was, to some extent, an exception. Nevertheless, having briefly reviewed Chałasiński's research programme referring to historical arguments, Kukiel (like Kieniewicz) finished his review with references to the "real ideology" of the intelligentsia which, according to him, did not correspond with Chałasiński's version regarding this issue. See Marian Kukiel, "J. Chałasińskiego Społeczna genealogia inteligencji polskiej [recenzja]," *Teki Historyczne*, no. 1 (1948): 54–57.
60 The formula created by one of the founders of German professional historiography, Leopold von Ranke (1795–1886), which showed that an objective description of the reality was the ultimate aim of historical research.
61 Regarding the role of Marxism in this period, see Chapter 4.
62 For the usage of this terminology, see, for example, Józef Chałasiński, "Socjologia i historia inteligencji polskiej," *Kuźnica*, no. 20 (1946): 3.
63 See more Otto Wilhelm Müller, *Intelligencija: Untersuchungen zur Geschichte eines politischen Schlagwortes* (Frankfurt am Main: Athenäum-Verlag, 1971).
64 Generally speaking, the research on the intelligentsia as a social phenomenon plays an important role in writing both Polish and Russian history up until now. See, for example, Maciej Janowski, *Birth of the Intelligentsia – 1750–1831* (Frankfurt am Main/Berlin/Bern/Bruxelles/New York/Oxford/Wien: Peter Lang, 2014); Magdalena Micinska, *At the Crossroads: 1865–1918. A History of the Polish Intelligentsia* (Frankfurt am Main/Berlin/Bern/Bruxelles/New York/Oxford/Wien: Peter Lang, 2016); Marta Zahorska, "Spór o inteligencję w polskiej myśli społecznej do I wojny światowej," in *Inteligencja polska pod zaborami*, ed. Ryszarda Czepulis-Rastenis (Warszawa: PWN, 1978), 188–190; about the Russian case, see Denis A. Sdvizhkov, "Ot obshhestva k intelligencii: istorija ponjatij kak istorija samosoznanija," in *Ponjatija o Rossii, K istoricheskoj semantike imperskogo perioda*, vol. 1 (Moskva: Novoe literaturnoe obozrenie, 2012), 382–427; Nathaniel Knight, "Was the intelligentsia part of the nation? Visions of society in post-emancipation Russia," *Kritika: Explorations in Russian and Eurasian History* 7,

no. 4 (2006): 733–758. See also Denis Sdvižkov, *Das Zeitalter der Intelligenz: Zur vergleichenden Geschichte der Gebildeten in Europa bis zum Ersten Weltkrieg* (Göttingen: Vandenhoeck & Ruprecht, 2006), 103–133.
65 See, for example, the writings of Aleksander Świętochowski as "Wywóz naszej inteligencji,(I)" *Przegląd Tygodniowy*, no. 32 (1874), 261–262; and "Wywóz naszej inteligencji,(II)" *Przegląd Tygodniowy*, no. 34 (1874), 281–283; in the interwar period, a similar debate was initiated by the journalist and poet Zdzisław Dębicki in his book "Kryzys inteligencji polskiej" (Zdzisław Dębicki, *Kryzys inteligencji polskiej* [Warszawa: [no publisher], 1918]). See also the case of the Russian empire: the term *Otshhepenstvo* was used in defining the intelligentsia by Peter Struve, see the famous discussion in the journal "Vekhi": http://www.lib.ru/POLITOLOG/XX/wehi.txt_with-big-pictures.html (23.03.2019).
66 In his article, Lewandowski remarks upon the fact that the arguments of Chałasiński had been based on the tradition of social criticism in terms of Brzozowski's writings (Lewandowski, "Dyskusja prasowa nad koncepcją inteligencjii," 100–101.); the same remark had been made by Maria Ossowska (Maria Ossowska, "Inteligent polski na tle grupy towarzyskiej Europy Zachodniej," *Myśl Współczesna*, no. 5 (1947): 137). I mean, in this case, the literary and journalistic tradition of 'responsibility' in a much broader sense than a given ideological attitude.
67 Of course, these virtues were not always in conflict with each other. For example, from Chałasiński's perspective, the entire sociological work was based on research on 'ideal types.' Thus, idealisation was not considered a vice (like it was with, for example, Kieniewicz) but the main analytical tool.
68 See Marcin Zaremba, *Komunizm, legitymizacja, nacjonalizm. Nacjonalistyczna legitymizacja władzy komunistycznej w Polsce* (Warszawa: Wydawnictwo TRIO, 2005).
69 See more Jochen August (ed.), *"Sonderaktion Krakau". Die Verhaftung der Krakauer Wissenschaftler am 6. November 1939* (Hamburg: Hamburger Edition 1997).
70 See Agata Zysiak, "Modernizing science: Between a liberal, social, and socialistic university – The case of Poland and the University of Łódź (1945–1953)," *Science in Context*, no. 28(2) (2015): 215–236.
71 Zygmunt Szymanowski, "O racjonalną politykę w dziedzinie szkolnictwa wyższego," *Kuźnica*, no. 1 (1945): 5.
72 Of course, in many respects, it was just a reference to the programme promoted by Kotarbiński, see Chapter 1.
73 Włodzimierz Sokorski, "Reorganizacja wyższego szkolnictwa," *Kuźnica*, no. 13 (1947): 5.
74 Ibid.
75 Ibid., 5.
76 Józef Chałasiński, "O społeczny sens reformy uniwersytetów," *Kuźnica*, no. 24 (1947): 4.
77 Ibid., 3.
78 Ibid., 3. Chałasiński's idea was closely connected to his idea of the 'public opinion' which was discussed in Chapter 1.
79 See more about the testing of the limits of the acceptable in the public sphere, which characterised Chałasiński's strategy in the early post-war years in Chapters 1 and 5.
80 About Chałasiński's programme on the post-war university, see the publications of Agata Zysiak (in addition to her book to which I repeatedly referred in this thesis): Agata Zysiak, "Modernizing science: Between a liberal, social, and socialistic university – The case of Poland and the University of Łódź (1945–1953)," *Science in Context* 28, no. 2 (2015): 215–236; Kamil Piskała and Agata Zysiak, "Świątynia nauki, fundament demokracji czy fabryka specjalistów? Józef Chałasiński i powojenne spory o ideę uniwersytetu," *Praktyka teoretycna* 9, no. 3 (2013): 271–297; nevertheless, it is important to emphasise that Agata Zysiak, as a sociologist, worked with different models

of university but not with the public discourse on educational reform. Therefore, for Zysiak, Chałasiński embodies the model of a 'social university' and the changes in his discourse on this topic did not play a decisive role for the narrative of Zysiak, while for me this perspective is more important.
81 See more about it in Chapter 5.
82 See Galina M. Ivanova, "Social'nye aspekty razvitija sovetskoj sistemy obrazovanija 1950-e – 1960-e" (URL), https://cyberleninka.ru/article/n/sotsialnye-aspekty-razvitiya-sovetskoy-sistemy-obrazovaniyav-1950-1960-gg.

5 Between 'Outdated' Marxism and 'Updated' Catholicism

'For [Émile] Durkheim, religion is a system of beliefs and rites that bind all members of a social group under pain of a sanction. [Religion implies] the conviction that, regarding the most important issues, all members of the group [should] believe in the same way, behave in the same way, and accept undoubtedly the same authority figures .... The [Marxian] doctrine fulfils its "religious" function just as ably in the strength of the belief of the social group and in the infallibility of the authority figures who are the guarantors of this doctrine.'[1] With these words, the sociologist Stanisław Ossowski examined, in 1947, the 'religious character' of Marxism. Since the project of 'gentle revolution' encouraged Polish scholars to promote their own idea of 'progressiveness,' the situation in the early post-war years was not the most pleasant for followers of the Marxist ideology. Due to the lack of strong political forces that would promote Marxism at the institutional level, the debates in the cultural and academic press became a platform upon which Marxists had to face their critics in an open discussion.

The authorities' aim to avoid any direct references to communism in the public discourse of governmental institutions and the state-run press meant that public discussions on Marxism, to some extent, were a problematic issue for Marxists themselves. The Łódź journal 'Kuźnica' became a centre of attraction for people with Marxist views. However, the forms of Marxism that became an issue in the post-war public debates had, in most cases, little to do with Soviet ideology in its Stalinist form. In fact, the early post-war debates on Marxism continued the discussions on this matter that had taken place in interwar Poland.[2] Paradoxically, even though the political context of this discussion significantly changed under the new conditions, Marxism still was in a defensive position and did not aim to replace all other forms of knowledge. Thus, 'Kuźnica,' which did not hide its Marxist orientation, did not reduce its agenda to solely Marxism. Many of those scholars who criticised Marxism were welcomed to publish their theoretical articles on the pages of this journal. 'Progressiveness' in place of a formal association with Marxism was not only the leitmotif of 'gentle revolution' but also a criterion for selecting materials for the leading left-wing journals.

DOI: 10.4324/9781003428251-6

Uncertain steps of Marxism

In one of his essays, with a telling title 'On the so-called Irrelevance of Marxism,' the philologist and leader of the 'Kuźnica' group Stefan Żółkiewski recognised that 'anti-Marxist views [were] common for the Polish intelligentsia.'[3] Although aiming to resolve this problem, Żółkiewski did not have an ambition to make Marxism a universal tool for the resolution of all scientific problems. From his perspective, Marxism was neither the only sign of progressiveness, nor the argument in itself, and thus, its relevance required justification through non-ideological argumentation. Even though Żółkiewski's discourse contained typical concepts from the Marxian vocabulary, such as 'reaction,' 'ideology of fascism,' and 'revisionism', his understanding of the correlation of forces in post-war Polish academia meant he could not argue that all non-Marxist views were non-scientific.

Meanwhile, Żółkiewski still had the ambition of 'modernising' Polish academia through Marxism. In his view, there were intellectual tendencies in Polish academia with which Marxists should argue in an open academic discussion. Among ideological opponents of Marxism, Żółkiewski specified the French philosophers of science, German new-Kantians, and American pragmatism, all of which had strongly influenced the Polish academic agenda in the interwar period.[4] This list was not unusual for a Marxist: by the French theorists of science, he referred to those who questioned the possibility of reaching objective truth[5]; Neo-Kantian thinkers were represented by Marxists as the chief propagators of idealism; and the works of the representatives of American pragmatism, with their interest in individual psychology, appeared to be a manifesto of individualism. These concepts stood in opposition to the cognitive optimism and the belief in the possibility of the human mind to conceive objective truth that were propagated by Marxism and thus by Żółkiewski. In his view, this cognitive optimism was among the most crucial 'innovations' of Marxism to be promoted in Polish academia.

It is worth noting how Żółkiewski described the camp of his 'allies' in the struggle for the scientific worldview. For example, the representatives of the former Viennese circle of logical positivism and the Warsaw logicians were, from Żółkiewski's perspective, those scholars with whom Marxists could cooperate fruitfully in the struggle against idealism.[6] This remark on the 'progressiveness' of the Warsaw School of Logics (the first rector of the University of Łódź, Tadeusz Kotarbiński, was one of the key figures associated with this philosophical tradition[7]) was not a minor fact. Both the Viennese circle and the Warsaw logicians had been deeply engaged in the agenda of the intellectual movements that Żółkiewski considered opponents of Marxism. Nevertheless, the participation of the Warsaw logicians in the project of the 'gentle revolution' and their senior position in post-war Polish academia were sufficient arguments to regard them as allies and describe their intellectual activity as 'progressive.'[8]

More importantly, the 'progressiveness' and the 'reactionary character' in the discourse of Żółkiewski did not have any geographical or political borders. The 'camp of Marxism' was, for Żółkiewski, an international phenomenon. Due to this, neither the political support of Marxists to the Soviet Union nor, on the contrary, the criticism against the Soviet path of socialism were criteria for the demarcation between the 'progressive' and 'reactionary' views in Żółkiewski's early post-war programme. He claimed that Marxism, in general terms, is nothing but a scientific worldview. All intellectual tendencies that were based on the rational approach to reality did not contradict Marxism.[9] Of course, this idea was typical for the Marxist discourse in different periods and could be interpreted differently in various political situations. Nevertheless, in the early post-war period, this statement could be read as a defensive argument rather than a sign of totalitarian ambition.

This careful strategy used in the defence of Marxism was also typical for its representatives in historiography. Many Polish historians publicly emphasised the limited character of the Marxian theory of history and highlighted that Marxism was not able to replace other methodological approaches.[10] The suspicion towards Marxism within historical circles was a challenge for those historians who promoted a Marxian turn in historiography. A prominent Polish historian, Witold Kula, was among those scholars who attempted to show the opportunities offered by Marxism for historical writing. In his publications, Kula omitted words such as 'reactionary,' 'fascist,' or 'idealistic.' His interest in Marxism was based on the purely academic idea of its usefulness in providing a new perspective on the old issues.

For Kula, Marx was the thinker who was able to represent history in scientific terms and turn the historiographical narrative to the analysis of social and economic processes. According to this view, Marx made historiography more scientific, and thus more progressive, than it previously was in the times when the main virtue of historians was a 'diligence in collecting anecdotes.' Kula argued that, thanks to Marx, the historiographical agenda could concentrate on research into objective factors rooted in social and economic history.[11] Moreover, Kula assured the reader that the Marxian approach to research on ideologies helped to find a compromise between extremely institutionalist approaches, which concentrated on the examination of great economic institutions, and studies on the social and political activity of people. Thus, Kula promoted not Marxism itself but the role of Marx in the invention of social and economic history, which changed the key virtues of historical work and moved historians away from describing facts and towards the analysis of objective processes.[12]

Additionally, according to Kula, Marxism as a form of socio-economic history was both progressive and democratic due to the subject of its research. Being a Marxist, that is, examining social–economical aspects of history, could help Polish historians to write a new history of Poland, which would oppose the traditional historical narrative that concentrated on the description of the dominant classes. Developing this idea, Kula wrote:

> A revision of the former historiography should be conducted [under the new political conditions]. It is necessary to conduct this [revision] based on as broad a source base as possible, at the highest possible scientific level. On this path, through the examination of social and economic history, we could

revise our political history, we could revise the entire picture of our past. new Poland will be able to see, comprehend, [and] understand the past without the narcotic of nobility's legend.[13]

Kula's vision of history was a national one. His main idea was to construct a narrative that could describe the history of the core of the nation, instead of reproducing the national mythology invented by the nobility. Of course, Kula did not mean that all his fellow historians saw Polish history through the prism of the 'noble mythology.' His point was that the socio-economic approach invented by Marx could be of importance for achieving the aims of the professional historians.

The publications of Żółkiewski and Kula reflected more influential trends in the strategies of Marxists in the public sphere of post-war Poland. Both strove to show (though in different ways) that Marxism could help Polish scholars to become more 'progressive' in their academic work. They were sure that the application of Marxist methodology to academic issues was, at the same time, a political issue since it made academic work serve the national interest. Meanwhile, they did not make the radical difference between Marxism and the Polish academic traditions the central point of their public discourse. According to them, Marxism was not an alternative word with its own conventions, but a set of epistemic techniques that could improve the existing forms of academic practice.

Meanwhile, the remote participation of the philosopher Adam Schaff[14] contrasted the uses of the early post-war years in the discussions on Marxism. Schaff did not hesitate to argue that Marxism and communism represented the only possible humanist theory and that it proposed the only 'truly democratic' programme. Schaff was not foreign to the sublime forms of promotion of Marxist ideology. He wrote in one of his articles:

Scientific socialism is a scientific system. But at the same time, exactly because it is a science, and because it leads with scientific accuracy to the most important goal that humanity has set for itself throughout its history, it [scientific humanism embodied in Marxism] is a poetry.[15]

From this holistic perspective, Marxism appeared to be the quintessence of true harmony and beauty, and therefore the final stage of the development of humanism and science. Schaff clarified that other intellectual movements, for example, liberalism and Christianity, could have been considered 'progressive' movements at certain stages of historical development, but that, after the appearance of Marxism and, later, communism, all other ideologies lost their humanistic role and scientific character. They did not respond to the new historical realities and, thus, became reactionary ones.[16]

Contrasting his colleagues based in Poland, Schaff did not avoid direct references to communism as the 'most humanist' programme, or the idea that it made all other theories 'outdated' and 'reactionary.' Developing this idea, he wrote:

Communists who stand firmly on the basis of Marxism are humanists in the best sense of the word. And the attempt to dress the right wing of social democracy in the false guise of 'humanism' is clearly a reactionary [act], and a cover for an attack on scientific socialism and the revolutionary wing of its supporters.[17]

This decisive attack on methodological and ideological attitudes outside of Marxism became a good illustration of what was atypical for the early post-war years. Against the backdrop of careful attempts to 'revise' the 'negative' image of Marxism in Poland, the decisive tone of the Moscow-based philosopher did not seem natural. Meanwhile, it was Schaff's version of Marxism (which had been primarily understood as a Soviet Marxism) that became the object of public criticism in the cultural and academic press; a criticism which had not been prevented either by censorship or by the politicians who were responsible for science and education in the new Polish state.

'Quasi-religion' and 'anti-progressive' Marxism

During the early post-war years, the Łódź group of Polish sociologists was in the centre of the debates on Marxism. Reconstructing the genealogy of Polish social sciences, Józef Chałasiński repeatedly emphasised the limited character of Marxist methodology. Since Chałasiński's teacher, Znaniecki, opposed the idea of making sociology a science about social and economic processes that excluded a humanistic element,[18] it was not possible to avoid a discussion on the paradigmatic contradictions between Marxism and Polish sociological heritage.[19] Frequently, Chałasiński referred to the works of Marxists whom themselves recognised the limitation of their ideology. For example, one of the founders of Polish sociology and statistics, Ludwik Krzywicki (1859–1941), and the prominent Polish Marxian economist Oskar Lange (1905–1965) were called to witness the inapplicability of Marxism to many sociological issues (which, according to Znaniecki's school, were the sphere of expertise for the humanities). The writings of Lange (who was then the ambassador of the Polish Republic to the USA) allowed Chałasiński to argue that 'the method of historical materialism can have only a limited application in the disciplines that involve researching the subjects created by individual human thought,'[20] while the texts of Krzywicki helped him to assert that 'historical materialism can be applied to [the humanities] <…> only from the perspective of … mass movements, and only to the extent to which the ideas that were expressed by these movements … have the character of social ideas.'[21] These references were supposed to show that the coexistence of many different approaches was possible, and that the reductionism of the whole agenda to Marxism was not desired by Polish Marxists themselves.

However, Chałasiński attacked Marxism in a more brutal way. In 1947, he published, in Borejsza's journal 'Odrodzenie,' a long article in which he criticised Marxism, not only as a research programme but also as a political ideology. Having repeatedly referred to the writings of Karl Mannheim,[22] Chałasiński questioned both the scientific status and democratic character of 'the classical Marxist theory.' As with his programme regarding the 'production' of the 'new intelligentsia,'[23]

Chałasiński discussed the ambitions of Marxism through the prism of 'democratisation.' According to him, the endeavour of Marxists to rule the social processes from above was a dangerous tendency that would lead, following the principles formulated by Montesquieu, to the monopolisation of power by the Marxian minority and represented, in fact, a false idea of progress.[24]

Developing this idea, Chałasiński paid special attention to the fact that the writings of Marx and Engels contain no theory of human life in a non-capitalist society. According to Chałasiński, the only scientific elements of Marxism were the theory of capitalism and the programme of the struggle against the domination of capitalist forms of oppression. Arguing so, Chałasiński wrote:

> Marxism was a theory of the path from capitalism to socialism, [but] not a theory of a society based on humanistic and social principles. Marx did not provide a theory of economic and social planning. Those who want to build a new, non-capitalist society must go beyond Marxism. The theories of Marx and Engels do not provide a sufficient basis for a planned democracy.[25]

Thus, Chałasiński asserted that the Marxists' aim to lead the process of democratisation in Poland was based on a flawed understanding of the very theory of the founders of Marxism.

Additionally, Chałasiński questioned the ability of the 'classical theory of Marxism' to provide an ideology for the formation of a society 'based on humanism.' Obviously answering the theses of Adam Schaff, Chałasiński directly referred to the writings of Engels and Lenin to show that the theorists of Marxism proposed a programme of moral relativism determined by the morality of a chosen class. In Chałasiński's view, this ideology could not be suitable for the Polish society that was to build socialism without the dictatorship of the proletariat. Chałasiński did not hesitate to argue that:

> The Marxist method of the implementation of the ideal [of the state of freedom], namely the [theory of the] dictatorship of the proletariat is an anti-humanist [theory].[26]

Thus, Chałasiński argued that Marxism, both as a 'scientific' and as a political programme, was not able to lead the 'humanisation' and 'democratisation' of the Polish state. Moreover, Chałasiński asked the reader of the main Polish cultural journal to prevent the transformation of Marxists into a new church, arguing that this would destroy the democratic character of the Polish state and replace 'progressiveness' with outdated social and political elements from the 19th century.[27]

In the popular science journal 'Myśl Współczesna (The Contemporary Thought),' another sociologist, Stanisław Ossowski, published a detailed examination of the Marxist ambition to represent 'the scientific worldview.' At the end of 1947, Ossowski could still provide an open criticism of the ideology that was supposed to unite the socialist bloc, which was in the early stages of its formation. He also delivered a blow against the idea that Marxism represents the embodiment of 'progressiveness.' In his view, the outdated character of Marxism (at least in its dogmatic version) was commonplace in academia and expressed surprise at the fact that the editors of 'Kuźnica' attempted to revise this idea. Ossowski referred to the works of the philosopher and first president of Czechoslovakia, Tomáš Masaryk (1850–1937), who, even in 1898, stated the theoretical and philosophical fiasco of Marxism,[28] and to the writings of the Polish Marxist sociologist Kazimierz Kelles-Krauz, who himself recognised the crisis of the Marxian ideology.[29]

Thus, in December 1947, Ossowski wondered: 'Where did this question [of the relevance of Marxism] come from today and why did it find a place in the first issue of the leading left-wing journal?'[30] On the eve of 1948, Ossowski was still surprised by the attempts to restart the debates on Marxism that, in his view, had lost their relevance in the early 20th century. Ossowski did not miss the opportunity to critically remark on the aspiration of 'Kuźnica' to teach the Polish intelligentsia and to re-educate all Poles in their 'misconception' regarding Marxism, which seemed to him not only inappropriate for the current agenda but just ridiculous.[31] Marxism, according to Ossowski, was not progressive but outdated.

Developing this idea, Ossowski argued that Marxists dogmatised the flexible and applied programme of Marx and Engels and, thus, hindered the scientific development of their ideas. Not without witticism, Ossowski referred to the popularity of the 'bourgeois scholar' and ethnologist Lewis H. Morgan (1818–1881) in Marxist literature, which still regarded him as a relevant author only because Marx and Engels based some of their ideas on Morgan's research.[32] Among other things, this irony was directed against the whole tradition of Soviet ethnography, in which Morgan was one of the central figures.[33] Ossowski did not hesitate to argue that it was not possible, in the mid-20th century, to base a scientific approach on works that lost their relevance thanks to the rapid development of disciplines such as ethnography.[34]

In a similar way, Ossowski criticised the Polish edition (conducted, according to him, with 'scholastic commentaries') of the classics of Russian Marxism. Concretely, Ossowski's criticism was directed against the publication of the philosophical writings of the Russian Marxist, Georgi Plekhanov (1856–1918). Since Vladimir Lenin said once that Plekhanov's philosophical works 'are the best ones in the whole international Marxist literature,'[35] the translation of Plekhanov's works seemed obvious for those who promoted Soviet Marxism in post-war Poland. Nevertheless, for Ossowski, the works of Plekhanov, without critical commentaries on the changes that had happened in science since the death of the author, 'could not bring [the reader] closer to Marx.'[36] According to Ossowski, the noncritical approach to Russian Marxism is the best way to make Marxism foreign to the Polish academic circles. For him, no 'scientific approach' could be based on the noncritical glorification of the authority of the 'classics.'[37] Thus, for Ossowski, it was not possible to be 'progressive' without being 'critical' of all the ideas that one defines as scientific.

This argument led Ossowski to the main point in his reflections on Marxism. Based on Émile Durkheim's theory, Ossowski argued that Marxism could be formally examined as a religion. Since, for Durkheim, religion was a purely sociological phenomenon, the claim of atheism did not change the religious form of Marxism. Besides 'common beliefs' of all members of this 'social group [i.e. Marxists]' and the idea that the followers of this 'religion' had to defend their ideals in front of external enemies, Marxism had, according to Ossowski, a coherent doctrine, which was to explain all phenomena, which helped to protect the coherency of this ideology. Additionally, Ossowski remarked upon the religious character of the vocabulary of Marxists, which contained concepts such as 'sectarianism,' 'orthodoxy,' and 'heresy.' This, in his view, protected the Marxian 'religious group' from decline.[38] The theoretical texts written by Marxists seemed, from Ossowski's perspective, very similar to religious tractates that would lose their relevance beyond the given 'religious group' that produced them.[39]

Ossowski also touched upon another sore point in the Marxist agenda. When dealing with the cult of authority figures, he inscribed Marxism into the history of the competition between 'science' and 'reactionary attitude.' In this story, Marxists were not on the side of 'science' and 'progress.' Their dependence on the 'classics' put them, from Ossowski's perspective, on a level with the professors at Pisa University who accused Galileo Galilei of contradicting Aristotle, and with those who did not accept William Harvey's invention for conserving the circulation of blood because of its contradictions with Galen and Hippocrates. From this perspective, Marxists not only failed to adopt the virtue of 'progressiveness' required for the development of science but also had a 'reactionary attitude' towards the newest scientific ideas.[40] Ossowski never tired of repeating that his criticism was directed not against Marx and Engels themselves, but against their followers – Marxists. Marx, according to Ossowski, also had significant difficulties with 'Saint-Simonists,' who dogmatised the programme of their teacher and could not accept his own innovative programme.[41] In this way, Marxism as a social phenomenon was represented not only as a quasi-religious ideology but also as a fundamentalist movement.[42]

The Marxian response

Of course, Marxian methodology could not help but influence the sociological practice in Poland. For example, the sociologist Julian Hochfeld (1911–1966) was one of the central representatives of so-called open Marxism[43] in Polish social sciences. In the interwar period, Hochfeld was an activist of the Polish socialist movement and, after his education at the University of Krakow, studied at the *École libre des sciences politiques* in Paris. Having spent a brief period in the Soviet Union, Hochfeld joined Polish troops in the Near East and later found himself in London until, after the war ended, he returned to Poland. This brief biographical remark shows that Hochfeld's approach to Marxism was rooted in the ideological agenda of Polish and French interwar discussions, and that this factor influenced his understanding of the very subject of the discussion.[44] Hochfeld recognised 'a lot of truth' in the words of the critics of Marxism. Nevertheless, he disagreed with the radical statements on the 'outdated' and 'anti-humanist character' of Marxism.

Hochfeld was convinced that dogmatism, religious belief in authority figures, and the doctrinal method of thinking were 'neither typical nor necessary' for Marxism.[45] At the same time, Hochfeld argued that he is 'far from believing that the criticism [of the opponents of Marxism] is groundless regarding some Marxists <...> especially regarding Marxist politicians,' for whom a quasi-religious discourse was very typical. Nevertheless, the comparison with religion is, in his view, a simplification. For Hochfeld, this comparison would relativise the essential difference between religion and science, which was a question of the highest importance for academic Marxism. Defending Marxism as a purely scientific theory, Hochfeld attempted to delineate between professionals and other Marxists, whose misconceptions were caused by lack of knowledge:

Marxists, to whom prof. Ossowski referred [in his article], are either politicians with a poor academic background but a great sense of the political needs of their group or party; or early-stage students of certain social issues; or people with cloudy minds who write all sorts of absurdities.[46]

This remark is very informative in itself. For Hochfeld, dogmatism and dependence on authority figures were examples of non-professional Marxism.

Among the most important postulations that had been proclaimed by Marxism, Hochfeld identified the recognition of reality and the possibility of comprehending this reality; the idea that different phenomena are connected to each other and stay in a position of mutual dependence; and the processual vision of development and the acceptance of the law of causality.[47] These ideas belonged to the principles that made scientific knowledge possible. Echoing Żółkiewski's programme, Hochfeld wrote:

Marxism just means science. Its greatest triumph will be when the word 'Marxism' itself loses its meaning .... This will be the greatest monument that social development will build to the titans of human thought: Karl Marx and Friedrich Engels.[48]

Thus, Hochfeld's Marxism required neither a religious worship of its classics, nor any radical changes in the forms of academic practice that were typical to post-war Polish academia.

This method of thinking forced Hochfeld to criticise Adam Schaff, who was, for him, a representative of Soviet philosophy in post-war Poland. Referring to the freshly published book by Adam Schaff, entitled 'The Introduction to the Theory of Marxism,' Hochfeld questioned Schaff's claim of Marxism as 'an integral and comprehensive theoretical system, which covers the knowledge of the reality in all its manifestations.' This 'too general and vague' definition of Marxism led Schaff, in Hochfeld's view, too many misconceptions. Developing this argument, he referred to Engels's *Anti-Dühring*[49] in his claim that no universal philosophy is possible.[50] Hochfeld argued that many research fields had not been developed by the classics of Marxism and yet represented a wide field for the scholarly creativity.[51] He wrote:

> Dialectical materialism or Marxian philosophical materialism and the Marxist dialectical method – [all this] is only a system of the most general theoretical-cognitive and methodological postulates.[52]

Moreover, this 'liberal' (as he called it) approach to Marxism was to be protected from any dogmatisation:

> To regard Marx as a mathematician, literary historian, poet, to regard Engels as a military theoretician, chemist, statistician, logician, etc. – this is more or less the same as regarding Einstein as a violinist or Napoleon as a lawyer.[53]

Thus, Hochfeld joined, in fact, the criticism against the totalitarian ambitions of Adam Schaff's 'Soviet Marxism.'

In 1948, Schaff was still very polite to his opponents from non-religious academic circles. He characterised Ossowski's articles as 'an attempt of the friend and sympathiser to point out, in a friendly manner, those defects in the theoretical development of Marxism that, in his opinion, can be seen in modern Marxism and which impede this development.'[54] Even though this sentence hardly reflects the intentions of Ossowski, it illustrates Schaff's aspiration to divide the academic field into two opposite camps (for Marxism and against it) and, in the early postwar years, Ossowski was regarded as an 'ally' of Marxism. Meanwhile, the aim of Schaff's publication was not a discussion with Ossowski. Schaff was going to examine 'the author's erroneous ideas, which often distort his positive thoughts and allow, against his will and intentions, the opponents of Marxism to cling to the words of his articles.'[55] Thus, Schaff brought a new feature to academic discussion: that is, not to use the discussion for an exchange of arguments, but to correct mistakes and to prevent the usage of Ossowski's 'partly correct ideas' by the ideological enemies.

It is not surprising that Schaff supported Ossowski in his criticism against 'Marxian dogmatism' – 'dogmatism' was considered a vice even in the official discourse of Stalinism, and the denial of a dogmatic attitude did not constitute a problem for the scholar trained in Soviet academia. As did Hochfeld, Schaff explained dogmatist tendencies as abuses conducted by non-professionals and, thus, Ossowski's criticism was reoriented to become a charge against 'bad Marxists.' Schaff argued: 'our roads [with Ossowski] were beginning to branch out, when prof. Ossowski started to look for the genesis of these sins and attempted to find the root of evil in Marxism itself.'[56] So, a good Marxist, for Schaff, was not an 'exegete' commenting on the 'Holy Scripture' of the classics, but a virtuous scholar who strives to be 'progressive' in his scientific statements, while all possible misconceptions were rooted in the lack of training among people calling themselves Marxists. Meanwhile, in his defence of the Marxian programme, Schaff referred to the idea of unity between theory and practice, which were necessary preconditions for the effectiveness of

Marxism as a social and economic programme. For Schaff, the amalgamation of proletarian ideology and the 'scientific programme' under the banner of Marxism was the proper way to make Marxism work. The 'only' reservation delivered by Schaff was that it may be impossible to make the academic agenda truly scientific and 'progressive' without connection to the ideology of proletariat dominance.[57]

Thus, even though Schaff formally agreed with Hochfeld's strategy of presenting Marxism as a non-dogmatic and creative scientific programme, Schaff's version of 'non-dogmatism' required much more dogmata than Hochfeld's. To him, Marxism represented not only general postulations of the belief in objective reality and the possibilities of knowledge, but also science about 'the objective laws of social development which ... allow us to understand the laws of social progress that became an ideological bond for the class [of proletariat] which is the social bearer of this progress.'[58] Ossowski's approach to Marxism as 'a religious social bond' was foreign to Schaff, not because it implied the connection between ideology and science (this was quite normal to him), but because Ossowski, in his view, abused the formal similarities of Marxism with religious groups while ignoring the content of these ideologies. Schaff did not deny that Marxism functioned as a 'social bond' or that it promoted the special destination of the proletariat. It was important for him to show that Marxism denied any religion or metaphysics and thus led people to the 'correct' and truly 'progressive' worldview. While, for Hochfeld, with science and 'progressiveness,' there was no need for Marxism, for Schaff, there was no 'progressiveness' and no 'science' without Marxism.[59]

Schaff also attempted to challenge the arguments regarding the outdated character of canonical Marxist thinkers, especially those who held fame in the Soviet Union. Schaff argued that the ideas of Plekhanov, formulated 50 years ago, were more progressive than some of the most recent publications in philosophy.[60] Moreover, Schaff brought into the discussion another argument that was only beginning to play a role in post-war academic discussions. Responding to Ossowski's caustic remark on the references made by Marxist ethnologists to the outdated works of Lewis Morgan, Schaff used the practice of the Soviet Union as evidence of the academic relevance of Morgan's legacy:

> Marxist ethnology has reached a very high level, especially in the USSR, where this discipline is by no means alien to the scientific achievements of the last 70 years. And, if Marxists base their research on the works of Engels and, thus, Morgan, this is neither dogmatism nor evidence of their exegetical attitude towards these authors, but evidence that they are convinced that the key ideas of Morgan remain relevant.[61]

Thus, the statement regarding the 'high level' of ethnology in the Soviet Union was, for Schaff, an argument in itself that proved the relevance of the classics of Marxism.

The Soviet Union as a source of truth took its place in Schaff's more general reflections on the future of Marxism as well. In his view, the development of Marxism in the Soviet Union became possible because of the occurrence of the deconstruction of the 'official science,' which was controlled by capitalism and was an obstacle to the rise of Marxists before the socialist revolution. Schaff wrote:

> One should be a professional Marxist scholar in order to write about scientific issues from the Marxist point of view with skill. But this [being a good Marxist] requires certain conditions. Historically, they [these conditions] were first implemented in the Soviet Union and in the countries of People's Democracy.[62]

Thus, the changes that had happened in Poland after the war became the conditions for being a 'good Marxist' and having 'truly progressive views,' which, earlier, could be possible only in the Soviet Union. These new conditions meant, for Schaff, an opportunity to extend Soviet 'correct philosophy' to the new socialist countries established under Soviet patronage.

In this way, Schaff explained the model of philosophical debate that he was going to promote in Poland. Firstly, his programme already had a tendency to claim that a socialist state must have one 'correct' methodology based on the new social–political reality, and this methodology was Marxism. Secondly, if Poland came to the 'new realities' only after the Second World War, the entirety of previous Polish philosophy and scholarship could be classified as a bourgeois one. Even those who represented themselves as Marxists did not avoid the bourgeois influences and, thus, could not be 'good' Marxists since this was only possible in a special milieu i.e. under the new political conditions.[63] Additionally, the 'non-dogmatism' of Schaff represented a very rigid structure, which made the discussion an opportunity to explain the 'correct views' to the audience and to fix the mistakes that had been committed by his opponents. Unlike other Polish Marxists, Schaff did not try to argue with those who accused Marxists of having a 'reactionary attitude'; he promoted an alternative vision of 'progressiveness' that made all his opponents 'reactionary fellows' instead.

In 1948, Schaff reconciliatorily expressed his hope that 'these exchanges of opinions will lead to learning about each other and to understanding each other [between Marxists and non-Marxists]; to the further crystallisation of Marxian thought and to <...> reducing the distance between the Marxian camp and the academic world.'[64] Indeed, several years later, this distance would be forcibly reduced. Nevertheless, in the early post-war years, Adam Schaff was only one of many participants in this debate and, in a sense, this foreshadowed of the coming changes. Under 'gentle revolution,' his idea of 'virtuous behaviour' was neither dominant nor official.

Unequal opponents: Catholics vs. Marxists

It was not an accident that Adam Schaff started his response to the comparison of Marxism with religion by referring to the 'opponents' who used this idea in their struggle against the 'scientific form of knowledge.'[65] These 'opponents' were Catholics. From Schaff's perspective, the Catholic groups represented a real threat, not only for the development of Marxism in post-war Poland, but also for the whole 'democratic' project that was to be implemented in the Polish state. In this regard, Schaff's position was the most radical expression of the moods that had dominated the socialist and communist milieu since the interwar period. Nevertheless, the post-war realities meant that an intellectual dialogue between the two camps became a necessary point in the public agenda of this period. For both the authorities and for Marxists who participated in the public discussions, Catholics were ideological enemies. Nevertheless, tolerance towards religion was still one of the basic principles proclaimed in the post-war Polish state.

One of the fundamental changes in the status of Catholics in post-war Poland, in comparison with the interwar period, was the ratio of the number of Catholic groups that were allowed to participate in public debates and the role of Catholicism in Polish society. Even though the general slogans of the Polish post-war political project did directly contradict the ideas promoted by most Catholics involved in the social agenda, the tense relations between Catholics and the authorities were obvious to all participants in the public debates.[66] Either way, the Catholic journals could not stay away from the discussion on Marxism and used this topic to secure their position in the intellectual landscape of post-war Poland.

It is not surprising that the prevention of Marxism from becoming a dominant ideology was a central issue to all Catholic groups involved in the public agenda in the early post-war years. For example, the 'programme declaration' of the Catholic group headed by Bolesław Piasecki promoted the idea of equalising the rights of 'materialists and idealists' for participation in the construction of the post-war Polish state. According to the declaration, 'we and the Marxists have a common service for the primary task of building and restoring the Polish statehood.' The 'progressive Catholics' called this collaboration a 'loyal ideological struggle,' which could bear fruit for the intellectual development of Poland. According to them, the discussion between Marxists and non-Marxists through the 'loyal confrontation' and 'loyal criticism' had to 'raise the [intellectual, ideological] level of both of the two sides [Marxists and Catholics].'[67] Besides the fact that 'loyal confrontation (*lojalna walka*)' and 'loyal criticism (*lojalna krytyka*)' are a good description of the post-war activity of Piasecki's group, these words illustrate that the opportunity to confront Marxism in the public sphere (at least in its materialist agenda) was a central issue also for those Catholics who put special emphasis on their loyalty towards the regime.[68]

One of the young Catholic activists from Piasecki's group, Andrzej Micewski (1926–2004), then a student at the University of Warsaw,[69] pointed out the 'dangerous popularity' of materialism among Polish students. According to Micewski, it was necessary 'to protect young people from the one-sided intellectual and ideological influence of Marxism.' More importantly, Micewski emphasised that the task of Catholics was to ensure Marxism did not receive a monopoly on such terms as 'radicalism, progress and science.'[70] Thus, Piasecki's group aimed to prepare a platform on which 'science' and 'progress' would mean neither Marxism nor struggle against religion.

The debates on the 'scientific character' of Marxism were, of course, a good opportunity for Catholics to challenge the ambitions of Marxists, who still had relatively weak positions in both the Polish public sphere and in academia. The literary critic and philosopher Jerzy Braun (1901–1975), associated with Zygmunt Kaczyński's Catholic group, prepared a considerable number of publications on this topic. Braun also asserted the similarity between Marxism and religion, but his approach to this issue was not identical with Ossowski's formal sociological programme. Braun referred to the philosophical roots of this issue. He pointed out that science deals with 'what exists, but not with how it should be.' The 'Marxian prophecy' regarding the struggle of classes, the special destination of the proletariat on the way to the new ideal world, and the 'laws of historical development' had, according to Braun, little to do with the 'scientific approach' to the real world. Braun described this as a kind of 'metaphysics.' Thus, he formulated a point which was, according to him, key to understanding the 'relations' between Catholicism and Marxism: Marxian teaching could not be compared with Catholicism as 'an objective science and a theological system.' In his view, these two ideologies could be discussed through such oppositions as 'metaphysics vs. metaphysics' or 'pseudo-religion vs. religion.'[71]

Developing his ideas, Braun claimed that the basic values to which Catholicism and Marxism referred in their discourse could not be 'harmonised' and brought to a compromise. For Braun, it was obvious that Christianity as a social doctrine would support all progressive social reforms if they were carried out 'within the framework of Christian values.' Nevertheless, Christianity, in his view, does not accept the idea of incorrigibility of any one social class. It is a duty of Christians to stand against evil and to strive towards justice; in this regard, Christianity does not contradict 'progressiveness.' Nevertheless, Christians always hope for the rehabilitation of persons who commit evil actions and do not categorise people in accordance with their class identity. Thus, Catholicism, according to Braun, represented a much fairer and more progressive social programme than Marxism. In his view, the collaboration with the representatives of the Marxian programme was possible only under the condition of the rejection of the most essential ideological tenets of Marxism.[72]

Braun's publications on the Marxist ideology formulated the ideas which were relatively common for Polish Catholics in the post-war period. Never before had a political situation required from them such intensive reflections on the possibility of collaboration with Marxism, nor on the limits of the acceptable in this collaboration.[73] Despite all the differences in the strategies undertaken by various Catholic groups, they found themselves in a camp opposed to Marxism, ideologically and politically. The debate on the relations between Marxism and Catholicism stood on the crossroad of academic and political agendas. The possibility of leading a public debate on this topic was one of the crucial facets of the 'gentle revolution' project.

However, discussions between Marxists and Catholics that implied an exchange of arguments from both sides were not an equal debate. The editorial boards of the left-wing journals regarded the new balance of forces as an opportunity to propagate 'knowledge' instead of 'beliefs,' 'science' instead of religion, and 'enlightenment' instead of 'obscurantism.' For them, all of these negative tendencies were embodied in Catholicism. While Catholics were forced, from the beginning, to use the idea of ideological plurality as a defensive tool,[74] many of the authors of the left-wing journals had a lower motivation in arguing with Catholics. Nevertheless, in the early post-war period, Catholics had an opportunity to oppose the tendencies that led to defining them as 'reactionary forces' due to their intellectual affiliation with Catholicism.

Reacting to the publications in the state-run press, one of the leaders of the Kraków Catholic group, the theologian Jan Piwowarczyk,[75] attempted to provoke a dialogue with Marxists and directly opposed the agenda that had been promoted (not least by Adam Schaff) in the left-wing journals. In his publications, Piwowarczyk presented a philosophical analysis of Marxist ideas and, in fact, challenged not only the scientific character but also the philosophical status of Marxism. Piwowarczyk's central argument referred to the fact that Marx did not invent something new as a philosopher, because neither Hegelian dialectic nor Feuerbach's materialism were original ideas. According to Piwowarczyk, the 'religious' charisma of the Marxian teaching would not be so powerful if Marx had not wanted to create a positive programme instead of a philosophical teaching.[76] This positive programme, wrote Piwowarczyk, made Marx a teacher and a prophet rather than a philosopher.

The philosophical aspects of Marxism were still important to Piwowarczyk in their historical perspective. It was Feuerbach who, in Piwowarczyk's view, had inspired Marx and Engels in cutting the Hegelian category of 'spirit' from the philosophical agenda, and introducing instead 'consciousness' as a key analytical category. Marxism, wrote Piwowarczyk, as both a political and philosophical programme, chose the path of materialism that was not so obvious from the perspective of Hegel's theory of history. Additionally, according to Piwowarczyk, Marx and Engels had been 'misled' by Feuerbach's conviction that there are only two opposite philosophical programmes: idealism as a rejection of matter; and materialism that understands ideas as a reflection of matter. According to Piwowarczyk, there was the third path of 'spiritualism,' which had been ignored by Marxists and promoted by the majority of Christian philosophers. For 'spiritualism,' both spirit and matter were real and differentiation between them presented an essential issue for Christian philosophy.

Developing this idea, Piwowarczyk argued that Marxism (as a 'prophetic movement'[77]) was opposed to religion because it had a wrong idea of religion. Piwowarczyk claimed that Marx's 'mistake' was rooted in his attempt to judge the religious form of knowledge through the analysis of Hegelian idealism. Meanwhile, in his view, the Hegelian 'absolute' was not a Christian approach to the metaphysical issues. According to Piwowarczyk, Christianity also disagreed with idealism because Christians claimed the real, but not ideal, character of the key theological categories that had been described in the Holy Scripture. Thus, according to Piwowarczyk, Christianity, like Marxism, struggles against idealism, while also promoting the 'third path' of spiritualism that had been mistakenly ignored by Marxists.[78]

Additionally, Piwowarczyk argued that the anti-religious programmes of Marx, Engels, and Lenin,[79] who regarded religion as a form of oppression and thus a 'reactionary ideology' by definition, were wrong in its crucial point. Religion is, for Piwowarczyk, a form of personality development and has nothing to do with exploitation, even though it had been used in such a way historically. In his view, there is nothing in the Catholic thought that would oppose the 'progressiveness' in social issues. Regarding the culture of public debates, Piwowarczyk sadly remarked on the lack of readiness among Marxist opponents to lead an equal discussion with Catholics. The hostility against religion was, in his view, an integral part of the Marxian programme in Poland and could not positively promote intellectual development:

> In the camp of Marx's students, there are two types of tactics of struggle against religion: [the first is a] more Marxist [and] deterministic tactic and [the second one is a] more revolutionary [and] impatient [tactic] … [the followers of] the first one claim we are creating a communist system, and religion will fall by itself. [According to the followers of] the second one, we should fight against religion because it will not disappear itself. Both directions pursue the same aim.[80]

Piwowarczyk lamented the fact that Marxists, due to their philosophical views, did not need any discussions with Catholics and thus there is no opportunity to find a compromise in open ideological competition.

The political contexts of the debates with Marxism did not lose their importance for Piwowarczyk. Developing his programme, he emphasised that there are no visible ideological limits in Marxism that could prevent violence, since the 'class struggle' and the ideas of society without religion, state, and private property seemed to be the only criteria for the morality of action in Marxism. Nevertheless, Piwowarczyk argued that the lack of readiness for a dialogue with Marxists in the past was a factor in the escalation of the radicality of Marxism. According to him, these mistakes of the past could make Catholicism the victim of violence:

> There are those who see only moral relativism in Marxism … they do not want to recognise a certain ethos in it. And this is the tragedy of the fight against Marxism, that [the opponents of Marxism] wanted to shoot the ideas [of Marxists] with a revolver. [Meanwhile,] it is necessary to present a true social ideal instead of a false one. Then the fight will be worthy of opponents. Any fight against an idea with the help of violence and police is unworthy of human being. This must be remembered ….[81]

Thus, Piwowarczyk emphasised that tolerance towards ideological opponents must also become a virtue in order to make a peaceful public discussion possible. According to him, this would prevent the development of Marxism to a phenomenon of the scale to threaten Catholicism. In this way, being in a defensive position,

Piwowarczyk appealed to tolerance as a helper in preventing a more radical anti-religious campaign in post-war Poland.

The last quotation became the starting point in Adam Schaff's answer to Piwowarczyk's reflections on Marxism. Schaff wittily remarked that 'Mr. Priest' was 'too late' with his reflections on tolerance and the non-acceptance of violence against Marxism.[82] Schaff stigmatised his opponent as a representative of the 'right-wing press' and, thus, classified him as an 'enemy' in the ideological struggle. To avoid oversimplifying the context of this debate, one should say that the interwar attitude of Piwowarczyk did not seem 'non-problematic,' not least for the realities of the early post-war period. On the one hand, the priest was always fond of radical agrarian and social reforms,[83] on the other, in the interwar period, Piwowarczyk had been among the fighters against the 'Jewish ideology' in Poland, and some of his publications contained an apologetic sentiment towards German antisemitism.[84] After the war, Schaff (still based in Moscow) felt himself to be in a dominant position over his opponent and did not feel any requirement for tolerance towards him.

Considering the 'uncertain steps' of Marxism in the public and academic life of post-war Poland, it is characteristic that Schaff wittily remarked that 'the right-wing press' discussed Marxism more frequently than the left-wing journals. Since Schaff apparently did not feel the tension that forced the Polish party and governmental functionaries to soften the contradictions between Catholicism and the new regime, he had more freedom to attack Catholics than his colleagues based in Poland. Schaff's narration was sarcastic and offensive at the same time. He proposed that Piwowarczyk should read the textbook for Marxism to learn more about Marxist ideas before writing theoretical articles on them. Schaff argued that the priest, having compared Marxism to religion with its prophets, Holy Scripture, and apostles, forgot to find an analogy for the inquisition present in the Marxian practice.[85] Schaff did not really debate the theses of Piwowarczyk, instead, he 'explained' to the reader the key principles of Marxian teaching and the reason why the 'right-wing' reactionaries could not recognise the correctness of Marxism. For him, the competition between Catholics and Marxists was not a discussion between two types of worldviews, but a war in which 'it is necessary to take the fight and to win or to lose.'[86]

Since Marxism was, for Schaff, an embodiment of science, and thus an opposition to religion, it not surprising that he was not interested in Piwowarczyk's argument regarding 'spiritualism' as the third path between idealism and materialism. He explained that there are only two options: materialism or faith, and if 'spirit' does not come from matter, it does not exist.[87] The contradictions between spiritualism and idealism were, for Schaff, nothing but a 'family dispute'[88] among idealists. Schaff was mocking Piwowarczyk's attempt to 'defend' Marxism and to find a 'Marxian morality' that would defend it against the accusation of moral relativism.[89] He argued that Marxism did not need an excuse from the Catholic side. For him, Marxism had its own idea of ethics, which had nothing to do with the Catholic equivalent, but instead was determined by the interest of the proletariat. Thus, Schaff attempted to convince the reading public that Catholics were not supposed to be equal opponents but should be considered enemies in post-war Poland.

The fragile 'compromise' on 'non-reactionary' Catholicism

Much like in many other debates, Schaff's offensive discourse on Catholicism contrasted with both the intentions of the organisers of the 'gentle revolution' and the mainstream of the early post-war period. The realities of this time required and allowed a dialogue between Catholics and Marxists. In 1946, Jerzy Borejsza became an organiser of several public debates between Catholics and left-wing intellectuals, which were hosted by the editorial board of the journal 'Odrodzenie,' based then in Kraków. Besides the fact that Borejsza still saw the necessity of bringing the opposing sides together and letting them discuss controversial issues, it is noteworthy that both sides of the debates publicly reported on these meetings and their results. Not only the discussions themselves but also the style of reports on them illustrated the difference between the form of debate promoted by Schaff and the realities of the 'gentle revolution.'

Kazimierz Wyka, a historian of literature, became a representative of the Marxist side in this debate and prepared a detailed review of the Kraków discussions between Catholics and Marxists. Wyka's description did not represent any polemical intention in itself; his narration described the differences in the positions that had been discussed in Kraków and followed the general idea of the 'gentle revolution' to soften internal contradiction.[90] In general terms, these debates (Jan Piwowarczyk also was among the disputants) became a meeting point for the ideas that had been discussed in both the Catholic and left-wing journals. The reader of Wyka's report did not see any accusations or radical disagreements between the two sides of the debate, though the lines of *non possumus* had been drawn during these discussions very clearly.

Wyka specified the arguments from various fields of knowledge, which determined the agenda of dispute between Catholics and Marxists. Regarding philosophical issues, both sides agreed that reason was more important than will and feelings but disagreed on the rationality of the programmes of the opposition. Regarding the social theory, Catholics claimed that 'Catholic sociology' recognised the class struggle but was particularly occupied with the facets of Marxism that questioned the value of individuality. Responding to this argument, Marxist sociologist and, then, the Minister of the Enlightenment, Władysław Bieńkowski, argued that 'Marxists do not question the right of an individual for his own development, but an individual is understood [by Marxists] as the social aim.' This emphasised the intention of Marxists to reshape the political conditions for the intellectual development of all individuals living in the country.[91] Either way, it was not the aim of this debate to avoid the contradictions between the two ideologies, and the differences between them were openly discussed during the Kraków dispute.

Meanwhile, there were signs of both sides' readiness to find a compromise between the representatives of the two opposing camps. According to Wyka, during the Kraków debates, Catholics recognised that the social reform that had been conducted in Poland was the achievement of Polish socialists, who had made the social life in Poland fairer than it was before. Marxists, in turn, agreed not to claim that the Catholics' drive towards internal and spiritual development was a sign of the protection of capitalism and a 'reactionary attitude.' In general terms, the representation of the discussion that was prepared by Wyka served as an illustration for the fact that the 'gentle revolution' 'was working' and bearing fruits. More importantly, the balance of forces that had been performed by Wyka was, from the perspective of Borejsza's project, an ideal form of 'collaboration' between Catholics and Marxists: Catholics recognised the social changes that had been conducted by the government, and Marxists gave 'progressive' Catholics a space for spiritual self-reflections without classifying them as 'reactionary forces.' In essence, this was the version of *modus vivendi* prepared by Borejsza for post-war Poland.

Reporting on the Kraków discussion, one of the most active young fellows from Piasecki's Catholic group, Wojciech Kętrzyński, highlighted that the dispute was the first time in post-war history when Catholics and Marxists were brought together to discuss the contradictions between their programmes. Of course, Kętrzyński put special emphasis on the importance of tolerance towards ideological opponents, as well as on the value of discussion itself as a way to mitigate contradictions. Developing this argument, he wrote:

> It can be said that, among the several dozens of people gathered in the hall, those who believed that one of the positive arguments in this discussion could be violence, coercion, a knife or a gun, a sentence or prison, represented an absolute minority (or even nobody [thought so] at all). Although not so long ago, on both sides, this view would have been a dominant one![92]

Thus, the very opportunity to publicly debate their contradictions to Marxists and, more importantly, the readiness of Marxists to give an impression of tolerance towards their opponents were the key issues for Catholics under the post-war conditions.

Nevertheless, Kętrzyński did not fail to mention that Catholics took these discussions much more seriously than Marxists and were much more interested in finding an understanding with their opponents. Developing this argument, he remarked:

> It should be objectively recognised that the representatives of Catholic groups gathered [in this meeting] showed, without doubt, more knowledge of the ideology of their opponents. There is also no doubt that Marxism, [the general ideas of] its classical thinkers and their works, were known to the most of Catholics who participated in the debate, while the basic ideas of Christian worldview and the teaching of the Catholic Church were known to Marxists only in a general form.[93]

Kętrzyński deplored the fact that Marxists had limited motivation in the discussions on the Catholic ideals of the early post-war years. Kętrzyński never tired of repeating that 'it is not possible to build a new regime, which would be better than the old one without Christianity; without Christianity, one could only destroy everything.'[94]

The Kraków dispute, as well as the reaction to it in the cultural press, was an important sign that, from the perspective of the 'gentle revolution' project, 'progressiveness' as a virtue could be seen beyond the opposition between 'religion' and 'atheism.' Of course, the space afforded to the public activity of Catholics was still very limited. In fact, the privilege of Polish Catholics was not to be officially defined as 'reactionary fellows' for their disagreement with historical materialism, under the condition of accepting the 'progressive social reforms' conducted in Poland. This did not mean that the Catholic groups (though in different forms) did not go beyond this framework or refrain from criticising the politics conducted by the authorities.[95] Additionally, the virtue of tolerance, which was intensively promoted in the public sphere by the Catholics, at least was not denied at the official level. Borejsza's strategy showed his readiness to accept this virtue under the condition that it did not oppose 'progressiveness,' even though the promotion of tolerance as a virtue did not receive the status of an official programme.

In any case, this compromise was a fragile one. The Catholic scholars and writers sensitively reacted to all attempts to exclude them from the debate on scholarly relevant issues. With time, they had more and more reasons for concern. For example, Kaczyński's Catholic group indignantly responded to the discussion on the 'new Polish encyclopaedia,' which was supervised by Adam Schaff. In one of his articles devoted to this project, Schaff argued that the defeat of fascism in the war meant 'the victory of materialism over idealism in the minds of people.' An unknown author from the Warsaw group asked Schaff a rhetorical question: 'Were there only materialists who defeated fascism and Hitlerism?' Schaff's programme for the liquidation of idealism in Polish philosophical praxis led the author to a further question: 'Does Adam Schaff want to eliminate the whole idealist tradition, including Plato and Socrates, from the philosophical agenda of post-war Poland?' Developing this idea, the author regarded Schaff's programme as a call for 'the abolition of the teaching of Christ and the whole heritage of the rich Christian philosophy.'[96]

The idea that neither a political theory nor a philosophical agenda is possible without Christianity was, for understandable reasons, a leitmotif in the discourse of the Catholic press. For example, the lawyer and philosopher, Stanisław Stomma, in one of his articles published under the pseudonym Marian Jedlicz,[97] argued that the 'sociological laws' that force people to disagree with inequality had to be distinguished from the laws of human nature, in which the Catholic Church had more experience than Marxists. Arguing so, Stomma referred to the corruption of human nature that had to destroy the 'optimism' of Marxists.[98] Stomma expressed an opinion (which was more or less common to the Catholic circles) that the Catholic social programme was openly an 'anti-humanist' one, since it denied the human origin of moral principles.[99] Nevertheless, this fact did not make it 'reactionary' in terms of social and political issues. On the contrary, the belief in the ontological roots of justice could be an important resource for reconstructing the Polish state. Catholics, with their extensive experience in reflections on the 'human nature,' could find a better path to the stability desired in 'new Poland.'[100]

Nevertheless, the Marxist authors did not show any desire to be supervised by Catholics regarding the knowledge of human nature. Since the struggle for the materialist worldview was the key component of their political and academic programme, they did not seem to be interested in the issues of original sin, nor in Catholic solutions for healing the moral diseases. In 1947, the publication of anti-religious feuilletons and caricatures in the journal 'Kuźnica' provided evidence that the readiness to simulate a 'respectful' dialogue with Catholics was slowly losing its relevance in the changeable political conditions. The pictures of Saint Peter telling Gott about the success of his party (Christian Democracy) on the last election, fat priests exploiting naïve believers, and bishops raising hands in Nazi salutes found their place in the pages of the journal, together with quotations from Voulter's *Dictionnaire philosophique* regarding the 'right for stupidity.'[101] This style of anti-religious discourse showed the fragility of the dialogue with Catholics as a principle of 'gentle revolution.'

The reaction of Catholics to the anti-religious programme of 'Kuźnica' illustrates their endeavour to maintain the *modus vivendi* formulated during the Kraków discussion. The offensive tone of the Marxist authors and the departure of the readiness for open dialogue, which was desired by Catholics, forced an anonymous author of the journal to accuse Marxist opponents of breaking the principles upon which the new Polish state had been based. Reacting to the anti-religious feuilletons and caricatures published in 'Kuźnica' under the title 'Don Basilio,' the author wrote:

> Kuźnica is – and has every right to be – an anti-religious and anti-Catholic group. But the boundless naivety and the absence of any sense of this publication ['Don Basilio'] is regrettable. At a time when most responsible people in Poland are concerned about the constant relaxation of dangerous and unnecessary tensions in society; when many people in the ruling camp, like many Catholics, would like to achieve a *modus vivendi* regarding the Catholic issue, considering this issue is one of the most fundamental political problems for now; Kuźnica – the leading Marxist journal – ... with a giggle adds fuel to the fire.[102]

The move from theoretical reflections about the struggle against idealism, to the anti-religious propaganda, including caricatures depicting fat priests and feuilletons mocking shameless clerics who deceive naïve people, was a bad sign for Catholics.

Even though political developments in 1948 did not fill Catholics with optimism, they attempted to answer the feuilleton in kind. Nevertheless, the unhappiness of the situation could be felt by the reader, who hardly found any witticisms in the article '*About Marx and Marxists. A Marxian feuilleton.*' The main idea of this publication was not new. After several quotations from the works of Lenin and Stalin, with claims of 'non-dogmatic Marxism' that were chosen as epigraphs, the reader could find a caustic remark on the difference between the slogans of Marxists and their practice. The example of such a contradiction was the publication of the Manifesto of the Communist Party in the theoretical journal of the Workers' Party 'Nowe Drogi (The New Paths).' This, according to the Workers' party functionaries, 'is a sharp [sword] [which is currently] sharper than it was a hundred years ago.' The point of the feuilleton's author was simple: the central thesis of Marxism was historical determinism in approach to ideas, and the remark on the actuality of a century old text stood in contradiction to this thesis. So, the feuilletonist wrote: 'Although our dear Marxists will undoubtedly have a thousand reasons for the justification [of their attitude]. I just wonder what Marx would say, miraculously resurrected in 1948 and forced to read the jubilee press.'[103]

It is highly unlikely that such feuilletons could hurt the Marxists much. Nevertheless, the debates between Marxists and Catholics still became one of the most important markers of the 'gentle revolution.' Even though the 'respectfulness' and 'tolerance' of the state-run press towards Catholics was not quite apparent, the Catholic journals and Catholic thinkers were part of the intellectual agenda in the early post-war years. The 'unequal' debates were still a form of discussion.

*

Paradoxically, both Marxists and Catholics entered the early post-war period in a defensive position. Both Marxism and Catholicism had to justify the 'progressiveness' of their ideological attitudes. The 'virtues politics' of the 'gentle revolution' did not imply any paternalist or governmental regulation of the correct way to be 'progressive.' In combination with the idea that scholars were to determine their agenda independently, this led to public accusation that Marxism was promoting an 'outdated' and 'anti-humanist' ideology instead of science. Due to this, Marxists were under suspicion of having a 'reactionary attitude' towards the recent achievements in science and scholarship. Most of those scholars who attempted to defend the Marxist approach as a scientific methodology assured their opponents that Marxism did not imply any radical changes to the forms of scientific practice that their opponents thought 'progressive.' In a sense, the struggle against religion and, concretely, Catholicism was the main argument with which Marxists wanted to win the sympathies of the anti-religious sections of Polish academia and the reading public. For the Catholics in turn, the refutation of the scientific status of Marxism became the crucial point in their public discourse. Publicly claiming the 'progressiveness' of their social doctrine, Catholics insisted on an equal dialogue with Marxists. Fortifying their defensive positions, Catholics made the promotion of tolerance towards ideological opponents an important tool in their survival strategy. Despite the unwillingness of the leftist (not only Marxian) scholars to seek compromise, Catholics were able to get official recognition that being Catholic did not necessarily mean possessing a 'reactionary attitude.' However, this temporary 'success,' much like the entire project of the 'gentle revolution,' was not eternal.

**

'Progressiveness' as a virtue, promoted by the organisers of the 'gentle revolution' project, became a framework for the early post-war years. It was not my intention to argue that all the participants of the public debates adopted this virtue. On the contrary, my point is that most scholars involved in the public agenda immediately after the war did not feel any conflict between their forms of virtues behaviour and the official discourse on this issue. The idea that scholars were to determine their agenda independently could not help but lead to a plurality of public manifestations of 'progressiveness,' some of which stood in conflict to each other. Additionally, in terms of its 'virtues politics,' the state did not pretend to be a teacher of virtuous behaviour. This constellation of factors made the early post-war public debates a platform on which, despite the close control of Soviet officials, the ideas that stood in contradiction to the Soviet realities, as well as to authoritarianism in general, could be promoted publicly. However, the institutional platform for these debates was fully dependent on the state and thus could be easily deconstructed. But were the scholars so mouldable like institutions?

Notes

1 Stanisław Ossowski, "Doktryna marksistowska na tle dzisiejszej epoki," *Myśl Współczesna*, no. 12 (1947): 505.
2 Marci Shore, *Caviar and Ashes: A Warsaw Generation's Life and Death in Marxism, 1918-1968* (New Haven/London: Yale University Press, 2006), 10–152.
3 Stefan Żółkiewski, "O tak zwanej nieaktualności Marksizmu," *Kuźnica*, no. 1 (1945): 3.
4 Ibid., 2.
5 The matter concerned, first of all, the philosophers of science who developed the concept of experience as a condition of the possibility of knowledge. One of the central figures in this line was the famous mathematician and philosopher of science, Henri Poincaré (1854–1912).
6 Żółkiewski, "O tak zwanej nieaktualności Marksizmu," 3.
7 See Chapter 1.
8 In a very unusual way for the Marxian discourse, Żółkiewski referred to the writings of Karl Popper to show the fallacy of relativism. Even though Popper had some sympathies with the left-wing ideologies (see Malachi Haim Hacohen, *Karl Popper, the Formative Years, 1902-1945* [Cambridge: Cambridge University Press, 2000]), his post-war writings had strong anti-communist and anti-Marxist character. Moreover, for Polish sociologists, Popper became a referent author in their struggle against Marxists (see Chapter 1). See Stefan Żółkiewski, "O Emilu Meyersonie," *Kuźnica*, no. 9 (1945): 6.
9 Generally speaking, this was the main point of Żółkiewski's apologia of Marxism (Żółkiewski, "O tak zwanej nieaktualności Marksizmu," 2–4).
10 Tadeusz Rutkowski, *Nauki historyczne w Polsce 1944–1970: Zagadnienia polityczne i organizacyjne* (Warszawa: Wydawnictwo Uniwersytetu Warszawskiego, 2007), 129–131.
11 Witold Kula, "Uwagi o historii gospodarczej," *Kuźnica*, no. 10 (1945): 4.
12 Ibid., 5.
13 Kula, "Uwagi o historii gospodarczej," 5.
14 See more about his remote (from Moscow) participation in the public debates of post-war Poland in Chapter 1.
15 Adam Schaff, "Humanizm socjalistyczny (II)," *Kuźnica*, no. 8 (1947): 3.
16 Adam Schaff, "Humanizm socjalistyczny (I)," *Kuźnica*, no. 7 (1947): 1–2.
17 Adam Schaff, "Humanizm socjalistyczny (II)," 3.
18 See Chapter 1.
19 See about the development of his discourse on the tradition of Polish sociology: Aleksei Lokhmatov, "Auf dem Weg zur 'Einheit': Józef Chałasiński und die Suche nach einer 'erlaubten' Genealogie der Soziologie im Nachkriegspolen (1945–1951)," *NTM Zeitschrift für Geschichte der Wissenschaften, Technik und Medizin* 4, no. 28 (2020): 524–528.

20 Józef Chałasiński, "Zasadnicze stanowiska we współczesnej socjologii Polskiej," *Przegląd Socjologiczny* 3, no. 1–4 (1946): 13.
21 Ibid.
22 In Chapter 1, I mentioned discussions on Mannheim's publications in the Polish sociological journal.
23 See Chapter 4.
24 Józef Chałasiński, "Problemy Demokracji," *Odrodzenie*, no. 14–15 (1947): 8.
25 Ibid., 9.
26 Józef Chałasiński, "Problemy Demokracji," 9.
27 Ibid., 9.
28 He referred to Masaryk's book: Tomáš Garrigue Masaryk, *Die wissenschaftliche und philosophische Krise innerhalb des gegenwärtigen Marxismus* (Wien: Die Zeit, 1898).
29 See about him: Timothy Snyder, *Nationalism, Marxism, and Modern Central Europe: A Biography of Kazimierz Kelles-Krauz* (Cambridge, MA: Harvard University Press, 1998).
30 Stanisław Ossowski, "Doktryna marksistowska na tle dzisiejszej epoki," *Myśl Współczesna*, no. 12 (1947): 501.
31 Ibid., 501–502.
32 About the influence of Morgan on Marx and Engels, see William H. Shaw, "Marx and Morgan," *History and Theory* 23, no. 2 (1984): 215–228; Erhard Lucas, "Die Rezeption Lewis H. Morgans durch Marx und Engels," *Saeculum* 15 (1964): 153–176.
33 See Anna Zaczkowska, "'Ten, który stał się Mostem:' Wpływ Lewisa H. Morgana na rosyjską antropologię," *Laboratorium Kultury*, no. 3 (2014): 139–156.
34 Ossowski, "Doktryna marksistowska na tle dzisiejszej epoki," 502.
35 Vladimir I. Lenin, *Polnoe sobranie sochinenij* (Moskva: Izdatel'stvo politicheskoj literatury, 1967), 42: 290.
36 Ossowski, "Doktryna marksistowska na tle dzisiejszej epoki," 503–504.
37 Later, Ossowski specified the elements of the Plekhanov's programme which had, in his view, a definitively outdated character. Stanisław Ossowski, "Teoretyczne zadania marksizmu. Szkic programu," *Myśl Współczesna*, no. 1 (1948): 4–11.
38 Ossowski, "Doktryna marksistowska na tle dzisiejszej epoki," 505–506.
39 Ossowski referred, among others, to the article: Jan Tański, "O marksistowskie podstawy w ocenach estetycznych," *Odrodzenie*, no. 43 (1945): 4, 5. Ossowski, "Doktryna marksistowska na tle dzisiejszej epoki," 508.
40 Stanisław Ossowski, "Doktryna marksistowska na tle dzisiejszej epoki," 510–513.
41 Ibid., 508.
42 Ossowski did not hesitate to emphasise that the post-war publications of Adam Schaff embodied, in his view, the tendencies that he criticised in Marxism. The post-war publications of Adam Schaff became, for Ossowski, an example of the ambition of Marxists to influence the post-war academic agenda in Poland. Besides articles published in the cultural press, there was Adam Schaff's book 'Introduction to the History of Marxism' that was published in 1948 and represented, in fact, an overview of the 'correct point of view on Marxism,' see Adam Schaff, *Wstęp do teorii marksizmu* (Warszawa: Książka, 1948). This book also became a key point in Ossowski's criticism.
43 After the war, he was a member of the Polish Socialist Party but not of the Polish Workers' Party. See more Maciej Gdula, "The Warsaw School of Marxism," *Stan Rzeczy*, no. 13 (2017): 197–225.
44 See more about Hochfeld and his biography: Mirosław Chałubiński, "Powroty do Juliana Hochfelda," *Studia Socjologiczno – Polityczne. Seria Nowa* 6, no. 1 (2017): 27–41.
45 Julian Hochfeld, "O znaczeniu marksizmu," *Myśl Współczesna*, no. 4 (1948): 72.

46 Ibid., 74.
47 Ibid., 81–87.
48 Ibid., 92.
49 One of the most influential works of Engels was directed against Eugen Dühring, German antisemitic thinker, see Friedrich Engels, *Herrn Eugen Dührings Umwälzung der Wissenschaft* (Leipzig: Genossenschaftsdruckerei, 1878).
50 Schaff was to know this point, since this argument was used by Zhdanov during the campaign against Soviet philosopher Grigori Alexandrov, see Chapter 6.
51 Among other fields that had not been developed by the classics of Marxism, Hochfeld referred to formal logic (Julian Hochfeld, "O znaczeniu marksizmu," 77.) that would be one of the subjects of cruel criticism during the wave of Stalinisation, see Chapter 6.
52 Julian Hochfeld, "O znaczeniu marksizmu," 78.
53 Ibid., 80.
54 Adam Schaff, "Marksizm a rozwój nauki," *Myśl Współczesna*, no. 6–7 (1948): 245.
55 Adam Schaff, "Marksizm a rozwój nauki," 246. For Schaff, Catholics were implacable enemies of Marxism and their references to Ossowski's ideas were a strong argument for Ossowski. The discussions between Catholics and Marxists will be thematised in this chapter.
56 Adam Schaff, "Marksizm a rozwój nauki," 247.
57 Schaff, "Marksizm a rozwój nauki," 246–254.
58 Ibid., 248.
59 Ibid., 247–253, 255.
60 Ibid., 259–260.
61 Schaff, "Marksizm a rozwój nauki," 254.
62 Ibid.
63 This is not only an intention which could be assumed from the works of Schaff. He followed this logic when explaining the 'misconceptions' of the prominent Polish Marxist Ludwik Krzywicki, see Schaff, "Marksizm a rozwój nauki," 254.
64 Schaff, "Marksizm a rozwój nauki," 263.
65 Ibid., 245–246.
66 See more in Chapter 1.
67 Bolesław Piasecki, *Kierunki 1945–1960* (Warszawa: Wydawnictwo PAX, 1981), 10.
68 See more about this group in Chapter 1.
69 Later, he became the historian of Piasecki's group. See his book: Andrzej Micewski, *Współrządzić czy nie kłamać? PAX i Znak w Polsce 1945–1976* (Paryż: Libella, 1978); it is noteworthy that 'historian' became later his pseudonym in the documents of the security services, when he started his collaboration with them: "'Historyk' na usługach SB," *Dziennik Polski*, August 14, 2006.
70 Andrzej Micewski, "Nowe aspekty problematyki młodzieowej," *Słowo Powszechne*, February 7, 1948.
71 Jerzy Braun, "Marksizm – nauka – objawienie," *Tygodnik Warszawski*, no. 30 (1947): 1–2. In his article, Braun also referred to the publication of Józef Chałasiński with his anti-Marxist programme and claimed that Marxism was an immoral and anti-humanist ideology, see Jerzy Braun, "Marksizm a społeczenstwo przyszłości," *Tygodnik Warszawski*, no. 19 (1947): 7.
72 Braun, "Marksizm a społeczenstwo przyszłości," 7.
73 Of course, the issue of the relations between Marxism and Catholicism was present in the interwar discourse of Catholics (primarily affiliated with the French milieu, see Piotr H. Kosicki, *Catholics on the Barricades. Poland, France, and "Revolution", 1891–1956* [New Haven/London: Yale University Press, 2018], 46–59). Nevertheless, the balance of forces in Poland was then different.
74 See Chapter 1.

75 Piwowarczyk had been one of the key figures of the underground teaching at the Kraków Spiritual Academy and one of the leading theologians of the time.
76 Piwowarczyk remarked that Marx's programme denied critical nihilism and thus became a reason for his conflict with the anarchist Mikhail Bakunin. Ks. Jan Piwowarczyk, "Filozofia marksizmu," *Tygodnik Powszechny*, no. 31 (1945): 1.
77 Regarding the religious nature of Marxism, which also was an important point for Piwowarczyk, he referred, among others, to the books that characterise his approach to Marxism: Antonin-Dalmace Sertillanges, *Socialisme et Christianisme* (Paris: Librairie Victor Lecoffre, 1905); Jacques Maritain, *Humanisme intégral* (Paris: Fernand Aubier, 1936); Paul Piechowski, *Proletarischer Glaube in sozialistischen und kommunistischen Selbstzeugnissen* (Berlin: Furche Verlag, 1928).
78 Piwowarczyk, "Teologia marksizmu," *Tygodnik Powszechny*, no. 32 (1945): 2.
79 It is noteworthy that Piwowarczyk referred to the French language editions of Lenin's works.
80 Piwowarczyk, "Teologia marksizmu," 2.
81 Ks. Jan Piwowarczyk, "Etyka marksizmu," *Tygodnik Powszechny*, no. 34 (1945): 2.
82 Adam Schaff, "Ks. Piwowarczykowi w odpowiedzi (I)," *Kuźnica*, no. 15 (1945): 3.
83 See Chapter 1.
84 Jacek Leociak, *Młyny Boże. Zapiski o Kościele i Zagładzie* (Wołowiec: Czarne, 2018), 59–63.
85 It is difficult to say if Schaff really thought that finding an analogy for the inquisition in the history of Marxism would constitute a problem, or if he just was convinced of the sacrality of the image of the Soviet Union and the national perspective on Marxism among Catholics.
86 Adam Schaff, "Ks. Piwowarczykowi w odpowiedzi (I)," 3.
87 Ibid., 4.
88 This concept was very important for Schaff and the process of Stalinisation would show that the family of idealism became much bigger than it was for him in the early post-war years, see Chapter 6.
89 Adam Schaff, "Ks. Piwowarczykowi w odpowiedzi (II)," *Kuźnica*, no. 16 (1945): 4.
90 Kazimierz Wyka, "Socjalizm, komunizm i katolicyzm," *Odrodzenie*, no. 27 (1946): 9.
91 Ibid.
92 Wojciech Kętrzyński, "Na marginesie krakowskich dyskusji," *Dziś i Jutro*, no. 29 (1946): 3.
93 Ibid., 3.
94 Kętrzyński, "Na marginesie krakowskich dyskusji," 3.
95 See more about the checking the limits of the permissible in post-war Poland in the previous chapters.
96 [agr.], "Likwidacja idealizmu?," *Tygodnik Warszawski*, no. 6 (1948): 4.
97 Przemysław Pazik, *Spory i wybory ideowe katolików świeckich w okresie narodzin komunistycznego systemu władzy w Polsce (1945-1948)* (PhD thesis, University of Warsaw, 2019), 177. See more in the book: Przemysław Pazik, *Spory i wybory ideowe katolików w Polsce 1942-1948* (Warszawa: Neriton, 2022).
98 Marian Jedlicz, "Kompleks walki z 'mieszczaństwem'," *Tygodnik Warszawski*, no. 25 (1946): 2.
99 Ibid., 3. See other articles with criticism against the concept of humanism: Jerzy Kubin, "Dlaczego nie jestem humanosocjalistą," *Tygodnik Warszawski*, no. 11 (1947): 11; [H.K.], "Pogrobowiec wolterianizmu," *Tygodnik Warszawski*, no. 8 (1947): 5; Jan Gerard, "W poszukiwaniu pewności: Mit moralności społecznej," *Tygodnik Warszawski*, no. 26 (1946): 4.
100 Of course, the idea that Catholics could 'complete' the social-economic theory of Marxists with 'spiritual aspects' was one of the central issues in the post-war Catholic discourse. See more in Chapter 3 and in Aleksei Lokhmatov, "Pol'skaia katolicheskaia

intelligentsiia i ideologiia marksizma: Stanovlenie 'otnoshenii' (1945–1948)," *Clioscience: Problemy istorii i mezhdistsiplinarnogo sinteza*, no. 6 (2016): 186–193.
101 "Don Basilo," *Kuźnica*, no. 5 (1947): 5.
102 [dh], "Niestety znowu 'Kuźnica'," *Dziś i Jutro*, no. 7 (1947): 6.
103 Krzystof R. Gawor, "O Marksie i marksistach. Felieton marksistowski," *Dziś i Jutro*, no. 12 (1948): 5.

6 The 'Failed' Quest for Unity

In an interview several years after the downfall of the socialist regime in Poland, the Polish philosopher Bohdan Chwedeńczuk (1938–) told Adam Schaff, the organiser of Stalinisation in Poland: 'Let us talk about you, who was seen as a man of the authorities and thus one having wealth and privileges.' Adam Schaff replied to his former assistant Chwedeńczuk[1]: 'All this was just shit [but] not wealth, I had nothing. I had a lot of power instead.'[2] This was true; one of the main factors that determined the changes in the public sphere of Stalinisation was the reformation of both the balance of forces in the academic world and the organisation of public debates. The period of Stalinisation has usually been seen as the key point in 'introducing the Soviet (Stalinist) model' in post-war Poland. The (partial) imitation of the Soviet academic and political system, in conjunction with the radical changes in the discourse on the key issues of the public agenda, have been regarded as evidence that Poland was being made a part of the 'Soviet empire.'[3] Moreover, the form of 'public debates' that was promoted in Poland during Stalinisation is usually described as the destruction of all forms of discussion in the public sphere.[4]

These points are not unreasonable. Nevertheless, there are several reservations that could present a new perspective on the processes that happened in the public representation of cultural and academic life in Poland. First, the 'Soviet' or 'Stalinist' model is a problematic concept in itself. If institutional aspects of Stalinisation, such as the governmentalisation of both academia and the official discourse on science and scholarship as part of the 'industrialisation' project, were the clear signs of Soviet influence in post-war Poland, the area of academic practice was a more problematic issue. The phenomenon that is sometimes called a 'Stalinist science' was a very complex one.[5] Even Soviet scholars did not have direct 'instructions' on how they should think or what they should say in any given situation. The basic ideological guidelines were so general that, sometimes, the same scientific or scholarly approaches could be regarded during one period of Stalin's rule as the vanguard of Soviet science and as a reactionary and non-Marxist tendency several years later.[6]

The early post-war years brought significant changes in the cultural and academic life of the Soviet Union. The guiding spirit of late Stalinism 'to discipline' Soviet scholars and writers after their contact with 'Western culture' during the war resulted in several ideological campaigns against the leading Soviet writers

DOI: 10.4324/9781003428251-7

and scholars. These took place, primarily, between 1946 and 1951.[7] These campaigns aimed to emphasise that the position of the leading scholars and scientists did not always guarantee that their approach would not be accused of deviation from 'Marxian teaching,' and that the programme of their opponents would not become the new vanguard of Soviet science.[8] Most importantly, late Stalinism was accompanied by 'public discussions' that showed how Soviet academics should 'virtuously' behave in front of the official criticism of their approaches.[9]

During the Stalinist purges of the 1930s, the scholars who became the target of smear campaigns usually had little chance of avoiding arrest and, at best, imprisonment in a concentration camp.[10] On the contrary, after the war, Soviet academia was predominantly made up of scholars and scientists who had gone through the 'reforging' of the 1930s. This kind of 're-education' made most of them much more 'responsive' to the norms of 'virtuous behaviour' promoted by the Soviet authorities. Ideological campaigns against individual scholars and their public 'repentance' for 'mistakes,' which was called self-criticism (*samokritika*),[11] did not necessarily result in arrests, executions, or destroyed careers. More frequently, these campaigns were tests to determine whether the scholar in question adopted the virtue of 'modesty' and 'discipline,'[12] i.e. loyalty to the current political need of the communist leadership. Having adopted this virtue, Soviet academics could make 'the right decision' every time they faced public criticism or radical changes to the official line on 'correct views.'

Most importantly, since virtues implied a certain independence in conduct, the principles of late Stalinism provided a certain space for 'initiatives' from 'below.'[13] The foundations of 'virtuous behaviour' in Soviet academia include not only accepting the dominant idea of 'correct views' but also a constant search for 'reactionary elements' in the conduct of oneself and others. This also concerned the struggle for a 'correct Marxism' among Soviet scholars and scientists, who used the political request for a new wave of ideological campaigns (*prorabotki*) to fight their academic competitors.[14] Even though all Soviet academics were 'united' under the banner of Marxism–Leninism, which became the main 'brand' of Soviet academia, the struggle against 'distortions (*iskazhenia*)' and 'dogmatism (*nachetnichestvo*)' in Marxism shaped a space for competitions between various schools and approaches.[15] The declaration of methodological unity among Soviet scholars did not mean the absence of plurality in their academic practice. On the contrary, the methodological unity alongside the 'virtues politics' of the Soviet regime made the quest for 'true virtuousness' an instrument in the internal struggle among academics. It was possible to accuse opponents of not being 'virtuous' enough, which made their errors not only a mistake but also a quasi-moral misconduct. Thus, 'public' scholarly discussions regarding a certain methodological approach were an integral part of this 'moral court.'

Most Soviet scholars knew that 'public discussions' on scholarly issues (organised with permission from the authorities) were, in fact, not an exchange of arguments but a kind of 'disciplinary work.' This trait of Stalinist academia made most ideological campaigns against individual scholars a 'successful' undertaking, since 'the correct point of view' was supposed to 'win' in the end. In this regard, adhering to the virtue of loyalty to political need, whilst publicly denying 'individualism' and 'egoism,' was a clue to this 'success.' Since, from the perspective of Soviet Marxism, there was only one correct point of view on all scientific matters, for the representative of 'wrong views,' the 'good thing to do' was to go through the purging fire of 'self-criticism.'

In the newspaper 'Pravda' from June 1928, Stalin wrote:

> Self-criticism is a special method of the Bolshevik education (*vospitanie*) of the cadres of the party and the working class in the spirit of revolutionary development... we need not every kind of self-criticism. We need the self-criticism that rises the culturedness of the working class; that develops its fighting spirit; that strengthens its belief in the victory; that makes it stronger and helps it to became the true owner of the country.[16]

Besides the fact that 'self-criticism' was closely associated with the categories of discipline and education, it was a technique of 'self-couching' that was supposed to lead to a kind of proletarian *eudaemonia*,[17] which was the ultimate aim of the Ancient 'virtue engineering.' This was not possible without all scholars sharing the virtue of *concordia* (harmonic unity and full agreement with each other), which, since antiquity, had been considered a precondition of stability within a political regime.[18] The ability to 'recognise' publicly the rightness of critics who (with the permission of the party leadership) led ideological campaigns against individual Soviet scholars was the only form of 'virtuous behaviour' for those whose mistakes became the objects of public criticism. Of course, this does not mean that all Soviet scholars believed in the rightness of the 'dominant' views, even though it was officially required to be 'sincere' (but not opportunistic) in conducting 'self-criticism.'[19] Nevertheless, the Soviet authorities possessed instruments for creating the illusion of harmony and 'virtuousness' in Soviet academia.

The situation in Polish academia was much more troublesome. It entered the period of 'Stalinisation' from a completely different starting position. Since the reformation of the academic system in Poland was still to be conducted by scholars themselves, it was not easy to force them to share the virtues that made the Soviet 'public' scholarly discussions possible. The transition from the early post-war period to Stalinism was problematic, not least because the 'gentle revolution' was not designed for this aim and, in fact, promoted very different virtues that were difficult to apply to the realities of Stalinisation. Additionally, the Polish case became a good illustration of the limited impact that the radical reconstruction of institutions had on the 'knowledge production.' The fact that radical changes in academic practice were to happen within a very short period and, more importantly, in the absence of mass repressions as 'preparatory measures,' made the quest for the new virtues uneasy. There were few barriers to imitating the names of Soviet research institutions and filling the Polish public sphere with iconic Soviet figures. The problem was how to 're-educate' Polish scholars to be capable of making 'right decisions' in accordance with the new standards of 'virtuous behaviour.'

Soviet propaganda on academic issues was based on the postulate that the Soviet Union was the stronghold of the most progressive tendencies in contemporary thought. Obviously, this idea stood in contradiction to Polish scholarship.[20] To accept the supremacy of Soviet science and scholarship, Polish scholars were to become Soviet scholars. This did not seem like a realistic plan. Therefore, the Stalinisation of Poland was not, and could not be, Polish academia becoming a part of the Soviet academic landscape. The rise of the political pressure of the Soviet Union forced the Polish authorities to begin this process without clear guidelines or instructions. The only obvious task for the organisers of Stalinisation was to destroy the institutions created during the 'gentle revolution,' which provided a platform for the public scholarly debates and made the plurality of various approaches visible. This task seemed much more concrete and realistic. Thus, the early stages of Stalinisation were aimed at destruction rather than creation.

The Cold War context and the tightening of the regime

The escalation of the relationship between the Soviet Union and the other members of the Anti-Hitler-Coalition could not go unnoticed by the countries situated in the zones of influence of opposing camps. The return of militaristic rhetoric to the public discourse of official propaganda in Poland, which, in the early post-war years, was primarily orientated towards the idea of the 'peaceful reconstruction' of the country, was one of the most visible signs of the changes in the political realities. The propaganda of the Soviet Union and, later, that of the countries from the zone of Soviet influence changed to a more brutal criticism of 'the Western countries.'[21] The so-called Marshall plan, which was meant to organise financial assistance in the form of loans for the reconstruction of European countries, had already become a controversial issue by the time of its preparations in 1947. The idea that this plan was directed against the spread of Soviet influence in Europe irritated Stalin himself and spurred changes in Soviet politics towards the countries in the sphere of Soviet influence.[22]

One of the key political events that determined the path taken by the authorities in post-war Poland was the creation of the Information Bureau of the Communist and Workers' Parties (Cominform), as well as its first conference in the Polish town of Szklarska Poręba in September 1947. After the Communist International had been disbanded by Stalin in order to show that the Soviet Union did not threaten the European political regimes,[23] the Cominform became the new organisation that had to coordinate the activity of all the communist parties. The very creation of the Cominform was a political step that demonstrated a break with the politics of dialogue. Of course, this affected the 'limits of the acceptable' in the countries under Soviet domination. The conflict with the 'Western allies' led to the mobilisation of all the methods of struggle against the 'West' that the Soviet Union had at its disposal.

The key issues that were discussed in Szklarska Poręba concerned the discipline in the communist camp. Both Soviet representatives, Vyacheslav Molotov and Andrei Zhdanov, who moderated the meeting, spoke about the escalation of the situation in the world. Instead of an alliance with the Western countries, Soviet delegates returned to the representation of the current realities through the prism of the separation of the world into two opposing camps: the 'imperialistic' camp headed by the USA and the 'democratic one' headed by the Soviet Union.[24] In his speech, Zhdanov made clear that the main aim of disciplining the communist parties in other countries was the enforcement of the Soviet Union as 'the main bastion of democracy and socialism.'[25] Thus, the key point of Zhdanov's speech was to condemn 'special paths' to socialism, which he characterised as an 'underestimation of the achievements of the Soviet Union.'[26] According to Zhdanov, the 'intentional (*narochitoe*) emphasising of the independence from Moscow' (which was one of the principles of the early post-war project designed by Stalin) 'played into the enemies' hands' and had to be stopped.[27]

The idea of mobilisation in the 'camp' headed by the Soviet Union provided new opportunities for an increase in the role of the security services under the new conditions. The whole security system in post-war Poland had been constructed in close collaboration with the NKVD.[28] This direct link to the Soviet executive branch made the Polish security services, to some extent, independent even from Polish communist leaders, with whom Moscow still spoke in the language of 'brotherly recommendations.' Characteristically, the government funding for the Ministry of Public Security in Poland exceeded the budget for fields such as education, labour, and public health.[29] If the first steps of the Polish security services were focused on the struggle against the relics of the Home Army units, the development of their apparatus and the escalation of the international situation led to the expansion of the issues that were included in the competence of this institution. Primarily, the matter concerned the struggle against the 'internal enemies' whose 'number' increased proportionally with the tightening of the regime. Although the security services still did not directly regulate academic debates, the news about arrests and executions was a part of the information space in which the debates covered in this chapter took place.

Meanwhile, even the political establishment of Poland did not have a clear idea of what exactly was expected in Moscow, nor what the limits of the acceptable under the new conditions were. The leader of the Workers' Party, Władysław Gomułka, continued to emphasise the peculiarity of the 'Polish path' to socialism in his public discourse. He even proposed his mediation for the reconstruction of the relationship between the Soviet Union and Yugoslavia after the conflict between Stalin and the Yugoslavian dictator Josip Broz Tito (1892–1980).[30] However, Gomułka's programme became more and more problematic. The idea of the mobilisation of all communist forces under the supervision of the Soviet Union implied the necessity of emphasising loyalty to Moscow. The new realities were to change the whole image of 'public discussions,' which had to be organised by fundamentally different principles. Thus, the new status of the Soviet Union in the Polish public sphere became the central marker of the changes that were happening in the Polish public sphere.

Disciplining 'public discussions': All roads lead to the Soviet Union

The idea of mobilisation for the struggle against 'the capitalist camp' under the supervision of the Soviet Union made all other issues secondary. In general terms, the new approach to representing the Soviet Union had been formulated after the creation of the theoretical journal of the Workers' Party 'Nowe Drogi (The New Paths)' in 1947. Initially, this journal was only one of many other periodicals and had a very limited influence on the intellectual agenda beyond communist circles. Nevertheless, this journal played an important role in disciplining the discourse within the Workers' Party. This was the first step towards the spread of this discourse to the entire Polish public sphere. The image of the Soviet Union constructed in the pages of 'Nowe Drogi' was meant to replace the 'misconceptions' that dominated the public debates under the 'gentle revolution.'

Since the editor-in-chief of 'Nowe Drogi,' Franciszek Fiedler (1880–1956), was a historian, the readers of the first issue could make themselves familiar with a 'historical' approach to the 'failures' of the interwar Polish state in its politics towards the Soviet Union.[31] In fact, the entire modern history of Poland was represented by Fiedler as a history of unforgivable mistakes in its relationships with Soviet Russia. Fiedler argued that 'the destruction of the Soviet Union was [according to the reactionary regime of Józef Piłsudski] in the Polish "state's interest" in the 20th century.'[32] More importantly, according to Fiedler, the Polish–Soviet War (which started with the Soviet invasion of Polish territories) was nothing but an 'attempt to implement this plan [of the destruction of the Soviet Union].'[33] Developing this idea, Fiedler claimed that Piłsudski strove for the 'fascistisation of Europe' and, in fact, 'stood behind Hitlerism' and that his main conviction was that, 'just a Soviet Union and just a Red Army having officers of worker and peasant origin would not be able to handle Hitler's hordes led by Prussian Junkers.'[34] His main point was not a sophisticated one: there were two camps in the interwar period – the 'fascist' camp of aggression and the Soviet camp of peace. Since Poland under Piłsudski was opposed to the Soviet Union, 'logically,' it was in the camp of 'fascism.'

Remarkably, Fiedler could find simple solutions for the most problematic issues. So, for example, the main opponent of Piłsudski, Roman Dmowski, was the leader of the Polish nationalist movement, but, at the same time, his activity became a symbol of 'pro-Russian' orientation in Polish foreign policy.[35] On the one hand, Dmowski's National Democracy was a forbidden ideology in post-war Poland. On the other, his idea of friendship with Russia in the struggle against the German threat made him a kind of 'prophet' for the post-war realities. Fiedler resolved the problem in an 'elegant' way and wrote:

> In one of his works published after 1918,[36] Roman Dmowski, reviewing his politics towards Russia in the inter-war and war period (1914 – 1918), characterised them as absolutely correct, [nevertheless, he] recognised only one mistake: he could not foresee the victory of the Russian revolution in 1917.[37]

Thus, it was not Dmowski's nationalist views but his 'disbelief' in the victory of the Russian revolution that made him a reactionary thinker. Thus, transgressions against the Soviet Union became the main criterion for the demarcation between 'progressive' and 'reactionary' ideas. It was not anti-socialist or anti-Marxist views but the wrong idea of the Soviet Union that was the most dangerous misconception.

Of course, it is difficult to imagine that anybody in Poland could be convinced by Fiedler's arguments. Obviously, the depiction of the Polish–Soviet War as a campaign organised by the 'reactionaries' who aimed to destroy the Soviet Union could not work as a propagandistic strategy intended to win the sympathies of the Polish audience. On the contrary, the narrative of Fiedler did not refer to the traditional Polish stereotypes nor to any issues that would seem more attractive for the Polish reader. Moreover, Fiedler did not avoid the themes that could potentially cause significant problems with promoting Polish–Soviet friendship. For example, the inclusion of the eastern regions of the former Polish republic into the Soviet Union after the beginning of World War II was discussed as follows:

> Only the Polish democracy, only the working class, which, in alliance with the peasantry, made great changes of historical importance in the life of the people... only they could [make] and had the courage to make a historic turn in relationships with the great Eastern neighbour. Because it was necessary to have courage in order to defend the right of the Ukrainian and Belarusian republics to possess their land against [the attitude of Polish] public opinion.[38]

If one read these sentences as an election programme, one would have an impression that the key electorate was situated outside of Poland. This reorientation of the propaganda, for which Moscow was becoming a more important reader than the Polish audience, was a typical feature that spread to many other segments of the public sphere during the process of Stalinisation. The Soviet Union became not a topic for reflections but a 'monument,' and the description of this 'monument' had to follow a very strict genre. The key element of this genre was the glorification of the self-image of the Soviet Union.[39]

After the clear message delivered by Zhdanov and Molotov in Szklarska Poręba in September 1947, the usage of the Soviet Union became an issue of much higher political importance. The anniversary of the October Revolution in November 1947[40] became an occasion for collective admirations of the Soviet Union under the new political conditions. In a characteristic way, the journal 'Nowe Drogi' demonstrated its ability to deal with the image of the Soviet Union 'independently.' Since the editorial board of the Workers' Party journal had much more experience with Soviet propaganda realities than other participants in the public debates, they were able to depict the 'correct image' of the Soviet Union. The publications prepared by Polish communists for the anniversary issue characterised the Soviet Union as the 'bastion and guide of progress'[41] that embodied the 'most humanist' and 'most progressive ideas.'[42] The quotations from the works of Marx, Engels, Lenin, and, more abundantly, Stalin decorated all the publications and did not contain any adaptation to the peculiarities of the Polish context.

The article written by Jerzy Borejsza was, to some extent, an exception, which only emphasised the difference between his idea of public debate and the new realities. In his article devoted to the October Revolution, Borejsza still strove to emphasise the 'real independence' of Poland as a key issue in the Polish–Soviet relationship.[43] Of course, the words of Lenin and Stalin played a role in Borejsza's discourse, but the main point of his argument was that the October Revolution liberated Poland from the dominance of other states. Borejsza represented the key conflict of the early 20th century between Józef Piłsudski and Roman Dmowski as a competition between two concepts of a fictive freedom. Unlike Fiedler, Borejsza was not satisfied with mentioning a 'misbelief in the victory of the Russian Revolution' and argued that Dmowski's failure was that he did not believe that Poland could be 'truly independent.' According to Borejsza, Dmowski asked reactionary czarism to protect Poland against Germany, which put him in the same boat as Piłsudki, who chose the opposite strategy and did not believe that a 'true freedom' was possible.[44] In either case, Borejsza still attempted to use the image of the Soviet Union to protect the ideas that made the 'gentle revolution' project possible.[45] The disordered combination of the lofty glorification of the Soviet Union with the ideas of Polish 'independence' in the publication of Jerzy Borejsza was a sign of the confusion concerning the possible promotion of his programme under the new conditions.

Borejsza's 'press empire' also had to become much more careful in dealing with Soviet and Russian culture. It was a logical strategy to give the floor to Russian (Soviet) scholars themselves. The 'dam' that Borejsza had built to make Polish scholars the creators of the image of the Soviet Union was breached. There was no longer a need to refer to the French intellectuals for comments both on Russian culture and the heritage of revolutionary thinkers. In the pages of the state-run cultural press, Vladimir Lenin introduced Leo Tolstoy,[46] while Maxim Gorky (1868–1936) explained to the Polish audience the role of Vladimir Lenin in Russian and world culture.[47] Along with the icons of Communist Russia such as Lenin and Gorky, less official Soviet philologists like Yury Tynyanov explained to the Polish reader the issues related to Russian literature.[48] So, at this stage, it was not the official status of any one Soviet author but the idea to make 'Russians' present Russian culture that was crucial for the moderators of the Polish cultural press. This seemed to be a safer strategy under the extremely changeable political conditions.

This tendency became more and more visible. The list of authors whose names appeared on the pages of the cultural journals stopped having any significant differences with the school programme for literature in the Soviet Union. In line with the 'classics' from the 19th century, the works of the officially recognised poets and writers of late Stalinism made the Polish reader familiar with Russian and sometimes even world literature and culture.[49] Thus, the supervision of the Polish cultural agenda passed from the hands of the French to the Soviets. The 'cultural ambassador' of the Soviet Union, Ilja Erenburg (whose name did not appear earlier in the state-run press), became one of the key figures who formulated and defined the directions of the cultural development under the new conditions of the Cold War.[50] The acceptance of most of the materials proposed by the Sovinformburo, which the editors of Polish state-run press[51] used as a tool for meeting Soviet expectations, showed that the project of 'gentle revolution' was about to meet defeat.

The Wrocław Congress and the defeat of the 'gentle revolution'

The 'World Congress of Intellectuals in Defence of Peace,' which took place in August of 1948, became one of the key events in the early post-war history of Poland. In front of an international audience, Jerzy Borejsza still wanted to present his achievements in creating the new intellectual profile of the post-war Polish state. The international convention of intellectuals, which was formally initiated by the Cominform and aimed at the mobilisation of pro-communist forces, became, on Borejsza's initiative, an attempt to promote the pluralistic vision of leftist culture at the international level. Against the backdrop of the tendencies that threatened his entire project, Borejsza still attempted to publicly promote a non-violent version of socialism. The list of the delegates invited to participate in the Congress was diverse and included the representatives of very different directions within left-wing ideology.[52] Support for the Soviet Union was not a criterion for the selection of delegates to the Congress, which was intended to unite the intellectuals from the entire world under the banner of the fight for peace.

By 1948, congresses in 'Defence of Peace' had already their history. Milan (1907), London (1909), Basel (1912), Amsterdam (1932), Paris (1935), and Brussel (1936) became the 'capitals' of the pacifist movement. Albert Einstein, Maxim Gorky, Heinrich Mann, and Romain Rolland were among the key figures in these congresses and became the faces of the struggle against 'imperialism,' as well as the wars provoked by the bearers of 'imperialist ideologies.' The fact that the next Congress took place in Wrocław (formerly Breslau), which belonged to the so-called Recovered Territories of the Polish Republic, played a key role in the representation of the regime established in Poland after the war. Polish Wrocław was to become an antipode to German Breslau through the opposition between the new peaceful 'socialist ideology' and 'militaristic fascism.' Borejsza, as one of the organisers of the convention, which was informally called 'Borejsza's Congress,'[53] strove to convince his guests from the entire world that Poland had the internal resources to become not only a new capital of the pacifist movement but also an example of a peaceful and non-violent form of political organisation. Generally, it was not the representatives of the Soviet Union but the members of the Western delegations that were still the target audience of the Wrocław Congress.

The core of the organising committee consisted of French and Polish fellows who still attempted to promote the vision of the leftist culture that became the guiding spirit of the 'gentle revolution.' Additionally, the Congress committee was going to invite many delegates from the Anglo-Saxon countries, many of whom did not sympathise with the Soviet Union and its form of socialism. The new political situation of 1948 made most of Borejsza's ideas very problematic. The official proposal of the Congress was 'to defend European culture against American imperialism,' which made it a political action directed against the USA. Moreover, even during the preparatory meetings, it was required to add statements regarding the leading role of the Soviet Union and 'Slavic countries' in this process, which caused difficulties in recruiting the delegates from Western countries.[54] However, Borejsza's group still tried to keep some autonomy from the Soviet official discourse and, for safety reasons, it was decided 'not to make [this congress an event] of too official character'[55] in order to reduce the intersection of 'Soviet comrades.'

Nevertheless, this 'informal' Congress became one of the biggest international meetings of intellectuals in the post-war history. Borejsza was able to attract to Wrocław people of very different political and philosophical backgrounds: the prominent French writer Julien Benda, who was famous for his criticism against the European intellectuals as 'betrayers of democracy'[56]; Georg Lukács, one of the most prominent Hungarian left-wing philosophers and the theorist of literature[57]; Ruth Benedict, one of the key figures in social anthropology, and the Catholic philosopher and priest Jean Boulier, who represented French 'progressive Catholics.' These were all among Borejsza's guests in Wrocław and could deliver their speeches on the necessity of defending peace in the world and condemn the militaristic tendencies in the politics of the USA. Moreover, Albert Einstein passed his greetings on to the delegates of the Congress and complained about the fact that the American authorities did not allow him to come to Wrocław because of his access to state secrets.[58]

The Polish delegation of the Congress also represented the plurality of the intellectual landscape of post-war Poland. Tadeusz Kotarbiński, Józef Chałasiński, and Stanisław Ossowski, together with Marxists from the 'Kuźnica' group,[59] were among the Polish delegates at the Congress. In his speech delivered to the international audience, Chałasiński claimed:

> The division of Europe into two worlds: one for socialism and another one against it, is a nonsense and contradicts the idea of European culture; dividing Europe into two hostile camps which will be turned against each other represents a deadly danger, and [could lead to] the complete destruction of European culture.[60]

Thus, in his public speech, Chałasiński (obviously unintentionally) characterised the new programme of the socialist block proclaimed by Zhdanov and Molotov in Szklarska Poręba several months ago as a 'nonsense.' His idea of the new realities was still not influenced by the changes that were about to happen in the public sphere of post-war Poland. In the summer of 1948, Chałasiński described the intellectual agenda of scholars in their struggle against militarism through the prism of competition between 'progressive' and 'reactionary' views that did not have any geographical implications.

Nevertheless, the clash between the new realities of the Cold War and the programme of 'gentle revolution' could not be delayed. The participation of a Soviet delegation in the Congress could not go without consequences for the agenda of the Congress. Soviet scholars and writers who had already experienced the new wave of 'disciplining' in the Soviet Union could not support the pluralistic vision of 'progressive thought' represented in the Congress. Unlike Chałasiński, they knew very well the 'Soviet point of view' on this issue: the world is divided into two opposite camps and the leader of the socialist camp is the Soviet Union. So, it is not surprising that the speech of a Soviet delegate provoked a scandal that escalated during the Congress. The General Secretary of the Union of Soviet Writers, Alexander Fadeyev (1901–1956), delivered his speech in a style that was quite typical in the Soviet Union. Criticising 'Western culture,' Fadeyev claimed:

> Reactionary writers, screenwriters, philosophers, and artists will do everything to serve their masters [imperialists and capitalists]. They put murderers and drug addicts, sadists, pimps, provocateurs and degenerates, spies and bandits on a pedestal... If jackals could learn to type, and hyenas could handle a fountain pen, they would probably create something similar to the books of such Millers, Eliots, Malrauxs, and other Sartres.[61]

The list of names mentioned in this speech shows that all the members of the international delegations could see a reason to be hurt by Fadeyev's words. Of course, Sartre, with his authority among left-wing intellectuals, took a special position in this line. Both the content and the form of the speech delivered by the Soviet delegate contrasted his attitude with the general ideology of the Congress.

One can learn about the reaction that Fadeyev's speech provoked among the audience from the book of the French writer and journalist Dominique Desanti, who participated in the Congress as a member of the French delegation. According to Desanti, French delegates reacted ironically to the general theses of Fadeyev's speech, saying 'These Soviets! Their dogmatism!' Nevertheless, after Fadeyev had mentioned Sartre, the situation escalated. According to Desanti, Borejsza emotionally said then: 'they have spoiled my congress,' while Pablo Picasso, who also was among the guests of the Congress, threw away his headphones with a similar interpretation. Moreover, the leading members of the French delegation and some other delegates decided to leave the Congress.[62] It was a great task for Borejsza to resolve this conflict. Even though his diplomatic skills helped to soften the situation, this incident was evidence that the project of 'gentle revolution' was about to become a fiasco. The fact that Soviet delegates refused to make corrections to their speeches for the preparation of a common declaration of the Congress[63] was a sign that the programme proclaimed in Szklarska Poręba was a mandate rather than a recommendation.

Reshaping the public life

The increasing role of the security services in the new realities made them active participants in reforming the public image of the post-war Polish state. The first and most obvious 'enemy' in the intellectual landscape of the early post-war years was the Warsaw Catholic group of Zygmunt Kaczyński. Kaczyński's public activity and his attempts to gather Christian scholars and politicians from the Labour Party, which had been destroyed by the security services, were regarded as a threat to the regime. In July 1948, the economist Kazimierz Studentowicz was arrested when trying to leave Poland. After his interrogation, the security services decided to arrest the whole group. The leader of the Warsaw Catholic collective, Zygmunt Kaczyński, was sentenced to ten years in prison[64] but, several years later, died (he was possibly killed by the security services) in jail.[65] The fact that the Warsaw group became the main target of the security services, while the Kraków group and Piasecki's collective continued their existence, showed that the key concern for the security services was the threat of potential political influence beyond the 'Catholic ghetto.'

The Kraków group continued their line on avoiding political issues in their public discourse and further reduced their activity in the political field in comparison to the early post-war period. Piasecki's fellows, on the contrary, made support for all the political and social initiatives of the authorities the key point of their public activity.[66] Piasecki, who closely collaborated with the security services, got an opportunity to make his organisation 'PAX' and 'secular Catholics' a tool of the authorities in their struggle against the official Church hierarchy after 1948. During the period of Stalinisation, it became the aim of the authorities to rapidly reduce any influence of Catholics beyond the 'Catholic ghetto.' The security services felt strong enough to attack the Church with a new energy. Even those Catholics (like Piasecki's group) who chose collaboration with the authorities ceased to be opponents in discussions and became an instrument of control over society.[67]

The situation was becoming unpleasant, not only for Catholics but also for most of the active opponents of Soviet influence in science. The leader of the sociological group, Józef Chałasiński, whose blow against Marxism in 1947 provoked an irritated response from Marxists,[68] was also to read the writing on the wall. The changes in his post-war political agenda threatened both his discipline and him personally. The anniversary of the journal 'Przegląd Socjologiczny' was a good occasion for Chałasiński to represent the achievements of his discipline in accordance with the new political realities. In an anniversary issue that was published in early 1949, Chałasiński presented sociology not as an opponent but as an ally of Marxism in the 'progressive camp.' Protecting the heritage of his teacher Florian Znaniecki, Chałasiński assured the reader that the ideological attitude of sociologists from his milieu 'did not correspond with the ideology of both "endecja's" intellectual circles [endecja – from ND – National Democratic Party; Polish nationalist movement] and "Sanational" fascists [from the regime of Sanation of Józef Piłsudski].'[69] Meanwhile, Chałasiński conducted a certain criticism of the American professor Znaniecki, whose name disappeared from the list of the editors of the journal. Zaniecki's group were characterised as 'Polish Europeans' with 'foreign education' who were 'the liberals of Franco-Anglo-Saxon type (*liberałowie francusko-anglosaskiego pokroju*)' without an active participation in social movements.[70] This 'gentle' criticism against the interwar attitude of sociologists was obviously meant to save space for the development of sociology under the new conditions.[71]

Nevertheless, 'gentle criticism' was not the style of the realities that Polish scholars faced during the period of Stalinisation. The fate of sociology as a discipline and of the sociological journal was an illustration for that. The last anecdote that concluded the celebration of the restart of sociology in post-war Poland was devoted to a conversation that took place between Chałasiński and famous Polish sociologist Stefan Czarnowski in 1934. During one of the discussions on the fate of 'Przegląd Socjologiczny,' Czarnowski said sceptically: 'the publication of a sociological journal cannot be successful in Poland if it failed in France, where *L'année sociologique* ceased to be published.'[72] From the perspective of 1948,[73] Chałasiński responded to his opponent: 'Nevertheless, it was possible. We are celebrating now the anniversary of the faith in Polish opportunities and Polish forces.'[74] In a sadly ironic way, it was the last issue of 'Przegląd Socjologiczny' that was published before its closure by the organisers of Stalinisation in Poland. The gentle methods of reorganising the intellectual image of post-war Poland were left behind.

The changes in the geopolitical agenda provoked an intense struggle between different groups within the Workers' Party. The attitude of Władysław Gomułka under the new political conditions gave his opponents within the party the opportunity to accuse him of 'nationalist bias.' Gomułka's attempt to keep the status quo of the early post-war period, especially regarding the emphasis on independence from the Soviet Union, did not meet the requirements of the post-Szklarska Poręba reality. Soviet representatives in Poland, who did not like the post-war Polish 'privileges' from the early post-war years, took the opportunity to intensify their criticism of the 'nationalist' attitude of 'Polish comrades.' Soviet ambassador Viktor Lebedev reported to Moscow on 'the shamefaced attitude (*stydlivaja linija*) [of Gomułka's men] towards the propaganda of the rapprochement with the Soviet Union.'[75] Since Gomułka did not change his line and continued to speak publicly about the 'Polish path to socialism' and the 'independence of Poland,' his political opponents informed the Soviet ambassador that the Politburo did not share his 'nationalist' attitude.[76] Finally, the anti-Gomułka party won the competition and (obviously, after an informal 'permission' from Moscow) dismissed Gomułka from his position; later, he was arrested.[77] Thus, Bolesław Bierut, who was one of the most loyal friends of the Soviet Union, was appointed as the new head of the party and held both the governmental and party leadership.[78]

The changes in the party leadership had personal consequences for the constructors of the early post-war realities. The key organisers of 'gentle revolution' were the first to learn the new forms of 'virtuous behaviour' – the public repentance for 'misconceptions.' The Workers' Party[79] started the 'disciplining' project among their own members. The chief designer of 'gentle revolution' Jerzy Borejsza and the leader of the 'Kuźnica' group Stefan Żółkiewski were to go through the procedure of 'self-criticism' in front of their comrades from the party. Borejsza excused himself for 'liberalism in relation to the snobbish intelligentsia and that he allowed pseudo-Marxist voices in the press,'[80] while Żółkiewski recognised the 'erroneous tendency' of 'Kuźnica' in 'the overestimation of Western inventions and the underestimation of the achievements of the Soviet Union.'[81] This path of 'repentance' was meant to become universal for the participants in the public debates since they all were, in one way or another, guilty of the 'underestimation of the achievements of the Soviet Union.'

One year later, both official journals of the 'gentle revolution' – 'Odrodzenie' and 'Kuźnica' – were closed and, in their place, the new journal 'Nowa Kultura (The New Culture)' emerged. This journal was designed to unite cultural and literary discourse in Poland. The title 'Nowa Kultura' referred to the tradition of the interwar communist magazine[82] and this new continuity intended to show a less 'shamefaced' attitude of the authorities towards communist ideology. Jerzy Borejsza was deposed from the throne of the 'Pope of the Press' and soon was dismissed from all significant party posts.[83] This meant the cardinal change in the organisation of the system of the official press.

The reformation of the censorship system made the continuation of all discussions that had formed the intellectual profile of the early post-war period impossible. The end of 1949 became a turning point in this regard. In his public speeches, Bolesław Bierut proclaimed an uncompromising struggle against those who 'are licking the boots of their American bosses.'[84] The vice-director of the Department of the Press and Publishing Houses, Ferdynand Chaber, spoke to the members of the censorship apparatus that had to destroy the legacy of 'gentle revolution': 'We are in the stage of the escalation of the class struggle. The enemy is attacking us more and more fiercely and insidiously… the enemy is shouting that he [belongs to the] left-wing [camp] … You are the apparatus that should expose the enemy.'[85] This approach to control over the public expression of ideas finished the project initiated by Jerzy Borejsza. Under the new conditions, the enemies were to be found among those who 'disguised' themselves as friends.

An unfortunate quest for '*concordia*'

The format of the scientific Congress became one of the most characteristic features of Stalinisation. The idea of public activity of scholars under the banner of 'progressive ideology' as part of a political struggle implied that *concordia* regarding both political and scholarly issues became the aim of all scientific events. The loyalty to the current political need, and thus Marxism–Leninism as an embodiment of the interest of the 'working masses,' became the central virtue that was to be rapidly adopted by Polish scholars under the new conditions. Polish writers,[86] philologists,[87] historians,[88] and other scholars[89] organised their own congresses at which they were expected to proclaim unity regarding the 'progressive methodological principles' of their disciplines. The preparations for the creation of the Polish Academy of Sciences, which was to organise Polish science and scholarship from above, became a part of the institutional project of Stalinisation.

Logically, Stalinisation began within professional groups. It appeared to be simpler to reach the desired '*concordia*' through the 'critical discussions' among representatives of the same discipline. Remarkably, this logic significantly influenced the interactions between the representatives of various disciplines. Along with the destruction of the institution of public debates, this led to a deeper fragmentation of knowledge even though the methodological unity of all sciences was a significant point in the Marxist propaganda.[90] The disciplinary principle in the creation of the centralised scientific institutions resulted in the fact that Stalinisation became a task of professional corporations.

Nevertheless, rapid institutional changes did not mean that people changed together with institutions, nor in accordance with the aims that had been formulated by the political leadership. The limited number of scholars who were deeply experienced in Soviet realities, coupled with significant contradictions in the general ideas of 'Stalinisation,' made this process very problematic. There were two basic contradictions that made the 'quest' for methodological unity an irresolvable puzzle. Firstly, the new realities required from scholars both 'synthesis' with the national (Polish) 'progressive' intellectual tradition and also the recognition of the dominance of the Soviet Union, with Marxism–Leninism as the 'only scientific approach.' Considering anti-Soviet and anti-Marxist (at least in its Soviet version) tendencies in Polish academia, it was not easy to find a solution for this contradiction. Secondly, a 'progressive universal methodological programme' was to be found by the Polish scholars themselves who (unlike their Soviet colleagues) did not have special 'training' in the 'correct' form of public discussion and did not know a lot about the necessity of achieving *concordia* at the end of every discussion.

The First Congress of Polish Science (1951) became the main international event that was supposed to demonstrate the achievements of 'Stalinisation.' Chopin's 'heroic (heroiczny)' Polonaise *As-dur* accompanied the documentary chronicle that reported on the opening of this Congress in the summer of 1951. Against the backdrop of the Polish capital, still bearing signs of the devastation of the war, Warsaw Polytechnic (the headquarters of the Congress) was represented by Polish filmmakers as a centre of enlightenment and progress in the recovering Polish state.[91] The profiles of Nicolaus Copernicus and Maria Skłodowska-Curie were chosen to embody the scientific achievements of the Polish nation and celebrate the Congress on postal stamps. The Polish Prime Minister, Józef Cyrankiewicz, welcomed the academic audience of the Congress by saying, 'Continuing the wonderful traditions of its glorified predecessors, serving the nation and Poland and through it progress and humanity, Polish science will be a creator of the greatness of its nation.'[92]

Thus, the Congress was expected to bring to its natural conclusion the idea that science should be governmentally reorientated to the service of the nation. Against the backdrop of the escalation of the political situation, the 'unity' of the scholars became a political issue. Nevertheless, the achievement of this aim, even under the strong political pressure, would be possible only in the case of a radical change in the forms of 'good scientific practice.' To the disappointment of the political leadership, the Section for the Social Sciences and Humanities of the Congress failed, in fact, to fulfil its main mission – to claim unity regarding methodological issues. Against the backdrop of overall unity depicted in sublime reports from the Congress, it seems striking that the official report of this Section praised Marxism–Leninism but still recognised the absence of compromise in methodological and theoretical approaches to understanding their research fields.[93]

Such an 'unpleasant' result, which was recognised in the face of international delegations, was rooted in the preparation process that had been started several years before the solemn ceremony in 1951.[94] The constellation of participants in the preparatory meetings of the Congress demonstrated the aim of the organisers not to 'purge' Polish academia from all non-loyal people but to force the established Polish scholars to work differently. In general terms, the core of the Section for the Social Sciences and Humanities contained the figures who shaped the intellectual agenda during the early post-war years. Not Marxists but the leading members of Polish academia took the key positions in the event committee that was meant to reform Polish scholarly practice.

So, for example, one of the main critics of Marxism in the early post-war period, Józef Chałasiński, became the chief of the section and played a leading role in the executive committee. However, unlike many of his colleagues, Chałasiński significantly changed his attitude under the influence of the fluid political situation. By this time, Chałasiński had already acquired a new status. He replaced Tadeusz Kotarbiński in the position of the rector of the University of Łódź and showed an extraordinary 'flexibility' in his views. Chałasiński, who, during the early post-war period, had become one of the key theorists of 'public opinion' as a necessary precondition of the anti-authoritarian form of democratisation and considered the Marxian programme to be an anti-humanist ideology due to its concept of 'class struggle,' wrote in the Kraków popular science journal 'Życie Nauki (The Life of Science)':

> The pursuit of truth and the use of freedom, in fact, was never undirected, but was always associated with a positive program defined by the direction of the interests of the epoch <...> the University not only stands on the field of class struggle, it also participates in it.[95]

Thus, Chałasiński reorientated his whole programme to promote the idea of the 'conditionality' of any freedom and ideology of class struggle. These points, which had been the key targets of his criticism several years before,[96] made him a 'model student' from the perspective of the organisers of Stalinisation.

Nevertheless, such 'flexibility' was not a precondition for taking key positions in the event committee of the Congress. For example, the prominent philosopher–logician Kazimierz Ajdukiewicz,[97] who could hardly be characterised as a sympathiser of Marxism–Leninism, became the chair in the Subsection for Philosophy and the Social Sciences. It is not surprising that this section became the main source of problems for the organisers of the Congress. In general terms, these problems were determined by the very formulation of the task that the scholars had to fulfil. The political leadership wanted them to synthesise a 'progressive tradition' in the history of philosophy and the social sciences in Poland, which would result in Marxism–Leninism. Moreover, the scholars were asked to come to Marxism–Leninism themselves through an 'open discussion.'

Among those who were invited to the Congress, there were scholars of very different professional and political backgrounds. Some of them had been already

The 'Failed' Quest for Unity 157

suspended from teaching for their 'idealist' views.[98] Nevertheless, it was not an obstacle for inviting them to fulfil the mission of the Congress. The idea that stood behind this event was to 're-educate' Polish academics. It was not a formal declaration of loyalty (which could be organised without real participation of scholars), but the adoption of new forms of 'good academic practice' that was the main point in the agenda of the political leadership.

The statements of Kazimierz Ajdukiewicz regarding the principles that he considered central for any discussion showed that the fulfilment of the task of the Congress, from the beginning, was highly problematic. Among other things, Ajdukiewicz said:

> It was decided not to force the speakers [of the subsection], who are primarily not Marxists, to conduct their criticism [of Polish intellectual tradition] from the Marxist position, but [to allow them] to conduct criticism [against this or that tendency in Polish academia] from their own point of view.[99]

From this starting point, the path towards methodological unity under the banner of Marxism–Leninism did not seem to be the shortest one. The main idea that only the correct (Marxist) had to win at the end did not fit in the paradigm presented by Ajdukiewicz.

Responding to this statement, the Marxist sociologist Julian Hochfeld, who still attempted to promote his version of 'open' Marxism, asserted that he did not understand the division between speaking 'from the Marxist point of view' and 'from his own.' Hochfeld argued:

> If someone is not convinced of the justice of this [Marxist] view of the world, it is his right, and even his duty not to support the positions of Marxism and to prove clearly that he [the opponent of Marxism] is right.[100]

This attitude seemed logical from the perspective of Hochfeld's idea of Marxism as just an embodiment of science.[101] He still believed that the task of the scholars was just to organise an open discussion that would lead to the 'correct' decision on all questions regarding the 'progressive tradition' in the Polish thought. For him, the Congress was an opportunity to unify all sciences since it 'should not be the sum of the congresses of individual disciplines [...] but] an act of unity of science.'[102]

Hochfeld did not stop promoting the idea that the Congress could help to develop the existing academic tradition. He saw the reason for the 'certain stagnation,' which he diagnosed in the work of the Section,[103] in the lack of readiness to formulate 'concrete questions' and to give to them 'concrete answers.' From Hochfeld's perspective, it did not seem problematic to find a 'progressive tradition,' for example, in the activity of interwar sociology. Developing this argument, he said, 'progressive sociological groups played an exceptional role and criticised the canons of scholars [who were] completely immersed in idealism.' Hochfeld argued that 'the progressive role of at least a section of Polish sociologists, such as [Ludwik]

Krzywicki... Chałasiński, [and] Ossowski' was in 'showing the social conditionality of ... other disciplines' and taking a step towards scientific progress.[104]

Nevertheless, even Hochfeld's broad approach to the demarcation between 'progressive' and 'reactionary' tendencies could not help to move the discussion along. Besides the fact that the very task of dealing with the past from the perspective of the current ideological tasks was not the most usual form of academic work for most participants in the discussion, the struggle against idealism did not seem to them to be the aim in itself nor the sole criterion of the scientific character of a given approach. During the preparation meetings, the members of the subsection were not able even to find a common basis for a substantive discussion on the matter.

The political pressure on the scholars who participated in the preparation meetings had a very specific character. The discussions of the 'humanistic' Section, which was visited by the professional geographer, Sejm deputy and member of the Main Council for Science and Higher Education (*Rada główna nauki i szkolnictwa wyższego*), Stanisław Leszczycki, were an example of the intersection between scholars and politicians. Leszczycki scolded the scholars and social scientists for their passivity in reaching '*concordia*' and induced them to take example from the natural sciences, which were much better in claiming their loyalty to Marxism–Leninism and glorifying the achievements of Soviet natural scientists.[105] During one of the meetings, he said:

> Are the scholars in Poland more overworked than scientists? <...> the number of scholars [dealing with the humanities] is, of course, more than that of mathematicians... but the number cannot play a role in this issue. I think that the reasons should be sought in ideology [...and] in the mentality of the fellows.[106]

Thus, Leszczycki saw the reason for this passivity in reaching unity not as a problem with the unrealistic task that the scholars received from politicians, but as an issue with the 'mentality' or, in other words, with the character traits of scholars. These character traits had to be changed to reach the aim that had been set.

Leszczycki repeatedly emphasised that it was a task for scholars but not for politicians to fulfil the mission of the Congress. He made crystal clear that the aim of the Congress would be reached only if scholars changed their academic ethos, which could not be done from above. Developing this idea, he said:

> If this [academic discussion] were directed [by politicians], there would be no need of conferences <...> the aim of subsections [of the Congress] is not to write reports for the authorities, but to specify errors [in their disciplines] through mutual criticism [between the representatives of different views].[107]

Thus, it was the central issue for the organisers of the Congress to make scholars themselves 'virtuous' men and women in performing the tasks formulated by the political leadership. Scholars were repeatedly called to come to the methodological unity 'through discussions' and 'virtuous' forms of 'criticism' and 'self-criticism.'[108]

Nevertheless, there were no instruments to force scholars to work differently. The arguments of politicians did not seem convincing. They could not make the discussion (especially among the members of the 'humanistic' section[109]) a productive one. During one of the discussions, the philosopher Tadeusz Kotarbiński described the situation in Polish academia as follows:

1 the social and party demand for the philosophy of Marxism–Leninism determined by the understanding of philosophy as an instrument of political struggle;
2 the postulation of taking an example, in academic work, from the philosophers of the Soviet Union;
3 the undisguised (sic!) [governmental] support for one philosophical attitude: Marxism–Leninism;
4 reorganisation of departments [in accordance with the new ideology]; the collectivisation of academic research; the dependence on the all-national Six-Year Plan.[110]

In fact, all these points described tendencies that Kotarbiński did not consider positive. There were two points that played a special role for Kotarbiński: the issue of freedom of discussion, and the new role of the Soviet Union in establishing the current academic agenda. Responding to the political request to find a 'progressive tradition' in Polish academia, Kotarbiński claimed that the best legacy of the interwar period was 'free discussion between the representatives of different views' and thus promoted not only a free format of discussion but also plurality in the intellectual arena.[111] Moreover, he did not see the example of the Soviet Union as a relevant criterion for defining 'good scientific practice.' He said, 'it would be very desirable and useful for both sides to strengthen the exchange of views between Polish and Soviet philosophers. However, this exchange should be seen as a partnership, not as one-way imitation.'[112] Thus, Kotarbiński questioned the basic ideas that were a precondition for fulfilling the mission of the Congress.

The discussion around Kotarbiński's statements was a characteristic one. No other but Józef Chałasiński dealt the most aggressive blow against Kotarbiński's attitude. In his speech, Chałasiński characterised the ideas of Kotarbiński as 'ahistorical.' Chałasiński argued that 'the tolerance of the authorities to philosophical research [and its idea of 'freedom of discussion'] was determined by the class-political conditions of the social system,' since the authorities supported the tendencies of 'isolation from historical reality' practiced by philosophical circles, which made them foreign to Marxism. Thus, Chałasiński accused Kotarbiński of maintaining the ideas that had been the cornerstone of his own public discourse during the early post-war years. In 1951, Chałasiński argued:

Before the war, [Poland] was stuck in the era of capitalism; we were on the periphery of the world, while today, in alliance with the Soviet Union, we are in the vanguard [of the world].[113]

The former theorist of 'public opinion' and intellectual freedom, Chałasiński, continued his speech by saying:

> Only correct methodological and substantive statements arise from <...> the diagnosis [of social processes] based on the only scientific method—Marxism. Then [when this idea has been accepted] the path of philosophy is clear...The implementation of the Six-Year Plan as the basis of the new system is an issue of much more great importance than any intellectual freedom.[114]

When attacking Kotarbiński, Chałasiński showed an example of how other scholars should abandon their own previous views and adopt the virtue of loyalty to the current political line in their academic work. Meanwhile, Chałasiński still wanted to secure some piece of his own freedom and argued that the principle of freedom of discussion could be accepted only 'in a narrow circle of professors.' According to him, 'in the wide circles of students,' the freedom of discussion should be abandoned because it could become a factor in the 'demobilisation of youth social forces.'[115]

Discussions around the Congress became one of the first public events at which Adam Schaff gained a more authoritative position for the promotion of his idea of the 'only scientific method.' Schaff 'explained' to Kotarbiński (who, being a rector in Łódź, had given Schaff a job after his return to Poland[116]) the reason for his misconception, which 'could give an absolutely wrong impression that the interwar period was a better time than the current period.' The issue of freedom of discussion and thus plurality in the academic field was interpreted by Schaff as follows:

> The postulation of freedom of discussion introduced by Professor Kotarbiński is another result of his non-sociological [and] abstract approach. It could be accepted only if there were no foreign agents of the class enemy, reactionary gangs, and if in fact there was an abstract situation of an equal number of bourgeois and Marxist scientists. [Nevertheless,] the class struggle continues, and, [in Polish academia], we have <...> on the one hand, the large camp of phenomenologists, neo-Thomists, etc., on the other, the Marxist camp, which is great in its prospects but still small in its size – meaning freedom of discussion [in this case] would be the biggest negligence, more - a social crime.[117]

Schaff's paternalist tendencies from the early post-war period received a new weight during the wave of Stalinisation. Nevertheless, Polish scholars still did not recognise him as a teacher of new virtues.

The attempts of politicians and scholars like Schaff and Chałasiński to force their colleagues to change their academic ethos were, in fact, not successful. The mission of the Section and thus of the Congress would be fulfilled only if all its participants would adopt the new forms of 'virtuous behaviour.' Kotarbiński openly said that he did not consider the arguments of Chałasiński and Schaff plausible and insisted on the necessity of maintaining plurality in the intellectual field.

Of course, Kotarbiński was not alone. For example, the new chair of the subsection for philosophy and the social sciences, Stanisław Ossowski (who took over this position from Ajdukiewicz in his absence), argued that the violation of freedom of discussion could make it impossible to implement the main slogan of Stalinisation – mobilisation of the best human resources for the service of the nation:

> The mobilisation of intellectual forces <...> is impossible without freedom of discussion...one who cuts down an apple tree in order to pick apples as quickly as possible does not follow the rules of rational production.[118]

Thus, the participants in the preparation meetings for the Congress made no progress in reaching 'unity' on methodological issues by the official start of the Congress. This reflected the impossibility of quickly changing the foundations of their academic practice. The official report that was prepared by the members of the section described the Polish academic heritage of both philosophy and sociology as reactionary one.[119] Nevertheless, the public accusations against both the past and present of Polish academia did not help to resolve the main problem. Polish scholars did not adopt the virtues that made 'public discussions' successful in the Soviet context. The understanding of this defeat was a new challenge for the organisers of Stalinisation in Poland.

*

The process of Stalinisation was a problematic undertaking from the very beginning. The conference of the Cominform and the speeches delivered by Molotov and Zhdanov formulated the general guidelines on what the new realities would mean for the countries in the zone of Soviet influence. Nevertheless, the significant difference between the Polish political project supported by Stalin and the new requirements also confused those who took central positions both in the political establishment and in the hierarchy of the Polish United Workers' Party. Nevertheless, Soviet representatives never tired of clarifying the new rules of the mobilisation around the Soviet Union. The changes in party leadership were a clear sign that the early post-war project had failed, and the new realities required a new project. The defeat of 'gentle revolution' meant that other people and other principles would regulate the public sphere of post-war Poland.

The idea of political mobilisation under the supervision of the Soviet Union broke all the conventions that made the 'gentle revolution' project possible. The official claims of loyalty to the Soviet Union became the most visible change in the Polish public sphere.[120] The Soviet Union replaced French left-wing intellectuals in their 'teaching' position[121] on cultural and theoretical issues. The party journals practiced ekphrasis when describing the achievements of the Soviet Union as a monument, while the cultural journals let Soviet scholars and writers transmit their own self-image to the Polish reader.

Nevertheless, it was much easier to close journals and to fire the chiefs of the publishing institutions than to reforge the people who constituted the core of Polish academia. The First Congress of Polish Science played a special role among other congresses, which became routine under Stalinism. The political mission that

Polish scholars had during the Congress was to resolve all methodological contradictions and to come to a '*concordia*' under the banner of 'Marxism–Leninism.' It was a task to write a 'mathematical equation' with a known result and several mandatory elements, such as 'the mobilisation of the best scholars,' 'the basing on the progressive national tradition,' 'Marxism–Leninism,' and the 'Six-Year Plan.' However, without adopting the new forms of 'virtuous behaviour,' all scientific debates on this topic seemed to be a multiplication by zero. Polish scholars did not show (with some exceptions) any readiness to adopt the new virtues. After the deconstruction of the institutions of public debates and the failure of the quest for the unity within the Congress, the organisers of Stalinisation had no other choice but to try to construct the 'correct' 'public discussion' artificially. This task required a new teaching programme in Stalinist virtues.

Notes

1 Between 1961 and 1968, Bohdan Chwedeńczuk was an assistant of Adam Schaff.
2 Bohdan Chwedeńczuk, *Dialogi z Adamem Schaffem* (Warszawa: Iskry, 2005), 13–14.
3 Basically, though with many reservations, this is the paradigm of most of the research on the spreading of the Soviet 'model' in Eastern Europe, see, e.g., Michael David-Fox and György Péteri, eds., Academia in Upheaval: Origins, Transfers, and Transformations of the Communist Academic Regime in Russia and East Central Europe (Westport: Information Age Publishing, 2000).
4 See more about the complex character of the issue: Piotr Hübner, "Stalinizacja polskiej nauki," in *Oblicza polskiego stalinizmu*, ed. Ryszard Studziński (Włocławek: Wyższa Szkoła Humanistyczno-Ekonomiczna, 2000), 37–56.
5 Of course, 'Stalinist Science' is just an attempt to catch the tendencies in Soviet Science under Stalinism. For the critical reflections on this concept, see Michael D. Gordin, "Was There Ever a 'Stalinist Science'?," *Kritika: Explorations in Russian and Eurasian History* 9, no. 3 (2008): 625–639.
6 Two more famous examples were the changes in the role and status of the linguistic theory of Nikolai Marr (see Vladimir M. Alpatov, *Istoriya odnogo mifa. Marr i Marrizm* [Moskva: URSS], 2004) and the fate of Stalin's favourite, the historian Mikhail Porshnev, see Vladimir Ryzhkovskij, "Sovetskaja medievistika and Beyond," *Novoe literaturnoe obozrenie*, no. 3 (2009). https://magazines.gorky.media/nlo/2009/3/sovetskaya-medievistika-and-beyond.html.
7 In fact, these campaigns happened parallel to the attempts to re-educate the Soviet academia in Central and Eastern Europe.
8 This was the case both with the opponents of Nikolai Marr's theory and with the group of Soviet medievalists who had been attacked by Mikhail Porshnev during the 1930s and, after the war, organised a campaign against him, see Anton N. Afanasev, "'Bor'ba za nauchnost'' v pozdnestalinskoj medievistike: k istorii odnoj teoreticheskoj diskussii 1951–1953 gg.," *Logos* 32, no. 6 (2022): 111–128.
9 Alexei Kojevnikov, "Rituals of Stalinist Culture at Work: Science and the Games of Intraparty Democracy circa 1948," *The Russian Review* 57 (January 1998): 28–40.
10 See more: Sheila Fitzpatrick, *The Cultural Front: Power and Culture in Revolutionary Russia* (New York: Cornell University Press, 1992): 209–233.
11 See more on the concept of self-criticism (*samokritika*) in Chapter 7. For the comparision of Soviet self-criticism and Catholic confession, see Berthold Unfried, *"Ich bekenne": Katholische Beichte und sowjetische Selbstkritik* (Frankfurt am Main: Campus, 2006). For a more general overview of research on the phenomenon of 'self-criticism' see,

Malte Griesse, "Soviet Subjectivities: Discourse, Self-Criticism, Imposture," *Kritika: Explorations in Russian and Eurasian History* 9, no. 3 (2008): 609–624.
12 In this case, it does not matter that many Soviet scholars were not party members. This virtue was supposed to be adopted by all Soviet citizens.
13 See Juliane Fürst, *Stalin's Last Generation: Soviet Post-War Youth and the Emergence of Mature Socialism* (Oxford: Oxford University Press), 22.
14 See about the ideological campaigns ('*prorabotki*') in historiography: Vladimir Tihonov, *Ideologicheskie kampanii "pozdnego stalinizma" i sovetskaja istoricheskaja nauka, seredina 1940-h–1953 g.* (Moskva: Nestor-istorija, 2016); in philosophy and biology: Kojevnikov, "Rituals of Stalinist Culture at Work," 28–40.
15 See more about the tendencies of the 'Thaw' in Soviet Academia: Benjamin Tromley, *Making the Soviet Intelligentsia: Universities and Intellectual Life under Stalin and Khrushchev* (Cambridge, UK: Cambridge University Press, 2014), 187–216.
16 Iosif Stalin, "Protiv oposhlenija lozunga samokritiki," *Pravda*, no. 146, 26 June 1928. https://www.marxists.org/russkij/stalin/t11/t11_14.htm
17 *Eudaemonia* (from εὐδαιμονία) – means in English a special state of 'good spirit' or 'happiness,' 'welfare.' *Eudaemonia* has been the central concept of the virtue theory since antiquity. Those who succeeded in cultivating virtues were supposed to come to *eudaemonia*.
18 See, e.g., Robert Brown, "Livy's Sabine Women and the Ideal of Concordia," *Transactions of the American Philological Association* 125 (1995): 291–319.
19 Stalin himself emphasised that 'self-criticism' should not become only a 'formalist' thing but had to be conducted consciously: Stalin, "Protiv oposhlenija lozunga samokritiki."
20 See the previous chapters.
21 See about the escalation of the conflict: Fraser Harbutt, "American Challenge, Soviet Response: The Beginning of the Cold War, February–May, 1946," *Political Science Quarterly* 96, no. 4 (1982): 623–639.
22 Geoffrey Roberts, "Moscow and the Marshall Plan: Politics, Ideology and the Onset of the Cold War, 1947," *Europe-Asia Studies* 46, no. 8 (1994): 1371–1386.
23 See Kevin McDermott and Jeremy Agnew, *The Comintern: A History of International Communism from Lenin to Stalin* (London: Macmillan International Higher Education, 1996), 191–211.
24 Grant M. Adibekov, *Soveshhanija Kominforma 1947, 1948, 1949. Dokumenty i materialy* (Moskva: Rosspen, 1998), 20. (Zhdanov declared as the main purpose of this institution the exchange of information among the Communist parties. See Adibekov, *Soveshhanija Kominforma*, 297, 298.)
25 Adibekov, *Soveshhanija Kominforma*, 300.
26 Ibid., 13.
27 Ibid., 300.
28 See the description of this collaboration in the memoirs of Ivan Serov: Ivan Serov, *Zapiski iz chemodana. Tajnye dnevniki pervogo predsedatelja KGB, najdennye cherez 25 let posle ego smerti* (Moskva: Olma, 2020), 214–253. The human resources activity of the Polish security services was controlled and confirmed by the NKVD (see, e.g., Izabela Wagner, *Bauman: A Biography* [Cambridge: Polity], 115).
29 See Krzysztof Szwagrzyk, "Aparat bezpieczeństwa w latach 1944–1956," in *Aparat bezpieczeństwa w Polsce: Kadra kierownicza*, vol. 1, *1944–1956*, ed. Krzysztof Szwagrzyk (Warszawa: Instytut pamięci narodowej, 2005), 19.
30 Tatyana Volokitina, Galina Murashko, and Albina Noskova, eds., *Stanovlenie politicheskih rezhimov sovetskogo tipa, 1949–1953: Ocherki istorii* (Moskva: ROSPJeN, 2002), 499–510.
31 Franciszek Fiedler, "Ideologiczne koncepcje reakcji," *Nowe Drogi*, no. 1 (1947): 31–64.
32 Ibid., 31–32.
33 Ibid., 32.

34 Ibid., 36.
35 See more about the difference in the programmes of Dmowski and Piłsudski: Władysław Bułhak, "Dmowski – Rosja a kwestia polska: U źródeł orientacji rosyjskiej obozu narodowego 1886–1908," *Roczniki Humanistyczne* 53, no. 2 (2005): 181–200.
36 Though other quotations in this text usually contained exact references to the literature, in this case, the author did not specify what kind of publication he meant.
37 Fiedler, "Ideologiczne koncepcje reakcji," 40.
38 Ibid., 58.
39 In 1947, when the article was written, various approaches to the image of the Soviet Union still coexisted in the public sphere of post-war Poland. Nevertheless, the tendency reflected in Fiedler's publication became, later, the basis for constructing a new image of the Soviet Union.
40 The October Revolution happened on 25th October according to the Julian calendar (Old Style) and on 7th November according to the Gregorian calendar. Therefore, some of the Polish publications on this issue celebrated the 'November Revolution.'
41 Jakub Berman, "Twierdza i drogowskaz postępu," *Nowe Drogi*, no. 6 (1947): 5–11.
42 Roman Werfel, "Państwo humanizmu socjalistycznego," *Nowe Drogi*, no. 6 (1947): 12–43.
43 Jerzy Borejsza, "Niepodległość nieurojona," *Nowe Drogi*, no. 60 (1947): 113–134.
44 Ibid., 117.
45 It should be mentioned that this idea was, on the one hand, the continuation of the programme formulated by Borejsza in the very beginning of the post-war period (in 1945, he published an article with a very similar title, see Jerzy Borejsza, "Nieurojona suwerenność," *Kuźnica*, no. 4–5 [1945]: 15–17.), on the other hand, in late 1947, Borejsza already felt the necessity of integrating the fragments glorifying the achievements of the Soviet Union, which sometimes did not have much to do with the core of his argumentation.
46 Włodzimierz Lenin, "Lew Tołstoj," *Kuźnica*, no. 40 (1947): 1.
47 Maksym Gorki, "Włodzimierz Lenin," *Kuźnica*, no. 40 (1947): 2.
48 So, for example, Tynianov's article on the literary tricks of the Russian poet and diplomat Alexander Griboyedov (1795–1829) in his prominent satirical poem 'Woe from Wit' was published in the cultural press: Jurij Tynianow, "Tematyka komedii 'Bieda z tym rozumem'," *Kuźnica*, no. 40 (1947): 7–8.
49 See, for example, the translation of the article of Boris Pasternak which preceded his translations of the works of Shakespeare: Borys Pasternak, "Przedmowa do przekładów Szekspira," *Kuźnica*, no. 40 (1947): 9–10.
50 Ilja Erenburg, "Kultura jest niepodzielna," *Kuźnica*, no. 43 (1947): 1–2.
51 Patryk Babiracki, *Soviet Soft Power in Poland: Culture and the Making of Stalin's New Empire, 1943–1957* (Chapel Hill: University of North Carolina Press, 2015), 77.
52 See the project of the Congress: AAN, Akta Kongresów Pokoju, sygn. 1, K. 2–7; see, the list of participants: AAN, Akta Kongresów Pokoju, sygn. 11, K. 25–32.
53 Eryk Krasucki, *Międzynarodowy komunista. Jerzy Borejsza: Biografia polityczna* (Warszawa: Wydawnictwo naukowe PWN, 2009), 160.
54 Zygmunt Woźniczka, "Wrocławski Kongres Intelektualistów w obronie pokoju," *Kwartalnik Historyczny* 94, no. 2 (1987): 138.
55 AAN, Akta kongresów pokoju. Światowy Kongres Intelektualistów, sygn. 157/1, K. 23.
56 Julien Benda, *La Trahison des clercs* (Paris: Les Éditions Grasset, 1927).
57 See about him: Galin Tihanov, "Revisiting Lukács' theory of realism," *Thesis Eleven* 159, no. 1 (2020): 57–63.
58 Woźniczka, "Wrocławski Kongres Intelektualistów w obronie pokoju," 139.
59 See AAN, Akta Kongresów Pokoju, sygn. 11, K. 25–32.
60 Woźniczka, "Wrocławski Kongres Intelektualistów w obronie pokoju," 146.
61 AAN, Akta kongresów pokoju. Światowy Kongres Intelektualistów, sygn. 5. K.23.

62 Dominique Desanti, *Les staliniens, 1944–56. Une expérience politique* (Paris: Fayard, 1975), 113–115.
63 See the projects of the manifesto: AAN, Akta kongresów pokoju. Światowy Kongres Intelektualistów, sygn. 9, K. 1–6.
64 Other members of the group had to spend more than six years in prison or were sentenced to life imprisonment.
65 He was possibly killed by the security services in 1953. See more: Tomasz Sikorski and Marcin Kulesza, *Niezłomni w epoce fałszywych proroków: Środowisko "Tygodnika Warszawskiego" 1945–1948* (Warszawa: Wydawnictwo von Bonowiecky, 2013), 71–124.
66 See Mikołaj S. Kunicki, *Between the Brown and the Red: Nationalism, Catholicism, and Communism in 20th-Century Poland; The Politics of Bolesław Piasecki* (Athens: Ohio University Press, 2012), 77–180.
67 The matter concerns the group of Piasecki, who became the most active enforcer of the governmental line among Catholics, see Kunicki, *Between the Brown and the Red*, 77–180.
68 See Stefan Jędrychowski, "Walka o wolność nauki czy o utrzymanie starego porządku?," *Kuźnica*, no. 24 (1947): 1–2.
69 Józef Chałasiński, "Trzydzieści lat socjologii Polskiej 1918–1947," *Przegląd Socjologiczny*, no. 1 (1949): 15.
70 Ibid., 13–14.
71 Aleksei Lokhmatov, "Auf dem Weg zur ‚Einheit': Józef Chałasiński und die Suche nach einer ‚erlaubten' Genealogie der Soziologie im Nachkriegspolen (1945–1951)," *NTM Zeitschrift für Geschichte der Wissenschaften, Technik und Medizin* 28 (2020): 528–531.
72 Chałasiński, "Trzydzieści lat socjologii Polskiej 1918–1947," 54.
73 The issue was prepared in the late 1948 and published in 1949.
74 Chałasiński, "Trzydzieści lat socjologii Polskiej 1918–1947," 54.
75 Additionally, in March 1948, Lebedev wrote that the group gathered around Gomulka was 'obviously infected by Polish chauvinism.' See *Sovetskij faktor v Vostochnoj Evrope 1944–1953 gg.: Dokumenty*, ed. Tatyana Volokitina, Galina Murashko, and Albina Noskova, vol. 1, *1944–1948* (Moskva: ROSSPJeN, 1999), 562–564.
76 Tatyana Volokitina, ed., *Vostochnaja Evropa v dokumentah rossijskih arhivov 1944–1953 gg.* Vol. 1 (Moskva: Sibirskij hronograf, 1997), 900–902.
77 Moscow supported the decision of the Politburo of the Workers Party, emphasising that 'the line of the distrust towards the Soviet Union conducted by com. Wieslaw [Gomułka], caused serious damage to the interests of Poland, weakening her political positions.' (See Tatyana Volokitina et al., eds., *Moskva i Vostochnaja Evropa: Stanovlenie politicheskih rezhimov sovetskogo tipa, 1949–1953. Ocherki istorii* [Moskva: ROSSPJeN, 2002], 510–513.)
78 It is difficult to say if the arrest of Gomułka was confirmed in Moscow. Stalin, who obviously had some sympathies towards Gomułka, wrote in a telegram to Bierut: 'it is better to let c[omrade] Gomułka stay in the Central Committee, but not [let him be] in the Politburo. The Party would only benefit from this' (See Gennadi Matveev et al., eds., *SSSR – Pol'sha. Mehanizmy podchinenija, 1944–1949* [Moskva: AIRO-HH, 1995] 271–278).
79 In December 1948, the Polish Workers Party and the Polish Socialist Party were united in the Polish United Workers Party.
80 "Przemówienie tow. Borejszy," *Nowe Drogi*, no. 11 (1948): 124, 125.
81 "Przemówienie tow. Żółkiewskiego", *Nowe Drogi*, no. 11 (1948): 106.
82 Marci Shore, *Caviar and Ashes: A Warsaw Generation's Life and Death in Marxism, 1918–1968* (New Haven/London: Yale University Press, 2006), 34.
83 Borejsza died in 1952, see Krasucki, *Międzynarodowy komunista*, 281, 282.

84 "III Plenum Komitetu Centralnego PZPR," *Nowe Drogi*, no. 6 (1949): 4.
85 Kamila Kamińska-Chełminiak, *Cenzura w Polsce, 1944–1960: Organizacja, kadry, metody pracy* (Warszawa: Oficyna Wydawnicza ASPRA, 2009), 104.
86 See about the Congress of Polish writers: Paweł Knap (ed.), *Wokół zjazdu szczecińskiego 1949 r.* (Szczecin: Instytut Pamięci Narodowej, 2011).
87 See Stefan Żółkiewski, "Na marginesie Zjazdu Polonistów 8–12 maja 1950 r.," *Pamiętnik Literacki* 41, no. 2 (1950): 308–328.
88 About the congress of historians that took place in Wrocław in 1949 and gathered, first of all, Marxist historians, only a few famous historians came to participate in this event. Jann Kott wrote about this congress: '[this congress] was a demonstration of a small group of assistants, junior teaching fellows, and journalists against professors,' see Rafał Stobiecki, *Historia pod nadzorem. Spory o nowy model historii w Polsce – druga połowa lat czterdziestych – początek lat pięćdziesiątych* (Łódź: Wydawnictwo Uniwersytetu Łódzkiego, 1993), 97.
89 According to the metaphor of Mariusz Zawodniak, the calendar of Congresses became a calendar of cultural life, see Mariusz Zawodniak, "Zjazdy, narady, konferencje literackie," in *Słownik realizmu socjalistycznego*, ed. Zdzisław Łapiński and Wojciech Tomasik (Kraków: Universitas, 2004), 404.
90 Piotr Hübner, *Polityka naukowa w Polsce w latach 1944–1953: Geneza systemu* vol. 2 (Wrocław: Zakład Narodowy im. Ossolińskich, 1992), 628–829.
91 "Wytwórnia Filmów Dokumentalnych Warszawa 1951: I Kongres Nauki Polskiej w Warszawie," *Repozytorium* https://repozytorium.fn.org.pl/?q=pl/node/6746.
92 *I Kongres Nauki Polskiej* (Warszawa: Państwowe Wydawnictwo Naukowe, 1953), 19.
93 *I Kongres Nauki Polskiej* (Warszawa: Państwowe Wydawnictwo Naukowe, 1953), 110.
94 See Piotr Hübner, *I Kongres Nauki Polskiej jako forma realizacji założeń polityki naukowej państwa ludowego* (Wrocław: Zakład Narodowy im. Ossolińskich, 1983), 73–87.
95 Józef Chałasiński, "Od liberalnej do socjalistycznej idei Uniwersytetu," *Życie Nauki*, no. 7–8 (1950): 526–529.
96 See more about Chałasiński's programme: Kamil Piskała and Agata Zysiak, "Świątynia nauki, fundament demokracji czy fabryka specjalistów? Józef Chałasiński i powojenne spory o ideę uniwersytetu," *Praktyka teoretyczna* 9, no. 3 (2013): 290–291.
97 Archiwum PAN, I Kongres Nauki Polskiej, Sygn. 13, K. 115.
98 See, the list of participants in the preparations from philosophy and the social sciences: Archiwum PAN, I Kongres Nauki Polskiej, Sygn. 13, K. 110–115. See also, for example, the session about the Polish Enlightment (Archiwum PAN, I Kongres Nauki Polskiej, Sygn. 13, K. 71–78.) Nevertheless, Ajdukiewicz remarked in his talk that most of the philosophers who organised the Congress were Marxists: Archiwum PAN, I Kongres Nauki Polskiej, Sygn. 117, K. 91.
99 Archiwum PAN, I Kongres Nauki Polskiej, Sygn. 117, K. 91.
100 Archiwum PAN, I Kongres Nauki Polskiej, Sygn. 117, K. 154. The idea of an open debate between "two worldviews" played an essential role in the discourse of Marxist speakers. Similar arguments were used by the Marxist philosopher Adam Schaff, see Archiwum PAN, I Kongres Nauki Polskiej, Sygn. 127, K. 104–105.
101 See more in Chapter 5.
102 Archiwum PAN, I Kongres Nauki Polskiej, Sygn. 117, K. 151.
103 Archiwum PAN, I Kongres Nauki Polskiej, Sygn. 117, K. 154.
104 Archiwum PAN, I Kongres Nauki Polskiej, Sygn. 117, K. 158.
105 The names of Ivan Pavlov and Trofim Lysenko started to dominate all academic journals for the Natural Sciences in Poland and thus shaped a space for the claim of 'unity' during the congress, see Piotr Köhler, "Lysenko Affair and Polish Botany," *Journal of the History of Biology*, no. 44 (2011): 305–343; it is noteworthy that the journal 'Myśl

Współczesna,' which had hosted the key discussion on Marxism during the early postwar years, reoriented towards glorifying Soviet achievements in biology during the period of Stalinisation. See, e.g., Włodzimierz Michajłow, "Biologia radziecka – nauka epoki socjalizmu," *Myśl Współczesna*, no. 3 (1950): 374–384; Kazimierz Petrusewicz, "Światopoglądowe znaczenie nauk Pawłowa," *Myśl Współczesna*, no. 3 (1950): 391–412.
106 Archiwum PAN, I Kongres Nauki Polskiej, Sygn. 117, K. 134.
107 Archiwum PAN, I Kongres Nauki Polskiej, Sygn. 117, K. 134–135.
108 This form of participation by professional scholars and scientists who held political offices at the same time in the meetings of the section was not a one-time thing. The philologist and politician Eugenia Krassowska-Jodłowska also participated in one of the meetings of the section and criticised the scholars for their passivity in reaching methodological unity. Then, she claimed: 'Nobody proposes to enforce any rules and regulations or impose these rules and regulations on scientific fellows. That is an absolutely wrong way. Science itself will develop its scientific norms in the struggle, in the fight between different views.' (Archiwum PAN, I Kongres Nauki Polskiej, Sygn. 117, K. 162.)
109 In my narrative, I will concentrate on the subsection for Philosophy and Social Sciences, because, on the one hand, interdisciplinary character of this subsection, on the other, the very strong positions of non-Marxist philosophers made the discussion in this subsection more contradictory. The striving not to soften but to thematise internal contradictions made this subsection a platform for very intense debates. About other section, from a more typical perspective, see Hübner, *Polityka naukowa w Polsce w latach 1944–1953*, 476–573.
110 Rps BUW nr aks 4228, I Kongres Nauki Polskiej, K (2).
111 Rps BUW nr aks 4228, I Kongres Nauki Polskiej, K (2).
112 Rps BUW nr aks 4228, I Kongres Nauki Polskiej, K (3).
113 Rps BUW nr aks 4228, I Kongres Nauki Polskiej, K (3).
114 Rps BUW nr aks 4228, I Kongres Nauki Polskiej, K (3).
115 Rps BUW nr aks 4228, I Kongres Nauki Polskiej, K (5).
116 See John Connelly, "Internal Bolshevisation? Elite Social Science Training in Stalinist Poland," *Minerva* 34, no. 4 (1996): 323–346.
117 Rps BUW nr aks 4228, I Kongres Nauki Polskiej, K (4).
118 Rps BUW nr aks 4228, I Kongres Nauki Polskiej, K (5).
119 The text was not confirmed by all the participants in the discussion and stood, in fact, in contradiction to what was debated during the preparation meetings, see Lokhmatov, "Auf dem Weg zur 'Einheit'," 538–539.
120 The image of the Soviet Union replaced the 'German question' and the discourse on the 'Recovered Territories' in its role in the official propaganda. With the beginning of Stalinisation, the 'German Question' ceased to be the core of governmental propaganda and, at the same time, the central issue of public discussions. The creation of the German Democratic Republic in 1949, and the idea of mobilisation of all socialist forces under the supervision of the Soviet Union made the anti-German discourse a dangerous issue. Even though the 'German Question' was still an important issue both for the authorities and for Polish society, the public debates on this issue were very limited. See more about the changes in the role of this issue in historiography: Maciej Górny, *The Nation Should Come First. Marxism and Historiography in East Central Europe* (Frankfurt am Main: Peter Lang, 2013), 36.
121 The review of French journals was still a part of the official discourse. Nevertheless, during Stalinisation, Polish journals reviewed primarily French communist journals which just transmitted the key ideas of Stalinism. In any case, the Soviet Union started to dominate the public sphere of Poland and France played an incomparably smaller role than it had in the public sphere of Poland under Stalinism.

7 The School of 'New Virtues'

'My long-term efforts to change the Zionist sympathies of my father, Maurycy Bauman, did not yield results <…> I solemnly declare to the party that I am breaking off all contact with my father.'[1] With these words, the young Workers' Party member, Zygmunt Bauman, showed an example of how a virtuous man should prefer loyalty to the current political need over loyalty to his own family. At this time, Bauman was experiencing a transitional period in his life and changed his occupation from an officer of the security services to a scholar. In a sadly ironic way, the virtues that the representatives of these both professions were forced to share under Stalinism were the same. On the wave of Stalinisation, the breaking of 'all contacts' with 'fathers' as a sign of loyalty was a political task for Polish academia as well. In this regard, it could seem that Bauman did not need to change his political ethos much, when beginning his scholarly career.

The power and powerlessness of institutions

The changes in the image of the Polish academic institutions gave an impression of a triumphant Stalinism. The closing of the Polish Sociological Institute, university departments of sociology, and the leading sociological journal was only one of the markers of this visible 'success.' Most probably, it was not the anti-Marxist discourse of Polish sociologists but the simple fact that Stalinist academy did not consider sociology a separate discipline that was the reason for these institutional changes. In the Soviet Union, sociology was stigmatised as a 'bourgeois science' and this decided the fate of this discipline in Poland under Stalinism. Of course, it did not mean that sociology entirely disappeared from the university syllabus and research practice. Those sociologists who were not deprived of teaching[2] continued to give seminars on 'the History of Social Thought.'[3] Nevertheless, the persistence of these islands of sociological thought did not change the fact that Polish sociology became, in a sense, one of the main victims of the attempts to imitate the institutional aspects of the Soviet academic model in Poland.

Meanwhile, the changes in the names of departments and the closing of the journals could not satisfy those who saw the future of Polish science and scholarship under the sovereignty of Soviet academia. The 'disappointing' results of the First Congress of Polish Science required a new campaign that aimed to change

DOI: 10.4324/9781003428251-8

the core of academic practice. It was necessary not only to force Polish scholars to criticise publicly the legacy of the 'fathers' of Polish academic disciplines, but also to show their 'virtuousness' in leading an open academic discussion in a new way. However, the lack of specialists in Stalinism trained in the Soviet Union could not help but influence the process of Stalinisation in Poland. After the creation of the Polish Academy of Sciences (October 30, 1951), the academic field was strictly divided into research institutes that were asked to fulfil the 'Six-Year Plan' within individual disciplines. Thus, Stalinisation was, in fact, split into many local 'Stalinisations' that had been led by selected scholars.

For example, Stefan Żółkiewski, the former editor of 'Kuźnica,' became a central figure in the Stalinisation of Literary Studies. The fact that Żółkiewski had publicly recognised his 'guilt' in 'underestimating the achievements of the Soviet Union' at the early stage of the 'reconstruction' of the Polish public sphere was not an obstacle for him in playing a central role in this process. On the contrary, his 'virtuous behaviour' showed that he was a suitable candidate for fulfilling this mission. In his public discourse under the new conditions, Żółkiewski repeatedly claimed that Soviet scholarship is the most 'creative and productive [scholarship] of our days.'[4] He wrote that the Soviet Union archived the level of intellectual development at which both fiction and literary studies had been united in their struggle for the class interest of the proletariat. He did not hesitate to take over the task of publicly praising the 'genius' works of Stalin that, according to him, 'revised the previous views on Marxism' and, thus, opened a new chapter in Marxist scholarship.[5]

Meanwhile, Żółkiewski obviously used the name of Stalin and references to the publications of Soviet scholars to promote his previous agenda, though in a slightly modified form. During the wave of Stalinisation, he intensified his criticism against those scholars whose agenda radically opposed realism in general and Marxist scholarship in particular.[6] Meanwhile, Żółkiewski attempted to show that his colleagues from the former group of 'Kuźnica' were the best representatives of the tendencies that he found 'progressive' and 'innovative' in the writings of Stalin.[7]

Due to his party status, Żółkiewski enjoyed strong governmental support during Stalinisation. The Institute of Literary Studies (Instytut Badań Literackich) became the institutional body that was supposed to help him to reform Polish philology. This institute was founded in 1948 and, in 1952, joined the structure of the Polish Academy of Sciences. From the beginning, Żółkiewski (who only received his PhD in 1952) supervised the Institute (he was its director until 1953), and it is no wonder that the key figures of the former 'Kuźnica' group (Kazimierz Wyka and Jan Kott among them) assisted him in governing literary studies under Stalinism.[8] Under the banner of this institute, Żółkiewski's group prepared a considerable number of publications that critiqued the 'nationalism' and romantic sentiments of Polish literary studies.[9] Meanwhile, the core activity of the institute was still focused on the diligent search for 'progressive' traits in a very traditional version of the Polish national canon.[10]

Like all other organisers of Stalinisation, Żółkiewski had significant problems with the unwillingness of Polish scholars to be 're-educated.' Understandably,

Żółkiewski's attempts to transmit the party's line both to the writers and literary scholars faced a passive scepticism among his potential 'students.'[11] It is noticeable that Żółkiewski, even in his reports on the 'personal issues' in Polish studies, did not show any optimism regarding the non-Marxist Polish philologists being able to adopt the new virtues.[12] So, for example, when attacking the prominent historian of literature Stanisław Pigoń, Żółkiewski proposed to suspend him from teaching when he would reach the age of 65 and let him focus on research and publishing activity, in which he could be very 'useful.'[13] Moreover, the journal 'Pamiętnik Literacki (Literary Memoir)' that, since 1952, had been supervised by the Institute of Literary Studies did not cease publishing the works of Pigoń and other philologists that did not show readiness to change their academic ethos in accordance with the new standards.[14] While diligently decorating their publications with the canonical names of Marxism–Leninism and publicly criticising the non-Marxist scholars, Żółkiewski's group tried to promote their own agenda rather than to forcibly re-educate all Polish philologists.

The case of Polish historiography was even more problematic than that of literary studies from the perspective of Stalinisation. While Żółkiewski had passed the test for 'virtuousness' required for holding a leading position in academia, historiography had other supervisors. It was none other than Tadeusz Manteuffel who was asked to lead the reorganisation of historical studies in Poland and to head the Institute of History of the Polish Academy of Sciences. Besides the fact that Manteuffel enjoyed significant professional authority among Polish historians, he could hardly be characterised as an admirer of dogmatic forms of Soviet Marxism.[15] Characteristically, the historians Celina Bobińska and Żanna Kormanowa, who received their professional training in the Soviet Union, were prohibited from leading positions in the reconstruction of Polish historiography.[16] This determined the 'special path' of the development of Polish historiography under Stalinism: the key figure of Stalinisation did not see his aim in destructing the forms of 'good academic practice' typical to Polish historians.[17] Of course, Manteuffel and his colleagues (among whom Witold Kula played a distinctive role) attempted to use the opportunity to modernise the historiographical practice and to implement big research projects on the history of Poland.[18] Nevertheless, this 'modernisation' concerned the focus of research and the set of relevant topics rather than the destruction of previous professional conventions.

Interestingly, Polish historians had an unexpected ally in their attempts to defend their idea of scholarly virtues. The so-called 'First Methodological Conference of Polish Historians' that took place in Otwock, a town near Warsaw, at the turn of 1951 and 1952, in many respects, determined the future of Polish historiography under Stalinism. The decisive roles in this conference were played by the Soviet historians Boris Grekov, Evgenii Kosminski, Arkady Sidorov, and Piotr Tretiakov. Despite the ritual claims of loyalty to Marxism–Leninism, this conference became a platform for a kind of coalition between Polish and Soviet historians against the ideological invasion into historical sciences. Thus, for example, the famous medievalist of Polish origin, Kosminski, wrote in one of his reports on this conference that Polish historians discussed with him the issue of the struggle against dogmatism and 'quotology (cytatologia).'[19] By 'quotology,' he meant speculations with quotations from the classics of Marxism–Leninism that did not have direct implications to historical sources.

It is not unimportant that, earlier, Kosminski himself had been accused of 'bourgeois objectivism' in the Soviet Union. Therefore, for him (much like for some other Soviet historians), this agreement with his Polish colleagues was, in a sense, an alliance of 'professionals' against non-qualified 'careerists.' Soviet historians themselves used the post-war changes in Soviet academia to openly attack those whom they considered quotologists.[20] In this regard, the critique of the misuse of Marxism at the Otwock conference was beneficial for both sides. The idea of 'concrete historical research' became an umbrella under which the previous historical practice could develop with only a few modifications. Even 'self-criticism' conducted by some historians during this conference concerned very concrete historical issues. For example, the Polish Marxist historian Stanisław Arnold excused himself for a false chronology in research on Polish feudalism and thanked the Soviet delegates for drawing his attention to these methodological mistakes.[21] Meanwhile, the Soviet historians did not support more radical attacks on the foundations of the academic practice.[22] Thus, the Polish historians got a 'blessing' from the Soviet colleagues and, most probably, this helped them to prevent putting historiography under the supervision of the radical proponents of re-education of Polish historians.[23]

Remarkably, an association with historians became a part of the survival strategy of Polish sociologists. After the closing of the leading journal on social sciences,[24] the leader of the Łódź sociological group, Józef Chałasiński, created a new periodical '*Przegląd Nauk Historycznych i Społecznych* (Review of the Historical and Social Sciences) instead. In the first issue of the journal, the editorial board assured the reader that the institutional transformation of the Polish sociological press was caused by the necessity of bringing together social and historical sciences, 'which have been, in our [the members of the editorial board] view, artificially divided.'[25] In fact, this turn towards historiographical themes helped some Polish sociologists to continue their academic practice under the new banner.

Nevertheless, historiography was not an affiliation prescribed for sociologies from above. It was not an accident that, during the preparation meetings for the First Scientific Congress, the social sciences and philosophy shared one subsection. From the perspective of the Stalinist ideology, there could not be another 'sociology' than the Marxist theory of socio-economic formations in its Soviet (Stalinist) version. Due to their subject, the social sciences were supposed to become the domain of Marxist philosophy. Therefore, the legacy of Polish sociology was doomed to go through the purging fire of 'criticism' and 'self-criticism' under the supervision of Marxist philosophers.

The missionaries of new virtues

The new stage of Stalinisation became a turning point in the career of the Marxist philosopher Adam Schaff. Contrasting well-established Polish philosophers and sociologists, Schaff was one of a few scholars who had both a deep knowledge of the Soviet academic realities and an enormous ambition to reform Polish academia. The deep knowledge of 'the original' and 'conscientiousness' in fulfilling his mission made Schaff's activity the most effective attempt to change not the banner under which the scholarly practice continued in Poland, but the foundations of this practice. While the representatives of other disciplines used the smokescreen of glorifying Marx, Lenin, and Stalin to preserve their academic practice from changes or to improve it in accordance with their own idea of 'progressiveness,' Schaff did not look for a compromise. He knew that the only public evidence of Polish scholars having adopted new virtues would help the Polish academics to reach the desired *concordia*, under which all non-Marxist scholars would confess their readiness to rebaptise themselves as Marxists.

Even though the figure of Adam Schaff had frequently appeared in the public debates of the early post-war period, Stalinisation made him the central figure of the academic landscape of Poland, and a discussion about this period requires a brief look at Schaff's biography. Adam Schaff (1913–2006) was born to a Jewish family in Lwów (now, Lviv) and would recall later that antisemitism in his native milieu was among the reasons for his early fascination with communism. He studied political economy at the University of Lwów and, later, moved to the Soviet Union to study philosophy at Moscow State University and prepare a dissertation at the institute of philosophy of the Academy of Sciences of the USSR.[26] Having finished his studies and having received a doctoral degree, Schaff came back to Warsaw in 1948, when academic and cultural life had already been reconstructed. He had got a job at the University of Łódź, although professional philosophers at the time had doubts regarding the credibility of his Soviet degrees. So, for example, Tadeusz Kotarbiński, then the rector of the university, thought that Schaff could not receive a professorship without a Polish *habilitation* degree.[27] Nevertheless, against the backdrop of the beginning of Stalinisation, his knowledge of Soviet academic realities became an extremely valuable asset. Having such a person on board was important, first of all, for the leaders of the Polish United Workers' Party, who had previously left academic issues for scholars to discuss and had themselves a very limited idea of the Soviet academic landscape.[28]

Nevertheless, Schaff could not fulfil his mission himself and required a team for fighting the vices and 'wrong' habits of Polish scholars. Since the established members of Polish academia did not fit Schaff's design, he decided to prepare young new scholars who would be able to lead public discussions in a form desired by Schaff. In 1950, Schaff created the Institute of the Formation of Academic Cadres (*Instytut Kształcenia Kadr Naukowych*), which was to start preparing an alternative 'intellectual elite' for Polish universities and research institutes. Following the tradition of the 'Institute of Red Professors (*Institut krasnoj professury*)' created by the Bolsheviks and partly imitating the 'Higher Party School of the Communist Party of the Soviet Union' created in 1946, Schaff attracted to his institute many young and talented students who would become the core of his young gourd designed to help him in conducting Stalinisation in Poland.[29]

The Institute began as a graduate school, but the routine of this institution seemed more like that of a military unit. In due time, all students had to be within the institute-building, while entering and leaving the territory were strictly registered. Along with the theoretical classes, the students had to watch films together and developed a 'progressive' cultural agenda.[30] Interestingly, this kind of isolation from the external world also implied some privileges. The students had access to 'both progressive [pieces of culture] and those that witnessed the decline of the bourgeois culture,' [31] which was not the case for the rest of the society. Already during their studies (this institution was the first to adopt the Soviet format of *aspirantura* instead of Polish traditional doctoral studies), some of the students were delegated to give seminars on philosophical subjects at the University of Warsaw.[32] Thus, Schaff's institute, from the moment of its foundation, represented a kind of Marxist order that was supposed not only to cultivate new virtues behind the 'monastery walls,' but also to preach these virtues for the laity.

The increase of Adam Schaff's influence was also reflected in the landscape of the academic press in Poland. Since the previous philosophical scholarship seemed hopeless from the perspective of Stalinisation, the 'best' way to reform philosophical press was to close the main philosophical journal '*Przegląd Filozoficzny* (The Philosophical Review)' (this happened in 1949) and to create a new periodical instead. It did not come as a surprise that Adam Schaff became the editor-in-chief of the newly established journal '*Myśl Filozoficzna* (Philosophical Thought)' that became the stronghold of Stalinisation. This periodical was the main educational toll of the teachers of new virtues.

In its introductory article,[33] the editorial board of 'Myśl Filozoficzna' addressed the Polish audience with a new programme of philosophy, which was still only an ideal to be reached through 'academic discussions.' Since Soviet philosophy was predominantly a tool of political struggle, the editorial board had to repeat the basic principles to be learned by Polish scholars:

> The world is divided into two camps. On the one side – the camp of peace and socialism headed by the Soviet Union… which attracts millions of ordinary and honest workers around the world. On the other side – the imperialist camp trying to start a new military conflagration in the interests of the Anglo-American aggressors … a camp that wants to stop and reverse the development of the world in order to save a dying capitalism.[34]

From this passage, it was clear that there were two kinds of philosophy – a bourgeois one and a correct one. This transition of the principles proclaimed in Szklarska Poręba by Zhdanov and Molotov to academic practice was an important point in the programme of the new journal led by Adam Schaff.

Referring to the Stalinist definition of a nation as 'the unity of territory, language, and historically formed psychological structure,' the editorial board had to recognise the problems with 'true socialism' in the 'Polish psychological structure.' Nevertheless, the lack of success in finding a Polish 'progressive intellectual tradition' during the previous public discussions did not confuse the members of the editorial board. They, based on quotations from the works of Vladimir Lenin, still believed that 'every nation [obviously including the Polish one] has two cultures – a democratic-socialist and a bourgeois one' within itself.[35] So, the aim that the editorial board of the new philosophical journal formulated for the new stage of Stalinisation was to win the competition held between Poland's bourgeois and socialist worlds.

The institutional destruction of Polish sociology was not a satisfactory result from the perspective of the organisers of Stalinisation in philosophy. The relics of Polish sociological legacy still had to be removed through an 'open criticism.' The reader of 'Myśl Filozoficzna' could read the following statement:

> A necessary condition for the success of this work [Stalinisation of Polish scholarship] is a critical coverage of the foundations of Polish academic sociology, whose research activities were burdened with a ballast of false ideological and methodological assumptions.[36]

So, it was not enough to close research institutions and sociology departments for the success of Stalinisation. The idea was to vanish all the relics of the 'wrong' character traits of the scholars who had been affiliated with 'reactionary' Polish sociology.

From the whole sociological group, Schaff's crew found only one 'virtuous man.' The former critic of Marxism, Józef Chałasiński exemplified what Schaff expected from the rest of Polish academia. Even though Chałasiński was not especially skilful in using the quotations of Marx, Engels, Lenin, and Stalin, he showed his 'modesty,' discipline, and loyalty to the 'current political need' and publicly condemned the legacy of Polish sociology. Of course, in Chałasiński's case, this could not work out without 'self-criticism.' He publicly characterised his own previous misconceptions and the heritage of his teacher Florian Znaniecki as reactionary misconduct. Chałasiński virtuously gave up his own 'individualist ambitions' and publicly defined Polish sociology as a research programme 'based on idealistic philosophy [that] was objectively related to the function of preserving the capitalist system, [and] did not lead to scientific knowledge.'[37]

Since the new form of 'virtuous behaviour' implied not only 'self-criticism' but also changes in the academic practice, Chałasiński also revised all his key research projects from the early post-war period. The new publications of Chałasiński on the 'intelligentsia' repeated, in fact, the governmental propaganda on producing a 'new intelligentsia' and lost all the anti-authoritarian aspects of his early post-war research programme.[38] Of course, Chałasiński was to change his approach to the concept of humanism. He did not insist anymore on the idea that Marxism was an 'anti-humanist' ideology. On the contrary, Chałasiński 'virtuously' changed his 'wrong' views and assured the reader that Marxism represented the main driving force of humanism.[39]

Nevertheless, the success of individual scholars in adopting the new virtues was not the aim of Adam Schaff and his colleagues. He knew that the mission could be fulfilled only in the case that all scholars (or at least the overwhelming majority of them) would become 'virtuous' men and women. Something that we can (with many reservations[40]) call a 'Stalinist science' was not a set of ideas but a form of collective practice. The *concordia* among all scholars, in combination with the victory of 'the only correct' opinion at the end of all discussions, was the only result that could be considered satisfactory. Schaff's group did not hide that their final aim was 'to imbue the whole of Polish science with a Marxist-Leninist worldview'[41]; a vision that did not imply any plurality.

Of course, the organisers of Stalinisation were 'realists' and (based on quotations from Lenin) recognised that collaboration with non-communist scholars was still possible. Nevertheless, such generosity was not unconditional. The only possibility of this collaboration depended upon the readiness of non-Marxist scholars to convert to Marxism. After the institutional disbanding of sociology and Chałasiński's 'virtuous' self-criticism, the representatives of the prominent Lvov–Warsaw school of logics (with which most of the established Polish philosophers had been associated in one way or another) started to be seen as the main bastion of 'anti-Marxism' and the object of the future 're-education' measures.[42] It is difficult to say if prominent philosophers such as Tadeusz Kotarbiński, Władysław Tatarkiewicz, and Kazimierz Ajdukiewicz took Schaff's philosophical attitude seriously before the beginning of Stalinisation, but, in 1951, he kindly offered them the 'assistance [of the editorial board of the journal] on the way to Marxism.'[43]

According to Schaff's programme, Polish scholars had to learn to do their job in the interest of the political need of the working class, which was the only criterion to distinguish a 'scientific approach' to philosophical issues from a 'non-scientific approach' to them. More importantly, the loyalty to the interest of the working class was defined by the interest of the Soviet Union as its vanguard. Having witnessed the beginning of the new wave of Stalinist repressions and the struggle of late Stalinism against so-called 'cosmopolitanism'[44] in the Soviet Union, Schaff repeatedly assured the reader that there was no place for the 'cosmopolitan attitude' in Polish science and scholarship.

Since by 'cosmopolitanism,' all 'Western sympathies' were meant, in the context of the international orientation of Polish academia, it was a very problematic claim. Nevertheless, Schaff's group had an ambition to explain to the Polish scholars that the political enemy embodied in the 'Anglo-American imperialism' had to become a scientific enemy. There was no possibility anymore to support scholars from the hostile countries through developing their academic agenda. All scientific relations with the 'Western' scholars, who did not join 'the camp of progress' led by the Soviet Union, had to be broken. Schaff's group assured the Polish scholars that the new Polish philosophy could go perfectly well without the 'Western bourgeois sciences' since they had the brilliant example of the Soviet Union to admire.[45]

It is noteworthy that the struggle against the 'western' affiliations was not an integral part of the Soviet academic programme during the whole period of Stalinism. Of course, the opposition between 'bourgeois scientists' and 'Soviet scientists' was always a central issue in the Soviet propaganda. Nevertheless, the idea of cooperation with 'progressive scientists' allowed Soviet academics to collaborate with their foreign colleagues when it was considered useful by the political leadership.[46]

The struggle against 'cosmopolitanism' was a political decision taken after the escalation of the Cold War; in other words, it was only one of many changes in the official line on this issue. The main point of this campaign was to force scholars and scientists to be virtuous and to show their loyalty to the current political need in their academic affiliation.

In post-war Soviet academia, 'public discussions' (which represented a prototype for Schaff's project) became a central academic event of the early post-war years. During his time in Moscow, Schaff could not help but witness a series of such discussions. In the field of philosophy, the most prominent 'public discussion' was organised around the textbook 'History of Western Philosophy' (1946) written by the superstar of Stalinist philosophy Georgy Aleksandrov (1908–1961).[47] Aleksandrov's 'History of Western Philosophy' was initially awarded the Stalin prize (November 1946) but, several weeks later, against the backdrop of the escalation of the Cold War, Stalin expressed displeasure with the non-patriotic character of Aleksandrov's book.

The Soviet ideologist Andrei Zhdanov (1896–1948), during an 'open discussion,' criticised, among other things, the lack of understanding that Marxism divided philosophy into 'before' and 'after' periods,[48] Alexandrov's neglect of Russian philosophy, which gave the impression that Marxism was only a Western phenomenon,[49] and, more importantly, the 'vegetarianism' towards bourgeois philosophers whom Aleksandrov, according to Zhdanov, 'burned incense for' at every opportunity.[50] Of course, the 'open discussion' 'convinced' Aleksandrov of the falsity of his position. He accepted the 'correct' point of view and went through the procedure of 'self-criticism' showing his 'virtuousness.'[51]

The 'open discussion' around Aleksandrov's book became a prime example of the academic form of 'self-criticism' at work. Despite the Stalinist innovations,[52] the idea of 'criticism' and 'self-criticism' (*kritika* and *samokritika*) had deeper roots in the theory of Marxism–Leninism. Lenin's scientific optimism and his belief in the partisanship character of objective knowledge implied that every question can be answered scientifically and can have only one correct solution. Epistemologically, the concepts of critic and self-critic in turn were a kind of modernisation of the Hegelian development principle: thesis – anti-thesis – synthesis. Though, there was one significant 'innovation': in its modernised Stalinist version, there was no need for a real synthesis. If the party leadership decided what side they take in the 'academic discussion' (this was not always the case), the 'correct' point of view just replaced the 'wrong' one.

In the historiography, this kind of Stalinist public discussion is frequently characterised as a ritual or a game in the sense of a 'creative' form of following certain rules. This 'game' was possible only if all the players follow these rules. [53] However, it is much more important that all these 'public discussions' aimed to check if Soviet scholars and scientists were ready to prefer loyalty to the current political line (expressed by the side supported by the party leadership) over loyalty to an 'abstract (i.e. non-partisan)' truth, to his own convictions (a 'Bolshevik modesty' and 'party discipline' were required), and to his colleagues and friends. For a game, it is not important if you are sincere in following the rules. Soviet scholars and scientists were asked to be sincere in following the virtues praised by the authorities.[54]

Therefore, the ultimate (though utopian) aim of Schaff's group was not only to force Polish scholars to accept the new rules of the 'game' but also to change their character, in other words, to make them other persons.

Fighting the 'stubbornness' of non-Marxist scholars

Since all Polish scholars were supposed to join the 'party of truth' at the end of the campaign, the most important task of Schaff's group was to show why one cannot have correct views if they are not a Marxist. Polish logicians were the first most obvious target for the organisers of Stalinisation. The first blow against the Lvov–Warsaw School was dealt by one of Schaff's students, Bronisław Baczko (1924–2016), who became one of the first fellows at the Institute of the Formation of Academic Cadres. The young officer Baczko was sent to Schaff's institute by the military command as a very promising cadre. His struggle on an ideological front started with a Marxist examination of the views of Tadeusz Kotarbiński, as a key representative of the logical tradition in post-war Poland. As all students of Schaff's institute, Baczko knew that there are only two philosophies – materialist (i.e. Marxist) and idealist. Thus, the first task of Baczko was to find out to which camp Kotarbiński really belonged.[55]

To find idealism in the works of Kotarbiński, who, since the interwar period, declared his materialist attitude was not an easy task. Nevertheless, understanding that the logician was not a Marxist inspired Baczko in his search. The concept of *'reizm (from lat. Res - thing),'* which described Kotarbiński's programme of rationalisation of the academic discourse, became an object of Baczko's examination. Being a part of the European logical movement, Kotarbiński thought that rational reductionism in the language used for academic communication, i.e. speaking in non-ideological and concrete language, would help to resolve most philosophical contradictions. Thus, according to Kotarbiński, 'good semantics would be a good treatment'[56] for contemporary philosophy. This programme gave Baczko a good argument with which to accuse Kotarbiński of reducing the essential philosophical issues to the matter of language and, thus, making philosophy a *façon de parler* rather than a science about objective laws of social and economic development, as it should be according to Marxism–Leninism. According to Baczko, this was not only philosophical misconduct from Kotarbiński's side but '[an act of] opening the door for idealism' since 'any blurring of the basic dividing line in philosophy and the introduction of some additional dividing lines depending on the acceptance of one or another "language"… makes the path of idealism easier, makes the smuggling of idealistic ideas under the banner of 'the language of thing' easier.'[57]

The young scholar Baczko was strict and, at the same time, indulgent towards the prominent professor Kotarbiński:

> It can be thought that, subjectively, Prof. Kotarbiński would not himself accept extremely conventionalist views. However, this does not change the objective fact that the conventionalist conclusions, which had been rejected by Prof. Kotarbiński, could be consistently derived from his views.[58]

Thus, though unaware of it, Kotarbiński, according to the author, supported idealism, while believing himself to be a materialist.

Meanwhile, the main point in Baczko's programme and also of Schaff's group concerned not exclusively with the realm of Kotarbiński's ideas. Baczko claimed that, politically, after the appearance of Marxism, there was no need for less radical materialist programmes. Developing this idea, Baczko referred to Lenin's interpretation of 'reflection theory,' which claimed that people reflect objective reality in their mind and that correct intellectual work is nothing but the comprehension of this objective reality. This uncompromising approach did not contain any idealism and, according to Baczko, perfectly resolved all the vacuous philosophical questions Kotarbiński was aware of.[59] Since the theory of Lenin was the pinnacle of progressive thought, the lack of Lenin's cognitive optimism in the works of Kotarbiński appeared to be not just a mistake from his part but a kind of stubbornness in accepting a more progressive ideological programme.

The examination of the 'social-political attitude' of Kotarbiński could only help Baczko to prove his point. In the interwar period, Kotarbiński had published his articles, among other journals, in 'The Rationalist (*Racjonalista*)' and was among the active fighters against metaphysics and irrationalism, both in the academic sphere and in the public debates. Baczko found many 'praiseworthy' traits in the previous public activity of Kotarbiński and especially emphasised his courage in the struggle against 'fascism and Catholic obscurantism.' His atheist attitude, claims of materialism, the fight against antisemitism in the universities, and the opposition to Józef Piłsudski's regime were, without doubt, 'relatively progressive' for the interwar Polish realities. Nevertheless, Baczko argued that Kotarbiński did not have the brevity required to recognise that his views were not 'truly progressive' when considered against the backdrop of the programme of the Bolsheviks. The political ideas of Kotarbiński were, according to Baczko, 'outdated' already in the interwar years. The aspiration of the philosopher to distinguish his 'intelligentsia's liberalism' from the movement of the workers' masses was a sin of backwardness even for the political realities of the Second Polish Republic. Thus, the academic 'backwardness' of Kotarbiński was only a reflection of his political 'backwardness.'[60]

More importantly, the main problem with Kotarbiński after the war was that he did not change his views when facing the new realities. Baczko wrote:

> In the philosophical and social views of Kotarbiński, there were certain points which could lead to the evolution towards dialectical materialism, towards the rejection of his anachronistic individualistic liberalism…unfortunately such an evolution did not take place until now.[61]

While the misconceptions of the past could be forgiven because of the 'relative progressiveness' of Kotarbiński's views, his stubbornness in not adopting the new forms of academic practice under the conditions of the victory of socialism in Poland was not acceptable. According to Baczko,

Kotarbiński had to change both his philosophical view and his political/scholarly ethos:

> As a whole, as a system, the philosophical and social views of Prof. Kotarbiński remained out of the way, fenced off to those ideological changes that occurred and are occurring in our reality, in our scholarship, among our intelligentsia. There is a task which Polish philosophers face now they should overcome all obstacles and barriers, all relics of idealism…[Polish philosophers should contribute] to the great struggle for peace and the Six-Year plan, the struggle for the future of our fatherland.[62]

Kotarbiński was, according to Baczko, only one example of the bearers of the vice of 'stubbornness' in refusing to accept more 'progressive' views preached by Schaff's group. Baczko's publication, in turn, was to 'help' the prominent professor to understand his mistakes and, through 'self-criticism,' to join the 'party of truth,' i.e. to become a 'virtuous man.'

The mentor of the campaign against the Lvov–Warsaw School, Adam Schaff, took over the analysis of the philosophical and ideological misconceptions of another prominent logician, the former chair of the subsection for the social sciences and humanities within the First Congress of Polish Science, Kazimierz Ajdukiewicz. When Kotarbiński openly claimed that he was a materialist, an atheist, and believed in the possibility of finding a rational explanation for all phenomena, the task of Schaff's crew was to explain why, without becoming a loyal Marxist, these beliefs of Kotarbiński continued to be only an illusion. The case of Ajdukiewicz appeared to be much easier. In the interwar period, Ajdukiewicz was among those scholars who questioned the optimism of Kotarbiński regarding the possibility of finding a non-conventional method of rational argumentation. Ajdukiewicz's argument was that every language is a kind of convention, and it would be highly problematic to find a meta-language for the rationalisation of academic discourse. It did not mean for him that rationalisation was a futile project; Ajdukiewicz – as many European logicians of his time – was deeply involved in the agenda of linguistics and had attempted to find a linguistically acceptable method of rational argumentation. Either way, the word 'conventionalism' was a marker in the vocabulary of Schaff's group and meant idealism.

As it was shown in the case of Kotarbiński, after the appearance of Marxism–Leninism, 'conventionalism' and 'idealism' were no longer just theoretical mistakes but became quasi-moral misconducts. Therefore, Schaff started his examination of Ajdukiewicz's philosophical views from the constatation of a sad fact that Ajdukiewicz not only was not a 'virtuous man' but also did not show any readiness to change his attitude:

> Ajdukiewicz is a conventionalist *tout court,* and he is a radical conventionalist. The line of his development is clear and remains unchangeable: Ajdukiewicz was a conventionalist in the interwar period …[he] has not changed his attitude now.[63]

Developing this idea, Adam Schaff strove to expose the 'mythology' that prevented Ajdukiewicz and other members of the school from seeing the faultiness of their attitude. 'The myth of scientific exactness' became the main object of Schaff's criticism. According to him, the 'esoteric mist' of the approach of the logicians had an extremely negative influence, not only on Polish academia, but also on the Polish intelligentsia, and thus represented a political threat under the new political conditions.[64]

Exposing the hidden political contexts, Schaff asked the public not to be misled by the self-representation of the Lvov–Warsaw School. He argued: 'Marxism teaches us that one should examine individuals and social groups not according to what they say or think about themselves, but according to what role they are objectively playing.' Schaff saw the foundation of the 'myth of exactness' in the references of logicians to mathematics. The abundance of mathematical equations played, in his view, a significant role in creating a 'curtain of smoke' around their argumentation. The critical and 'objective' Marxist position of Schaff allowed him to show that all mathematical formulae merely disguised idealistic semantics, conventionalism and, thus, bourgeois ideology. Historically, wrote Schaff, the Lvov–Warsaw School was at the centre of bourgeois influence. Among the negative influences that shaped the bourgeois profile of the school, there were English empiricism embodied in Bertrand Russell, the Austro-German neo-positivism of Moritz Schlick (1882–1936), Rudolf Carnap (1891–1970), Otto Neurath (1882–1945), and American pragmatism in the person of Charles W. Morris (1901–1979).[65]

The contacts with neo-positivism and, more precisely, with the Vienna circle was, from Schaff's perspective, a telling fact in itself. Developing this idea, Schaff used an irrefutable argument when showing that most of the scholars affiliated with these intellectual tendencies had left continental Europe for the USA and England in the late 1930s. Though Schaff failed to mention the reason why all these scholars had to leave the continent, it was enough, for him, to show that they were not in the Soviet Union and thus out of the camp of progress. The location in the USA and UK was, of course, an aggravating circumstance and good evidence of them becoming 'the flagship philosophy of world reaction.' So, Polish logicians became, due to their 'unvirtuous behaviour,' not just philosophers with wrong views, but agents of world imperialism. 'The bourgeoisie is well aware of the mobilising power of Marxist theory,' wrote Schaff, 'therefore, the ideological fire of the bourgeoisie is directed against it.'[66] In this situation, not to be a loyal Marxist meant to defend the world reaction.

Nevertheless, Schaff did not lose hope that it was possible to change the foundations of the academic practice of Polish scholars in general and Ajdukiewicz in particular. Additionally, he did not want to be unfair towards Ajdukiewicz and claimed that his opponent never wanted to defend obscurantism but sincerely believed in the rationality of his research programme. Schaff expressed certain empathy towards the representatives of the Lvov–Warsaw School but still was strict with them:

> Psychologically, the indignation of people who believed in the scientific myth of their position is quite understandable when this myth has been exposed. Nevertheless, this is the truth, and no indignation can help against this truth. [67]

Thus, if, earlier, Ajdukiewicz and the whole school were drugged by their mythology, after Schaff's ideological treatment, there was no excuse for any stubbornness. The path down which Polish scholars were asked to go was through repentance. Schaff was not tired of repeating that the criticism of non-Marxist views, and the self-criticism of non-Marxists, would be a healing balm for all the wounds of Polish academia.[68] In accordance with the Leninist concept of partisanship,[69] Schaff made it clear that, only upon adopting the new form of 'virtuous behaviour,' could the scholars join the 'party of truth.'

The blow against the founder of the Lvov–Warsaw School Kazimierz Twardowski (1866–1938) was supposed to complete the ideological destruction of the non-Marxist milieu in Polish academia. The young fellow of Schaff's institute Henryk Holland (1920–1961), who was honoured to conduct the examination of the works of Twardowski from the 'Marxist point of view,' had already had an experience in 'improving' the Polish academic landscape. Together with Leszek Kołakowski (1927–2009) and some other young intellectuals, he belonged to the group of the members of the Polish United Workers' Party who had organised a student protest against the teaching strategy of another representative of the Lvov–Warsaw School, Władysław Tatarkiewicz. During a seminar, the students read out their letter with accusations against Tatarkiewicz concerning his 'hostile claims against Poland constructing socialism,'[70] and the professor was suspended from teaching at the University of Warsaw.[71] Two years later, Holland continued the public struggle against the 'myth' of the Lvov–Warsaw School and exposed the 'legend of Kazimierz Twardowski.'[72]

The relevance of the critical examination of Twardowski's works was obvious because of the position that this figure held in Polish academia, even after his death. In fact, most Polish philosophy professors in the interwar period were Twardowski's students. The situation did not change much after the Second World War. The representatives of academic philosophy, Kotarbiński, Ajdukiewicz, and another famous Polish phenomenologist Roman Ingarden (1893–1970), according to Holland, developed and promoted the myth about the scientific exactness of the research programme of their teacher.[73] Twardowski had been a student of the prominent German philosopher Franz Brentano (1838–1917), and his interest in empirical psychology became a good target for Holland's criticism. Following his teacher – former priest and theologian Brentano – Twardowski, according to the author, wanted to distract philosophy from the social and economic examination of objective reality and instead deal with 'psychological facts,' which were a cover for metaphysics.

In such a way, Holland wrote that he 'could not deny himself the pleasure' of making the reader familiar with one of Twardowski's ideas 'from the field of the clear and unambiguous clarification of his concepts by which his students are so inspired.' In the fragment quoted by Holland, Twardowski – in an article published in 1897 – argued that there is no proof that thinking is conducted exclusively with the brain, and psychology as a discipline could prevent philosophy from reducing itself to physiology.[74] Following the spirit of his milieu, Holland was rough in his opinion: 'One should not argue with a scholar who at the turn of the 19th and 20th centuries contradicts the fact that people are thinking with their brain, one should laugh at him.'⁷⁵ Thus, all publications of Twardowski in which he disagreed with the theses of metaphysics not only seemed to Holland 'non-scientific' but merely disguised the subjective idealism that helped to maintain the metaphysical way of thinking. The German publications of Twardowski in which he characterised 're-flection theory' as a 'primitive psychology'⁷⁶ gave Holland a rich source of material for proving the opposition of Twardowski to the 'truly scientific' methods.⁷⁷

Of course, the publications of Twardowski in which he reflected on the possibilities of the immortality of the soul represented the most fertile ground for Holland's criticism. For him, it was obvious that any scholar who allowed the idea of the existence of God played into the hands of reaction. 'The blow of Twardowski against materialism,' wrote the author, 'and the defense of the Catholic faith represented an extraordinary obscurantism even for idealistic philosophy.'⁷⁸ Thus, the whole tradition of the Lvov–Warsaw School was represented by 'medieval' and 'scholastic' wordplays; 'the philosophy of Twardowski,' wrote Holland, 'was not a scientific philosophy but an extremely obscure, fideistic, clerical one.'⁷⁹

Following the genre, Holland repeated the call upon the representatives of the Lvov–Warsaw School to join the 'party of truth and historical materialism' and leave the 'party of reaction.' A public exposure of Twardowski's ideas was supposed to become an integral part of the self-purification of Polish academia. Baczko's contribution was only to show the path that the Polish scholars themselves were expected to follow to destroy the legacy of the teacher.⁸⁰ Thus, from the perspective of Schaff's group, not only a personal conversion, but also the renunciation of the 'fathers' was required for meeting the new standards of 'good academic practice.'

Can a 'non-virtuous' scholar write a textbook?

Following Chekhov's principle that 'if in the first act you have hung a pistol on the wall, then in the following one it should be fired,' the last episode of the offensive campaign against the Lvov–Warsaw School directly referred to a 'spectre' that was haunting the whole Stalinisation process in Poland. By the time of the campaign against Polish academic philosophers, the spirit of Zhdanov and his critic of the Soviet philosopher Aleksandrov received physical form in the Polish translation (1951) of Zhdanov's speech delivered during the 'open discussion' on Aleksandrov's '*History of Western Philosophy*.'⁸¹ Reference to the source of inspiration for the whole campaign did not appear in the public discussion until the publication of a review of the three-volume '*History of Philosophy*' written by one of the students of Twardowski, Władysław Tatarkiewicz.

However, the similarity between the cases of Tatarkiewicz and Aleksandrov was very superficial, even though both were formally criticised for their textbooks on the history of philosophy. Aleksandrov was a child of Stalinism, which had helped him to make a career. The campaign against Aleksandrov was rather an example of how a 'virtuous' member of Stalinist academia should behave when facing the changes in the political line promoted by the authorities. Tatarkiewicz was, on contrary, not only one of the representatives of non-Marxist Philosophy but also not a stranger to the Catholic agenda, continuing to publish his articles in Catholic journals even after the war.[82] By the time of the publication of the review, Tatarkiewicz was already suspended from teaching by the initiative of his students.[83] Either way, he still was the author of a three-volume textbook on the history of philosophy that was one of the biggest philosophical projects of the post-war years.

The reviewer of Tatarkiewicz's work, Tadeusz Kroński, was also associated with the Institute of the Formation of Academic Cadres, though not as a student but as a teaching fellow and specialist in German thought. More importantly, Kroński had been a student of Kotarbiński and Tatarkiewicz at the University of Warsaw, where he had studied philosophy. This provided a special context for his position as a critic of the Lvov–Warsaw School. Having started with the statement that bourgeois history of philosophy and bourgeois philosophy are different issues, Kroński asked himself if the textbook written by 'the bourgeois philosopher' Tatarkiewicz could be allowed for academic practice in the new socialist Polish state. Thus, the author from the beginning determined the practical implication of his review, which had to 'decide' if the book, written by a 'non-virtuous' scholar, could have any academic relevance in a socialist Poland.[84] 'The textbook of Tatarkiewicz was not different from other bourgeois textbooks on the history of philosophy,' wrote Kroński, 'but could this be useful under the conditions of People's Poland?'[85]

Having already learned which was the only 'scientific history of philosophy,' Kroński did not experience any difficulties in showing that the work of Tatarkiewicz did not respond to the key criteria of scientific character. Tatarkiewicz had written his textbook as a traditional history of philosophical ideas without any attention to the 'political and social views' of philosophers. In such a way, 'the striking anti-historicism of Tatarkiewicz was,' argued Kroński, 'one of the sources of the distortion of the development of philosophy in his textbook.'[86] The main mistake of which Tatarkiewicz was accused by his former student would be obvious for all readers of the prominent Lenin article *'Three Sources and Three Components of Marxism.'*[87] Though, for Lenin, Marxism as a principle of human thought had been rooted in German classical philosophy, English political economy, and French utopian socialism, none of these trends in European thought received a proper place in Tatarkiewicz's History of Philosophy.[88]

It was not difficult for Kroński to show that the 'non-virtuous' character of Tatarkiewicz had a direct impact on his philosophical work. So, for example, Tatarkiewicz's philosophical ethos did not allow him to see the roots of the materialist attitude of Thomas Hobbes, Baruch Spinoza, and – no less important – Mikhail Lomonosov (1711–1765) in the progress of the natural sciences and the scientific worldview as an opposition to idealism. Additionally, the whole Renaissance tradition was not, for Tatarkiewicz, a philosophical phenomenon. 'Strict fanatic immanentism[89] in the selection of philosophical facts forced Tatarkiewicz to refuse the philosophical originality of the Renaissance' though, according to Kroński, this period was extremely productive for the development of the materialist worldview.[90] More importantly, Tatarkiewicz – who was finishing his book after the war – 'falsified,' according to Kroński, the real history of materialism through attempts to represent such Christian thinkers as Tertullian and Thomas Aquinas as materialists.[91] Kroński also saw a sign of relativism in Tatarkiewicz's attempt to distinguish between 'minimalist' and 'maximalist' tendencies in philosophy. Tatarkiewicz introduced these concepts to define the thinkers who tended to speak exclusively about real objects and, conversely, those who attempted to make broader suggestions. Such a strategy exposed, according to Kroński, Tatarkiewicz's tendency to legitimise 'non-scientific' tendencies in philosophy and demonstrated his 'deeply reactionary character.'[92]

Kroński did not fail to examine another hidden consequence of Tatarkiewicz's 'spoiled' scholarly character – his 'cosmopolitan' and 'non-patriotic' tendency in writing the history of philosophy. According to Kroński, although the three volumes of Tatarkiewicz's writing contained 1362 pages, only 43 of them were devoted to Polish philosophy. More importantly, there was 'no word' about Russian philosophers in the *History of Philosophy*, which could be regarded as an attempt to overestimate the 'Western' intellectual tradition and to underestimate the achievements of the Soviet Union. For Kroński, it was crucial to show that this was a direct implication of Tatarkiewicz's academic ethos. For example, according to him, being a reactionary, Tatarkiewicz unconsciously attempted to conceal that Polish non-fascist thinkers were revolutionaries but not mystics and reactionaries.[93]

Developing this idea, Kroński came to the central point of the campaign for re-educating Polish scholars – a 'non-virtuous' thinker like Tatarkiewicz cannot be an author of an 'objective' history of philosophy because of his fear of losing popularity in reactionary circles. The hatred of progressive and socialist views as well as the exclusion of Russia and the Soviet Union from the narrative were, according to Kroński, examples of the world reaction destroying the Polish nation ideologically through its agents like Tatarkiewicz:

> In [his] hatred of the Soviet Union and constant fear of this natural ally [of Poland] and its support for the broad working masses of the [Polish] nation, [Tatarkiewicz] feverishly sought evidence of [Polish thought] belonging to the 'Christian,' 'European,' 'Western' culture, thinking that with the help of this propaganda it would be possible to cut a quiet natural bond that connects the Polish nation with the Russian one.[94]

The fact that Tatarkiewicz started the third volume of his *History* by claiming an intention to devote a separate volume to the philosophy of the Slavic countries[95] was not a problem for the argumentation of Kroński. He warned the reader against naivety in looking for cosmopolitans among scholars, when writing:

> Cosmopolitans are not always those who do not want to write about the culture of their nation (you can be a good patriot and deal with, for example, Spinoza and Thomas Aquinas the whole of your life), but first of all are those who dealt [with the culture of their nation] but did not specify its rightful position in the world.[96]

Developing this argument, Kroński literally copied the argument of Zhdanov from his speech against the Marxist Aleksandrov, which concerned the underestimation of the role of Marxism in the history of philosophy. Even though Tatarkiewicz never defined himself as a Marxist, Kroński critically remarked that the reader of his *History* may get the impression that Marxism is only one of many philosophical trends rather than the only scientific method.

Kroński's criticism can be reduced to one simple idea: no one can be a 'good scholar' and write a 'truly scientific texts' without becoming a loyal Marxist, i.e. changing the foundations of academic practice. The texts written by 'non-virtuous' scholars cannot be considered proper for preparing the new generation of Polish philosophers.[97] Thus, Kroński's blow against Tatarkiewicz was supposed to show to all scholars who opposed the new virtues that they had no choice but to change their scholarly ethos to be able to write 'truly scientific' texts.

The headstrong 'students' and failed teaching

Even though Adam Schaff and his group did their best to explain what it meant to be 'truly virtuous,' Polish scholars did not seem ready to follow the prescriptions of 'self-criticism' and rebaptise themselves as Marxists. Most importantly, Kotarbiński and Ajdukiewicz, who continued teaching at Polish universities, were allowed to publish their responses to the criticisms both against their academic ethos and against the whole academic tradition of the Lvov–Warsaw School. However, the ultimate aim to re-educate Polish scholars was not forgotten. The publications of the philosophers were accompanied by an extensive commentary from the editorial board and a special article prepared by one of the 'virtuous' scholars. These measures were obviously aimed to defend the reader, who could not be relied upon to be strong enough in the new faith, from the temptation to agree with the non-Marxist scholars. Either way, the hope that Kotarbiński and Ajdukiewicz would follow the virtuous example of Józef Chałasiński seemed increasingly elusive.

Responding to the arguments of Baczko (who had argued that the materialism of Kotarbiński was, in fact, idealistic although it contained some materialistic elements), Tadeusz Kotarbiński wrote: '[to say that] my works contain some traits of materialism [is as correct as] to say that the works of a father-Abbot contain certain traits of Catholicism.'[98] Moreover, Kotarbiński did not hesitate to say: 'I dare say that [my somatic semiotics are] the only consequently materialistic semantics in these territories.' He argued that his attempts to rationalise the academic discourse and his idea to represent words as bodies were the most effective path towards materialism. Concerning the accusations of his speculation with words that replaced the research on objective phenomena, Kotarbiński briefly remarked that he 'had never participated in such a party (*impreza*)' and did not see the necessity of refuting something that he had never said.

Responding to the accusation of conventionalism Kotarbiński did not hide his irony and argued that he could imagine like 'a bomber circling around this area ['conventional' elements of Kotarbiński's philosophy] – with the critic inside,

186 The School of 'New Virtues'

angrily throwing bombs on me.'[99] From two options, 'to fire back' or 'to wave a white flag,' Kotarbiński chose the former and thus disregarded the kind of answer that was strongly recommended by the group of 'educators.'

Kotarbiński confessed that he did not understand what his critic meant to say by accusing him of the separation of language from the socio-historical context:

> I am deeply convinced that language comes from history as a social construct. Since I was a teacher of classic philology, the elements of the historic-philological catechism are well integrated in my mind.[100]

Kotarbiński allowed himself even a certain witticism towards his critic. He said that Baczko had accused him of the metaphysical character of his research programme, though 'in a very specific, Marxian, understanding of this word.' In fact, according to Kotarbiński, his opponent had created 'a mannequin, a wax figure' in the place of his real dynamic and practical approach, and then repeatedly attacked this dummy.[101] Regarding dialectics, which represented the core of historical materialism, Kotarbiński argued that his research programme had no contradictions with this discipline, which he understood as a framework for explaining the process of development.[102] Thus, Kotarbiński attempted, on the one hand, to refute the key points of his opponent, and, on the other, to show that historical materialism, which was depicted on the 'red flag' of Schaff's group, referred to other issues than logic and could not be a criterion for judging logical studies.

Additionally, Kotarbiński made an important clarification concerning the whole philosophical tradition in Poland. According to him, the very concept of 'the Lvov–Warsaw School,' which had become the object of criticism, led to confusion. He found it more accurate to speak about two different schools: the Lvov and the Warsaw ones. While Twardowski, a teacher for most of the Polish philosophers, was a philosopher 'in the full sense of the word,' his students who developed logic in Warsaw made it under the banner of 'anti-philosophy.' This division was necessary for Kotarbiński to show that Twardowski's engagement in the debates on ontological issues was foreign to the Warsaw philosophers, who wanted to conduct concrete research while avoiding vague philosophical categories. While the Warsaw school dealt with mathematical logic, Twardowski strove to make philosophy more scientific, though not in the English and French sense of *science,* but rather as was exemplified in the German *Wissenschaft.*[103] Kotarbiński recognised that the ontological tendencies in Twardowski's programme, 'from the sociological point of view, could be labelled as escapism.' Meanwhile, Kotarbiński emphasised that Twardowski possessed a virtue of 'extreme tolerance' that he thought crucial both for a scholar and for a citizen. According to Kotarbiński, Twardowski did not force his agenda on his students, which was an example to follow.[104] Thus, when answering to the arguments of his opponents, Kotarbiński did not fail to mention his disagreement with the basic virtues promoted by Schaff's group.

It is noteworthy that Kotarbiński deemed it necessary to respond to the attacks of Schaff's institute through the prism of 'the issues of good and evil.'

He remembered that one of the key arguments of his critics was his 'stubbornness' in changing the foundations of his academic practice despite the changes that had happened in the political landscape of Poland. Kotarbiński did not hide his irony when writing that his views 'had been ossified and did not move, even though the society rushes forward, carried away by the progressive movement.' Obviously referring to the campaign promoted by Adam Schaff, the author wittily said: 'it is true that I do not participate in the class struggle organised politically...but it is not true that I am away from practice.' Kotarbiński argued that he was ready to improve his views but only when these improvements would correspond with his moral convictions, otherwise he preferred to characterise the changes required by his critics as timeserving (*koniunkturalizm*), which he considered a vice both for a scholar and for a citizen. He referred to the example of Socrates, whose views maintained their relevance despite all the political and social changes that had occurred over thousands of years. Developing this idea, Kotarbiński himself thematised the connection between political and scholarly virtues. Without refusing his key moral principles, Kotarbiński as an 'academic liberal' was ready to serve 'the new socialist academia and to participate in the education of proletariat.'[105] Nevertheless, Kotarbiński preferred to stay a 'virtuous' man in his own understanding of 'virtuousness' rather than accept the forms of academic practice promoted by Schaff's group.

None other than sociologist Józef Chałasiński was chosen to 'shame' Kotarbiński in the eyes of the reader. It is no coincidence that Chałasiński, who himself 'virtuously' followed the 'requirements' of the 'new times,' showed a special diligence in proving that the post-war publication of Kotarbiński contained no response to the social changes in post-war Poland. Chałasiński, who a few years earlier had flaunted his liberalism,[106] wrote that Kotarbiński's concept of *reizm* was interesting to him only as a form of 'liberal-individualistic escape' from historical reality and as a 'claim for a moral purity of the historical role of the scholar in our revolutionary epoch.'[107]

The reader of the texts written by Chałasiński immediately after the war would be surprised to read in the article of the same author the following lines:

The [social and moral] criteria of these liberal moralists...had some moral disagreements with capitalism but, after various moral reservations, have solidarity with the dictatorship of capitalism...this is their moral catastrophe.[108]

Moreover, Chałasiński did not hesitate to accuse Kotarbiński of actively opposing the new political realities. Chałasiński went beyond the texts written by his opponent and referred to the oral presentation delivered by Kotarbiński at the meeting of the Łódź Scientific Society: 'concerning the Marxian movement, he [Kotarbiński] said that every scholar had to take from this movement what corresponds with his conscience.'[109] This reference to the conscience was especially irritating for Chałasiński. He argued: 'none of them who wanted to take part in the reconstruction [of Poland into a socialist state] could avoid self-determination towards the theory and methodology of historical materialism.' This led Chałasiński to the main point of his new ideology:

> The conscience of the intellectual which is detached from the course of history is a broken compass. One should not trust it when, in order to avoid a decision, it says that ... there is a compromise, a third 'gentlemen' path ... a path of the peace of conscience. There is no third way. History has greatly simplified the matter of choice. There is either a path of criminal capitalism or a socialist revolution.[110]

Characteristically, this 'commentary' by Chałasiński had been published before Kotarbiński's article, although it contained the criticism of Kotarbiński's text which was supposed to be read later. Additionally, when the readers of the journal, despite all the warnings, read the article of Kotarbiński, they had to face the section 'From the editorial board.'[111] In the text apparently written by Schaff or, at least, under his close guidance, the 'editorial board' made clear that this was the end of the debate on the views of Kotarbiński.[112] Having reviewed the *pro et contra* arguments of Kotarbiński's research programme, they expressed regret concerning the stubbornness of the philosopher who claimed 'only a partial solidarity' with historical materialism. Kotarbiński had failed to conduct 'critical and self-critical examination of his own views' and continued to promote 'views the fallacy of which had been demonstrated.'[113] Schaff's group was not able to do anything about it and they washed their hands.

However, the name of Kotarbiński appeared during the discussion on the heritage of the Lvov–Warsaw School once again. This time, Kotarbiński attempted to defend his teacher Kazimierz Twardowski against the criticism of Henryk Holland. There was no place for such a contribution in the main part of the journal anymore, and the opinion of Kotarbiński was published in the section 'Letters to the editorial board.' In any case, the tone of this text had changed since his last contribution, which was full of witticisms. This time, Kotarbiński was obviously very annoyed. He did not hesitate to characterise the article of Holland as abusive and wrote that the 'contempt, mockeries, and humiliation' towards Twardowski that were published in Holland's article were unacceptable. More importantly, he claimed that the editorial board should watch the language of their publications and reflect on what kind of discussion they had been promoting.[114]

The editorial board was apparently a bit concerned by Kotarbiński's pressure and even recognised that they probably had to remove 'some most cruel' passages from Holland's contribution. Nevertheless, they clarified again that their idea of scholarly discussion implied the struggle against the bourgeois and idealistic attitude. Thus, the cruelty in the formulation could be understood as an instrument of this struggle.[115] Either way, with this commentary, Kotarbiński not only refused the requirement to renounce the disciplinary 'fathers' but also openly characterised the form of 'discussion' proposed by the organisers of Stalinisation as rude and unacceptable. He did so at the highest point of Stalinisation.

Kotarbiński's 'stubbornness' was not a unique case. Kazimierz Ajdukiewicz also got an opportunity to answer to the criticism of Adam Schaff against his research programme. Much like Kotarbiński, Ajdukiewicz attempted to rationalise the arguments that were used by Schaff. Not without witticism, Ajdukiewicz wrote that 'after reading [his ideas in the interpretation of his opponent], the reader of the article of prof. Schaff would get a very unflattering option on the state of the sanity of the author who had been criticised.'[116] In the best traditions of his discipline, the logician Ajdukiewicz systematised the accusations of Schaff and replied to them in a very detailed contribution. He asserted that the thesis of 'radical conventionalism' was rooted not in the idealism that Schaff desired to find in his publications but in the nature of the language. At the same time, Ajdukiewicz pointed out that, much like Kotarbiński, he never argued for the fetishisation of language nor the break with the social reality in logical studies.[117]

Additionally, Ajdukiewicz did not show any progress in comprehending the role of Marxism–Leninism as the 'only scientific method.' On the contrary, he continued to argue that he did not see any essential contradictions in his approach with 'the doctrine of Marxism.' He wrote:

The criticism of prof. Schaff did not convince me of the need to revise any of the opinions he criticised in his article… I even think that some of my works … would not be without relevance for the justification of the Marxist method of practicing philosophy.[118]

The main argument of Ajdukiewicz was simple: 'The issues with which I was dealing and the issues with which Marxist philosophers were dealing are different. Different issues require different methods.'[119] Most importantly, Ajdukiewicz's public discourse confirmed the fiasco of Schaff's 'teaching' project: the central representatives of Polish academia failed to become 'virtuous scholars' in accordance with the new standards.

It is noteworthy that Ajdukiewicz received a gentler 'supervision' from the editorial board than was the case with Kotarbiński. To conclude the debate on the Lvov–Warsaw School, Leszek Kołakowski (1927–2009), then one of the activists in Schaff's institute and later one of the key European anti-Marxist thinkers,[120] was chosen to comment on the response of Ajdukiewicz. The style of Kołakowski's narration was noticeably more polite than that of his other colleagues from the Institute of the Formation of Academic Cadres. Of course, all necessary concepts such as 'reactionary character,' 'bourgeois idealism,' and 'the class nature of Ajdukiewicz's ideas' were present in the contribution of Kołakowski. Nevertheless, at that moment, it was already clear that re-education of Polish philosophers failed. In this situation, Kołakowski preferred a philosophical criticism against the whole of the conventionalist tradition over attacking Ajdukiewicz individually.

In his article, Kołakowski conducted an in-depth examination of various approaches in conventionalism.[121] Based primarily on the works of the prominent mathematician and philosopher Édouard Le Roy (1870–1954), the mathematician and astronomer Henri Poincaré (1854–1912), as well as the physician and historian of science Pierre Duhem (1861–1916), Kołakowski showed that relativism concerning the possibility of reaching objective reality and a constructivist approach to the definition of scientific fact was a very influential movement in philosophy.[122] Commenting on this tendency, Kołakowski could just argue that relativisation of the issue of objective truth made science helpless in its struggle against prejudices. Developing this idea, Kołakowski (who was one of the main experts in exposing Catholic philosophy during the wave of Stalinisation[123]) claimed that this kind of relativism, coupled with agnosticism, led to the fact that 'bourgeois scientists' could not find arguments in their struggle against religion.[124]

The impossibility of re-educating the famous Polish philosophers made Kołakowski's contribution, first of all, a declaration of the ideas that attracted him and many of his young colleagues to Schaff's campaign. Marxism–Leninism seemed, to them, a much more effective tool in their struggle against the 'obscurantism'[125] that they had faced in interwar Poland and wanted to destroy under the new political conditions. From their perspective, only belief in the objective truth could help science to complete its mission, since, as Kołakowski put it, 'waking people have one common world and each come back to her or his own world only while sleeping.'[126] Nevertheless, the fact that the Polish philosophers (who had struggled against clericalism themselves) got the opportunity to argue with their accusers did not allow Schaff's group to organise an information blockade and to achieve the state of *concordia* under which the forms of academic practice they promoted would seem the only correct ones. Much like his colleagues, Kołakowski was forced to come to a sad conclusion that the ideological campaign did not bring any changes in the scholarly ethos of leading Polish scholars.

*

The radical reconstruction of Polish academia under Stalinisation significantly changed its image. Nevertheless, the changes hardly corresponded with the expectations of the ideologists and activists of Stalinism. While many Polish scholars asked to rule this process focused on preserving the forms of academic practice they considered 'progressive,' Schaff's qualifications made his campaign the most 'professional' attempt to force Polish scholars to adopt the new forms of 'virtuous behaviour.' Nevertheless, this attempt obviously failed. Schaff was confronted with a scholarly ethos that was not to break in a non-violent way. Polish philosophers and social scientists were forced to openly defend themselves therefore making the inapplicability of Schaff's programme a public fact. Schaff's opponents never tired of repeating that rationality, the opposition to 'obscurantism,' and even materialism, played an important role in their research and political agenda. Nevertheless, they did not recognise Schaff's monopoly over these categories. More importantly, academic discussion as an exchange of arguments and the plurality of various opinions in the academic field were, for them, the only precondition for academic development. This kind of discussion had to divide questions into those that were pointless and those that were relevant and, thus, to lead to 'rationality.' Therefore, during the whole campaign, the logicians attempted to 'translate' the arguments against them into arguments and to respond to the concrete points they had extracted from the polemical texts of their opponents, which were written in another genre. They praised tolerance towards other opinions as both a political and academic virtue and considered the loyalty to the views that they found wrong a 'timeserving'; in other words, a vice and not a virtue.

The radical changes in the foundations of academic practice promoted by the organisers of Stalinisation did not work and were not supposed to work beyond the paradigm of 're-education.' Since virtues imply a practice orientated to a community (in the sense of a reference group) that considers them valuable, Schaff, who strove to break the barrier between the political leadership and Polish academia, could not succeed in this aim without destroying other communities within Polish academia and their own conventions. Despite the political pressure at the highest point of Stalinisation, the project, which was aimed at extending the Communist party principles in this field to the whole of Polish academia,[127] did not work. Polish soil showed again its unpleasant conditions for the seeds of this kind of academic practice. Interestingly, despite the political context, both 'virtuous' Józef Chałasiński and many 'non-virtuous' scholars attacked by the activists of Stalinisation received an honourable membership of the newly created Polish Academy of Sciences.[128] Either way, it was becoming increasingly clear that the official fiasco of Stalinism in Poland was about to be declared openly.

Notes

1 Izabela Wagner, *Bauman: A Biography* (Cambridge, UK: Polity Press, 2020), 167.
2 For example, Julian Hochfeld and Nina Assorodobraj-Kula gave seminars on 'Historical Materialism' and 'The History of Social Thought' at the University of Warsaw. Stanisław Ossowski and Maria Ossowska were deprived of teaching. See (URL): https://ws.uw.edu.pl/wydzial/historia/
3 Besides the foundation of the Chair for the History of Social Thought at the University of Warsaw, Józef Chałasiński restructured his department at the University of Łódź and continued sociological studies, interestingly, under the banner of the history of journalism. See more about this below.
4 Stefan Żółkiewski, "Na marginesie Zjazdu Polonistów 8-12 maja 1950 r.," *Nowe Drogi*, no. 3 (1950): 103.
5 Stefan Żółkiewski, "Tezy Stalina o języku a metodologia badań literackich," *Pamiętnik Literacki* 42, no. 2 (1951): 345.
6 For example, Żółkiewski was very critical towards the works of the famous Polish philologist and specialist in romanticism, Juliusz Kleiner: Żółkiewski, "Tezy Stalina o języku a metodologia badań literackich," 347.
7 Żółkiewski referred to the publications of Jan Kott, Kazimierz Wyka, see Żółkiewski, *Tezy Stalina o języku a metodologia badań literackich*, 345–346.
8 Janusz Sławiński, "Instytut Badań Literackich," in *Słownik realizmu socjalistycznego*, ed. Zdzisław Łapiński and Wojciech Tomasik (Kraków: Universitas), 74–75.
9 See, e.g., Henryk Markiewicz, *Krytyka literacka w walce o realizm socjalistyczny, 1944–1954* (Warszawa: Państwowy Instytut Wydawniczy, 1955). Markiewicz, in fact, developed Żółkiewski's ideas that had been expressed earlier in his book: Stefan Żółkiewski, *Stare i nowe literaturoznawstwo. Szkice krytyczno-naukowe* (Wrocław: Zakład Narodowy im. Ossolińskich, 1950).
10 See, e.g., Stefan Żółkiewski, *Spór o Mickiewicza* (Wrocław: Zakład Narodowy im. Ossolińskich, 1952). More about the project: Janusz Sławiński, *Instytut Badań Literackich*, 77–78.

11 See more about the reactions of Polish writers on Żółkiewski's speech, earlier, at the writers' congress in Szczecin in 1949: Danuta Dąbrowska, "Zjazd szczeciński 1949 r. w dokumentach osobistych pisarzy," in *Wokół zjazdu szczecińskiego 1949 r.*, ed. Paweł Knap (Szczecin: Instytut Pamięci Narodowej, 2011), 30–31.
12 See more about John Connelly and Teresa Suleja, ""Projekt reformy personalnej polonistyki uniwersyteckiej" Stefana Żółkiewskiego z 1950 roku," *Arcana*, 2 (1997): 93–113.
13 Grzegorz Wołowiec, "Filologia i nacjonalizm. Stanisław Pigoń jako ideolog kultury ludowo-narodowej," *Teksty drugie*, no. 6 (2017): 112; John Connelly and Teresa Suleja, "Projekt reformy personalnej polonistyki uniwersyteckiej," 106.
14 See, e.g., Stanisław Pigoń, "Z dziejów dawnego teatru szkolnego," *Pamiętnik Literacki* 43, no. 1–2 (1952): 287–311.
15 See more about Rafał Stobiecki, *Historia pod nadzorem. Spory o nowy model historii w Polsce – druga połowa lat czterdziestych – początek lat pięćdziesiątych* (Łódź: Wydawnictwo Uniwersytetu Łódzkiego 1993), 93–98.
16 Stobiecki, *Historia pod nadzorem*, 109. Maciej Górny, *The Nation Should Come First. Marxism and Historiography in East Central Europe* (Frankfurt am Main: Peter Lang Edition, 2013), 54. Of course, both Bobińska and Kormanowa actively published under Stalinisation and promoted the Soviet scholarship as an ideal model of science. Moreover, Kormanowa became the head of the Department of Modern History at the Institute of History of the Polish Academy of sciences.
17 See Rafał Stobiecki, "Stalinowska unifikacja nauki historycznej (przykład Polski)," *Acta Universitatis Lodziensis. Folia Historica*, no. 55 (1996): 30–31.
18 See Stobiecki, *Historia pod nadzorem*, 99–128.
19 See Volodymyr Ryzhkovskyi, *Soviet Occidentalism: Medieval Studies and the Restructuring of Imperial Knowledge in Twentieth-Century Russia* (PhD-thesis, Georgetown University, Washington, 2019), 335. In Polish historiography though it has been supposed that the struggle against 'quotology' was a phenomenon of the de-Stalinisation process, see Elżbieta Orman, "O paradoksach historiografii w czasach PRL-u na przykładzie korespondencji Stefana Kieniewicza i Henryka Wereszyckiego," in *Stefan Kieniewicz – Henryk Wereszycki. Korespondencja z lat 1947–1990*, ed. Elżbieta Orman (Kraków: Instytut Historii PAN, 2013), 38.
20 So, for example, Boris Porshnev, who made his career thanks to Stalinism and was among the critics of Kosminski, later, about the time of Kosminski's visit to Poland, was cruelly criticised in the academic press for his 'quotology,' i.e. the usage of the quotations from Marx and Lenin for 'non-scientific speculations.' See more about Ryzhkovskyi, *Soviet Occidentalism*, 333–337; Volodymyr Ryzhkovskyi, "Sovetskaja medievistika and Beyond (k istorii odnoj diskussii)," *Novoe literaturnoe obozrenie* 3 (2009) (URL, accessed: 14.07.2021), https://magazines.gorky.media/nlo/2009/3/sovetskaya-medievistika-and-beyond.html.
21 Stanisław Arnold, "Niektóre aspekty periodyzacji dziejów Polski," in *Pierwsza Konferencja Metodologiczna Historyków Polskich. Przemówienia. Referaty. Dyskusje*, vol. 1, ed. Stanisław Herbst, Witold Kula, Tadeusz Manteuffel (Warszawa: Państwowe wydawnictwo naukowe, 1953), 168–174.
22 Górny, *The Nation Should Come First*, 54.
23 Stobiecki, *Historia pod* nadzorem, 109.
24 See about structural changes in Polish academia: Piotr Hübner, *Polityka naukowa w Polsce w latach 1944–1953: geneza systemu*, vol. 2 (Wrocław: Zakład Narodowy im. Ossolińskich, 1992), 628–829.
25 See "Od redakcji," *Przegląd Nauk Historycznych i Społecznych*, no. 1 (1950): 7.
26 About the formative years of Adam Schaff and his early experiences with communism, see Mateusz Kuryła, "Adam Schaff – droga do komunizmu (1913–1939)," *Przegląd Humanistyczny* 3 (2018): 167–189.

27 After Schaff's return from the Soviet Union, Kotarbiński considered his Soviet degree insufficient for receiving a professorship in Poland and thought that a new (Polish) habilitation was required, see John Connelly, "Internal Bolshevisation? Elite Social Science Training in Stalinist Poland," *Minerva* 34, no. 4 (1996): 326.
28 Schaff remarked later that Bolesław Bierut (1892–1956), who became the leader of the Polish Workers' Party after the accusation against Władysław Gomułka (1905–1982) of nationalist bias, very much appreciated the competencies of Schaff, see the interview with Adam Schaff: '*Nie ma innej drogi*,' https://www.youtube.com/watch?v=mMBkGFEukq4.
29 See more about this institute: Beata Bińko, "Instytut Kształcenia Kadr Naukowych przy KC PZPR – narzędzie ofensywy ideologicznej w nauce i szkolnictwie wyższym," *Kultura i Społeczeństwo* 2 (1996): 199–214.
30 Beata Bińko, "Skąd przychodzili, dokąd zmierzali... aspiranci pierwszego rocznika Instytutu Kształcenia Kadr Naukowych przy KC PZPR," in *Komunizm: ideologia, system, ludzie*, ed. Tomasz Szarota (Warszawa: "Neriton" – Instytut Historii PAN 2001), 185.
31 AAN VI, ANS 5/7, K. 215–216 (185).
32 Bińko, "Skąd przychodzili, dokąd zmierzali," 178.
33 There is no author in the article entitled 'From the Editorial Board,' but the listed members of the editorial board as well as the content of the text show that this article was highly likely to have been written by Schaff himself.
34 "Od Redakcji," *Myśl Filozoficzna*, no. 1 (1951): 7.
35 Ibid., 8–9.
36 Ibid., 12.
37 Józef Chałasiński, "Z zagadnień metodologii badań społecznych," *Myśl Filozoficzna*, no. 1 (1951): 77. This time, Hochfeld 'assisted' Chałasiński in his self-criticism and helped him to explore all the 'mistakes' in his research programme and the programme of his teacher, Znaniecki, see Julian Hochfeld, "O niektórych aspektach przeciwstawności materializmu historycznego i socjologii burżuazyjnej," *Myśl Filozoficzna*, no. 1–2 (1951): 106–154.
38 See Józef Chałasiński, "Inteligencja ludowa – Naukowy pogląd na świat – upowszechnianie wiedzy i oświaty," *Nauka Polska*, no. 4 (1954): 130–148.
39 Józef Chałasiński, "Humanizm socjalistyczny i rewolucja kulturalna," *Przegląd Nauk Historycznych i Społecznych*, no. 3 (1953): 11–28.
40 Michael D. Gordin, "Was There Ever a 'Stalinist Science'?," *Kritika: Explorations in Russian and Eurasian History* 9, no. 3 (2008): 625–639.
41 *Od Redakcji*, 11.
42 Ibid., 15.
43 Ibid., 13.
44 This campaign had very strong antisemitic connotations. Meanwhile, using the slogans of 'patriotism' and 'native culture,' the organisers of this programme put special emphasis on the struggle against 'Western influences.' See Gennadij Kostyrchenko, *Tajnaja politika Stalina. Vlast' i antisemitism* (Moskva: Mezhdunarodnye otnoshenija, 2003), 310–350.
45 *Od Redakcji*, 15.
46 The example of Soviet genetics is very telling in this regard. See, for example, Nikolai Krementsov, "A 'Second Front in Soviet Genetics: The International Dimension of the Lysenko Controversy, 1944–1947," *Journal of the History of Biology*, no. 29 (1996): 229–250.
47 Grigorij F. Aleksandrov, *Istorija zapadnoevropejskoj filosofii*, Moskva, Leningrad: Izdatel'stvo AN SSSR, 1946.
48 Andrej A. Zhdanov, *Vystuplenie na diskussii po knige G.F. Aleksandrova "Istorija Zapadnoevropejskoj Filosofii" 24 ijulja 1947* (Moskva: Gospolitizdat, 1952), 12–13.
49 Zhdanov, *Vystuplenie na diskussii po knige G.F. Aleksandrova*, 14.

50 Ibid., 17–19.
51 See, for example, Alexei Kojevnikov, "Rituals of Stalinist Culture at Work: Science and the Games of Intraparty Democracy circa 1948," *The Russian Review*, no. 57 (1998): 28–40.
52 See more in Chapter 6.
53 See, for example, Kojevnikov, "Rituals of Stalinist Culture at Work," 25–28.
54 For example, Leon Orbeli was accused of being 'not sincere' in conducting 'self-criticism': Kojevnikov, "Rituals of Stalinist Culture at Work," 34.
55 Bronisław Baczko, "O poglądach filozoficznych i społeczno-politycznych Tadeusza Kotarbińskiego," *Myśl Filozoficzna*, no. 1–2 (1951): 247–248. The publication of Baczko was a summary of his small book that was published by the Institute of the Formation of Academic Cadres – Bronisław Baczko, *O poglądach filozoficznych i społeczno-politycznych Tadeusza Kotarbińskiego* (TKKN: Warszawa 1951).
56 Tadeusz Kotarbiński, "Logika dla nauczycieli a logika matematyczna," *Ruch filozoficzny* 9, no. 9–10 (1925): 124.
57 Baczko, "O poglądach filozoficznych i społeczno-politycznych Tadeusza Kotarbińskiego," 250–251.
58 Baczko, "O poglądach filozoficznych i społeczno-politycznych Tadeusza Kotarbińskiego," 257.
59 Ibid., 269–275.
60 Ibid., 260–261; 281–287.
61 Ibid., 289.
62 Ibid.
63 Adam Schaff, "Poglądy filozoficzne Kazimierza Ajdukiewicza," *Myśl Filozoficzna*, no. 1 (1952): 210.
64 Schaff "Poglądy filozoficzne Kazimierza Ajdukiewicza," 210.
65 Ibid., 212.
66 Ibid., 254.
67 Ibid., 256.
68 Ibid. About the Soviet culture of academic criticism, see, e.g., Sergei R. Matveev, "'Uchenyj-bol'shevik prizvan ocenivat' objektivno': recenzii v sovetskoj istoricheskoj periodike 1930–1950-h godov," in *Nauchnoe recenzirovanie v gumanitarnyh disciplinah*, ed. Natal'ja M. Dolgorukova and Aleksei A. Pleshkov (Moskva: Izdatel'skij dom NRU HSE, 2020), 113–124. It is noteworthy that the communist journal 'The New Paths (Nowe Drogi)' published a special article on 'criticism and self-criticism' in the subsection 'consultations': Celina Budzyńska, "Krytyka i samokrytyka niezawodny oręż partii," *Nowe Drogi*, no. 7 (1952): 117–127.
69 Lenin's usage of the word *partijnost'* was very unusual both for Russian and Polish languages and apparently represented both the direct translation of the word *Parteilichkeit* into Russian (see, for example, Vladimir I. Lenin, *Polnoe sobranie sochinenij* vol. 12 [Moskva: Izdatel'stvo politicheskoj literatury, 1967], 138) and – a normal meaning in Russian – belonging to a party.
70 "List grupy uczestników seminarium filozoficznego profesora Władysława Tatarkiewicza," *Przegląd Filozoficzny*, no. 2 (1995): 88. This happened on March 27, 1950, see Wiesław Chudoba, *Leszek Kołakowski. Kronika życia i dzieła* (Warszawa: Wydawnictwo IFiS PAN, 2014), 75.
71 Bronisław Dembowski, *Spór o metafizykę i inne studia z historii filozofii polskiej* (Włocławek: Włocławskie wydawnictwo diecezjalne, 1997), 306–307.
72 Henryk Holland, "Legenda o Kazimierzu Twardowskim," *Myśl Filozoficzna*, no. 3 (1952): 260–312. This article (in the extended version) was published later as a small book, see Henryk Holland, *Legenda o Kazimierzu Twardowskim* (Warszawa: Książka i Wiedza, 1953). In this text, I will refer to the journal version of Holland's publication.
73 Henryk Holland, "Legenda o Kazimierzu Twardowskim," 260–263.

74 Kazimierz Twardowski, *Rozprawy i artykuły filozoficzne* (Lwów: 1927), 8–9.
75 Henryk Holland, "Legenda o Kazimierzu Twardowskim," 267.
76 Of course, Twardowski did not 'know' that this was 'Lenin's theory.' He referred to the works of his opponents from the camp of empirical psychology (Kazimierz Twardowski, *Zur Lehre vom Inhalt und Gegenstand der Vorstellungen. Eine psychologische Untersuchung* [Wien: Alfred Hölder, 1894], 67).
77 Henryk Holland, "Legenda o Kazimierzu Twardowskim," 272–278.
78 Ibid., 288.
79 Ibid., 311.
80 Ibid., 311–312.
81 Andrzej A. Żdanow, *Przemówienie wzgłoszone w dyskusje nad książką G. Aleksandrowa „Historia zachodnoewropejsrkiej filozofii" 24 czerwca 1947 r.* (Warszawa: Książka i Wiedza, 1951).
82 See, for example, Władysław Tatarkiewicz, "Szczęście ludzi przyszłych," *Tygodnik Warszawski*, no. 17 (1946): 1–2.
83 See above.
84 Tadeusz Kroński, "O "Historii filozofii" W. Tatarkiewicza," *Myśl Filozoficzna*, no. 4 (1952): 249.
85 Ibid., 254.
86 Tadeusz Kroński, "O "Historii filozofii" W. Tatarkiewicza," 255.
87 Vladimir I. Lenin, *The Three Sources and Three Component Parts of Marxism*,(URL): https://www.marxists.org/archive/lenin/works/1913/mar/x01.htm.
88 According to Kroński, all socialist thinkers were, for Tatarkiewicz, only sociologists but not philosophers: Tadeusz Kroński, "O „Historii filozofii" W. Tatarkiewicza," 256.
89 By the term 'immanentism,' Kroński meant a non-historical logic of Tatarkiewicz's approach.
90 Tadeusz Kroński, "O „Historii filozofii" W. Tatarkiewicza," 257–259.
91 Ibid., 260.
92 Ibid.
93 Ibid., 266.
94 Ibid., 266.
95 Władysław Tatarkiewicz, *Historia filozofii* vol. 3 (Warszawa: Czytelnik, 1950), 6.
96 Tadeusz Kroński, "O „Historii filozofii" W. Tatarkiewicza," 269.
97 Ibid., 271.
98 Tadeusz Kotarbiński, "Odpowiedź," *Myśl Filozoficzna*, no. 2 (1952): 315.
99 Ibid., 318–319.
100 Ibid., 319.
101 Ibid., 322.
102 Ibid., 223.
103 Kotarbiński obviously meant the influence of Edmund Husserl with his project of philosophy as rigorous science (see Edmund Husserl, *Philosophie als strenge Wissenschaft* [Hamburg: Meiner Verlag, 2009]), see Kotarbiński, "Odpowiedź," 329.
104 Kotarbiński, " Odpowiedź," 328.
105 Ibid., 329–330.
106 Aleksei Lokhmatov, "Auf dem Weg zur ‚Einheit': Józef Chałasiński und die Suche nach einer ‚erlaubten' Genealogie der Soziologie im Nachkriegspolen (1945–1951)," *NTM Zeitschrift für Geschichte der Wissenschaften, Technik und Medizin* 4, no. 28 (2020): 530.
107 Józef Chałasiński, "Rzecz z powodu 'Humanistyki bez hipostaz'," *Myśl Filozoficzna*, no. 2 (1952): 309, 310.
108 Ibid., 312.
109 Ibid., 313.
110 Ibid., 314.

111 "Od redakcji," *Myśl Filozoficzna, no. 2* (1952): 331–337
112 Ibid., 331.
113 Ibid., 337.
114 Tadeusz Kotarbiński, "Listy do redakcji: W sprawie artykułu 'Legenda o Kazimierzu Twardowskim'," *Myśl Filozoficzna*, no. 4 (1952): 356–358.
115 Ibid., 357–358.
116 Kazimierz Ajdukiewicz, "W sprawie artykułu prof. A. Schaffa o moich poglądach filozoficznych," *Myśl Filozoficzna*, no. 2 (1953): 292.
117 Ibid., 292–315.
118 Ibid., 316.
119 Ibid., 334.
120 He was the author of the fundamental work on the history of Marxism: Leszek Kołakowski, *Main Currents of Marxism*, Vol. I: *The Founders*, Vol. II: *The Golden Age*, Vol. III: *The Breakdown* (Oxford: Oxford University Press, 1978).
121 Leszek Kołakowski, "Filozofia nieinterwencji," *Myśl Filozoficzna*, no. 2 (1953): 335–373.
122 It is striking that Kołakowski did not mention the book of the Polish biologist Ludwik Fleck (Ludwik Fleck, *Entstehung und Entwicklung einer wissenschaftlichen Tatsache. Einführung in die Lehre vom Denkstil und Denkkollektiv* [Basel: Schwabe, 1935]), which is currently regarded as a key work in the field of the constructivist approach to the social facts.
123 Kołakowski was the key figure of the 'Myśl Filozoficzna' group dealing with the disclosure of 'religious philosophy.' In his articles, Kołakowski, with witticism, showed the failure of religious philosophy (see, e.g., Leszek Kołakowski, "Mitologia księdza Kłósaka," *Myśl Filozoficzna*, no. 1–2 [1951]: 315–322). In an interesting way, many years later, after he changed his views, he would be considered a philosopher of religion, which is well accepted in Catholic circles. See, e.g., the collection of his essays published by the Catholic published 'Znak': Leszek Kołakowski, *Chrześcijaństwo* (Kraków: Znak, 2019); regarding the anti-religious programme of Schaff, there was a special section in the journal called 'Ideological Faces of Reaction' which published materials on the 'struggle' of Vatican against the 'scientific world view,' see, e.g., Mieczysław Mannell, "Watykan przeciwko nauce," *Myśl Filozoficzna*, no. 1–2 (1951): 313–322.
124 Leszek Kołakowski, "Filozofia nieinterwencji," 335–373. For a more detailed analysis of this campaign, see Aleksei Lokhmatov, "The Academic Virtues in Public Discussion: Adam Schaff and the Campaign against the Lvov-Warsaw School in Post-War Poland," *Studia Historiae Scientiarum*, 20 (2021): 711–753.
125 Ibid., 351.
126 Ibid., 372.
127 See Celina Budzyńska, "*Krytyka i samokrytyka niezawodny oręż partii*," 117–127.
128 For example, Tadeusz Kotarbiński, Kazimierz Ajdukiewicz, Władysław Tatarkiewicz; all of them became full members of the Polish Academy of Sciences, which, according to the Soviet sample, was to become the highest form of recognition of academic achievements.

8 '1956' as a 'Diagnosis' and 'Prognosis'

'We were able to get information about the circumstances of the arrival of the Soviet state leader in Warsaw. Mr. Khrushchev, according to the unanimous testimony of eyewitnesses, completely lost control of himself. As soon as he got off the plane, he exclaimed to the Polish leaders: "We have shed our blood to liberate this land, and now you want to give it to the Americans, but it will not succeed, it will not take place!"'[1] With these words, Philippe Ben, the French correspondent of '*Le Monde*,' who specialised in the Polish political agenda, reported on the visit of the Soviet delegation to Warsaw in 1956, where the situation had obviously got out of control.[2] The verbal crossfire that happened between Nikita Khrushchev, the leading figure of the Soviet Union after Stalin's death, and Władysław Gomułka, the newly (re-)elected head of the United Polish Workers' Party released from prison during the wave of 1956, was an alarming sign. The readiness of Soviet troops based in Poland for a violent solution to the conflict showed that the situation was not far from a dramatic escalation.

Reporting on the Polish events, Philippe Ben described a story which became a topos in the historiography of '1956.' Khrushchev allegedly asked the Soviet ambassador Panteleimon Ponomarenko, pointing at Gomułka: 'Who is that?' and Gomułka, without hesitating, said: 'This is me, Gomułka, whom you kept in prison for more than three years.'[3] Even though it is very unlikely that the dialogue between Gomułka and Khrushchev contained these words,[4] the conversation between the Soviet leader and the main hero of the 'Polish October'[5] was certainly highly intense.[6]

'1956' became a symbol of the crisis of the whole socialist system. After Stalin's death on March 5, 1953, the Soviet leadership looked for another form of governmentality than that of Stalin's dictatorship. In February 1956, during the 20th Congress of the Communist Party of the Soviet Union, the new party leader Khrushchev delivered a 'secret speech' 'On the Cult of Personality and Its Consequences.' In this speech, Khrushchev criticised primarily the repressions against party members that had been conducted during the rule of Stalin. This change in the political line of the Soviet leadership had huge consequences that were unexpected, not least for Soviet leaders themselves.[7] The military crisis and Soviet invasion of the Hungarian People's Republic in the late 1956 resulted in a full-fledged military operation with thousands of victims and became one of the most famous bloody

DOI: 10.4324/9781003428251-9

illustrations of the crash of the foundations Stalinism was based on. The Polish opposition movement of 1956 and its open support to the Hungarian Revolution showed in turn that the crisis could lead to a complete deconstruction of the Eastern Bloc. Even though, in 1956, most Central and East European communist regimes managed to suppress the opposition movement without Soviet invasion, one feeling was common for all people living behind the iron curtain in 1956: the post-war realities could not stay unchanged.

Losing the control over the public sphere

In June 1956, the workers of the western Polish city Poznań (Posen) went on the streets chanting slogans like 'Down with the Bolsheviks,' 'Down with Russians,' and 'Down with Moskals' adjoined such trivial but vital claims as 'We want bread,' 'We want to live like human beings,' and 'We are hungry.'[8] The anti-Soviet (Russian) mood became the key factor which determined the political developments of '1956.' The idea of 'new independence' dominated the public sphere during the wave of demonstrations in Poland. The martyr's halo which Gomułka had in the Polish society because of his resignation on the wave of Stalinisation brought him an extraordinary 'symbolic capital.' Gomułka became a people's hero of 1956 due to the idea that he suffered for the independence of Poland. The very fact of the enormous popularity of the communist Gomułka showed that the idea of independence played a much bigger role than, for example, his anti-Catholic attitude, which did not correspond with the religious beliefs of the majority of population.[9]

The reaction of the leaders of the Polish United Workers' Party to the demands of the demonstrators showed that the situation was very unclear for the chief representatives of the leading party themselves. The minutes of the meetings of the party functionaries testify that, among the strategies which were proposed for solving the crisis, the idea of using a positive image of Gomułka took one of central positions in their agenda. Nevertheless, not all communists accepted this idea. In a very characteristic way, one of the leading 'Soviet Poles,' the writer Jerzy Putrament, claimed that the promotion of Gomułka could have very dangerous consequences. Putrament (who obviously understood that this conversation would be described in Soviet reports to Moscow) argued that the nomination of Gomułka as a party leader would be seen as support for those who shared anti-Soviet 'prejudice':

> Promoting Gomułka to the leadership could lead to a counterrevolution or to a horrible Machiavellianism which would mean to delude these people and these unconscious layers [of the population] who do not understand what the alliance with the Soviet Union means for us; to delude them by opposing Gomułka to the Soviet Union ... this is the political sense of this proposition [to bring Gomułka to the leadership].[10]

Of course, Putrament and the other organisers of Gomułka's dismissal were so 'sentimental' about this situation not because they did not tolerate lies or Machiavellianism. The return of the party leader with such a reputation among the Polish population would give him broad opportunities to dismiss from the leading positions those who put him in prison a few years earlier.[11]

Not only the fact that debates within the party showed huge contradictions between its members, but also the break of the information blockade in the Polish public sphere could not go unnoticed in Moscow. In August of 1956, the Committee for Information of the Soviet Foreign Office wrote in its report regarding 'the situation on the ideological front' of Poland:

> The discussion which unfolded in Polish society and the press after the 20th Congress of the Communist Party of the Soviet Union took an unhealthy character and, in fact, resulted in a campaign which is foreign to the people-democratic regime ... the hostile campaign against the Polish United Workers' Party and the political system is closely intertwined with the slanderous anti-Soviet propaganda which is aimed at tarnishing the Soviet Union and undermining and discrediting Soviet-Polish relations.[12]

Thus, the Soviet government had on their desks the report which showed that the Workers' Party could not handle the situation. This could have severe consequences if the Soviet government took a decision regarding the 'fraternal help' of Soviet troops to Polish comrades.

The development of the situation in summer 1956 showed that the party leaders could not control the public expression of ideas. The apparatus of censorship was also confused regarding the new rules of public discussions. It was clear that obvious 'anti-Soviet attacks' were not allowed in the public press, but public criticism of Stalinism broke all the censorial principles elaborated in the period of Stalinisation.[13] For the Soviet embassy, this uncertainty in the actions of the Polish authorities seemed to be a weakness in the struggle against 'counterrevolution.' In his report on the public debates in the Polish press, the Soviet representative Nikolai Ponomarev wrote:

> All these [publications in Polish periodicals] show that the serious negative phenomena observed in Poland in the first half of 1956 continue to occur ... the party organisations of the Polish United Workers' Party continue to treat liberally various types of attacks [conducted] by hostile elements and do not take sufficient measures to ensure proper party leadership of ideological work.[14]

Characteristically, for Ponomarev, the 'anti-Sovietism' of the Polish public sphere in 1956 meant the lack of competence of the Polish Workers' Party leaders in vanishing the 'reactionary elements' from the public life of the Polish state which caused the crisis.

In this situation, Polish communists were caught in the crossfire. The Soviets required the struggle against anti-Soviet moods, while the emphasis on the friendship with the Soviet Union could make the demonstrators angry. Attempting to manage the situation, Edward Ochab, who became the leader of the Workers' Party after the death of Bolesław Bierut (March 1956), spoke to one of the key Soviet functionaries, Anastas Mikoyan (1895–1978), and asked him to withdraw all Soviet advisors from Poland because their presence provoked essential difficulties for Polish party leaders in their attempts to stabilise the situation.[15]

Moreover, Ochab himself started a discussion among the members of the Politburo of the Workers' Party on the necessity of reducing Soviet influences in Poland.[16] This point provoked a negative reaction by Konstantin Rokossowski, the military minister of Poland. Rokossowski, as one of the key figures of the Second World War and a Soviet marshal, was chosen for the position of Polish military minister because of his Polish origin and, at the same time, positive reputation among Polish and Soviet soldiers.[17] Nevertheless, for Poles, his presence in the Polish government was not understood, of course, as a sign of Soviet military domination over Poland. Certainly, Rokossowski maintained constant contact with the 'centre,' and his opposition to the party line of the Polish communists meant, at the same time, conflict with Moscow.[18]

Khrushchev wrote in his memoirs that he called Ochab by phone and asked directly if Gomułka had returned to the Polish Politburo 'with the help of anti-Soviet forces' and without waiting for an answer expressed his wish to come to Poland in person. Having received a negative response, Khrushchev, according to his memoirs, lost his trust in 'Ochab's honesty.'[19]

Considering the violent temper of Khrushchev, one can only guess what the Soviet leader really said to Gomułka when they met at the airport.[20] In any case, the Soviet delegation had not been allowed to participate in the plenum and waited for Gomułka for a special conversation regarding the new principles of the Polish–Soviet relationship. During this (highly emotional) discussion, the members of the Soviet delegation repeatedly referred to the role of the Soviet Union in the liberation of Poland and accused the Poles of betrayal. The Polish leaders attempted to explain to the Soviets that their brutal intervention can only escalate anti-Soviet moods.[21] The answer of Vyacheslav Molotov was simple and concrete: 'this means that your ideological work is bad.'[22] Regarding the references to the public opinion and critical publications in the press, Lazar Kaganovich (1893–1991) remarked that '[in the Soviet Union,] the Party rules the ideological front and the press' and Khrushchev added: 'you have lost your control of the press.'[23] So, for Soviet leaders, the problem with Polish 'public opinion' was the lack of government control over the public sphere and its instruments.

The difference between Polish and Soviet perspectives on the results of the 20th Congress and its meaning for the future of the socialist bloc is also a noteworthy issue. When Gomułka said that the information about Khrushchev's 'secret speech' was, in fact, the main reason for the current critical situation in Poland, Mikoyan immediately responded: 'the cult of personality did not entirely concern Poland.'[24] For Mikoyan, Khrushchev, and other Soviet high-ranking party fellows, the issue of the cult of personality was the problem of the fear with which they lived in the epoch of Stalin. The criticism against the repressions, which contained the core of Khrushchev's speech at the 20th Congress, was directed, first of all, against the 'unfair killing' of high-ranking Communist Party members.[25] There was no place for Poland in this story, and Soviet leaders did not see a connection between this 'internal' issue of governing principles and the 'counter-revolutionary' 'anti-Sovietism' in Poland.

When emotions settled down, the positions of the two sides were, in fact, the same: Polish leaders agreed that anti-Sovietism had to be vanished from the Polish public sphere but wanted to do it themselves, while Soviet representatives claimed their recognition of the 'independence' of Poland and expressed confidence in their Polish colleagues. When Gomułka said: 'I think that all internal problems we will solve ourselves.' Mikoyan and Kaganovich answered together with the words which Gomułka had already heard from the mouth of Stalin immediately after the war: 'of course, we will say our opinion and you will decide.'[26] Saying goodbye, Khrushchev tried to mitigate the situation and said: 'Comrade Gomułka, we regard you as an extraordinary figure ... the decision regarding your arrest, comrade Gomułka, was taken in Warsaw. We were doing everything to defend you.'[27] Even though Gomułka was still convinced that his arrest had been discussed with Stalin, this final point served as an attempt to defuse the situation.

The quest for honesty

The political crisis and its reception at the level of the Workers' Party was only a small piece of the reality of 1956. The processes which had started with rumours regarding the changes in the post-Stalinist ruling principles in the Soviet Union and accelerated with the release of Gomułka from prison touched very different areas of Polish cultural and academic life. It was March of 1956 when the meeting of 'the Council on Culture and Art,' which took place in Warsaw, showed that the style of public discussion prescribed by Stalinism had lost its relevance. During this meeting, Stefan Żółkiewski, who had become by the moment one of the most influential figures in the educational policy, repeatedly referred to the 'party principle' in cultural politics and still promoted the governmental approach to ruling culture. Nevertheless, his friend and assistant in Stalinising Polish literary studies, Jan Kott, not only openly criticised the realities of Stalinism but also attacked the very idea of governance in the field of culture. This was a very important sign of breaking with the visible loyalty to the Stalinist discourse that dominated literary studies over several years.

In his speech entitled 'Revolution and Modernity,' Kott criticised any governmental intersection in the field of cultural practice, considering it a programme opposed to the left-wing idea of culture. According to Kott, the very programme of 'Socialist realism' was based on the glorification of 'everything that happened under the socialist regime,' which led, according to him, to lies and thus the corruption of the whole political system. For Kott, Lenin's principles of cultural development had nothing to do with the literary programme which had been implemented in Poland after the Second World War. Developing this argument, he claimed that honesty and artistic freedom are a necessary condition of the cultural development of any society. Moreover, Kott argued that the very principle of 'the leading role of the party' in the cultural field was a big obstacle for cultural progress.[28]

In general terms, Kott's speech reflected the ideas which determined the intellectual atmosphere of '1956.' The activity of the 'Crooked Circle Club (Klub Krzywego Koła),' an organisation of young academics and writers that appeared in early 1955, became an illustration of the readiness of young intellectuals to challenge the official discourse they considered hypocritical. This club presented itself as a platform for an honest debate about the issues that could not be discussed in the press due to the censorship. The members of the Club represented various political attitudes[29] but were united by the idea of promoting intellectual and artistic freedom as a key principle of the new realities. The most prominent Polish scholars, independently from their 'official' status in the eyes of the authorities, were invited to give lectures for the members of this club.[30] Looking for honesty in the public debate, the intellectuals involved in the agenda of the Club did not avoid thematising political issues such as the 'quasi-socialist character' of the regime established in the Soviet Union and the necessity of conducting an independent policy towards the Eastern neighbour.[31]

Of course, the security services, which were in particular danger in this situation as the key organisers of Stalinisation, attempted to influence the situation, using very different methods. For example, it is highly likely that the activity of the leader of 'secular Catholics,' Bolesław Piasecki, during the crisis of 1956, was initiated by the security services as an attempt to bring the public sphere back under government control. In his article entitled 'The State Instinct,' Piasecki, in fact, threatened those who broke the limits of the permissible in the public sphere. He wrote: 'if we do not lead discussions within the framework of responsibility, we will provoke the necessity of brutal implementation of the state interest.'[32] Thus, Piasecki, whom the Soviet embassy thought a sympathiser of the Soviet Union,[33] tried to put the 'state interest' (of course, in the form promoted by the security services) over the 'honesty' desired by the young intellectuals. Nevertheless, this act had the opposite effect and provoked a great indignation in the public sphere. The Crooked Circle Club not only publicly criticised Piasecki's opportunism but also demanded the dismissal of Piasecki from all governmental positions.[34]

More importantly, Piasecki's blow against honesty led to a split in his group and became a turning point in the history of the public activity of Catholic scholars and writers. The group of Catholics led by Tadeusz Mazowiecki (later, the first non-communist prime minister of post-war Poland) declared the termination of their relations with Piasecki and the creation of a separate Catholic group.[35] Mazowiecki's followers returned to the legacy of French personalism with its idea of engagement with the current political reality, but, in his version, engagement did not mean collaboration with the authorities.[36] On the contrary, his activity was based on the aspiration of publicly challenging the official discourse. Developing his own political agenda, Mazowiecki was not ready to follow the tactics of the 'escape to culture' that had been associated with the Kraków group.[37] Thus, the crisis of 1956 created the impetus to formulate new principles of political activism for Catholics that could allow them to make political alliances with non-Catholics and, therefore, to be a part of the broader political and intellectual debate beyond the 'Catholic ghetto' created under Stalinism.[38]

The symbol of Stalinisation in the Polish public sphere, the journal 'Nowa Kultura,' which had been founded 'on the grave' of the 'gentle revolution' project, also took a leading position in the movement of '1956.' This story began with a disciplinary campaign against the editorial board of the journal. Paweł Hoffman, who had been one of the key figures during the period of Stalinism, was dismissed from his position for publishing an article which broke the ideological conventions of Stalinisation. One of the leading left-wing activists of the early post-war years, Adam Ważyk, published in 'Nowa Kultura' his poetic work entitled 'A Poem for Adults.' In this publication, Ważyk depicted the everyday life of workers who constructed the symbol of the new regime, 'Nowa Huta (literally The New Steel Mill).' This was a district (not far from historical Kraków) which had to become the prototype of a 'workers' paradise' in new Poland.[39] In his poem, Ważyk presented not a glorious picture in the style of Socialist realism but described the difficult life of workers whose real existence was far from that depicted in official reports.[40] This unauthorised quest for honesty provoked an immediate reaction from the leaders of the Workers' Party, who made the decision to dismiss Paweł Hoffman for his 'anti-Party' and 'anti-socialist' editorial policies.

It may seem symbolic that the new editor-in-chief who was chosen by the party leadership was none other than Stefan Żółkiewski, the former leader of the 'Kuźnica' group. After his public repentance for his pro-Western orientation in 1948, the coming of Żółkiewski to the position of the editor-in-chief of 'Nowa Kultura' could be seen as a revival of the tradition of 'Kuźnica' under the new conditions. Nevertheless, the beauty of this symbolism can be misleading. Żółkiewski, an advocate of strong control over the public sphere and 'the principle of partisanship' in cultural politics, was asked to discipline the editorial board which had allowed the publication of Ważyk's poem. Though, during the early post-war years, it was quite typical for 'Kuźnica' to discuss the disadvantages of the work of individual functionaries and governmental projects, by 1955, this kind of honesty seemed too dangerous for the foundations of the system.

Nevertheless, the 'spirit' of '1956' did not leave unchanged the editorial politics of 'Nowa Kultura.' Żółkiewski was not able to resist the reformation of the ideas regarding the public debates, and the political movement of this period made the journal one of the strongholds of strong criticism against the legacy of Stalinism.[41] The opportunity to criticise 'the cult of personality' opened the door for criticism of the very foundations on which the Stalinist regime had been based. It is characteristic that Żółkiewski (who had repented for underestimating the role of the Soviet Union in 1948), in April 1956, repented for the misconceptions of Stalinism in front of the audience of the central cultural journal. Żółkiewski openly recognised the 'errors' of the cultural politics which had been conducted in Poland when writing:

> Our struggle for the development of the revolutionary theory, our fight against the distortions of cultural life, was poorly conducted. We spent more energy fighting the danger of foreign ideological influences, [and] far less, far too little, fighting our own mistakes .... I say this with self-criticism – our journalists and philosophers could not keep up with the criticism of the mass participation of cultural life in Poland.[42]

In this way, the party functionary Żółkiewski attempted to respond to the public request for 'honesty' and thus stabilise the situation. Meanwhile, Żółkiewski attempted to assure the reader that the dogmatisation of Marxian classics, 'anti-people' politics, the abuse of functionaries, and all other problems were solved by the 20th Congress. Developing this idea, he wrote:

> Examples of complete, sharp, and fair criticism were given by the 20th Congress. This kind of criticism clears our starting positions in the discussion. The 20th Congress removed this dam of stupidity in the face of Communist thought in matters of culture, [removed the] barrier before which our half-hearted criticism had been stopped.[43]

Of course, it is difficult to draw such implications from the actual content of the materials of the 20th Congress. Nevertheless, the key idea of Żółkiewski was to use the image of this event for bringing the situation back under control.

Of course, this kind of 'honesty' was hardly satisfactory, especially for the young intellectuals who were among the key drivers of the 1956 movement. Thus, the struggle against the hypocrisy of the authorities became the core ideology of the prominent student journal 'Po Prostu (*Simply said*).' Initially, this journal (founded in 1947) was designed as a stronghold of the Workers' Party's influence over the academic life of students. The title 'Po Prostu' referred to the communist periodical that had been published in Vilnius (then, Polish Wilno) in the interwar period.[44] Before 1955, it was not among the most readable periodicals in Poland. The activist Elgiusz Lasota (1929–2001), who was an editor of the journal, wittily remarked: 'The main concern of the team [of the editorial board] was what to do so that [the published exemplars of the journal which were] in unopened packages did not fill all the windowsills in the rooms of the youth organisations at universities.'[45] Nevertheless, the quest for honesty considerably changed the public image of 'Po Prostu.'

The editorial article published in September 1955 demonstrates that '1956' began in Poland before the calendars in the country turned to 1956. The editorial board claimed:

> We are a group of young people/students and graduates of higher educational institutions. [We are] people who cannot help but interfere in everything that happens around us. We are a group of dissatisfied people – we would like [to have] more, smarter and better. We edit the journal of students and young intellectuals – we want it to be a platform for all young people with a warm heart and an open head.[46]

The key point of the programme of 'Po Prostu' was an archetypal striving to return back to the sources of 'true socialism,' to its prophets and ideals. One of the articles published in the journal was entitled '*There socialism has been forgotten.*' Much like the editors of 'Nowa Kultura,' the young intellectuals published a report from one of the factories in a small town, Zambrów, that described the everyday life of simple workers, which had little to do with the official propaganda of the regime.[47] Thus, the struggle for honesty became not only a slogan but also a journalistic programme of 'Po Prostu.'[48]

The academic experience which the leaders of the movement had during Stalinisation and, more precisely, the smear campaigns in which they participated[49] were, in a sense, their school of activism. However, this activism was turned against its organisers. The students and young scholars from 'Po Prostu' did not change their negative attitude towards religion, which, in their view, according to Marxian metaphor, 'worked as opium' and distracted people from social problems.[50] They still strove towards the enlightenment of the people and wanted to participate in the ideological struggle. Nevertheless, they openly opposed the forms of virtuous behaviour promoted under Stalinism.[51]

The quest for honesty led to the reformulation of the 'national' agenda in a form that seemed extremely threatening from the perspective of the authorities. For example, the arrest of the leaders of the Home Army and the Moscow trials of them made the topic of the Home Army an issue which, during the period of Stalinism, became a taboo in the public sphere of the Polish state. The 'Po Prostu' activists Jerzy Ambroziewicz, Walery Namiotkiewicz,[52] and Jan Olszewski[53] argued that the official image of the anti-Nazi resistance was not fair. In their article, which was later published as a book, they wrote:

> The white and red armband with the inscription AL [People's Army – Soviet-backed underground units] or AK [Home Army] was only a measure of political consciousness, but it could not be a criterion of readiness for sacrifice, perseverance and courage. From the point of view of basic moral values, the blood and labour of each soldier of the conspiracy should be considered equally.[54]

Thus, it was not only the 'basic moral values' that were preferred over the differences in ideology, but also sharing one national history stood above ideological issues.

Between France and the Soviet Union, there is … Poland

The resistance to Soviet domination was not the only catalyst of the reinforcement of national sentiments among Polish scholars engaged in the public agenda. The French communists who had been the crucial figures in the post-war public agenda also expressed their dissatisfaction with the rebellion of the Poles against the Soviet Union and thus made the all-national alliance between the representatives of different ideologists even stronger. According to the Soviet embassy attaché Roman Bogdanov, the head of the delegation of the French communists Étienne Fajon told the activists of the 'Polish October' in Warsaw: 'we treat critically the events in Poland. You [Poles] have forgotten that the main conflict of our days is the conflict between socialism and capitalism. You blame everything on the party and forget the subversive activities of imperialism. We disagree with it.'[55] In this way, the French communists (most of whom were convinced Stalinists) did not hesitate to publicly attack the Polish movement of '1956' and to join the Soviets in accusing the Polish 'anti-Soviet' moods.[56]

In the pages of the leading communist journal '*L'Humanité*,' the communist politician Marcel Servin, directly accused the Polish party leadership of following 'bourgeoise ideology' and the 'transition of power' into the hands of the 'opportunist forces.' Moreover, Servin claimed that the 'clerical' and 'antisemitic' groups were the leaders of the movement which took place in Poland in 1956.[57] For him and other French communists, Polish 'anti-Sovietism' could threaten the unity of the communist movement, which had to lead the proletariat in the world. Thus, from the perspective of French communists, Poland, through its disloyalty to the Soviet Union as the stronghold of 'progress,' played into the hands of world capitalism.[58]

Responding to this accusation, the former member of Adam Schaff's group, Leszek Kołakowski, published one of the most decisive answers to Servin's publications. In the pages of 'Sztandar Młodych (*Banner of Youth*),' Kołakowski argued that Servin did not even try to understand the processes which had been happening in Poland during the wave of '1956.' The accusations of antisemitism, antirevolutionary character, and clericalism to which Servin and other French communists referred in their public discourse were, according to Kołakowski, further evidence of the fallacy of the attitude of French communists. More importantly, Kołakowski's answer became a manifesto of the priority of loyalty to the nation over ideology. He wrote:

> A counter-revolution supported by the whole nation is impossible. The idea that it is possible to build socialism against the nation and [with the help of] a military-police clique based on terror is not just cynical. This is harmful and pernicious to the cause of socialism .... The world labour movement has paid a price of crime and shame for this opinion that it will never want to pay again.[59]

Being outraged about the dishonesty of the French view of the 1956 movement, Kołakowski publicly opposed not only the position of his French colleagues, but also the basic ideas of Stalinism to liberate the Polish nation from the domination of 'reactionary views.' The Polish nation but not the Marxist ideology became a fundamental category in Kołakowski's argument.

Of course, Kołakowski's reaction to the campaign of the French communists was not an isolated case. Many other Polish journals published articles that accused the French communists of ignorance of the situation in Poland. Additionally, according to the young Marxist scholars, the French ignored a simple fact: since the regime in Poland was not a capitalist one, the 'will of the nation' could not represent the interests of the bourgeoise.[60] The young sociologist Jan Strzelecki took the next step in 'defending' the movement of '1956' in the face of French communists. In the pages of 'Nowa Kultura,' Strzelecki argued that the Communist Party of France shared the responsibility for the crimes which had been committed by Stalinism. In a very emotional manner, Strzelecki wrote:

> You [the French communists] supported ... the political idea ... which nearly brought our country and the whole of our [socialist] bloc to tragedy. You supported the idea of people who provoked, among the masses of their nation, only one feeling – the feeling of fear.[61]

Developing this idea, Strzelecki argued that the Polish example would help French communists to better understand the need of the proletariat and peasants in their own country. He wrote: 'we are convinced that, neither more nor less, the future of the socialist idea in the entire world depends on the success of the modernisation of the socialist system [in Poland].'[62]

This conflict with the French communists did not mean a rejection of the authority of French culture. Interestingly, the trick of the early post-war years, when the texts of the French thinkers had been used to depict an ideal image of the Polish state, was used in '1956,' too. During the wave of '1956,' the left-wing intellectual and editor of '*France Observateur*,'[63] Claude Bourdet, took over the role of a French intellectual who admired the Polish future. According to an editorial note, Bourdet wrote his article especially for the Polish journal 'Nowa Kultura' and regarded this as an opportunity to speak to the Polish reader directly on behalf of 'French left-wing intellectuals.'

When delivering, in fact, the message of the Polish editors, Bourdet wrote: 'All significant events in the life of the Polish people excite the French in a special way.'[64] Developing this unsophisticated idea, Bourdet argued that not only strong historical and cultural ties between Poland and France but also the uniqueness of 'the Polish Revolution' of '1956' attracted the attention of French left-wing intellectuals. He painted a sad picture of leftist culture in post-war France which had faced plenty of splits within the left-wing camp and complained about the fact that neither socialists nor communists were able to unite the working people for the common struggle against the 'new rise of capitalism.' According to Bourdet, the conflict between freedom and loyalty to the Soviet Union was a core issue also for the French intellectuals: for socialists, the Soviet experiment was an example of a dictatorship which had destroyed all liberties, while, for communists, the Soviet Union had become the organiser of the world communist movement. Thus, Poland could become again an example of a compromise between the two extremes.[65] Generally, Bourdet's message could be seen as a plea for the development of the idea of the Polish special path, from which France or even the 'Western world' could learn.

Of course, the plurality of approaches to socialism was not the only issue in the Polish–French agenda after 1956. Polish scholars readily published their articles in French journals and, when it became possible, went to Paris to visit research and cultural institutions,[66] but these trips also created new opportunities to participate in the non(anti)-socialist discourse outside the socialist bloc. Thus, '1956' became a crucial stage in the history of Polish émigré institutions. The prominent role that the exile would play in Polish history by the 1960s would not have been possible without the changes brought with the Polish October. Additionally, the Parisian journal 'Kultura' intensified their attempts to reach the Polish public through the Iron Curtain and thus started to play a much more important role in the intellectual life of Poland.[67] More importantly, the journal became a platform for the development of the Polish national discourses of 'the West' and 'Civilisation' that, under the conditions of the Cold War, played a significant role in strengthening both the coherent vision of the Polish nation and its intellectual association outside the socialist bloc.[68]

France still had a large 'symbolic capital' in the Polish public sphere which was hardly comparable with any other country.[69] Nevertheless, '1956' brought a new feature to the relationships between French and Polish intellectuals. The outrage of the left-wing Polish scholars regarding the unfairness of the French communists' account of the Polish October and their loyalty to the idea of Soviet dominance made the defence of a national path a central issue in the public agenda. Moreover, contrasting the project of the 'gentle revolution' in which France played the role of the apostles of socialism, post-1956 'France' increasingly became a window to 'The West' and 'Civilisation' rather than a bearer of the virtue of 'progressiveness.'

Polish academics and the fiasco of Stalinisation

The political crisis of 1956 could not help but radically change the academic agenda of post-war Poland. The fellows from the research institutions which had been formed on the wave of Stalinisation organised new open discussions and, under the banner of 'the struggle against the cult of personality,' criticised the very foundations of the academic practice promoted under Stalinism. 'No one can rule science from outside. It can only rule itself .... No one can replace a real scholar in the work of linking science with the realisation of socialism.'[70] These words caught the eye of the reader of the newly created popular science journal 'Kultura i Społeczeństwo (Culture and Society).' One of the involuntary organisers of Stalinisation in historiography, Witold Kula, emphasised that the worst tendency which had been brought by 'the ruling of the strong hand' was the degradation of the culture of discussion between representatives of various ideological attitudes. Kula argued that 'substantive academic discussion' had been destroyed and had to be reconstructed.[71] For him, the 'scientific point of view' and 'discussion' promoted in Poland after 1948 were neither 'scientific' nor a discussion.[72]

While the attempts to teach Polish scholars new virtues were not successful even at the time of the dominance of Stalinism, '1956' destroyed most of Schaff's 'achievements' in this area. Using the new opportunities, Tadeusz Kotarbiński concluded one of his essays with the following words:

> Let us hope that all the organisational issues that have been tormenting scholars will be fully clarified ... whatever the [academic] system that will be established, there must be conditions in which gifted people can develop

their creative abilities. And we will not be mistaken if we name among these conditions, among other things, the atmosphere of spiritual freedom, the cult of truth, respect for the creative personality, as well as [praising] the merits earned by hard work.[73]

Of course, for Kotarbiński, the attempts to destroy all these principles both in academia and in the public sphere were associated with Stalinisation. In 1956, Kotarbiński could openly celebrate the victory of his values over Stalinism.

Meanwhile, it is noteworthy that Kotarbiński delicately described Stalinisation as 'an unpleasant period of mistrust [between logicians and Marxists].' Developing this argument, he wrote:

There was a fear [from the Marxist side] that, from the side of logicians, some harmful social theories may come, since they [logicians] had grown up in an atmosphere of environments [which were] alien to materialism, dialectics, social revolution, and socialism. In [their] turn, logicians feared obstacles to their subject and distortions of its content, which had a source in the tendencies of that [Marxist] group [which was] quite alien to the object [of logic] itself.[74]

In any case, Kotarbiński saw only one possible solution to the problems caused by Stalinism:

It is necessary to allow it [logic] to live and act according to its own nature and use it for public education purposes. It is enough [to write] memorials, [to] intervene in its field of activity, it is enough [to write] articles convincing [people] of what logic is and for whom it can be useful. Regarding this issue, everything that can be said has been said already, and it has been said many times. It is time to make decisions.[75]

In other words, Kotarbiński hoped that the period of the intervention of Marxism in other fields of knowledge was at the end. Polish scholars could just do their job without wasting time with pointless discussions on the limits of the Marxian approach. '1956' was important for Kotarbiński, not only as a return to a 'normal' academic work, but also as an opportunity to implement the ideas which had been formulated before but could not become a reality because of Stalinism.[76]

The sociologist Józef Chałasiński also greeted the changes of 1956 with undisguised joy.[77] According to the report on the conference of the members of the Academy, Chałasiński, a full member of the Polish Academy of Sciences, publicly claimed that the members meetings of the Academy, which used to be so boring during Stalinisation, and from which 'nobody used to expect something interesting in terms of science and in intellectual terms in general' were going to become exciting scientific events thanks to the results of the 20th Congress of the Communist Party of the Soviet Union.[78]

Of course, for Chałasiński, the movement of '1956' was an event of special importance not least because it led to the restarting of the scientific institutions that he created immediately after the war. Chałasiński declared the reopening of both the Sociological Institute and the sociological journal and invited the reader to share his joy regarding the return of sociology to the public sphere of Poland.[79] Chałasiński wrote not without sarcasm:

> The restart of the [journal] '*Przegląd Socjologiczny*' is not the only sign of normalisation in the field of sociology .... The section of sociology modestly hid in the philosophical society, so as not to irritate the monopolists of sociological omniscience, who gathered at the Institute of Social Sciences [i.e. Schaff's institute] as well as at the departments of historical materialism [at universities]. The 'Thaw' rehabilitated <...> sociology.[80]

Thus, Chałasiński not only emphasised the importance of the new conditions for developing sociology but also did not hide his witticisms regarding the activity of Schaff's institute, which had become the stronghold of Stalinisation.

Chałasiński, who had appeared to be the most loyal students of the virtues promoted under Stalinism, represented himself, in 1956, as a defender of sociology against Stalinism. The role of a victim was extremely important to Chałasiński. Describing (very selectively) his 'unpleasant' experiences under Stalinism, Chałasiński called himself ironically a 'bourgeois sociologist' who had become a member of the Academy of Sciences despite his affiliation with reactionary sociology.[81] Additionally, Chałasiński described a 'courageous act' of his own that could be seen as a 'struggle' against the dominant ideology. According to this story, the weekly 'Świat (The World)' asked Chałasiński to write an article on Stalin's approach to sociology. His 'resistance' was not manifested in a rejection of this order; Chałasiński wrote this article and sent it to the editorial board. After that he received a letter from the editor-in-chief which Chałasiński partly quoted in his essay. The editor asked him 'to specify the influence of Stalin's thought on the development of the social sciences in general and in Poland in particular' and added 'Thank you in advance.' This had been a line of *non possumus* for Chałasiński and he wrote: 'as old people answered to thanks, "there is nothing to thank me for." In this case, there really was nothing to thank me for, since the editorial board did not receive corrections and the article was not published.'[82] In this way, Chałasiński showed how his uncompromising courage helped sociology to survive Stalinism.

This survival owed, according to Chałasiński, the 'liberal tradition of the University of Łódź.' In his view, the rebirth of sociology in Poland was the best answer to the Stalinists who had argued that sociology represented 'revisionism and opportunism of a socio-democratic type.'[83] More importantly, Chałasiński, who himself had proclaimed the struggle against the legacy of Florian Znaniecki in Polish academia, endorsed the importance of Znaniecki's works in the pages of the restarted '*Przegląd Socjologiczny*.' The 75th birthday of Znaniecki was a good occasion for Chałasiński to mention that his humanistic approach to sociology had 'a great impact on the development of sociological thought both in America and Europe' and represented 'the date of the coming of Polish sociology into contemporary sociological thought.'[84] The affiliation with European and American sociology was not shameful again.

Nevertheless, '1956' did not mean, for Chałasiński, a return to the programme of the early post-war years. Unlike in the times of the 'gentle revolution,' Chałasiński represented himself as a defender of 'true Marxism' against those who attempted to distort it. He used the opportunity to attack Adam Schaff and his institute with its monopoly on deciding what is right and what is wrong from the 'point of view of Marxism-Leninism.' The forms of discussion promoted by Stalinism (and adopted by Chałasiński), he sarcastically called 'a tournament on the topic "Who is the best Marxist?"'[85] Using references to Marx and Lenin, Chałasiński attempted to show (though not very convincing) that the sociological picture of the plurality of societies with different logics of development could be much better described as a true Marxism than Schaff's authoritarian model.[86] Continuing his criticism against Adam Schaff as the organiser of Stalinism, he wrote:

> Without solid historical knowledge, Marxism-Leninism becomes a formal, and, in extreme forms, a scholastic [approach]. [Thus,] the discussion, which began with the martial fanfare of class and ideological struggle and [was conducted] under the banner of the clash between the old generation of humanists ... and the young group of the Marxist vanguard, led not to an aggravation of methodological contradictions ... but, on the contrary, to a general softening of the difference between [their] methodological attitudes ....[87]

Using the opportunities opened by '1956,' Chałasiński attempted to promote his anti-authoritarian ideas under a new banner. He generously quoted fragments of Schaff's publications[88] proposing 'to drill students' and 'to instill [in them] a sense of duty and honour.' Commenting on them, Chałasiński sarcastically remarked that he had nothing against the sublime ideas of duty and honour, but no science is possible through indoctrination. In fact, referring to his ideas regarding the creation of a 'progressive' intelligentsia, Chałasiński argued that 'true Marxism-Leninism' required not an army but a creative milieu of intellectuals.

As an advocate of 'true Marxism,' Chałasiński also opposed the Stalinist (in fact, Leninist) idea of an absolute unity between science and politics. He wrote: 'We all understand that there is no apolitical science. But not everyone has understood yet that there would be no science at all if every cognitive act of the scholar contained exclusively political components.'[89] Developing this idea, Chałasiński told the reader a story about a 'young philosopher' (obviously, one of Schaff's students) who gave seminars at the University of Warsaw and explained to the students that 'Plato was an idealistic and reactionary obscurantist' and compared him with Józef Piłsudski. 'If Plato and Piłsudski belonged to the same idealistic reactionary movement, why one should read Plato in Greek when it is easier to read Piłsudski in Polish?' – Chałasiński ironically asked. Nevertheless, Lenin, according to Chałasiński, was not guilty of Schaff's misconduct: 'this operation [i.e. the classification of Plato and Piłsudski together in a reactionary camp] was possible [in the mind] of this "philosopher" but he learned this not from Lenin.'[90]

Chałasiński's strategy and his attempt to adopt to the extremely changeable political conditions illustrates one very important point about the crisis of 1956. It shows that the role of ideas themselves was, in fact, secondary. Due to the extraordinary flexibility of Chałasiński's views, his case demonstrates that, promoting very similar ideas and glorifying the same names (except for that of Stalin), Chałasiński attempted to challenge the forms of the virtuous behaviour promoted by Schaff's group. After '1956,' the names of Marx, Engels, and Lenin served as a weapon in this struggle.[91]

Adam Schaff and his good conscience

Adam Schaff's discourse also could not stay unchanged in 1956. 'It is perhaps no exaggeration to say that the problems of political life of great importance ... are centred around [the phenomenon which] we call the "cult of personality." This issue is difficult and painful. No Communist, no honest man, can pass by them with indifference.'[92] Writing these words, Adam Schaff, being full of noble indignation, decisively and uncompromisingly criticised the cult of personality as one of the most dangerous tendencies in the current agenda. Schaff's articles on the genius of Stalin and his insightful contributions to history, philosophy, and linguistics[93] had been left behind. The situation had changed, and the struggle against the cult of personality with 'its effects' and 'roots' became for him the issue of 'the fight against evil.'[94] The chief organiser of Stalinisation in Poland wrote in an article published in the official journal of the Workers' Party:

> Stalin, around whom the Leninist core of the party was centred after Lenin's death, began, with time ... to violate the Leninist norms of party life, and to abuse power ... [the cult of] Stalin – with his consent and with his support – was developed right up to idolatry. Stalin was considered not only a genius and infallible man, but, in fact, a real creator of history, a real author of the victories of socialism.[95]

Schaff failed to specify who these people were that had idolised Stalin through representing him as a 'genius' and 'creator of history,' but, in 1956, it was not an issue for him. Schaff's aim was to explain to the reader what the correct hierarchy under the new conditions was and how one should behave in the new realities. In fact, Schaff did not change his academic ethos a lot. The key intention of his publication was to explain to the Polish audience what the Communist Party of the Soviet Union really meant under the struggle against the cult of personality. In his article, Schaff strove to show that the 'true' message of the 20th Congress was misunderstood by the rebellious masses and did not change much regarding the issue of the party discipline.

The political ideal which, according to Schaff, had to become a guideline in the post-Stalin epoch referred to Lenin's political principles, which had been distorted by Stalin. Nevertheless, revolutionary cultural and political freedoms were not a part of Schaff's idea of Leninism. According to Schaff, the party was to rule the country based on the collective principle without the domination of a single person. Generally, Schaff just repeated the idea of de-Stalinisation that was promoted by Soviet leaders – the party leaders should take all decisions collectively and should not engage in repressions against its members.[96] Thus, from Schaff's perspective, the return to 'true democracy' did not require either demonstrations or claims of 'independence from the Soviet Union.'

More importantly, Lenin's writings helped Schaff to find an ethical explanation for the fact that he himself was one of the central figures of the indoctrination of the cult of personality in Poland. According to him, Lenin recognised that even the party is not infallible. Nevertheless, the denial of the principle of infallibility did not change, in Schaff's view, the principles of 'democratic centralism' and the leading role of the party:

> [Lenin] saw the sign of its [the Party's] strength not in the pose of infallibility, but in the open, public admission of every mistake. The denial of the infallibility of any institution does not violate its seriousness and authority, does not threaten the discipline that democratic centralism based on … the strength of this discipline is in the awareness and conscious submission to the will of the majority, not in blind faith in anybody's infallibility.[97]

Thus, for Schaff, there was no problem with the fact that the party was 'sometimes' wrong, since nobody promised that it would not be. Meanwhile, there was no individual responsibility for the 'mistakes' which were made by the party as a collective. According to Schaff's ideology, if you submitted to the will of majority without believing in its rightness, i.e. just followed the virtue of loyalty, you made the correct choice.

Of course, Schaff cared not only about the past but also about the present and, more precisely, about the solution to the crisis which Poland experienced in this time. His solution to the problem was simple but not easy. According to Schaff, the rejection of the idea of the infallibility of the party did not contradict 'the unity of the party which takes care of its Central Committee with respect and confidence.' This nearly familial approach to the role of the party leadership was accompanied with a not less sentimental statement that the Central Committee contained 'the best and most experienced people' of the party and, by all appearances, of the country (since the party members were the most progressive people in the country).[98] Thus, Schaff attempted to explain to his rebellious students that the centralised organisation of power was still relevant, and that they should let the party leadership decide what was right and wrong.

Developing his reflections on the new period in the Polish history, Schaff could not help but prepare a more 'scientific' paper that explained the new reality from the 'correct point of view.' During the wave of de-Stalinisation, Schaff published a small book with his new guidelines for 'cultural politics in philosophy and sociology.' Besides the general words on the obligation to struggle against the cult of personality, Schaff claimed that the rejection of the idea to unite all scholars under the banner of Marxism–Leninism did not belong to the list of changes which would take place in Poland after Stalinism. In his book, Schaff asked a rhetorical question:

> Does the Marxist camp continue its struggle for the complete victory of Marxist ideology? .... Were there any new reasons that would prompt us to reconsider our principled position in the direction of 'co-existence' with bourgeois ideology?[99]

And gave 'obvious' answer:

> On the contrary, the current situation requires an intensification of the ideological struggle in the sense of a comprehensive deepening of criticism of bourgeois ideology, which has been repeatedly emphasised in official party resolutions.[100]

Schaff did not revise either the idea of making everyone in Poland a Marxist or the uncompromising character of his project. His idea of Marxist ideology was not only to dominate Polish academia but also to reach the 'complete victory' over the tendencies which he understood as 'bourgeois culture.' Nevertheless, the balance of forces changed again, and the authority of Adam Schaff, during the crisis of the regime, was reduced. He was able neither to control the discourse of Polish scholars in the public sphere nor to maintain the loyalty of his own colleagues and students.

Schaff's students against Stalinist virtues

It seems very characteristically that the cruellest criticism of the forms of academic practice that Schaff continued to promote came from those whom he chose to become the driving force of Stalinisation. Remarkably, the young academics from his institute became the driving force of '1956' instead. The crash of the fragile Stalinist legacy was obvious even in the heart of the intellectual life of the Workers' Party. In the spring of 1956, Włodzimierz Sokorski, who was the Minister of Culture and Art during the period of Stalinisation, mentioned the 'Institute of the Social Sciences (a new reincarnation of Schaff's Institute of the Formation of Academic Cadres)' as one of the most rebellious institutions when he was sent to the Soviet Union for negotiations with the Soviet government. In a conversation with Soviet functionaries, Sokorski said:

> Unhealthy moods are very strong at the Institute of the Social Sciences of the CC [Central Committee] of the PUWP [Polish United Workers' Party] .... The institute not only failed to be a support of the party, but even became a citadel from which non-partisan, anti-national views on many issues of politics, literature, and art have been spreading.[101]

The experience of Stalinisation influenced Schaff's young guard in a very visible way. From the propagators of the governmental and patrician struggle against 'obscurantism,' they became the ideologists of intellectual freedom as a key precondition of scholarly work.[102]

Schaff's attempts to mountain the Stalinist *status quo* in Polish academia provoked indignation among the young Marxists. Zygmunt Bauman, Maria Hirszowicz,[103] Włodzimierz Wesołowski, and, finally, Jerzy Wiatr publicly attacked Adam Schaff and his vision of academic practice. All of them continued to call themselves Marxists and emphasised their membership in the Workers' Party, but their idea of the role of Marxism and the party in science and scholarship was different. Their publication 'Today and Tomorrow of our Sociology' became a manifesto of the young scholars involved in the developments of '1956.'

The starting point of the manifesto addressed the most general and most relevant problem of the Polish agenda – the damage which had been caused by Stalinism to philosophy and sociology. In this regard, Schaff's reaction to the crisis programme could provoke nothing but a 'feeling of deep regret, frustration, and bitterness.' The young scholars formulated very clear criteria for the points which they expected to see in the official agenda regarding the legacy of Stalinism:

a   highlighting the deepest roots of the evil [caused by Stalinism, which should be conducted] decisively and without any limits, from Marxist positions but not from mythological and subjective positions; and thus specifying the social roots of the Stalinist deformation of academia (*nauka*);
b   the formation of a future programme based not on quantitative changes but on the decisive rejection of Stalinism and all its relics ...[104]

The young scholars could not find all this in Schaff's publications, which was to determine the new guidelines for the development of the Polish academic world. As trained Marxists, they wanted to see the 'professional' (i.e. Marxist) analysis of Stalinism, which they regarded with conviction as a harmful and destructive period of Polish history.

Schaff's attempts to argue that the only problem with Stalinism was Stalin's usurpation of power, and that, after his death, the party would rule academia in the right way did not correspond with their idea of scientific Marxism. They wrote: 'it is difficult to call this analysis [which had been conducted by Schaff] either a scientific one or a Marxist one.' The young scholars wanted to see a 'scientific' perspective on the 'errors' of Stalinism.[105] The examination of the social and economic roots of all political phenomena belonged to the obligatory programme of university lectures on Marxism. Referring to their theoretical background, the young Marxists wanted to have an answer on the question of what social and economic processes had been hidden behind Stalinism.[106]

Of course, it was only a rhetorical question. The young scholars had a very concrete idea of what was wrong with 'Stalinist science,' and the brief answer to this question was: everything. They argued with conviction that 'what had been hidden under the name of scientific knowledge about society, scientific philosophy and sociology, was not science but ideology.'[107] There is no need to emphasise that this distinction between science and ideology stood in an insoluble contradiction with the official version of Marxism–Leninism for which these fields were indivisible.

Nevertheless, the official ideology lost any relevance in the agenda of the young Marxists. Science was, for them, not only separated from ideology but was also opposed to it. They wrote:

> Until we make it clear to ourselves that, during the Stalinist period, we cultivated not science but ideology, one of the main functions of which was precisely to stifle the science of society, we will not get even a starting point for a full-fledged but not partial restoration [of philosophy and sociology].[108]

Developing this idea, the young scholars returned to the arguments of the early post-war years and characterised the forms of knowledge which had been promoted during the wave of Stalinisation as a 'religious view' and a 'mystification.' They wrote:

> It [Stalinism] was an ideology that played the role of the organiser of the masses around a stratum that usurped political and economic power and used this power against the aspirations of the masses. This ideology did not have any relation to the scientific study of reality.[109]

Thus, the group of young Marxists accused Stalinism (read Marxism–Leninism in its Soviet version) of promoting a pseudo-religious programme opposed to Marxism as a scientific view of things.[110]

Developing this idea, the young scholars destroyed another pillar of Stalinism, when claiming all the privileges which Marxism had in recent years unfair:

> The fact that, in our political views, we are Marxists in ideology gives us no prerogatives in academic discussions, no *a priori* advantage over non-Marxist sociologists ... rightness must be documented by scientific achievements.[111]

Thus, not the loyalty to the current political need of the party, but an ability to argue within the framework of academic conventions was, for them, the cornerstone of academic activity. They claimed that, 'as Marxists and communists,' they were ready to struggle for the form of knowledge 'which is based on logical and empirical principles of thinking.'[112]

One of the most active members of Schaff's institute, Leszek Kołakowski, went in his criticism of Stalinism even further away from the Marxist dogmatics. In one of his articles published in 'Nowa Kultura,' Kołakowski continued his struggle against 'idealism' that he fought during Stalinisation, but, this time, the object of his criticism was different. Starting his article with a self-representation: 'we – Marxists,' Kołakowski conducted his analysis from the position of 'true Marxism' and criticised the distortions of the Marxian teaching. In 1956, not 'hidden idealism' in the works of materialist logicians, but the very basis of Stalinist academic and political practice became the main target of Kołakowski's criticism.

Having proclaimed the new stage in the struggle against 'Platonism' in its various forms (we can only guess if it was Kołakowski whom Chałasiński attacked for comparing Plato and Piłsudski), Kołakowski argued that 'the malicious spirit of Plato' had taken root in the political realities of the Polish socialist state. The striving of the regime to make the public sphere not a reflection of real problems and contradictions but an ideal picture of a faked unity was, according to Kołakowski, an example of Platonic believe in ideal forms to which, according to Platonism, everything in the world strives. So, the struggle against Plato's concept of 'eidos' as an ideal type of things (shadows of 'real things') existing in the world, which had been conducted by Marxists, was, in his view, hypocrisy in a state in which the entire ideology worked in accordance with this principle.[113]

This led Kołakowski to his next point – the critique of the Stalinist approach to science and scholarship, which he calls 'Marxist Platonism.' In his view, Stalinism produced 'pseudo-Marxian Platonic (*platonizująca*) historiography, Platonic sociology, Platonic political economy, Platonic politics.' Thus, according to Kołakowski, Stalinism conducted a kind of 'Platonisation,' i.e. idealisation of academic practice instead of fighting idealism. A theory which did not reflect the real world but violently inscribed its postulates into the current realities was, for Kołakowski, nothing but a mystification.[114]

This nontrivial approach both to Marxism and Platonism led Kołakowski to a more general sociological statement. He differentiated two concepts: 'the consciousness of the masses' and 'public opinion' which opened up a new perspective on 'social physiology,' which Kołakowski strove to analyse. According to him, 'the consciousness of the masses' is a much broader concept that referred to the 'kinds of reaction to the most essential issues' of social life. 'Public opinion,' on the contrary, referred to the opinion of the majority of individuals on very concrete issues that may have nothing to do with ideology, such as, for example, the lack of teapots in stores. So, one of the consequences of 'Platonic idealism' which conquered, according to Kołakowski, all spheres of public life was the destruction of the concept of 'public opinion.' According to him, only return to the analysis of the 'public opinion' can help to make the regime truly democratic and truly realistic.

The re-appearance of the central category of Polish liberal sociology of the early post-war years[115] in the discourse of a Marxist was not the only speciality of the state-run press during the crisis of 1956. In one of his articles for 'Nowa Kultura,' Kołakowski challenged the central Marxist thesis of the unity of science. He argued that philosophy has no special subject and belongs to the humanities. This point led him to the argument that philosophy is, in many respects, a worldview issue rather than a strict science.[116] Of course, such an approach to the philosophical agenda stood in direct opposition, not only to the Stalinist version of Marxism, but also to the most liberal interpretations of Marxism.

One of Kołakowski's colleagues, the Marxist philosopher of science, Władysław Krajewski (1919–2006), reacted to his article with some perplexity. Krajewski ironically remarked that he could take this article 'as showing a sense of humour which is so inherent in Kołakowski,' but decided that 'since "Nowa Kultura" is not a humorous journal, it should be taken seriously.'[117] However, Krajewski's criticism was only one more illustration of the crash of the legacy of Stalinism. It had nothing to do with the ideological campaigns of Stalinism and did not contain any quasi-moral accusations of serving capitalism or the betrayal of the loyalty to Marxism. Logically, the main concern was that Kołakowski's argument destroyed the Marxian idea of the universal 'scientific worldview' which helped to fight 'obscurantism.' With undisguised witticism, Krajewski wrote that Kołakowski was 'the first Marxist philosopher' who questioned this basic principle.[118] Krajewski argued that this opinion could threaten the 'achievements' of Polish Marxists in post-war Poland that 'had sunk into idealism' before the coming of the new regime. Either way, Krajewski believed that an academic debate but not the pressure of an authority could help to resolve this problem.[119]

This discussion showed that the crash of Stalinism exposed the fact that all the young Marxist scholars from Schaff's milieu agreed in only one point – the radical denial of the forms of academic practice that had been promoted under Stalinism. Regarding other questions, there was a plurality of views. Of course, for Kołakowski, like for many other scholars from Schaff's group, the crisis of 1956 became a time of critical reflection on his own activity during the wave of Stalinism.[120] Kołakowski's experience in fighting religion and thus his expertise in theological issues helped him to find an approach to defining socialism which could satisfy very different participants in the social movement. Following the strategy of the so-called apophatic or negative theology (which does not dare to say what Gott is and says what Gott is not instead), Kołakowski wrote one of the most famous texts of '1956,' 'What is socialism?' According to him, socialism was neither authoritarian ideology, nor the limitations of freedom and creativity, nor the prohibitions in the intellectual sphere. Having listed these and many other characteristics that were not typical to Stalinism, Kołakowski laconically concluded that 'socialism is a very good thing.'[121] In 1956, the young guard of Stalinisation showed their unity in condemning the virtues that were to be cultivated in Poland after 1948. For them, they were unfair, false, and non-academic. Therefore, they failed.

The wave of '1956' as a phenomenon in the public life of Poland did not last long. The emotional conversation with Soviet comrades and, more importantly, the lack of experience in ruling politics, economics, and the cultural area 'from below' led to the quick changes in the politics of the party. Gomułka, who had become a symbol of Polish 'sovereignty,' did not see another approach to governing the country except the ruling of it with a strong party apparatus that would determine the limits of the permissible in the public sphere. The fate of the youth journal 'Po Prostu' became an illustration of the processes that took place in Poland in 1957. The journal was accused of anti-Marxist views and thus the 'falsity' of its political and intellectual programme.[122] In a symbolic way, the journal was closed in October of 1957, a year after the apex of the 1956 movement. Nevertheless, everything which had been written and said was not forgotten and repeatedly appeared in the public discourse during the subsequent crises which the socialist regime would face in Poland before its fall.

*

'1956' united both Marxist and non-Marxist scholars in their struggle against the virtues promoted under Stalinism. The conflict between Adam Schaff and his students can illustrate both the defeat of the Stalinisation project and its 'achievements.' It was clear that even those who were supposed to become the vanguard of Stalinisation did not adopt the virtues which would made the re-education of Polish scholars possible. They were Marxists, Leninists, and socialists but radically opposed the forms of 'virtuous behaviour' promoted under Schaff's supervision. The loss of control over the public manifestations of 'progressiveness' resulted in a plurality of various forms of Marxism performed by the young scholars, some of which stood in conflict to each other. Remarkably, the young Marxist scholars themselves claimed all political privileges for Marxism unjust and harmful. They did not want to have any domination over non-Marxists and non-party members and strove to prove the rightness of their scholarly theories in accordance with the 'virtuous norms' accepted by other scholars. They strove for the virtue of honesty both in scholarship and in politics. Based on this aspiration, they even opposed ideology as an epistemic category and considered it a 'non-scientific' and 'quasi-religious' form of thinking.

Interestingly, while developing the concepts of public opinion and the idea that philosophy was a worldview issue, most young scholars involved in the public agenda still needed to identify themselves as Marxists. Most of the ideas which constituted the core of the 1956 agenda had been thematised during the early post-war period without any need of references to Marxism. The search for an original and pure Marxism was the paradigm through which the young scholars who had got their training under Stalinism saw the realities, and this was an effect of Stalinisation. All this did not change the main fact that, having adopted the Marxist ideas (though in a very specific form), they definitively rejected the forms of 'virtuous behaviour' preached by the propagators of Soviet Marxism. Additionally, '1956' also became crucial for the development of the idea of political activism. Students and young scholars started to extend their idea of 'good practice' to the field of politics and publicly oppose the views that they considered wrong and harmful. They broke the idea of belonging to one community with the political leadership.

There was another important effect of '1956.' The loyalty to the nation became the main driving and organising force of this crisis. Not to be 'progressive' but to be 'a good Pole' became the imperative of '1956.' 'Nation' became not only an epistemic category (there was nothing new in this), but also a category that was opposed to the authorities that chose the loyalty to the Soviet Union. The interference of the French communists in this story could only strengthen this tendency. More importantly, the increase in the epistemic weight of the concept of nation made an alliance between the representatives of the two opposite camps, Marxists (or broader socialists) and Catholics, possible. This alliance was directed against both the authorities and, explicitly, the Soviet Union. After '1956,' this constellation of factors challenged the basic principle which had determined the early post-war Polish political project, when the state strove to be a protector of those who were 'progressive' and struggled against 'non-scientific views' and 'obscurity.' The authorities lost both the role of supporters of 'progressiveness' that they pretended to play in the early post-war years and that of teachers of virtues that they failed to adopt during Stalinisation. Most importantly, 'progressiveness' ceased to be considered a virtue supposed to unite Polish academia and to motivate its improvement.

By 1968, the next significant crisis of the socialist bloc, those who were PhD-Students and young scholars during the wave of '1956' became established academics. Despite their political activism, the activists of '1956' were allowed not only to successfully continue their career, but also to go abroad for long-term scholarships at the most prestigious European and North American universities.[123] According to the unspoken compromise that helped to stabilise the regime in 1957, Polish academia maintained its relative autonomy, but anti-Soviet statements had to become a tabu once again. However, this compromise was a fragile one. Scholars and writers involved in the public agenda ceased to see the authorities as an ally. The 'failure' of Stalinisation and '1956' convicted academics of the possibility to publicly oppose the authority. This was a factor that made the post-war Polish history a chain of crisis[124] that required more and more brutal and violent intervention of the authorities. Thus, the measures that the authorities undertook in 1968 to stabilise the situation in academia were incomparable even with the measures undertaken during Stalinisation. Police and military forces came to university campuses, many scholars were fired (it was not the case during 'Stalinisation'),[125] scholars of Jewish decent were forced to leave the country (like Zygmunt Bauman), others chose emigration themselves (like Leszek Kołakowski), while many student activists were sent to prison.[126] The cruelty of 1968 and the fact that the state violence only caused new wave of crisis were not least the manifestation of the clash of virtues that was not and could not be hidden. A desired stability of a 'virtuous academia' was not and could not be achieved.

Notes

1 Philippe Ben, "M. Khrouchtchev aurait accepté l'élimination de Rokossowski Mais des mouvements de troupes soviétiques sont signalés des armes distribuées aux ouvriers et aux étudiants," *Le Monde*, October 22 1956, https://www.lemonde.fr/archives/article/1956/10/22/m-khrouchtchev-aurait-accepte-l-elimination-de-rokossowski-mais-des-mouvements-de-troupes-sovietiques-sont-signales-des-armes-distribuees-aux-ouvriers-et-aux-etudiants_3112985_1819218.html
2 It is noteworthy that the Soviet embassy attempted to find out why Philippe Ben is so well informed about internal Polish realities, see: RGANI, F. 5. Op. 49. D. 4, L. 5, 6. I thank Andrei Ilin for drawing my attention on these materials.
3 Philippe Ben, "Une entrevue dramatique," *Le Monde*, November 22, 1956, https://www.lemonde.fr/archives/article/1956/11/22/ii-une-entrevue-dramatique_2249278_1819218.html
4 It is hard to believe that Khrushchev had not met Gomułka before. In his memoirs, Khrushchev recalls in detail his conversation with Gomułka during Khrushchev's first visit to Poland (see Nikita S. Khrushchev, *Vremja. Ljudi. Sobytija (Vospominanija v 3-h*

tomah) [Moskva: Informacionno-izdatel'skaja kompanija 'Moskovskie Novosti', 1999], 584–586). Additionally, the answer of Gomulka, in this case, seems like a reference to the idea that Gomułka's arrest was requested by Moscow, which was extremely popular in Poland. Though Gomułka thought that his imprisonment was confirmed by Stalin (see below, the discussion with Soviet delegates), such sublime words do not seem reliable. Anyway, this story was reprinted in the book of British journalist of Polish origin Konrad Syrop (see Konrad Syrop, *Spring in October: The Polish Revolution of 1956* [London: Weidenfeld and Nicolson, 1957], 95.), which was translated into Russian (see Konrad Syrop, *Vesna v oktjabre. Pol'skaja revoljucija 1956 goda* [New York: Izdatel'stvo Frederik A. Preger, 1961]) and influenced Russian historiography, see: Aleksandr M. Orekhov, *Sovetskij Sojuz i Pol'sha v gody 'ottepeli': iz istorii sovetsko-pol'skih otnoshenij* (Moskva: "Indrik", 2005) 183–184.

5 'The Polish October' is a historiographical concept describing the crisis of '1956,' named so because escalation of the situation happened in October of 1956.
6 See, below, the speech of Gomułka at the plenum of the Central Committee of the Polish United Workers' Party.
7 For example, the 20th Congress provoked a significant conflict between the Soviet Union and China which affected the whole socialist agenda of the world, see: Donald S. Zagoria, *Sino-Soviet Conflict, 1956-1961* (Princeton: Princeton University Press, 1962).
8 Jerzy Eisler, *'Polskie miesiące' czyli Kryzys(y) w PRL* (Warszawa: Instytutu Pamięci Narodowej, 2008) 21.
9 See: Rafał Łatka, "Prymas Wyszyński wobec rzeczywistości politycznej doby Władysława Gomułki," in *Dzieje Kościoła katolickiego na Pomorzu Zachodnim*, ed. Michał Siedziako, Zbigniew Stanuch, Grzegorz Wejman (Szczecin–Warszawa: Instytut Pamięci Narodowej, 2018), 47–65.
10 Władysław Ważniewski, *Walka polityczna w kierownictwie PPR i PZPR 1944-1964* (Toruń: Wydawnictwo Adam Marszałek, 1991), 82–83.
11 He did that, when he got such opportunity: Andrzej Werblan, "Władysław Gomułka a ugrupowania w partii w Październiku 1956 roku," *Polska 1944/45–1989. Studia i Materiały* 3 (1997): 79–89.
12 Aleksandr M. Orekhov, *Sovetskij Sojuz i Pol'sha v gody 'ottepeli'*, 148.
13 Kamila Kamińska-Chełminiak, *Cenzura w Polsce 1944–1960: Organizacja. Kadry. Metody pracy* (Warszawa: Oficyna Wydawnicza ASPRA, 2009), 230–250.
14 Orekhov, *Sovetskij Sojuz i Pol'sha v gody 'ottepeli'*, 151.
15 Ibid., 152.
16 Antoni Dudek, Aleksander Kochański and Krzysztof Persak, eds., *Centrum władzy. Protokoły posiedzeń kierownictwa PZPR. Wybór z lat 1949-1970* (Warszawa: Instytut Studiów Politycznych PAN, 2000), 187.
17 See his memoirs in which he wrote, among other things, about this period: Konstantin Rokossovskij, *Soldatskij dolg* (Moskva: Voenizdat, 1988).
18 The very fact that this discussion between Ochab and Rokossowski, during a close meeting of the members of Politburo, was reflected in Soviet documents (see Aleksandr M. Orekhov, "*Sovetskij Sojuz i Pol'sha v gody "ottepeli'*, 162, 163.) is a good illustration of the mechanisms for the circulation of information between Moscow and Warsaw.
19 Nikita S. Khrushchev, *Vremja. Ljudi. Sobytija (Vospominanija v 3-h tomah)* (Moskva: Informacionno-izdatel'skaja kompanija "Moskovskie Novosti", 1999), 235.
20 See the minutes of the plenum of the Polish United Workers Party that contained Gomułka's 'summary' of Khrushchev's expressions: Antoni Dudek et al., *Centrum władzy. Protokoły posiedzeń kierownictwa PZPR*, 216.
21 To take one example, Polish leaders, in their discussion with the Soviet delegates, said that the speech of the Prime Minister of the Soviet Union Nikolai Bulganin (1895–1975) who, during his visit to Poland, had characterised the demonstrators in Poznań as 'reactionaries' who had been funded by the 'agents of Western forces,' was negatively

perceived in Polish society. This visit took place in July of 1956. The British ambassador wrote about the words of Bulganin: '... no Pole, including communists, would be happy to hear when a foreigner teaches them how they should act. Bulganin showed himself not only as a tactless man but as one who has no idea about Polish realities' (Marcin Kula, *Paryż, Londyn i Waszyngton patrzą na Październik 1956 r. w Polsce* [Warszawa: Instytut Studiów Politycznych Polskiej Akademii Nauk, 1992], 91, 92).

22 "Notatka z rozmów delegacji Prezydium KC KPZR i członków Biura Politycznego KC PZPR w Warszawie, 19 października 1956 r.," in *Przełom Października 56*, ed. Paweł Dybicz (Warszawa: Fundacja Oratio Recto, 2016), 290.

23 "Notatka z rozmów delegacji Prezydium KC KPZR i członków Biura Politycznego KC PZPR," 292–293.

24 "Notatka z rozmów delegacji Prezydium KC KPZR i członków Biura Politycznego KC PZPR," 279.

25 See the original text of the 'secret speech' in which Khrushchev specified this point: Nikita Khrushchev, *O kul'te lichnosti i ego posledstvijah. Doklad XX sjezdu KPSS*, http://lib.ru/MEMUARY/HRUSHEW/kult.txt

26 "Notatka z rozmów delegacji Prezydium KC KPZR i członków Biura Politycznego KC PZPR," 322.

27 Among other things, Khrushchev said: 'and you did not believe me when I characterised you positively at the airfield' ("Notatka z rozmów delegacji Prezydium KC KPZR i członków Biura Politycznego KC PZPR," 322.) which could also help characterise the publication in *Le Monde* as a artistically exaggerated story. Though this does not revise its importance for understanding the international interest to this situation and French sympathies for Gomułka.

28 The speech of Kott was described in detail in the reports of Soviet representatives who visited the meeting and characterised the speech of Kott as a 'slanderous' one, see: Aleksandr M. Orekhov, *Sovetskij Sojuz i Pol'sha v gody 'ottepeli'*, 94.

29 Wojciech Roszkowski, *Najnowsza historia Polski 1956-1970* (Warszawa: Świat Książki 2011), 129.

30 Witold Jedlicki, *Klub Krzywego Koła* (Paryż: Wyd. Instytut Literacki, 1963).

31 Vadim Volobuev, *Politicheskaja oppozicija v Pol'she. 1956-1976* (Moskva: Institut slavjanovedenija RAN, 2009), 22–27.

32 Bolesław Piasecki, "Instynkt państwowy," in *Kierunki, 1945–1960*, ed. Bolesław Piasecki (Warszawa: Wydawnictwo PAX, 1981), 256–261; see about this: Wiesław Władyka, *Na czołówce: Prasa w październiku 1956 roku* (Warszawa; Łódź: Państwowe Wydawnictwo Naukowe, 1989), 361.

33 RGANI, F. 5. Op. 49. D. 4, L. 173–174.

34 The declaration was published in the journal 'Po prostu' which will be discussed below, see: Eugeniusz Lasota and Ryszard Turski, "Polski październik," *Po prostu*, no. 44 (1956): 1–2.

35 Andrzej Micewski, *Współrządzić czy nie kłamać? Warszawa: Pax i Znak w Polsce 1945-1976* (Paris: Libella, 1978), 177–178. Interestingly, Mazowiecki initially wanted to join the group of 'Tygodnik Powszechny'. Having received no answer from Kraków, he joined Piasecki's group. Andrzej Brzeziecki, *Tadeusz Mazowiecki. Biografia naszego premiera* (Kraków: Znak Horyzont, 2015), 40–41.

36 Mazowiecki formulated his views in a theoretical article that he published several years later in a new theoretical journal 'Więź' created by his group: Tadeusz Mazowiecki, "Dlaczego Personalizm?," *Więź*, no. 3 (1958): 11–24.

37 In 1956, the leaders of the 'Tygodnik Powszechny' group also were much more involved in the current politics than it was the case before the closure of their journal in 1953 (formally, the journal was put under the supervision of Piasecki's group). See more about different stages in the development of the discourse: Roman Graczyk, "Realizm polityczny 'Tygodnika Powszechnego' (1945-1989)," *Politeja* 10 (2013): 79–112.

38 See more about the alliance between Catholics and socialists in the prominent book by Adam Michnik: Adam Michnik, *Kościół, lewica, dialog* (Paryż: Instytut Literacki, 1977).
39 Katherine Lebow, *Unfinished Utopia: Nowa Huta, Stalinism, and Polish Society, 1949-56* (New York: Cornell University Press, 2016).
40 See, Adam Ważyk, "Poemat dla dorosłych," *lewicowo.pl*, August 6, 2020, http://lewicowo.pl/poemat-dla-doroslych/
41 Żółkiewski himself participated in discussions with censorship officers to support this or that publication, see Kamila Kamińska-Chełminiak, *Cenzura w Polsce 1944–1960: Organizacja. Kadry. Metody pracy* (Warszawa: Oficyna Wydawnicza ASPRA, 2009), 217–230.
42 Stefan Żółkiewski, "O niektórych opóźnieniach krytyki," *Nowa kultura*, no. 14 (1956): 1.
43 Ibid.
44 The introductory article to the first issue of the journal was written by Stefan Jędrychowski, one of the members of the 'Po Prostu' group in the 1930s, and, after the war, a member of the Workers' Party: Stefan Jędrychowski, "Dawnej i dziś," *Po prostu*, no. 1 (1947): 1.
45 See: Stefan Bratkowski, ed., *Październik 1956: Pierwszy wyłom w systemie: Bunt, młodość i rozsądek* (Warszawa: Prószyński i S-ka, 1996), 48. See more about this journal under Stalinism: Krzysztof Wasilewski, "'Sztandar Młodych' i 'Po prostu' wobec Października 1956 r.," in *Przełom Października 56*, ed. Paweł Dybicz (Warszawa: Fundacja Oratio Recto, 2016), 197–199.
46 "Od redakcji," *Po Prostu*, no. 27 (1955): 1.
47 Jerzy Ambroziewicz and Rafał Wiśniowski, "Tam zapomniano o socjalizmie," *Po Prostu*, no. 39 (1955): 1.
48 The prominent Polish exile writer Marek Hłasko was also one of the authors of the 'Po Prostu' group. See his nearly autobiographic novel: Marek Hłasko, *Beautiful Twentysomethings* (DeKalb: Northern Illinois University Press, 2013).
49 See Chapter 7.
50 Janusz Kuczyński, "Urok wiary," *Po prostu*, no. 29 (1955): 1.
51 During one of the meetings with Gomułka, they claimed the necessity of 'freedom for press and radio,' 'the transparency of the economy and politics,' and 'their own [Polish] path [independent from the Soviet Union] to socialism,' see Krzysztof Wasilewski, "'Sztandar Młodych' i 'Po prostu' wobec Października 1956 r," 205.
52 Later, a personal secretary of Gomułka.
53 After the downfall of the communist regime, a prime minister.
54 Jerzy Ambroziewicz, Walery Namiotkiewicz and Jan Olszewski, "Na spotkanie ludziom AK," *Po prostu*, no. 11 (1956): 1, 2.
55 RGANI, F. 5. Op. 49. D. 4, L. 4.
56 The book of Konrad Syrop became a stage in the transition of this concept from a journalist usage to a historiographical topos, see Konrad Syrop, *Spring in October. The story of the Polish Revolution 1956* (Westport: Greenwood Press Publishers, 1958).
57 See more Michaela Kůželová, *Francouzští komunisté a Polsko v roce 1956* (M. A. thesis, University of Prague, 2011), 65–68; For more general context: Jarosz Dariusz and Maria Pasztor, *Polish-French relations, 1944–1989* (Frankfurt am Main: Peter Lang, 2015), 110–111.
58 Michaela Kůželová, *Francouzští komunisté a Polsko v roce 1956*, 72–74.
59 Leszek Kołakowski, "Na łamach "L'Humanite": Kontrrewolucja w Polsce?," *Sztandar Młodych*, no. 258 (1956): 2.
60 Edda Werfel, "Do towarzyszy z bratnich partii," *Przegląd Kulturalny*, no. 44 (1956): 1; Roman Zimand, "Sprawy robotników całego świata," *Po prostu* no. 45 (1956): 1–2.
61 Jan Strzelecki, "List otwarty do towarzyszy z 'Humanite'," *Nowa Kultura*, no. 45 (1956): 1.

62 Ibid. Of course, the example of Strzelecki was not the only one, see, e.g., Zbigniew Florczak, "Rozmowa z Zachodem," *Nowa Kultura*, no. 43 (1956): 1, 2.
63 See about the programme of the journal: Philippe Tétart, *France Observateur: 1950-1964. Histoire d'un courant de pensée intellectuel* (Paris: PhD thesis, Institut d'études politiques, 1995).
64 Claude Bourdet, "Lewica Francuzka a Polska," *Nowa Kultura*, no. 52 (1956): 1.
65 Ibid.
66 See, for example, about Kołakowski's trips to Paris and his publications in French: Wiesław Chudoba, *Leszek Kołakowski. Kronika życia i dzieła* (Warszaw: Wydawnictwo IFIS PAN, 2014), 126.
67 The philosopher Krzysztof Pomian, then student of philosophy supervised by Adam Schaff, told me that Schaff regularly read the journal 'Kultura' which was forbidden in Poland. The exile government in London and intellectual groups affiliated with it contained their position of boycotting the regime organised in Poland. See more about the impact of '1956' on the agenda of Polish émigré fellows: Rafał Habielski, *Życie społeczne i kulturalne emigracji* (Warszawa: Biblioteka Więzi, 1999), 145.
68 See more in Łukasz Mikołajewski's insightful research: Łukasz Mikołajewski, *Disenchanted Europeans: Polish Émigré Writers from Kultura and Postwar Reformulations of the West* (Peter Lang: Frankfurt, 2018).
69 Agnieszka Latosińska, "Stosunki polsko-francuskie w latach 1945–1970," *Krakowskie Studia Małopolskie* 23 (2018), 185–186; Małgorzata Kamecka, "Ludzie i instytucje. O współpracy historyków polskich i francuskich," in *Cała historia to dzieje ludzi*, ed. Cezary Kuklo and Piotr Guzowski (Białystok: Wydawnictwo Uniwersytetu w Białymstoku, 2004), 416–421; Patryk Pleskot, *Intelektualni sąsiedzi. Kontakty historyków polskich ze środowiskiem "Annales" 1945–1989* (Warszawa: Wydawnictwo IPN, 2015), 97–110. Of course, it does not mean that France was only country with which an academic exchange was possible. Even though France still had a huge 'cultural capital,' the post-1956 academic relations reflected the orientations of various discipline which I mentioned in Chapter 3. For example, thanks to the Ford foundation, Polish scholars and social scientists developed their contacts with academic institutions in the USA and UK, See Jarosław Kilias, *Goście ze Wschodu. Socjologia polska lat sześćdziesiątych XX wieku a nauka światowa* (Kraków: NOMOS, 2017).
70 Józef Chałasiński, "Drogi i bezdroża socjalizmu w nauce polskiej (1949–1954)," *Kultura i Społeczeństwo*, no. 1 (1957): 26.
71 Witold Kula, "W sprawie naszej polityki naukowej," *Kwartalnik Historyczny*, no. 3 (1956): 153.
72 Ibid.
73 Tadeusz Kotarbiński, "Dążenia zrzeszeń naukowych w toku dziejów," *Nauka Polska*, no. 2 (1957): 10.
74 Tadeusz Kotarbiński, "Sprawa logiki w przededniu rozstrzygnięć," *Myśl Filozoficzna*, no. 2 (1956): 124.
75 Ibid., 125–126.
76 After 1956, both Kotarbiński and Ajdukiewicz continued to promote the idea (which they had formulated during the yearly post-war years) that logic should become a school discipline as a school of scientific argumentation. Kazimierz Ajdukiewicz, "W sprawie programów logiki usługowej," *Myśl Filozoficzna*, no. 2 (1956): 127–131.
77 Chałasiński also published his articles in the youth journal 'Po Prostu' and thus looked for sympathies among most cruel critics of Stalinism, see e.g. Józef Chałasiński, "O światowej opinii moralnej," *Po Prostu*, no. 43 (1955): 1.
78 Halina Jarnuszkiewicz, "Czy początek nowego okresu w pracach PAN?," *Nauka Polska*, no. 4 (1956): 147.
79 Józef Chałasiński, "Polski Instytut Socjologiczny. 'Przegląd Socjologiczny'," *Nauka Polska*, no. 4 (1956): 202–205.
80 Ibid., 203.

81 Ibid., 203–204. See also abou his self-victimisation: Chałasiński, "Drogi i bezdroża socjalizmu w nauce polskiej," 22–25.
82 Ibid., 204.
83 Józef Chałasiński, "Od redakcji," *Przegląd socjologiczny*, no. 10 (1957): 7.
84 Ibid., 10.
85 Józef Chałasiński, "Z zagadnień kultury współczesnej," *Przegląd socjologiczny*, no. 11 (1957): 12.
86 Ibid., 12–15.
87 Chałasiński, "Z zagadnień kultury współczesnej," 15.
88 For example, this one: Adam Schaff, "Jak kształcić młode kadry naukowe," *Przegląd Kulturalny*, September 18, 1955.
89 Chałasiński, "Z zagadnień kultury współczesnej," 16–17.
90 Ibid., 17.
91 The 'flexibility' of Chałasiński became an issue for another Znaniecki's student: Tadeusz Szczurkiewicz, "Socjologia polska a stalinizm," in *Krytyka rozumu socjologicznego*, ed. Stanisław Kozyr-Kowalski, Andrzej Przestalski and Jan Włodarek (Poznań: Wydawnictwo Zysk i S-ka, 1997), 274–281. I thank Bartosz Kaliski for drawing my attention on this article.
92 Adam Schaff, "Z czym walczymy i do czego dążymy występując przeciwko 'kultowi jednostki'," *Nowe Drogi*, no. 4 (1956): 18.
93 See e.g. Adam Schaff, "O niektórych zagadnieniach filozoficznych w pracach J. Stalina o językoznawstwie," *Myśl Współczesna*, no. 11–12 (1950): 230–249.
94 Schaff, "Z czym walczymy i do czego dążymy występując przeciwko 'kultowi jednostki'," 18.
95 Ibid., 19.
96 Though Soviet leaders came to this thesis after they executed Lavrentiy Beria, see about this case: Vladimir Haustov, ed., *Delo Berija. Prigovor obzhalovaniju ne podlezhit* (Moskva: MFD, 2012), 420–423.
97 Schaff, "Z czym walczymy i do czego dążymy występując przeciwko 'kultowi jednostki'," 20.
98 Ibid., 20–21.
99 Adam Schaff, *Aktualne zagadnienia polityki kulturalnej w dziedzinie filozofii i socjologii* (Warszawa: Państwowe Wydawnictwo Naukowe, 1956), 38.
100 Ibid., 44.
101 Orekhov, *Sovetskij Sojuz i Pol'sha v gody 'ottepeli'*, 96.
102 Several concrete examples of the institute members who changed their position during the wave of 1956 will be given below in this and the next subchapter.
103 She was then a young sociologist and later became one of the heroes of 1968. It was Maria Hirszowicz who, many years later, wrote the book 'Pitfalls of Engagement' about the engagement of Polish intellectuals with the socialism regime; see Maria Hirszowicz, *Pułapki zaangażowania: Intelektualiści w służbie komunizmu* (Warszawa: Scholar historia, 2001).
104 Zygmunt Bauman, Maria Hirszowicz, Włodzimierz Wesołowski and Jerzy Wiatr, "Wczoraj i jutro naszej socjologii," *Nowa Kultura*, no. 46 (1956): 1.
105 Bauman, et al. "Wczoraj i jutro naszej socjologii," 1. This was one of Schaff's arguments when he attempted to convince Ajdukiewicz of the idealist nature of his materialist programme.
106 In a personal conversation, Krzysztof Pomian, who was then one of participants in the student movement, told me about the criticism of students who asked the administration of the university to teach Marxism–Leninism at a higher level than it was then taught at Polish universities.
107 Bauman, et al. "Wczoraj i jutro naszej socjologii," 1.
108 Ibid.
109 Ibid.

110 Of course, this programme seems very similar to the anti-Marxist discourse of the early post-war years. Nevertheless, if critics of Marxism referred to its outdated character, the young scholar of 1956 had a hope for the 'correct' solution for all these problems.
111 Bauman, et al. "Wczoraj i jutro naszej socjologii," 5.
112 Ibid.
113 Leszek Kołakowski, "Platonizm, empiryzmie i opinia publiczna," *Nowa Kultura*, no. 16 (1956): 1.
114 Ibid., 2, 7.
115 See Chałasiński's publications on the public opinion in the early post-war years in Chapters 1 and 5. A propos, the struggle against Plato (though primarily for his totalitarian tendencies) was an integral part of Karl Popper's research programme, see Karl Popper, *The Open Society and Its Enemies*, vol. 1, 2 (London: Routledge, 1945).
116 Leszek Kołakowski, "Z czego żyją filozofowie," *Nowa Kultura*, no. 3 (1956): 2.
117 Władysław Krajewski, "Czy filozofia jest nauką humanistyczną," *Nowa Kultura*, no. 7 (1956): 1.
118 Krajwski remembered that Kołakowski himself had criticised the idea of the differentiation between philosophy and natural sciences after 'his visit to Italy,' by which he obviously meant Kołakowski's trip to the Congress of Thomists, see Kołakowski's report on this trip: Leszek Kołakowski, "Kongres tomistyczny w Rzymie," *Myśl Filozoficzna*, no. 1 (1956): 233–239. See: Krajewski, "Czy filozofia jest nauką humanistyczną," 4.
119 Krajewski, "Czy filozofia jest nauką humanistyczną," 1, 4.
120 According to the memoirs of the communist philosopher Marian Dobrosielski (1923–) who was then a secretary of the local party organisation at the University of Warsaw, Kołakowski came to him in the spring of 1956 (when the article on public opinion was written) and asked him to accept his withdrawal from the party membership. Dobrosielski argued that it was the 20th Congress and the exposure of Stalinism that had so deeply impressed Kołakowski and changed his ideals. Dobrosielski convinced Kołakowski not to take such an emotional decision, and he did not leave the party. Nevertheless, his readiness to revise his previous convictions was obvious not only from his publications but also from other forms of his public activity (see Wiesław Chudoba, *Leszek Kołakowski. Kronika życia i dzieła* [Warszaw: Wydawnictwo IFIS PAN, 2014], 121). In October 1956, Kołakowski visited Paris and Maison Lafitte, where he met Jerzy Giedroyc and the whole group of 'Kultura.' All this significantly influenced his attitude regarding the political realities. Having learned about the Soviet invasion of Hungary, he abandoned his visit to Paris and came back to Poland in order to participate in writing a letter of protest to the Soviet ambassador (Chudoba, *Leszek Kołakowski. Kronika życia i dzieła*, 125–127).
121 Leszek Kołakowski, "Czym jest socjalnym?," *Po prostu* no. 47 (1956): 1. See more about the intellectual evolution of Leszek Kołakowski in this period: Krzysztof Pomian, "Leszek Kołakowski: jednostka, wolność, rozum (Introduction)," in Leszek Kołakowski, *Główne nurty marksizmu. Powstanie, rozwój, rozkład*, vol. 1 (Warszawa: Wydawnictwo naukowe PWN, 2009), VII–XXX.
122 Wasilewski, "'Sztandar Młodych' i 'Po prostu' wobec Października 1956 r.," 206.
123 Jarosław Kilias, *Goście ze Wschodu Socjologia polska lat sześćdziesiątych XX wieku a nauka światowa* (Kraków: Zakład Wydawniczy Nomos, 2017).
124 See Jerzy Eisler's famous book on the chain of crisis: Jerzy Eisler, *'Polskie miesiące' czyli Kryzys(y) w PRL* (Warszawa: Instytutu Pamięci Narodowej, 2008).
125 See more: Tom Junes, *Student Politics in Communist Poland. Generations and Dissent* (Lanham/Boulder/New York/London: Lexington books, 2015), 103–142.
126 Junes, *Student Politics in Communist Poland*, 103–122.

Epilogue
The Concept of Virtues as a Lens

Virtuous battles in post-war Poland

The famous Polish sociologist, Jerzy Szacki, wrote in the biography of Leszek Kołakowski:

> This seems to us unbelievable today, because [only] very few people understand that one can [sincerely] be a Communist. Well, once it was possible, and this was quite selfless. There were such people, although there were not so many of them. However, in many cases they quickly moved away from communism, [and] later became anti-Communists.[1]

Centring the act of belonging to this or that ideological camp in the post-war history of the socialist bloc became a natural way of dealing with the communist past of Europe both in the professional historiography and in the popular view of history. The association with communism or, more generally, with Marxism could be seen as a marker of 'sincerity,' that is moral characteristics of people. From this perspective, loyalty to Marxism was understood as loyalty to the political leadership and thus an opposition to the 'nation.' Of course, this perspective has its merits. Firstly, the aim to cultivate or, at least, to promote this or that virtue is closely connected with the ideology that tends to determine what the correct forms of 'virtuous behaviour' are. Secondly, a violent domination of a political doctrine usually makes its supporters a part of the repressive apparatus and thus collaborators in a violent distraction of opposition. Nevertheless, this book shows that the concept of virtues as a lens allows us to slightly change this perspective.

The project of 'gentle revolution' became one of the most important events in the post-war history despite its short duration. Using the unique constellation of political and social factors in the early post-war years, the organisers of this project were able to make public scholarly debates an island of certain autonomy from the direct political pressure of the authorities. Along with the idea of promoting 'progressiveness' as the central virtue and making scholars themselves the creators of the intellectual agenda, it made the post-war public sphere a field on which the plurality of academic and ideological approaches became visible. The official claim 'to be progressive' was understood not as a call for breaking with the forms of 'virtuous behaviour,' which scholars themselves considered crucial, but as a call for promoting them publicly. Thus, the diverse intellectual landscape of the early post-war years reflected not a mistake of the censorship but the 'virtues politics' of the 'gentle revolution.' Striving 'to be progressive,' both in their academic work and in the public activism, Polish scholars showed how different the public manifestations of 'progressiveness' could be. Some of them publicly promoted their anti-authoritarian vision of both academia and society, while the authorities did not prevent them from spreading publicly the ideas that stood in conflict with both the Soviet realities and the authoritarian project that was about to be implemented in the whole socialist bloc.

The public image of the Soviet Union created under the 'gentle revolution' also reflected the 'virtuous politics' conducted in this period. Not only the aspiration to keep distance from the Soviet realities but also the 'distortion' of the self-image of the Soviet Union showed how foreign the Soviet academic practice was for the Polish academics. Additionally, this method of dealing with the Soviet Union was more evidence of scholars seeing no conflict between their forms of 'virtuous behaviour' and the official discourse on this issue. The orientation of the early post-war public agenda towards France, which was intentionally opposed to the Soviet Union as a teacher of virtues, was a very important sign that the national tradition still played a central role in the public scholarly agenda. Moreover, it was clear that the aspiration 'to be a good Pole,' in other words, to follow the 'national virtues,' stood frequently in conflict with the virtues gained with professional training. In case of a conflict between these virtues, the national ones were preferred.

Either way, under the 'gentle revolution,' 'national virtues' were still limited by the dominant virtue of 'progressiveness.' Being designed as a technic of purifying the national intellectual tradition from 'reactionary elements,' the cultivation of 'progressiveness' was expected to determine the development of ideas that, in turn, were supposed to become relevant beyond the national borders and show how the unique milieu of post-war Poland can help to 'produce' most 'progressive' and internationally relevant ideas. It is not accidental that, under these circumstances, 'progressiveness' became a weapon against dogmatic Marxism. The reason for this was both the 'outdated' character of classical Marxism for the international scholarly agenda and its exclusive morality. Meanwhile, 'progressiveness' was supposed to become a meeting point for both Catholics and socialists. From the perspective of the project of 'gentle revolution,' being Catholic did not necessarily mean possessing a 'reactionary attitude.' All this still made the 'gentle revolution' a modernisation project that forced all the participants in the public debate to prove their 'progressiveness.'

The visible stability of the early post-war years was determined by the fact that the official discourse on virtues did not require any significant 're-education' of scholars regarding their academic work and public activity. The state pretended to be a protector of the virtues promoted by scholars themselves, as well as a helper in spreading these virtues among the reading publics. When striving to 'be progressive,' Polish scholars behaved very differently. Disciplinary background, ideological affiliation, political experiences – all this played a role in how they responded to the call for 'progressiveness.' The early post-war debates showed that this virtue (as any other) could have very different public manifestations.

The escalation of the Cold War resulted in an enormous increase in pressure from the Soviet government on other countries within its sphere of influence. Around 1948, the authoritarian tendencies became unrestrained across Central and Eastern Europe. Both the academic and public institutions created under the 'gentle revolution' were destroyed. The crucial point of Stalinisation, which came to replace the 'gentle revolution,' was to rapidly change the forms of 'virtuous behaviour' that determined the academic and scholarly practice of Polish scholars. Most importantly, the state attempted to change its role from protector and helper to a supervisor and teacher of virtues. Additionally, it strove to discipline and control the public manifestation of virtues. This could not help but lead to a clash between the new virtues and the forms of academic practice performed by Polish scholars. Although the adoption of the new virtues was a precondition for the success of Stalinisation and its potential failure a great danger, this project failed. The authorities were not recognised in the role of the teachers and the new virtues were rejected. Scholars publicly opposed the new forms of academic practice and thus did not allow the organisers of Stalinisation to even give an impression of a 'virtuous' academia. The desired stability, which was to be achieved through the claims of unity supported by the most scholars, could not be even faked.

The defeat of Stalinisation was one of the key steps towards the crisis of '1956' that shook the whole socialist block. During this crisis, most Polish scholars who were engaged politically demonstrated a rebellion not against Marxism and Marxist ideas, but against the forms of 'virtuous behaviour' promoted by the chief organisers of Stalinisation. By 1956, Marxism started to play a more important role in Polish academia than it had in the early post-war years, and this was an effect of Stalinisation. Nevertheless, most adepts of Marxism publicly opposed the forms of 'virtuous behaviour' promoted by the authorities in the previous years. All the institutions that had been created during the wave of Stalinisation became opposition centres. This illustrates the fact that neither ideology nor institutional changes were crucial for the reshaping the academic and public landscapes of the countries under Soviet domination. The Polish crisis of 1956 became a logical outcome of the failure to forcibly replace the virtues that had previously determined the academic practice with new ones.

The 'failure' of Stalinisation and, after 1956, the necessity to return to a stronger form of regulation of the public sphere had also another important consequence. It led to the defeat of the 'enlightenment project' proclaimed by the authorities immediately after the war. After '1956,' the authorities lost their role as supervisors and protectors of the virtue of 'progressiveness' that they had pretended to play under the 'gentle revolution.' Most importantly, 'progressiveness' itself started to play a decreasing role in the public agenda. After '1956,' not 'to be progressive' but 'to be a good Pole' in terms of loyalty to the national identity in front of the foreign threat became the new basis of the alliance between Catholics and left-wing intellectuals.

This tendency would play an increasingly significant role throughout the second half of the 20th century. The fate of the three most famous protagonists of this book,

Zygmunt Bauman, Leszek Kołakowski, and Adam Schaff, can illustrate this point. Having emigrated after the new crisis of the regime in 1968 to the UK, Kołakowski gained his international reputation as a critic of Marxism and, from being a leading fighter against religion, became, in a sense, a philosopher of religion with a deep critique of the 'enlightenment' rationalism.[2] Bauman, on the contrary, did not cease to develop his socialist ideas, striving to maintain his commitment to 'progressiveness.' While Kołakowski became a national hero of the anti-communist movement before and after the fall of the socialist bloc, Bauman was internationally celebrated in the left-wing circles but did not fit with the national pantheon and experienced assaults in Poland even long after 1989.[3]

Adam Schaff, in turn, found himself in increasing isolation from the late 1950s. Even developing a more liberal form of Marxism inspired by the atmosphere of 'the thaw,'[4] Schaff remained a figure of Stalinism for those of his students who still had left-wing sympathies. At the same time, the right-wing section of the Workers Party and academia used his affiliation with Stalinism to find an outlet for their antisemitic sentiments and to make Schaff the object of a smear campaign organised on the wave of the cruellest post-war antisemitic action in 1968.[5] Schaff continued to be a loyal defender of the regime until its collapse.[6] The philosopher and historian Krzysztof Pomian, who was a philosophy student in the 1960s and, later, emigrated to France, told me a story about his meeting with Schaff during one of the international philosophical conventions in the early 1980s. When Schaff noticed Pomian, he told to the people around him: 'Dear colleagues, that is my former student and the leader of our emigration.' Pomian politely replied: 'Professor, indeed, I was your student, but I am not a leader of YOUR emigration.'[7] Being stigmatised both in the right-wing circles and by Soviet scholars,[8] Schaff and the forms of 'virtuous behaviour' he promoted were foreign to the Polish academic agenda.

The project of forcible 're-education' of scholars changed a lot of how Polish academia worked. Stalinisation definitively succeeded in destroying the project of 'gentle revolution.' It created a lot of new academic institutions (some of which still exist now) and was strong enough to orientate many young people towards Marxism. Meanwhile, it radically disfigured the scholarly life and forced many scholars to make the self-defence from the external intersection the core of their academic practice. On the one hand, it showed that the forms of 'virtuous behaviour' that scholars defended, with the coming of a new political crisis, were brought to the field of politics. On the other, it reinforced the national categories both in the academic work and political activism that served as a mobilisational tool for the struggle against the regime. Stalinism did not achieve its aims in Poland. Nevertheless, its traces would be palpable for a long time.

Looking beyond Poland

'I cannot imagine science developing in only one country [...] I said that science knows no borders and has no homeland [...] If one takes any scientific problem and follows its development, can one really say that science has a homeland or can betray its homeland?'[9] With these words, the prominent Soviet physiologist Lina

Stern responded to the judge who asked her to publicly confirm her ideas that stood in conflict with the official line of 'Soviet science.' This happened during the process against the members of the Jewish Anti-Fascist Committee who were arrested during the new wave of repressions in the Soviet Union after the end of the Second World War. Stern not only refused to recognise her guilt[10] under the highest political pressure but also pursued her own idea of how to be 'a good scientist,' even facing the threat of execution.[11] Breaking the basic conventions of Soviet academia, Stern failed to claim that every science is determined by the political interest of the proletariat and that the Soviet Union overcame other countries, having created the unique social conditions for developing 'truly scientific' approaches. Even having experienced the imprisonment and exhausting interrogations, Stern still did not follow the forms of 'virtuous behaviour' prescribed by both the show trials of the 1930s and the ideological campaigns in Soviet science.

No authoritarian regime is capable of making all scholars (much like all citizens) 'virtuous' in accordance with its own idea of 'virtuousness.' For a visible 'success' of 'virtues politics,' the regime must control not only the process of cultivating virtues but also their public manifestations. If we do not consider virtues ontological categories that strove to a metaphysic ideal,[12] we should regard both the cultivation of virtues and striving for them as a part of the social and partly political practice. Being adopted (or being supposed to be adopted), all virtues (whether it is, e.g., wisdom or progressiveness) can have very different public manifestations. This is a more visible contradiction between virtue as an idealistic concept and as a foundation of a real social practice. Additionally, even a violent 're-education' of scholars[13] did not guarantee the achievement of the desired state of *concordia* and *eudemonia*, to which virtues are supposed to lead. Even an information blockade and full control over the public expression of ideas could not always give the impression that all scholars 'virtuously' show their unity and behave identically when following their virtues.

However, the strength of the information blockade should not be underestimated. The tendency to generalisations and idealisations inherent in our perception of the world push us to accept the harmonic and geometrically perfect pictures of academic practice constructed by the authoritarian regimes in their self-representation. We tend to associate this effect with 'national traditions' or 'cultural ethos' that are rooted in the 'nature' of the things and thus are 'natural.' All contradictions tend to be explained by atypical individual cases. All this makes the faked unity of academia under any authoritarian regime an important component of the stability of the regime. The impression that the majority supports the dominant forms of 'virtuous behaviour' is supposed to demotivate those who want to challenge these forms.

Of course, it does not mean that authoritarian regimes, under which the state attempts to monopolise the process of teaching virtues, can be 'successful' only in making illusions. Firstly, every attempt to use the political pressure for re-educating scholars led to a new reconstruction of academic hierarchies and appearance of activists, who became not only the best students of the new virtues but also use the quasi-moral pathos of new 'educational' campaigns for fighting their opponents. Secondly, the reference to virtues as, for example, that of 'patriotism' or 'loyalty' can be effectively manipulated for maintaining the stability of the regime. Of course, both these 'virtues' can be orientated to the protection of the regime or, on the contrary, to its destruction. In this regard, the cultivation of 'patriotism,' for example, in Soviet Russia and that in other Soviet republics could have very different consequences for the regime, not to mention other states from the socialistic bloc. In one case, the state may seem more natural in determining the ideas that had to be associated with the 'national interest'; in the other, the regime can be seen as an oppressor of 'national virtues.'

Either way, the main question is if the state succeeds in forcing scholars to become a part of one 'community' with a political leadership that can produce its own 'virtues' and fight the tendencies that they consider 'vices.' Besides the fact that academia itself is never coherent and monolithic in terms of the virtues cultivated under its banner, the creation of an alliance with the political leadership implies a significant revision of the hierarchy and constellation of virtues in comparison to that of academia.[14] The feeling of belonging to one 'community' with the political leadership and sharing the forms of 'virtuous behaviour' determined by the people having power had been diligently cultivated in authoritarian regimes. This was (is) supposed to legitimate not only the domination of 'national virtues' over all others but also loyalty to the political leadership that determines how the virtues must be manifested. In this regard, a radical change of the official ideology does not change much in the core of academic or political practice. While promoting very different views and ideologists, scholars can continue to feel themselves a part of one 'community' with the political leadership and thus, in some cases, legitimise the crimes committed by politicians.

This raises a set of questions that can be seen differently from the perspective of virtues. The fall of the socialist regimes in Central and Eastern Europe (partly) destroyed the social and political institutions that helped the authorities to forcibly teach scholars (and other citizens) how to be 'virtuous.' Nevertheless, it did not mean that conflicts regarding scholarly virtues were resolved. On the contrary, they became much more visible. The attempts to create a common academic space that would overcome the national and geographical borders and thus promote a set of common virtues faced a considerable resistance among many scholars, not least in Central and East European universities. The relative strength of the right-wing discourse in this region and the idea of dominance of 'national virtues' over all others made academia and scholarly public practice not only a battlefield of various ideologies but a platform for a new clash of virtues.

The case of post-Soviet Russia also represents fertile soil for research on this issue. The gradual destruction of the autonomy of academic institutions from the authorities (that happened with only a few attempts to resist), as well as the limited access to the broader publics, with their habit of consuming the state-run mass media, wrecked the attempts of some scholars to reach the broader publics with a form of discourse opposed to that of the authorities.[15] More importantly, for the considerable section of Russian scholars, especially those involved in teaching, the 'defence of the fatherland' on the 'scholarly front,' which in most cases implies

Epilogue 233

the sense of belonging to one camp with the people in power, is the corn of 'virtuous behaviour.' Thus, universities and research institutions tend to become the centres of repression against both the students who challenge the dominant forms of 'virtuous behaviour' and 'non-virtuous' scholars.

The question of which virtues stay behind academic practice, as well as what the field of tension between opposite virtues is, makes us think not only of (aggressive) ideologists that cause the current conflicts but also of forms of 'virtuous behaviour'[16] that make the appearance and relevance of these ideologists possible. Meanwhile, the perspective of virtues shows us the reasons for the resistance of academic practice to rapid change, which, in turn, can have both merits and, no less importantly, great disadvantages.

Should academia be inside or outside of the discourse of loyalty to a nation? Is it necessary for a scholar to be 'progressive' in terms of his or her political views? Should the 'good scholar' be politically engaged? These and many other questions refer not only to ideologies but also to virtues that determine our academic practice. Most importantly, these virtues are both epistemic and civic, which makes them crucial for the development of both academic and political agendas.

Looking at the scholarly and public practice through the lens of virtues does not give a simple and logical explanation for all the phenomena of scholarly and public life. On the contrary, it opens a complex and contradictory picture. It forces us to look behind the surface and makes us critically reflect on our own scholarly work and on that of others.

Notes

1 Jerzy Szacki, *Leszek Kołakowski: Marksizm, komunizm*, in *Leszek Kołakowski – myśliciel i obywatel*, ed. Piotr Kosiewski (Warszawa: Fundacja im. Stefana Batorego, 2010), 15.
2 See, for example, Zbigniew Mentzel, *Kołakowski: Czytanie świata; Biografia* (Kraków: Wydawnictwo Znak, 2020).
3 See Izabela Wagner, *Bauman: A Biography* (Cambridge, UK: Polity Press, 2020).
4 See one of the most prominent publications of Adam Schaff, which became a precondition for a smear campaign against him and accusations of 'revisionism': Adam Schaff, *Marksizm a jednostka ludzka: Przyczynek do marksistowskiej filozofii człowieka* (Warszawa: Wydawnictwo Naukowe PWN, 1965). This book had an international resonance. Erich Fromm wrote an introduction for the English translation of Schaff's book: Adam Schaff, *Marxism and the Human Individual* (New York: McGraw Hill, 1970).
5 Bolesław Piasecki was among those who publicly attacked Schaff in alliance with the right-wing section of the Workers' Party and security services, see Mikołaj S. Kunicki, *Between the Brown and the Red: Nationalism, Catholicism, and Communism in 20th-Century Poland; The Politics of Bolesław Piasecki* (Athens: Ohio University Press, 2012), 146; see about the 'anti-Zionistic' campaign: Dariusz Stola, *Kampania antysyjonistyczna w Polsce 1967–1968* (Warszawa, Instytut Studiów Politycznych PAN, 2000).
6 Interestingly, when the regime broke down, Adam Schaff criticised the Polish People's Republic as a totalitarian state that did not correspond with the Marxist idea of freedom: see one of the late interviews with Adam Schaff for the Chanel TVP: '*Nie ma innej drogi,*' https://www.youtube.com/watch?v=GxPkZzV5Hg0

234 *Epilogue*

7 According to Pomian, Schaff's answer was as follows: 'Do not be so modest!,' which also says a lot about the character of Schaff.
8 The cruel criticism of Adam Schaff as a bearer of 'American Sociology' was a part of Soviet sociological agenda. See, for example, the transcripts of the discussion on the dictionary of sociological concepts: *Sociologicheskaja drama v dvuh dejstvijah. Stenogramma obsuzhdenija kratkogo slovarja terminov. Stenogramma obsuzhdenija plana sbornika statej «Social'nye issledovanija»* [URL]: http://www.ras.ru/publishing/rasherald/rasherald_articleinfo.aspx?articleid=918ed6d3-a597-4dcf-aac7-6b7ad62a559e
9 Joshua Rubenstein and Vladimir P. Naumov, eds., *Stalin's Secret Pogrom: The Postwar Inquisition of the Jewish Anti-Fascist Committee* (New Haven: Yale University Press, 2005), 413.
10 To be precise, Stern recanted her statements given under the pressure of interrogators. See Rubenstein and Naumov, *Stalin's Secret Pogrom*, 400–416.
11 Many of the accused were executed, while Stern got a relatively light punishment. She was sentenced to three and a half years in jail. See Joshua Rubenstein, "Night of the Murdered Poets," in *Stalin's Secret Pogrom: The Postwar Inquisition of the Jewish Anti-Fascist Committee*, ed. Joshua Rubenstein and Vladimir P. Naumov (New Haven: Yale University Press, 2005), 1–64.
12 In fact, most political theories that refer to the concept of virtues imply striving for a concrete ideal that plays a role of a metaphysical destination: see, for example, Philip Pettit, *The Robust Demands of the Good: Ethics with Attachment, Virtue, and Respect* (Oxford/New York: Oxford University Press, 2015), 43–72.
13 Before being arrested, Stern experienced several critical campaigns against herself in the Soviet academic journals, see Alla A. Vein, "Science and Fate: Lina Stern (1878–1968), A Neurophysiologist and Biochemist," *Journal of the History of the Neurosciences* 17, no. 2 (2008): 195–206; See more about the academic career of Lina Stern: Jakov A. Rosin and Viktor B. Malkin, *Lina Solomonovna Shtern, 1878–1968* (Moskva: Nauka, 1987).
14 Of course, one can be a member of different communities at the same time. The question is as follows: what virtues start to play a dominant role?
15 Besides the activities of 'Memorial' and big public outreach projects such as 'Postnauka' and 'Arzamas Academy,' there was a community of historians called 'the Free Historical Society (Volnoe istoricheskoe obshechestvo)' that attempted to reach the broader publics with their expertise on the historical politics of the Russian authorities. Nevertheless, it had unfortunately a very small impact on the perception of the history in Russian society, see Jade McGlynn, *Memory Makers: The Politics of the Past in Putin's Russia* (London: Bloomsbury, 2023).
16 It is worth mentioning that the post-Soviet sociologists conducted one of the biggest sociological projects on so-called '*Homo sovieticus*' that was rooted in the late Soviet critique of Soviet society (see, e.g., Aleksandr Zinovyev, *Homo sovieticus* [New York: Grove/Atlantic, 1986]). About the project, see Klaus Gestwa, "Der Homo Sovieticus und der Zerfall des Sowjetimperiums Jurij Levadas unliebsame Sozialdiagnosen," *Zeithistorische Forschungen/Studies in Contemporary History* 10 (2013): 331–334; Alexei Yurchak, "Soviet Hegemony of Form: Everything Was Forever, Until It Was No More," *Comparative Studies in Society and History* 45, no. 3 (2003): 480–510. However, my idea of virtues as a research tool does not imply any holistic vision of 'Soviet,' 'Polish,' or any other specific kind of people. On the contrary, I suppose that virtues as a lens can be a much more flexible analytic tool focused on concrete tendencies but on generalisations and thus can give a more dynamic and complex picture of scholarly and political reality.

Bibliography

Archives:

Archiwum Akt Nowych (Warsaw) – AAN
Archiwum Polskiej Akademii Nauk (Warsaw) – APAN
Gabinet Rękopisów, Biblioteka Uniwersytetu Warszawskiego (Warsaw) – GR
Archiwum "Kultury" (Maisons-Laffitte)
Centre Scientifique de l'Académie Polonaise des Sciences (Archive) (Paris)
Société Historique et Littéraire Polonaise (Archive) (Paris)
Gosudarstvennyj arhiv Rossijskoj Federacii (Moscow) – GA RF
Rossijskij Gosudarstvennyj Arhiv Novejshej Istorii (Moscow) – RGANI

Published sources:

Adibekov, Grant M., ed. *Soveshhanija Kominforma 1947, 1948, 1949. Dokumenty i materialy*. Moskva: Rosspen, 1998.
Bąbiak, Grzegorz P., ed. *Na rogu Stalina i trzech krzyży: Listy do Jerzego Borejszy, 1944–1952*. Warszawa: Czytelnik, 2014.
Datner, Szymon, and Kazimierz Leszczyński, eds. *Zbrodnie okupanta w czasie powstania warszawskiego w 1944 roku (w dokumentach)*. Warszawa: Wydawnictwo MON, 1962.
Dudek, Antoni, Aleksander Kochański, and Krzysztof Persak eds. *Centrum władzy. Protokoły posiedzeń kierownictwa PZPR. Wybór z lat 1949–1970*. Warszawa: Instytut Studiów Politycznych PAN, 2000.
Herbst, Stanisław, Tadeusz Manteuffel, and Witold Kula eds. *Pierwsza Konferencja Metodologiczna Historyków Polskich. Przemówienia. Referaty. Dyskusje*. Vol. 1, 2. Warszawa: Państwowe wydawnictwo naukowe, 1953.
Kochański, Aleksander, ed. *Protokół obrad KC PPR w maju 1945 roku*. Warszawa: Instytut Studiów Politycznych PAN, 1992.
Matveev, Gennadi, Gennadi Bordyugov, and Andrzej Paczkowski, eds. *SSSR – Pol'sha. Mehanizmy podchinenija. 1944–1949*. Moskva: AIRO-HH, 1995.
Nekipelov, Aleksandr, ed. *Central'no-vostochnaja Evropa vo vtoroj polovine XX veka*. Vol. 1, Moskva: «Nauka», 2000.
Volokitina, Tatyana, Galina Murashko, and Albina Noskova, eds. *Sovetskij faktor v Vostochnoj Evrope: 1944–1953 gg.: Dokumenty*. Vol. 1: 1944–1948. Moskva: ROSSPJeN, 1999.

Volokitina, Tatyana, Galina Murashko, and Albina Noskova, eds. *Sovetskij faktor v Vostochnoj Evrope: 1944–1953 gg.: Dokumenty.* Vol 2: 1949–1953, Moskva: ROSSPJeN, 2002.
Volokitina, Tatyana, Galina Murashko, and Albina Noskova, eds. *Vostochnaja Evropa v dokumentah rossijskih arhivov: 1944–1953 gg*, vol. 1. Novosibirsk: Sibirskij hronograf, 1997.
Volokitina, Tatyana, Galina Murashko, and Albina Noskova, eds. *Vostochnaja Evropa v dokumentah rossijskih arhivov: 1944–1953 gg*, vol. 2. Novosibirsk: Sibirskij hronograf, 1998.

Interviews:

Jerzy W. Borejsza (1935–2019)
Krzysztof Pomian (1934–)
Wiktoria Śliwowska (1931–2021)

Key journals:

Dziś i Jutro (1945–1956)
Głos Ludu (1944–1948)
Kierunki (1956–1957)
Kultura (1947–1957)
Kultura i Społeczeństwo (1957)
Kuźnica (1945–1949)
Kwartalnik Historyczny (1946–1957)
Myśl Filozoficzna (1951–1957)
Myśl Współczesna (1946–1951)
Nauka Polska (1953–1957)
Nowa Kultura (1949–1957)
Nowe Drogi (1947–1957)
Nowiny Literackie (1947–1948)
Odrodzenie (1944–1949)
Pamiętnik Literacki (1946–1957)
Po Prostu (1947–1957)
Przegląd Filozoficzny (1946–1949)
Przegląd Kulturalny (1952–1957)
Przegląd Nauk Historycznych i Społecznych (1950–1956)
Przegląd Socjologiczny (1946–1949; 1957)
Przegląd Zachodni (1945–1957)
Słowo Powszechne (1947–1957)
Sztandar Młodych (1950–1957)
Teki Historyczne (1947–1957)
Trybuna Ludu (1948–1957)
Twórczość (1945–1957)
Tygodnik Powszechny (1945–1957)
Tygodnik Warszawski (1945–1948)
Wiadomości (1946–1957)
Więź (1958)
Znak (1946–1953; 1953–1957)
Życie Nauki (1946–1953)

Bibliography:

Alpatov, Vladimir M. *Istoriya odnogo mifa. Marr i Marrizm*. Moskva: URSS, 2004.
Aleksandrov, Grigorij F. *Istorija zapadnoevropejskoj filosofii*. Moskva, Leningrad: Izdatel'stvo AN SSSR, 1946.
Angle, Stephen Slote. *Michael Virtue Ethics and Confucianism*. New York/London: Routledge, 2013.
Annas, Julia. *Intelligent Virtue*. Oxford: Oxford University Press, 2011.
Apor, Balázs. "Sovietisation, Imperial Rule and the Stalinist Leader Cult in Central and Eastern Europe." In *The Shadow of Colonialism on Europe's Modern Past*, edited by Róisín Healy and Enrico Dal Lago, 228–244. London: Palgrave Macmillan, 2014.
Aristotle. *The Nicomachean Ethics*. New York and London: Penguin, 2020.
Avis, George. *The Making of the Soviet Citizen: Character Formation and Civic Training in Soviet Education*. New York & London: Routledge, 1987.
Bąbiak, Grzegorz P. ""Czytelnik" od Warszawy po Nowy Jork." In *Na rogu Stalina i trzech krzyży. Listy do Jerzego Borejszy, 1944–1952*, edited by Grzegorz P. Bąbiak, 5–76. Warszawa: Czytelnik, 2014.
Bąbiak, Grzegorz P. ""Czerwona Marianna" o polsko-francuskich związkach literackich na łamach "Odrodzenia" (1945–1950)," *Prace Polonistyczne* 70 (2015): 9–29.
Bąbiak, Grzegorz P. *"Odrodzenie" (1944–1950): Bibliografia zawartości*. Warszawa: Wydział Polonistyki Uniwersytetu Warszawskiego, 2017.
Babiracki, Patryk. *Soviet Soft Power in Poland: Culture and the Making of Stalin's New Empire, 1943–1957*. Chapel Hill: University of North Carolina Press, 2015.
Baehr, Jason. *Intellectual Virtues and Education: Essays in Applied Virtue Epistemology*. New York: Routledge, 2015.
Baehr, Jason. *The Inquiring Mind: On Intellectual Virtues and Virtue Epistemology*. Oxford: Oxford University Press, 2011.
Barboza, Amalia. *Karl Mannheim*. Konstanz: UVK Verlagsgesellschaft mbH, 2009.
Baron, Samuel H. *Bloody Saturday in the Soviet Union: Novocherkassk, 1962*. Stanford: Stanford University Press, 2001.
Behr, Valentin. *Powojenna historiografia polska jako pole walki. Studium z socjologii wiedzy i polityki*. Warszawa: Wydawnictwo Uniwersytetu Warszawskiego, 2021.
Bell, David Scott, and Byron Criddle. *The French Communist Party in the Fifth Republic*. Oxford: Clarendon Press, 1994.
Ben, Philippe M. "Khrouchtchev aurait accepté l'élimination de Rokossowski Mais des mouvements de troupes soviétiques sont signalés des armes distribuées aux ouvriers et aux étudiants," *Le Monde,* October 22, 1956, https://www.lemonde.fr/archives/article/1956/10/22/m-khrouchtchev-aurait-accepte-l-elimination-de-rokossowski-mais-des-mouvements-de-troupes-sovietiques-sont-signales-des-armes-distribuees-aux-ouvriers-et-aux-etudiants_3112985_1819218.html
Ben, Philippe M. "Une entrevue dramatique," *Le Monde,* November 22, 1956, https://www.lemonde.fr/archives/article/1956/11/22/ii-une-entrevue-dramatique_2249278_1819218.html
Benda, Julien. *La Trahison des clercs*. Paris: Les Éditions Grasset, 1927.
Bensaude-Vincent, Bernadette, and Eva Telkes-Klein. *Les identités multiples d'Émile Meyerson*. Paris: Honoré Champion, 2016.
Białkowski, Błażej. *Utopie einer besseren Tyrannis. Deutsche Historiker an der Reichsuniversität Posen (1941–1945)*. Stuttgart: Ferdinand Schöningh, 2011.

Biełaszko, Mirosław. "„Tygodnik Warszawski" i jego środowisko (1945–1948)." *Biuletyn IPN* 75, no. 4 (2007): 77–83.

Bielatowicz, Jan. *Literatura na emigracji*. Londyn: Nakład Polskiej Fundacji Kulturalnej, 1970.

Bielecka-Prus, Joanna. "The Social Roles of Polish Sociologists after 1945." *Comparative Sociology* 10 (2011): 735–765.

Bińko, Beata. "Instytut Kształcenia Kadr Naukowych przy KC PZPR – narzędzie ofensywy ideologicznej w nauce i szkolnictwie wyższym," *Kultura i Społeczeństwo* 2 (1996): 199–214.

Bińko, Beata. "Skąd przychodzili, dokąd zmierzali… aspiranci pierwszego rocznika Instytutu Kształcenia Kadr Naukowych przy KC PZPR." In *Komunizm: ideologia, system, ludzie*, edited by Tomasz Szarota, 192–204. Warszawa: "Neriton" – Instytut Historii PAN, 2001.

Borsuk, Wojciech, ed. *Był taki dziennik "Sztandar Młodych*. Warszawa: Nowy Świat, 2006.

Boterbloem, Kees. *The Life and Times of Andrei Zhdanov, 1896–1948*. Montreal: McGill-Queen's University Press, 2004.

Bratkowski, Stefan, ed. *Październik 1956: pierwszy wyłom w systemie: bunt, młodość i rozsądek*. Warszawa: Prószyński i S-ka, 1996.

Braun, Jerzy, Karol Popiel, and Konrad Sieniewicz. *Człowiek ze spiżu*. Londyn: Odnova, 1981.

Brożek, Anna, Friedrich Stadler, and Jan Woleński, eds. *The Significance of the Lvov-Warsaw School in the European Culture*. Cham: Springer, 2017.

Bruski, Jan. *Between Prometheism and Realpolitik: Poland and Soviet Ukraine, 1921–1926*. Krakow: Jagiellonian University Press, 2016.

Brzeziecki, Andrzej. *Tadeusz Mazowiecki. Biografia naszego premiera*. Kraków: Znak Horyzont, 2015.

Bucholc, Marta. *Sociology in Poland: To Be Continued?* London: Palgrave Macmillan, 2016.

Bujak, Waldemar. *Historia Storonnictwa Pracy 1937–1946–1950*. Warszawa: ODiSS, 1988.

Cain, Friedrich, Bernhard Kleeberg, Dietlind Hüchtker, and Jan Surman. "A New Culture of Truth? On the Transformation of Political Epistemologies Since the 1960s in Central Europe and Eastern Europe." *Stan Rzeczy* 17, no. 2 (2019): 9–21.

Cain, Friedrich, Bernhard Kleeberg, and Jan Surman. "The Past and Present of Political Epistemologies of (Eastern) Europe." *Historyka Studia Metodologiczne* 49 (2019): 7–13.

Cain, Friedrich. *Wissen im Untergrund. Praxis und Politik klandestiner Forschung im besetzten Polen (1939–1945)*. Tübingen: Mohr Siebeck, 2021.

Chałasiński, Józef. *Społeczna genealogia inteligencji polskiej*. Warszawa: Czytelnik, 1946.

Chałubiński, Mirosław. "Powroty do Juliana Hochfelda." *Studia Socjologiczno-Polityczne* 6, no. 1 (2017): 27–41.

Chłopek, Maciej. *„Zdumiewający świat". ZSRR i ludzie radzieccy w propagandzie Polski Ludowej lat 1944–1956*. Radzymin: Wydawnictwo von Borowiecky, 2014.

Chodakiewicz, Marek. *Between Nazis and Soviets: Occupation Politics in Poland, 1939–1947*. Lanham/Boulder/New York/Toronto/Oxford: Lexington Books, 2004.

Chudoba, Wiesław. *Leszek Kołakowski. Kronika życia i dzieła*. Warszaw: Wydawnictwo IFIS PAN, 2014.

Chwedeńczuk, Bohdan. *Dialogi z Adamem Schaffem*. Warszawa: Iskry, 2005.

Connelly, John and Teresa Suleja. ""Projekt reformy personalnej polonistyki uniwersyteckiej" Stefana Żółkiewskiego z 1950 roku," *Arcana* 2 (1997): 93–113.

Connelly, John. "Internal Bolshevisation? Elite Social Science Training in Stalinist Poland." *Minerva* 34, no. 4 (1996): 323–346.
Connelly, John. "Polish Universities and State Socialism: 1944–1968." In *Universities Under Dictatorship*, edited by John Connelly and Michael Grüttner, 185–212. University Park: Pennsylvania State University Press, 2005.
Connelly, John. *Captive University. The Sovietization of East German, Czech, and Polish Higher Education, 1945–1956*. Chapel Hill: The University of North Carolina Press, 2000.
Crawford-Brown, Douglas J. "Virtue as the Basis of Engineering Ethics." *Science and Engineering Ethics* 3 (1997): 481–489.
Czajowski, Jacek. *Kardynał Adam Stefan Sapieha*. Wrocław: Zakład Narodowy im. Ossolińskich, 1997.
Czarnowski, Stefan. *Społeczeństwo - Kultura*. Warszawa & Poznań: Polski Instytut Socjologiczny, 1939.
Czepulis-Rastenis, Ryszard, ed. *Inteligencja polska pod zaborami*. Warszawa: PWN, 1978.
Czepulis-Rastenis, Ryszarda, ed. *Inteligencja polska pod zaborami*. Warszawa: PWN, 1978.
Dagger, Richard. *Civic Virtues: Rights, Citizenship, and Republican Liberalism*. Oxford: Oxford University Press, 1997.
Daly, Gabriel. *Transcendence and Immanence: A Study in Catholic Modernism and Integralism*. O.S.A. Oxford: Clarendon Press, 1980.
Jarosz, Dariusz, and Maria Pasztor *Polish-French Relations, 1944–1989*. Frankfurt am Main: Peter Lang, 2015.
Daston, Lorraine, and Peter Galison. *Objectivity*. New York: Zone Books, 2007.
Daston, Lorraine, and Heinz. O Sibum. "Introduction: Scientific Personae and Their Histories." *Science in Context* 16, no. 1-2 (2003): 1–8.
Daston, Lorraine. "Historical Epistemology." In *Questions of Evidence: Proof, Practice, and Persuasion Across the Disciplines*, edited by James Chandler, Arnold Davidson and Harry Harootunian, 282–289. Chicago: University of Chicago Press, 1994.
David-Fox, Michael, Peter Holquist, and Alexander Martin. "The Imperial Turn." *Kritika* 7, no. 4 (2006): 705–712.
David-Fox, Michael, and György Péteri, eds. *Academia in Upheaval: Origins, Transfers, and Transformations of the Communist Academic Regime in Russia and East Central Europe*. Westport: Information Age Publishing, 2000.
David-Fox, Michael. *Revolution of the Mind: Higher Learning among the Bolsheviks, 1918–1929*. Ithaca & London: Cornell University Press, 1997.
Davies, Norman. *Rising '44: The battle for Warsaw*. New York: Macmillan, 2003.
Davies, Norman. *White Eagle, Red Star: The Polish-Soviet War, 1919-20*. London: Macdonald and Company, 1972.
de Rubercy, Eryck. "Le germaniste résistant communiste, Jacques Decour," *Revue des Deux Mondes*, June 2003, 161–166, https://www.jstor.org/stable/pdf/44189761.pdf
Dembowski, Bronisław. *Spór o metafizykę i inne studia z historii filozofii polskiej*. Włocławek: Włocławskie wydawnictwo diecezjalne, 1997.
Desanti, Dominique. *Les staliniens, 1944–56. Une expérience politique*. Paris: Fayard, 1975.
Dmitriev, Aleksandr, and Jan Levchenko. "Nauka kak priem: eshhe raz o metodologicheskom nasledii russkogo formalizma." *Novoe literaturnoe obozrenie* 50, no. 4 (2001): 195–247.
Dostal, Marina Ju. "Slavistika: mezhdu proletarskim internacionalizmom i slavjanskoj ideej (1941–1948)," *Slavjanovedenie* 2 (2007): 17–31.

Drozdowski, Marian M., Hanna Eychhorn-Szwankowska, and Jerzy Wiechowski, eds. *Zwycięstwo 1920. Warszawa wobec agresji bolszewickiej*. Paryż: Editions Dembinski, 1990.
Dudek, Antoni, and Grzegorz Pytel. *Bolesław Piasecki. Próba biografii politycznej*. Londyn: ANEKS, 1990.
Dudek, Antoni, and Ryszard Gryz. *Komuniści i Kościół w Polsce (1945-1989)*. Kraków: Wydawnictwo Znak, 2003.
Eisler, Jerzy. *"Polskie miesiące" czyli Kryzys(y) w PRL*. Warszawa: Instytut Pamięci Narodowej, 2008.
Engels, Friedrich. *Herrn Eugen Dührings Umwälzung der Wissenschaft*, Leipzig : Genossenschaftsdruckerei, 1878.
Erman, Lev. *V. I. Lenin o roli intelligencii v demokraticheskoj i socialisticheskoj revoljucijah, v stroitel'stve socializma i kommunizma*. Moskva: Znanie, 1970.
Feest, Uljana, and Thomas Sturm. "What (Good) Is Historical Epistemology? Editors' Introduction." *Erkenntnis* 75 (2011): 285–302.
Fijałkowska, Barbara. *Borejsza i Różański. Przyczynek do dziejów stalinizmu w Polsce*. Olsztyn: Wyższa Szkoła Pedagogiczna, 1995.
Fleck, Christian, Matthias Duller, and Victor Karády, eds. *Shaping Human Science Disciplines. Institutional Developments in Europe and Beyond*. London: Palgrave Macmillan, 2019.
Fleck, Ludwik. *Entstehung und Entwicklung einer wissenschaftlichen Tatsache*. Basel: Schwabe Verlag, 1935.
Fleishman, Lazar. *Boris Pasternak: The Poet and His Politics*. Boston: Harvard University Press, 2013.
Foucault, Michel. *Discipline and Punish: The Birth of the Prison*. New York: Pantheon Books, 1977.
Foucault, Michel. *Wrong-Doing, Truth-Telling. The Function of Avowal in Justice*. Chicago: The University of Chicago Press, 2004.
Friszke, Andrzej. *Druga Wielka Emigracja: Życie polityczne emigracji 1945–1990*. Warszawa: Więź, 1999.
Friszke, Andrzej. *Między wojną a więzieniem. 1945–1953. Młoda inteligencja katolicka*. Warszawa: Instytut Studiów Politycznych PAN, 2015, pp. 126.
Friszke, Andrzej. *Opozycja polityczna w PRL. 1945–1980*. Londyn: AN EKS, 1994.
Fritzsche, Peter, and Jochen Hellbeck. "The New Man in Stalinist Russia and Nazi Germany." In *Beyond Totalitarianism: Stalinism and Nazism Compared*, edited by Michael Geyer and Sheila Fitzpatrick. Cambridge, UK: Cambridge University Press, 2010.
Frizman, Leonid. "Pushkin i pol'skoe vosstanie 1830 – 1831 godov." *Voprosy literatury* 3 (1992): 209–237.
Fürst, Juliane. *Stalin's Last Generation: Soviet Post-War Youth and the Emergence of Mature Socialism*. Oxford: Oxford University Press, 2010.
Garaudy, Roger. *Komunizm i odrodzenie kultury francuskiej*. Łódź: Spółdzielnia Wydawnicza "Książka", 1945.
Gestwa, Klaus. "Der Homo Sovieticus und der Zerfall des Sowjetimperiums: Jurij Levadas unliebsame Sozialdiagnosen." *Zeithistorische Forschungen/Studies in Contemporary History* 10 (2013): 331–334.
Glanc, Tomáš. "Razvedyvatel'nyj kurs Jakobsona." In *Roman Jakobson: Teksty, Dokumenty, Issledovanija*, edited by Henryk Baran and Sergeej I. Gindin, 359–360. Moskva: RGGU, 1999.
Gordin, Michael. "How Lysenkoism Became Pseudoscience: Dobzhansky to Velikovsky." *Journal of the History of Biology* 45 (2012): 443–468.

Gordin, Michael. "Was There Ever a "Stalinist Science"?" *Kritika: Explorations in Russian and Eurasian History* 9, no. 3 (2008): 625–639.

Górny, Maciej. *Science Embattled: Eastern European Intellectuals and the Great War*. Stuttgart: Ferdinand Schöningh, Brill Deutschland, 2019.

Górny, Maciej. *The Nation Should Come First: Marxism and Historiography in East Central Europe*. Frankfurt am Main: Peter Lang, 2013.

Gosk, Hanna. *W kręgu "Kuźnicy": dyskusje krytycznoliterackie lat 1945–1948*. Łódź: Państwowe Wydawnictwo Naukowe, 1985.

Györkei, Jenő, Alexander Kirov, and Miklós Horvath. *Soviet Military Intervention in Hungary, 1956*. New York: Central European University Press, 1999.

Habermas, Jürgen. *The Structural Transformation of the Public Sphere: An Inquiry into a Category of Bourgeois Society*. Cambridge, UK: Polity Press, 1989.

Habielski, Rafał. *Druga Wielka Emigracja: Emigracja w polityce międzynarodowej*. Warszawa: Więź, 1999.

Habielski, Rafał. *Życie społeczne i kulturalne emigracji*. Warszawa: Biblioteka Więzi, 1999.

Hacohen, Malachi Haim. *Karl Popper: The Formative Years, 1902–1945*. Cambridge, UK: Cambridge University Press, 2000.

Hałas, Elżbieta. *Towards the World Culture Society: Florian Znaniecki's Culturalism*. Frankfurt am Main: Peter Lang, 2010.

Handelsman, Marceli. *Historyka. Zasady metodologii i teorii poznania historycznego*. Warszawa: Gebethner i Wolff, 1928.

Harbutt, Fraser. "American Challenge, Soviet Response: The Beginning of the Cold War, February-May, 1946." *Political Science Quarterly* 96, no. 4 (1982): 623–639.

Haslinger, Peter. "East Central European History: Still a Strategically Important Field of Research." *Journal of Modern European History* 16, no. 3 (2018): 295–300.

Haustov, Vladimir, ed. *Delo Berija. Prigovor obzhalovaniju ne podlezhit*. Moskva: MFD, 2012.

Hicks, Daniel J., and Thomas A. Stapleford. "The Virtues of Scientific Practice: MacIntyre, Virtue Ethics, and the Historiography of Science." *Isis* 107, no. 3 (2016): 449–472.

Hirszowicz, Maria. *Pułapki zaangażowania: intelektualiści w służbie komunizmu*. Warszawa: Wydawnictwo Naukowe Scholar, 2001.

Hłasko, Marek. *Beautiful Twentysomethings*. DeKalb: Northern Illinois University Press, 2013.

Holland, Henryk. *Legenda o Kazimierzu Twardowskim*. Warszawa: Książka i Wiedza, 1953.

Hrushhjov, Nikita S. *Vremja. Ljudi. Sobytija (Vospominanija v 3-h tomah)*, vol. 1, Moskva: Informacionno-izdatel'skaja kompanija "Moskovskie Novosti", 1999.

Hübner, Piotr. "Stalinizacja polskiej nauki." In *Oblicza polskiego stalinizmu*, edited by Ryszard Studziński, 37–56. Włocławek: Wyższa Szkoła Humanistyczno-Ekonomiczna, 2000.

Hübner, Piotr. *I Kongres Nauki Polskiej jako forma realizacji założeń polityki naukowej państwa ludowego*. Wrocław: Zakład Narodowy im. Ossolińskich, 1983.

Hübner, Piotr. *Nauka polska po II wojnie światowej: idee i instytucje*. Warszawa: Centralny Ośrodek Metodyczny Studiów Nauk Politycznych, 1987.

Hübner, Piotr. *Polityka naukowa w Polsce w latach 1944–1953: geneza systemu*, Volume 1, 2, Wrocław: Zakład Narodowy im. Ossolińskich, 1992.

Husserl, Edmund. *Philosophie als strenge Wissenschaft*. Hamburg: Meiner Verlag, 2009 [1910].

Janowski, Maciej. *Birth of the Intelligentsia – 1750–1831*. Frankfurt am Main/Berlin/Bern/ Bruxelles/New York/Oxford/Wien: Peter Lang, 2014.

Jaszczuk, Andrzej. *Ewolucja ideowa Bolesława Piaseckiego 1932-1956*. Warszawa: Wydawnictwo DiG, 2005.

Jazhborovskaja, Inessa, Anatolij Jablokov, and Valentina Parsadanova. *Katynskij sindrom v sovetsko-pol'skih i rossijsko-pol'skih otnoshenijah*. Moskva: ROSSPJeN, 2014.

Jedlicki, Witold. *Klub krzywego koła*. Paryż: Instytut Literacki, 1963.

Judt, Tony. *Postwar: A History of Europe Since 1945*. London: Vintage Books, 2010.

Kaleta, Andrzej, ed. *Chałasiński dzisiaj: Materiały z konferencji naukowej*. Toruń: Wydawnictwo Uniwersytetu Mikołaja Kopernika, 1996.

Kamecka, Małgorzata. "Ludzie i instytucje. O współpracy historyków polskich i francuskich." In *Cała historia to dzieje ludzi*, edited by Cezary Kuklo and Piotr Guzowski, 416–421. Białystok: Wydawnictwo Uniwersytetu w Białymstoku, 2004.

Kamińska-Chełminiak, Kamila. *Cenzura w Polsce 1944 - 1960: Organizacja. Kadry. Metody pracy*. Warszawa: Oficyna Wydawnicza ASPRA, 2009.

Karłowska, Grażyna. "Edukacja domowa dziewcząt w rodzinie polskiej XIX i na początku XX wieku w świetle pamiętników," *Biuletyn Historii Wychowania* 19/20 (2004): 23–38.

Kersten, Krystyna. *Jałta w polskiej perspektywie*. Londyn-Warszawa: Wydawnictwo ANEKS & NOWa, 1989.

Kersten, Krystyna. *Narodziny systemu władzy. Polska 1943–1948*. Lublin: Wydawnictwo Lubelskie, 1989.

Kersten, Krystyna. *The Establishment of Communist Rule in Poland, 1943–1948*. Berkeley, CA: University of California Press, 1991.

Kikeshev, Nikolai I. "Slavjanskoe dvizhenie v SSSR: 1941-1948 gody." PhD thesis, The Institute of Russian History of the Russian Academy of Sciences, Moscow, 2008.

Klafkowski, Alfons. *Umowa Poczdamska a sprawy polskie 1945–1970*. Poznań: Wydawnictwo Poznańskie, 1970.

Kleeberg, Bernhard. "Bad Habits and the Origins of Sociology." In *Rethinking Order. Idioms of Stability and Destabilization*, edited by Nicole Falkenhayner, Andreas Langenohl, Johannes Scheu, Doris Schweitzer and Kacper Szulecki, 47–62. Bielefeld: Transcript, 2015.

Kleeberg, Bernhard. "Post Post-Truth: Epistemologies of Disintegration and the Praxeology of Truth." *Stan Rzeczy* 17, no. 2 (2019): 25–52.

Knap, Paweł, ed. *Wokół zjazdu szczecińskiego 1949 r*. Szczecin: Instytut Pamięci Narodowej, 2011.

Knight, Nathaniel. "Was the Intelligentsia Part of the Nation? Visions of Society in Post-Emancipation Russia." *Kritika: Explorations in Russian and Eurasian History* 7, no. 4 (2006): 733–758.

Köhler, Piotr. "Lysenko Affair and Polish Botany." *Journal of the History of Biology* 44 (2011): 305–343.

Kojevnikov, Alexei. "Rituals of Stalinist Culture at Work: Science and the Games of Intraparty Democracy circa 1948." *The Russian Review* 57 (1998): 28–40.

Kokowski, Michał. "The Science of Science (naukoznawstwo) in Poland: Defending and Removing the Past in the Cold War." In *Science Studies During the Cold War and Beyond: Paradigms Defected*, edited by Elena Aronova and Simone Turchetti, 149–176. London: Palgrave Macmillan, 2016.

Kołakowski, Leszek. *Chrześcijaństwo*. Kraków: Znak, 2019.

Kołakowski, Leszek. *Main Currents of Marxism*, vol. I: *The Founders*, vol. II: *The Golden Age*, vol. III: *The Breakdown*, Oxford: Oxford University Press, 1978.

Korkuć, Maciej. "Wybory 1947 – mit założycielski komunizmu," *Biuletynie Instytutu Pamięci Narodowej* 1–2 (2007): 106–115.
Kosicki, Piotr H. *Catholics on the Barricades: Poland, France, and "Revolution", 1891 – 1956*. New Haven/London: Yale University Press, 2018.
Kosicki, Piotr H. *Personalizm po polsku. Francuskie korzenie polskiej inteligencji katolickiej*. Warszawa: Instytut Pamięci Narodowej, 2016.
Kostyrchenko, Gennadij. *Tajnaja politika Stalina. Vlast' i antisemitism*. Moskva: Mezhdunarodnye otnoshenija, 2003.
Kott, Jan. *Przyczynek do biografii. Zawał serca*. Kraków: Wydawnictwo Literackie, 1995.
Kraśko, Tadeusz. *Wierność. Rozmowy z Jerzym Turowiczem*. Poznań: SAWW, 1995.
Krasucki, Eryk. *Międzynarodowy komunista. Jerzy Borejsza. Biografia polityczna*. Warszawa: Wydawnictwo naukowe PWN, 2009.
Krementsov, Nikolai. *Stalinist Science*. Princeton: Princeton University Press, 1997.
Kruszyński, Marcin. "Wokół dyskusji o przedwojennej inteligencji, uniwersytetach i wreszcie robotnikach na uniwersytetach (1945–1956). Uwag kilka." *RES HISTORICA* 43 (2017): 207–232.
Kuciński, Julian. *Łódzkie Towarzystwo Naukowe w latach 1936-1996*, vol. 1, 2. Łódź: Łódzkie Towarzystwo Naukowe, 1996.
Kuhn, Thomas. *The Structure of Scientific Revolutions*. Chicago: University of Chicago Press, 1962.
Kula, Marcin. *Mimo wszystko bliżej Paryża niż Moskwy: Książka o Francji PRL i o nas historykach*. Warszawa: Wydawnictwo Uniwersytetu Warszawskiego, 2010.
Kula, Marcin. *Paryż, Londyn i Waszyngton patrzą na Październik 1956 r. w Polsce*. Warszawa: Instytut Studiów Politycznych Polskiej Akademii Nauk, 1992.
Kunakhovich, Kyrill. *Communism's Public Sphere: Culture as Politics in Cold War Poland and East Germany*. New York: Cornell University Press, 2023.
Kunicki, Mikołaj S. *Between the Brown and the Red: Nationalism, Catholicism, and Communism in 20th-Century Poland: The Politics of Bolesław Piasecki*. Athens: Ohio University Press, 2012.
Kuryła, Mateusz. "Adam Schaff – droga do komunizmu (1913–1939)," *Przegląd Humanistyczny* 3 (2018): 167–189.
Kurzman, Charles, and Lynn Owens. "The Sociology of Intellectuals." *Annual Review of Sociology* 28 (2002): 64.
Kůželová, Michaela. *Francouzští komunisté a Polsko v roce 1956*. MA Thesis, the University of Prague, 2011.
Kutuzov, Vladislav. "A.A. Zhdanov i postanovlenie CK VKP(b) o zhurnalah «Zvezda» i «Leningrad»," *Novejshaja istorija Rossii* 1 (2011): 146–152.
Kuźnicka, Maria, and Tadeusz Kotarbiński. *Poczta do Karmelu. Korespondencja Tadeusza Kotarbińskiego i Marii Kuźnickiej z lat 1945-1973*. Warszawa: Instytut Filozofii i Socjologii PAN, 2006.
Łapiński, Zdzisław, and Wojciech Tomasik. *Słownik realizmu socjalistycznego*. Kraków: UNIVERSITAS, 2004.
Łatka, Rafał. "Prymas Wyszyński wobec rzeczywistości politycznej doby Władysława Gomułki." In *Dzieje Kościoła katolickiego na Pomorzu Zachodnim*, edited by Michał Siedziako, Zbigniew Stanuch and Grzegorz Wejman, 47–65. Szczecin–Warszawa: Instytut Pamięci Narodowej, 2018.
Lebow, Katherine. *Unfinished Utopia: Nowa Huta, Stalinism, and Polish Society, 1949–56*. New York: Cornell University Press, 2016.

Lechicki, Czesław. "Polska prasa katolicka 1945–1948." *Kwartalnik Historii Prasy Polskiej* 22, no. 2 (1983): 65–87.
Leinwand, Artur. *Przywódcy Polski Podziemnej przed sądem moskiewskim*. Warszawa: Wydawnictwo "Placet", 1992.
Lekmanov, Oleg. *Mandelstam*. Boston: Academic Studies Press, 2010.
Lenin, Vladimir I. *Polnoe Sobranie Sochinenij*, vol. 16, 17. Moskva: Izdatel'stvo politicheskoj literatury, 1967.
Lenzer, Gertrud. *Auguste Comte and Positivism: The Essential Writings*. New Jersey: Transaction Publishers, 1998.
Leociak, Jacek. *Młyny Boże. Zapiski o Kościele i Zagładzie*. Wołowiec: Czarne, 2018.
Lepenies, Wolf, ed. *Geschichte der Soziologie: Studien zur kognitiven, sozialen und historischen Identität einer Disziplin*. Frankfurt am Main: Suhrkamp, 1981.
Leskiewiczowa, Janina. *Warszawa i jej inteligencja po powastaniu styczniowym 1864–1870*. Warszawa: Państwowe wydawnictwo naukowe, 1961.
Lewandowski, Czesław. "*Dyskusja prasowa nad koncepcją inteligencji polskiej J. Chałasińskiego w latach 1946–1948*." *Kwartalnik Historii Prasy Polskiej* 29, no. 3–4 (1990): 71–101.
Lokhamtov, Aleksei. "'Periodisations' in Intellectual History: On the Plurality of Continuities in the Post-War Public Debates of Poland." In *Rethinking Period Boundaries: New Approaches to Continuity and Discontinuity in Modern European History and Culture*, edited by Jade McGlynn and Lucian George, 149–174. Oldenburg: De Gruyter, 2022.
Lokhmatov, Aleksei M. "Obraz SSSR v refleksii Pol'skoi katolicheskoi intelligentsii (1945—1948)." In *Rossiia i mir glazami drug druga*, edited by Alexander V. Golubev, 201–214. Moskva: Institut rossijskoj istorii Rossijskoj akademii nauk, 2017.
Lokhmatov, Aleksei. "Auf dem Weg zur „Einheit": Józef Chałasiński und die Suche nach einer „erlaubten" Genealogie der Soziologie im Nachkriegspolen (1945–1951)." *NTM Zeitschrift für Geschichte der Wissenschaften, Technik und Medizin* 28, no. 4 (2020): 519–546.
Lokhmatov, Aleksei. "The "Scientific View" of the Intelligentsia: The Literary Roots of Scholarly Public Debates in Post-War Poland (1946–1948)." *HISTORYKA. Studia Metodologiczne* 49 (2019): 77–100.
Lokhmatov, Aleksei. "The Academic Virtues in Public Discussion: Adam Schaff and the Campaign Against the Lvov-Warsaw School in Post-War Poland." *Studia Historiae Scientiarum* 20 (2021): 711–753.
Lokhmatov, Aleksei. "Theory in Action: French Personalism in the Public Debates of Post-War Poland." *Reliģiski-filozofiski raksti* 25 (2019): 277–293.
Lossky, Nikolay. *History of Russian Philosophy*. London: George Allen and Unwin Ltd., 1952.
Lucas, Erhard. "Die Rezeption Lewis H. Morgans durch Marx und Engels." *Saeculum* 15 (1964): 153–176.
Machcewicz, Paweł. *Druga Wielka Emigracja: Życie społeczne i kulturalne emigracji*. Warszawa: Więź, 1999.
MacIntyre, Alasdair C. *After Virtue: A Study in Moral Theory*. Notre Dame: Univ. Notre Dame Press, 1984.
Mandelstam, Osip. *Stihotvorenija*. Leningrad: Sovetskij pisatel', 1973.
Mańkowski, Tadeusz. "Ossolineum pod rządami sowieckimi," *Czasopismo Zakładu Narodowego im. Ossolińskich* 1 (1992): 135–155.
Mannheim, Karl. *Ideologie und Utopie*. Frankfurt am Main: Vittorio Klostermann GmbH, 1985.

Maritain, Jacques. *Humanisme intégral*. Paris: Fernand Aubier, 1936.
Maritain, Jacques. *Trois réformateurs: Luther, Descartes, Rousseau, avec six portraits*. Plon: Paris, 1925.
Masaryk, Tomáš Garrigue. *Die wissenschaftliche und philosophische Krise innerhalb des gegenwärtigen Marxismus*. Wien: Die Zeit, 1898.
Massalski, Adam. "Nauczyciele języka francuskiego męskich szkół średnich rządowych Królestwa Polskiego w latach 1833–1862." *Studia Pedagogiczne: Problemy społeczne, edukacyjne i artystyczne* 14 (2003): 55–81.
Mateja, Anna, ed. *Ludzie Znaku*. Kraków: Wydawnictwo Znak, 2015.
Matveev, Sergej R. "«Uchenyj-bol'shevik prizvan ocenivat' objektivno»: recenzii v sovetskoj istoricheskoj periodike 1930–1950-h godov." In *Nauchnoe recenzirovanie v gumanitarnyh disciplinah*, edited by Natalja M. Dolgorukova and Aleksei A. Pleshkov, 113–124. Moskva: Izdatel'skij dom NRU HSE, 2020.
Mazur, Grzegorz. "Walcząc bez broni: Propaganda i prasa Armii Krajowej." In *Wielka Księga Armii Krajowej*, edited by Ewelina Olaszek, 151–186. Kraków: Znak Horyzont, 2016.
Mazur, Mariusz. *O człowieku tendencyjnym... Obraz nowego człowieka w propagandzie komunistycznej w okresie Polski Ludowej i PRL 1944–1956*. Lublin: Wydawnictwo Uniwersytetu Marii Curie-Skłodowskiej w Lublinie, 2009.
McDermott, Kevin, and Jeremy Agnew. *The Comintern: A History of International Communism from Lenin to Stalin*. London: Macmillan International Higher Education, 1996.
McGlynn, Jade. *Memory Makers: The Politics of the Past in Putin's Russia*. London: Bloomsbury, 2023.
Mentzel, Zbigniew. *Kołakowski: Czytanie świata; Biografia*. Kraków: Znak, 2020.
Micewski, Andrzej. *Współrządzić czy nie kłamać? PAX i Znak w Polsce 1945–1976*. Paryż: Libella, 1978.
Michelet, Jules. *La Pologne martyre*. Paris: Dentu, 1863.
Michelet, Jules. *Pologne et Russie*. Paris: La Librairie Nouvelle, 1854.
Michnik, Adam. *Kościół, lewica, dialog*. Paryż: Instytut Literacki, 1977.
Micinska, Magdalena. *At the Crossroads: 1865–1918. A History of the Polish Intelligentsia*. Frankfurt am Main/Berlin/Bern/Bruxelles/New York/Oxford/Wien: Peter Lang, 2016.
Mikołajewski, Łukasz. *Disenchanted Europeans: Polish Émigré Writers from Kultura and Postwar Reformulations of the West*. Frankfurt: Peter Lang, 2018.
Mikucki, Jerzy and Sławomir Gala. *Kalendarium Towarzystwa Przyjaciół Nauk w Łodzi w Latach 1936–1946 i Łódzkiego Towarzystwa Naukowego w latach 1946–2005*. Łódź: ŁTN, 2006.
Miłosz, Czesław. *The Captive Mind*. New York: Vintage Books, 1955.
Modzelewski, Karol. *Zajeździmy kobyłę historii. Wyznania poobijanego jeźdźca*. Warszawa: Iskry, 2013.
Mounier, Emmanuel. "L'ordre règne-t-il à Varsovie?." *Esprit* 123, no. 6 (1946): 970–1005.
Mounier, Emmanuel. *Be Not Afraid: Studies in Personalist Sociology*. New York: Harper, 1954.
Mounier, Emmanuel. *De la propriété capitaliste à la propriété humaine*. Paris: Desclée de Brouwer, coll. "Questions disputées", 1936.
Mounier, Emmanuel. *Manifeste au service du personnalisme*. Paris: Éd. Montaigne, 1936.
Mounier, Emmanuel. *Oeuvres de Mounier*, vol. 3. Paris: Éditions du Seuil, 1962.
Mounier, Emmanuel. *Révolution personnaliste et communautaire*. Paris: Éd. Montaigne, 1934.

Mulsow, Martin. "History of Knowledge." In *Debating Two Approaches to History*, edited by Marek Tamm and Peter Burke, 159–187. London: Bloomsbury, 2019.
Noskova, Albina, ed. *Pol'sha v 20 veke: ocherki politicheskoj istorii*. Moskva: Indrik, 2012.
Orekhov, Aleksandr. *Sovetskij Sojuz i Pol'sha v gody "ottepeli": iz istorii sovetsko-pol'skih otnoshenij*. Moskva: Indrik, 2005.
Orman, Elżbieta, ed. *Stefan Kieniewicz – Henryk Wereszycki. Korespondencja z lat 1947–1990*. Kraków: Instytut Historii PAN, 2013.
Osękowski, Czesław. *Referendum 30 czerwca 1946 roku w Polsce*. Warszawa: Wydawnictwo Sejmowe, 2000.
Ossowska, Maria, and Stanisław Ossowski. *Intymny portret uczonych. Korespondencja Marii i Stanisława Ossowskich*. Warszawa: Sic! 2002.
Paczkowski, Andrzej, ed. *Referendum z 30 czerwca 1946 r.: Przebieg i wyniki*. Warszawa: ISP PAN, 1993.
Paczkowski, Andrzej. *Od sfałszowanego zwycięstwa do prawdziwej klęski. Szkice do portretu PRL*. Warszawa: Wydawnictwo Literackie, 1999.
Paczkowski, Andrzej. *Pół wieku dziejów Polski*. Warszawa: Wydawnictwo naukowe PWN, 2007.
Paul, Herman. "Distance and Self-Distanciation: Intellectual Virtue and Historical Method Around 1900." *History and Theory* 50, no. 4 (2011): 104–116.
Paul, Herman. "Weak Historicism: On Hierarchies of Intellectual Virtues and Goods." *Journal of the Philosophy of History* 6 (2012): 369–388.
Paul, Herman. "What Is a Scholarly Persona? Ten Theses on Virtues, Skills, and Desires." *History and Theory* 53 (2014): 348–371.
Paul, Herman. *Historians' Virtues: From Antiquity to the Twenty-First Century*. Cambridge, UK: Cambridge University Press, 2022.
Paul, Herman. *How to Be a Historian: Scholarly Personae in Historical Studies, 1800-2000*. Manchester: Manchester University Press, 2019.
Pazik, Przemysław. *Spory i wybory ideowe katolików świeckich w okresie narodzin komunistycznego systemu władzy w Polsce (1945-1948)*. PhD thesis, University of Warsaw, 2019.
Pazik, Przemysław. *Spory i wybory ideowe katolików w Polsce 1942-1948*. Warszawa: Neriton, 2022.
Petrov, Nikita. *Po scenariju Stalina: rol' organov NKVD-MGB SSSR v sovetizacii stran Central'noj i Vostochnoj Evropy, 1945-1953 gg*. Moskva: ROSSPJeN, 2011.
Pettit, Philip. *The Robust Demands of the Good: Ethics with Attachment, Virtue, and Respect*. Oxford/New York: Oxford University Press, 2015.
Piasecki, Bolesław. *Kierunki 1945 – 1960*. Warszawa: Wydawnictwo PAX, 1981.
Piasecki, Bolesław. *Siły rozwoju*. Warszawa: Wydawnictwo PAX, 1971, pp. 5–16.
Piechowski, Paul. *Proletarischer Glaube in sozialistischen und kommunistischen Selbstzeugnissen*. Berlin: Furche Verlag, 1928.
Pietrow, Nikita. *Stalinowski kat Polski. Iwan Sierow*. Warszawa: Demart, 2013.
Pikhoja, Rudolf. *Moskva. Kreml'. Vlast'. Sorok let posle vojny. 1945–1985*. Moskva: AST, 2007.
Piskała, Kamil, and Agata Zysiak. "Świątynia nauki, fundament demokracji czy fabryka specjalistów? Józef Chałasiński i powojenne spory o ideę uniwersytetu." *Praktyka Teoretyczna* 9, no. 3 (2013): 271–297.
Platt, Jonathan Brooks. *Greetings, Pushkin! Stalinist Cultural Politics and the Russian National Bard*. Pittsburgh: University of Pittsburgh Press, 2016.

Pleshkov, Aleksei, and Jan Surman. "Book Reviews in the History of Knowledge." *Studia Historiae Scientiarum* 20 (2021): 629–650.
Pleskot, Patryk. *Intelektualni sąsiedzi. Kontakty historyków polskich ze środowiskiem „Annales" 1945–1989*. Warszawa: Wydawnictwo IPN, 2015.
Pomian, Krzysztof. *Leszek Kołakowski: jednostka, wolność, rozum* (introduction), in Leszek Kołakowski, *Główne nurty marksizmu. Powstanie, rozwój, rozkład*, Vol. 1, VII–XXX. Wydawnictwo naukowe PWN, 2009.
Pomian, Krzysztof. *Wśród mistrzów i przyjaciół*. Gdańsk: Słowo/Obraz terytoria, 2018.
Popiołek, Joanna. *"Polar Action" of Antoni Bolesław Dobrowolski in the interwar period*, Polish Polar Research 1998 no. 1–2, pp. 31–36.
Popper, Karl. *The Open Society and Its Enemies*. Vol. 1, 2. London: Routledge, 1945.
Ptaszyński, Radosław. *Stommizm. Biografia polityczna Stanisława Stommy*. Kraków: Społeczny Instytut Wydawniczy Znak, 2018.
Radziwon, Marek. *Iwaszkiewicz. Pisarz po katastrofie*. Warszawa: Wydawnictwo wab, 2010.
Rederowa, Danuta, Bohdan Jaczewski and Waldemar Rolbiecki. *Polska Stacja Naukowa w Paryżu w latach 1893 – 1978*. Wrocław: Zakład im. Ossolińskich, 1982.
Roberts, Geoffrey. "Moscow and the Marshall Plan: Politics, Ideology and the Onset of the Cold War, 1947." *Europe-Asia Studies* 46, no. 8 (1994): 1371–1386.
Roelcke, Volker. "Auf der Suche nach der Politik in der Wissensproduktion: Plädoyer für eine historisch-politische Epistemologie." *Berichte Zur Wissenschaftsgeschichte* 33 (2010): 176–192.
Rokossovskij, Konstantin. *Soldatskij dolg*. Moskva: Voenizdat, 1988.
Romek, Zbigniew. "Cenzura w PRL a historiografia – pytania i problemy badawcze." In *Metodologiczne problemy syntezy historii historiografii polskiej*, edited by Jerzy Maternicki, 287–294. Rzeszów: Wydawnictwo WSP w Rzeszowie, 1998.
Romek, Zbigniew. *Cenzura a nauka historyczna w Polsce 1944-1970*. Warszawa: Wydawnictwo Neriton - Instytut Historii PAN, 2010.
Room, Abram (director). *Veter s vostoka*, 1940 [movie], (URL): https://youtu.be/k2v3ou8eFAo (17. 08. 2020).
Rosin, Jakov A., and Viktor B. Malkin. *Lina Solomonovna Shtern, 1878-1968*. Moskva: Nauka, 1987.
Rostworowski, Mikołaj. *Słowo o Paxie 1945–1956*. Warszawa: Wydawnictwo PAX, 1968.
Roszkowski, Wojciech. *Najnowsza historia Polski 1956–1970*. Warszawa: Świat Książki, 2011.
Rubenstein, Joshua, and Vladimir P. Naumov, eds. *Stalin's Secret Pogrom: The Postwar Inquisition of the Jewish Anti-Fascist Committee*. New Haven: Yale University Press, 2005.
Rutkowski, Tadeusz. *Nauki historyczne w Polsce 1944–1970: Zagadnienia polityczne i organizacyjne*. Warszawa: Wydawnictwo Uniwersytetu Warszawskiego, 2007.
Ryzhkovskij, Vladimir. *Sovetskaja medievistika and Beyond*, Novoe literaturnoe obozrenie 2009 no. 3 (URL): https://magazines.gorky.media/nlo/2009/3/sovetskaya-medievistika-and-beyond.html (12.11.2020).
Ryzhkovskyi, Volodymyr. *Soviet Occidentalism: Medieval Studies and the Restructuring of Imperial Knowledge in Twentieth-Century Russia*. PhD thesis, Georgetown University, Washington, 2019.
Schaff, Adam. *Aktualne zagadnienia polityki kulturalnej w dziedzinie filozofii i socjologii*. Warszawa: Państwowe Wydawnictwo Naukowe, 1956.
Schaff, Adam. *Marksizm a jednostka ludzka: Przyczynek do marksistowskiej filozofii człowieka*. Warszawa: Wydawnictwo Naukowe PWN, 1965.

Schaff, Adam. *Marxism and the Human Individual*. Translated by Olgierd Wojtasiewicz. New York: McGraw Hill, 1970.
Schaff, Adam. *Narodziny i rozwój filozofii marksistowskiej*. Warszawa: Książka i Wiedza, 1950.
Schaff, Adam. *Wstęp do teorii marksizmu. Zarys materializmu dialektycznego i historycznego*. Warszawa: Spółdzielnia Wydawnicza „Książka", 1948.
Schulze Wessel, Martin. ""Loyalität" als geschichtlicher Grundbegriff und Forschungskonzept: Zur Einleitung." In *Loyalitäten in der Tschechoslowakischen Republik. 1918–1938. Politische, nationale und kulturelle Zugehörigkeiten*, edited by Martin Schulze Wessel, 1–22. München: Oldenbourg Wissenschaftsverlag, 2004.
Sdvizhkov, Denis. "Ot obshhestva k intelligencii: istorija ponjatij kak istorija samosoznanija," in *Ponjatija o Rossii*, vol. 1, 382–427. Moskva: Novoe literaturnoe obozrenie, 2011.
Sdvižkov, Denis. *Das Zeitalter der Intelligenz: Zur vergleichenden Geschichte der Gebildeten in Europa bis zum Ersten Weltkrieg*. Göttingen: Vandenhoeck & Ruprecht, 2006.
Sękowski, Paweł. "Francja wobec polskich uchodźców wojennych i dipisów w pierwszych latach po drugiej wojnie światowej," *Dzieje Najnowsze* 2 (2014): 71–83.
Semczyszyn, Magdalena, ed. *Nad Odrą i Bałtykiem. Myśl zachodnia: ludzie – koncepcje – realizacja do 1989 r.* Szczecin: Instytut Pamięci Narodowej, 2013.
Semyonov, Alexander. "Empire as a Context Setting Category." *Ab Imperio* 9, no. 1 (2008): 193–204.
Serov, Ivan. *Zapiski iz chemodana. Tajnye dnevniki pervogo predsedatelja KGB najdennye cherez 25 let posle ego smerti*. Moskva: Abris Olma, 2017.
Sertillanges, Antonin-Dalmace. *Socialisme et Christianisme*. Paris: Librairie Victor Lecoffre, 1905.
Shapin, Steven. *The Scientific Life: A Moral History of a Late Modern Vocation*. Chicago: University of Chicago Press, 2008.
Shaw, William H. "Marx and Morgan." *History and Theory* 23, no. 2 (1984): 215–228.
Shore, Marci. *Caviar and Ashes: A Warsaw Generation's Life and Death in Marxism, 1918-1968*. New Haven/London: Yale University Press, 2006.
Sienkiewicz, Henryk. *Krzyżacy*. Warszawa: Spółdzielnia Wydawnicza Czytelnik, 1946.
Sikorski, Tomasz, and Marcin Kulesza. *Niezłomni w epoce fałszywych proroków. Środowisko "Tygodnika Warszawskiego" (1945 – 1948)*. Warszawa: Wydawnictwo von Bonowiecky, 2013.
Słabek, Henryk. *Dzieje polskiej reformy rolnej 1944-48*. Warszawa: Wiedza Powszechna, 1972.
Śliwak, Katarzyna. "Activities of priest Zygmunt Kaczynski– Minister of Religious Affairs and Public Education in the Government-in-exile (1943–1945)," *Przegląd Historyczno-Oświatowy*, no. 3–4 (2016): 196–208.
Śliwowska, Wiktoria, and René Śliwowski. *Rosja, nasza miłość*. Warszawa: Iskry, 2008.
Snyder, Timothy. *Bloodlands: Europe Between Hitler and Stalin*. New York: Basic Books, 2012.
Snyder, Timothy. *Nationalism, Marxism, and Modern Central Europe: A Biography of Kazimierz Kelles-Krauz*. Cambridge, MA: Harvard University Press, 1998.
Snyder, Timothy. *The Reconstruction of Nations: Poland, Ukraine, Lithuania, Belarus, 1569–1999*. New Haven & London: Yale University Press, 2003.
Sosnowska, Anna. *Explaining Economic Backwardness: Post-1945 Polish Historians on Eastern Europe*. Budapest/New York: Central European University Press, 2019.

Śródka, Andrzej, and Paweł Szczawiński, ed. *Biogramy uczonych polskich, część I: Nauki społeczne*, vol. 2, Wrocław: Zakład Narodowy im. Ossolińskich, 1984.
Srokosz, Jacek. "Model państwa totalnego w myśli Bolesława Piaseckiego." *Studia Erasmiana Wratislaviensia* 4 (2008): 71–85.
Stankowska, Halina. *Literatura i krytyka w czasopismach Wielkiej Emigracji (1832–1848)*. Wrocław: Zakład Narodowy im. Ossolińskich, 1973.
Steiner, Peter. "Which Side Are You on? Roman Jakobson in Interwar Prague." In *Roman Jakobson, linguistica e poetica*, edited by Edoardo Esposito, Stefania Sini and Marina Castagneto, 75–86. Milano: Ledizioni, 2019.
Stobiecki, Rafał. "Historia i historycy wobec nowej rzeczywistości. Z dziejów polskiej nauki historycznej w latach 1945–1951." *Acta Universitatis Lodziensis. Folia Historica* 22 (1991): 163–187.
Stobiecki, Rafał. "Stalinowska unifikacja nauki historycznej (przykład Polski)." *Acta Universitatis Lodziensis. Folia Historica* 55 (1996): 27–36.
Stobiecki, Rafał. *Historia pod nadzorem: Spory o nowy model historii w Polsce – druga połowa lat czterdziestych – początek lat pięćdziesiątych*. Łódź: Wydawnictwo Uniwersytetu Łódzkiego, 1993.
Stobiecki, Rafał. *Historiografia PRL. Ani dobra, ani mądra, ani piękna..., ale skomplikowana. Studia i szkice*. Warszawa: Wydawnictwo TRIO, 2007.
Stola, Dariusz. *Kampania antysyjonistyczna w Polsce 1967-1968*. Warszawa: Instytut Studiów Politycznych PAN, 2000.
Sturdy, Steve. "Biology as Social Theory: John Scott Haldane and Physiological Regulation." *The British Journal for the History of Science* 21 (1988): 315–340.
Styczyński, Marek. "Sergei Hessen, Neo-Kantian." *Studies in East European Thought* 56 (2004): 55–71.
Syrop, Konrad. *Spring in October. The Story of the Polish Revolution 1956*. Westport: Greenwood Press Publishers, 1958.
Syrop, Konrad. *Vesna v oktjabre. Pol'skaja revoljucija 1956 goda*. New-Jork: Izdatel'stvo Frederik A. Preger, 1961.
Szacki, Jerzy. "Leszek Kołakowski: Marksizm, komunizm." In *Leszek Kołakowski – myśliciel i obywatel*, edited by Piotr Kosiewski, 15–25. Warszawa: Fundacja im. Stefana Batorego, 2010.
Szczepański, Jan. *Dzienniki z lat 1945 – 1968*. Ustroń: Offsetdruk i media, 2013.
Szczepański, Jan. *Inteligencja i społeczeństwo*. Warszawa: Książka i Wiedza, 1957.
Szczotka, Sylwia. "Wizerunek bolszewika w polskich plakatach propagandowych wojny polsko-rosyjskiej 1919-1920 ze zbiorów Muzeum Niepodległości w Warszawie." *Niepodległość i Pamięć* 19, no. 1-4 (37-40) (2012): 205–213.
Szumski, Jan. *Historia a polityka. ZSRR wobec nauki historycznej w Polsce 1945-1964*. Warszawa: ASPRA, 2016.
Szwagrzyk, Krzysztof, ed. *Aparat bezpieczeństwa w Polsce. Kadra kierownicza.1944-1956*. Warszawa: Instytut pamięci narodowej, 2005.
Szymański, Wiesław. *"Odrodzenie" i "Twórczość" w Krakowie (1945-1950)*. Wrocław: Zakład Narodowy im. Ossolińskich, 1981.
Tatarkiewicz, Władysław. *Historia filozofii*, vol. 3.Warszawa: Czytelnik, 1950.
Tétart, Philippe. *France Observateur: 1950-1964. Histoire d'un courant de pensée intellectuel*. PhD thesis, Institut d'études politiques, Paris, 1995.
Tihanov, Galin. "Revisiting Lukács' Theory of Realism." *Thesis Eleven* 159, no. 1 (2020): 57–63.

Tihanov, Galin. *The Birth and Death of Literary Theory. Regimes of Relevance in Russia and Beyond.* Stanford: Stanford University Press, 2019.

Tihonov, Vladimir. *Ideologicheskie kampanii «pozdnego stalinizma» i sovetskaja istoricheskaja nauka (seredina 1940-h–1953 g.* Moskva: Nestor-istorija, 2016.

Torańska, Teresa. *Oni.* Londyn: Agencja Omnipress, 1989.

Trockij, Lev D. *Literatura i revoljucija.* Moskva: Politizdat, 1991.

Tromley, Benjamin. *Making the Soviet Intelligentsia: Universities and Intellectual Life under Stalin and Khrushchev.* Cambridge, UK: Cambridge University Press, 2014.

Tucker, William T. "*Max Weber's "Verstehen","* *The Sociological Quarterly* 6, no. 2 (1965): 157–165.

Turajczyk, Leon. *Społeczno–polityczne organizacje polskie we Francji 1944–1948.* Warszawa: Książka i Wiedza, 1978.

Twardowski, Kazimierz. *Rozprawy i artykuły filozoficzne.* Lwów: Książnica-Atlas, 1927.

Twardowski, Kazimierz. *Zur Lehre vom Inhalt und Gegenstand der Vorstellungen. Eine psychologische Untersuchung.* Wien: Verlag von Carl Kohegen, 1894.

Vein, Alla A. "Science and Fate: Lina Stern (1878–1968), A Neurophysiologist and Biochemist." *Journal of the History of the Neurosciences* 17, no. 2 (2008): 195–206.

Vinogradov, Sergej N. *Logika.* Moskva: Gosudarstvennoe izdatel'stvo politicheskoj literatury, 1947.

Volkov, Vadim. "The Concept of Kul'turnost': Notes on the Stalinist Civilizing Process." In *Stalinism: New Directions*, edited by Sheila Fitzpatrick, 210–230. London: Routledge, 1999.

Volobuev, Vadim. *Politicheskaja oppozicija v Pol'she. 1956–1976.* Moskva: Institut slavjanovedenija RAN, 2009.

Volokitina, Tatyana, Galina Murashko, and Albina Noskova. *Narodnaja demokratija: mif ili real'nost'? Obshhestvenno-politicheskie processy v Vostochnoj Evrope 1944 – 1948 gg.* Moskva: «Nauka», 1993.

Wagner, Izabela. *Bauman: A Biography.* Cambridge, UK: Polity Press, 2020.

Wasilewska, Wanda. "Wspomnienia Wandy Wasilewskiej 1939 – 1944." *Archiwum Ruchu Robotniczego* 7 (1980): 339–432.

Wasilewski, Krzysztof. ""Sztandar Młodych" i "rostu" wobec Października 1956 r." In *Przełom Października 56*, edited by Paweł Dybicz, 197–199. Warszawa: Fundacja Oratio Recto, 2016.

Ważniewski, Władysław. *Walka polityczna w kierownictwie PPR i PZPR 1944-1964.* Toruń: Wydawnictwo Adam Marszałek, 1991.

Ważyk, Adam. *Poemat dla dorosłych*, lewicowo.pl (URL): http://lewicowo.pl/poemat-dla-doroslych/ (06.08. 2020).

Werblan, Andrzej. "Władysław Gomułka a ugrupowania w partii w Październiku 1956 roku." *Polska 1944/45–1989. Studia i Materiały* 3 (1997): 79–89.

Werblan, Andrzej. *Stalinizm w Polsce.* Warszawa: Towarzystwo Wydawnicze i Literackie, 2009.

Wierzbicki, Andrzej. *Konstytucja 3 Maja w historiografii polskiej.* Warszawa: Wydawnictwo Sejmowe, 1993.

Wincławski, Włodzimierz. "Okoliczności powstania i status czasopisma w socjologii polskiej." *Studia Socjologiczne* 200, no. 1 (2011): 11–38.

Władyka, Wiesław. *Na czołówce: prasa w październiku 1956 roku.* Warszawa; Łódź: Państwowe Wydawnictwo Naukowe, 1989.

Bułhak, Władysław. "Dmowski – Rosja a kwestia polska. U źródeł orientacji rosyjskiej obozu narodowego 1886-1908." *Roczniki Humanistyczne* 53, no. 2 (2005): 181–200.

Wojtczak, Leszek, ed. *Bunty i służebności uczonego: Profesor Józef Chałasiński*. Łódź: Wydawnictwo Uniwersytetu Łódzkiego, 1992.

Wolniewicz, Marcin. "On the Process of De-Stalinization of Polish Historiography – Stefan Kieniewicz (1907–92) and the Insurgent Tradition." *Acta Poloniae Historica* 115 (2017): 235–266.

Wolniewicz, Marcin. "W stronę *origines de la Pologne contemporaine* – poszukiwania metodologiczne Stefana Kieniewicza w latach 1946–1948." *KLIO POLSKA. Studia i Materiały z Dziejów Historiografi i Polskiej* 9 (2017): 87–88.

Wołowiec, Grzegorz. "Filologia i nacjonalizm. Stanisław Pigoń jako ideolog kultury ludowo-narodowej." *Teksty drugie* 6 (2017): 107–141.

Wrona, Janusz. "System polityczny w Polsce w latach 1944-1948." *Pamięć i Sprawiedliwość* 8, no. 2 (2005): 51–70.

Yurchak, Alexei. "Soviet Hegemony of Form: Everything Was Forever, Until It Was No More." *Comparative Studies in Society and History* 45, no. 3 (2003): 480–510.

Żabicki, Zbigniew. *"Kuźnica" i jej program literacki*. Warszawa: Wydawnictwo Literackie, 1966.

Zaczkowska, Anna. ",,Ten, który stał się Mostem". Wpływ Lewisa H. Morgana na rosyjską antropologię." *Laboratorium Kultury* 3 (2014): 139–156.

Zagoria, Donald S. *Sino-Soviet Conflict, 1956-1961*. Princeton: Princeton University Press, 1962.

Zamojski, Jan E. "La presse clandestine polonaise en France pendant la Seconde Guerre mondiale." *Acta Poloniae Historica* 56 (1987): 85–126.

Zaremba, Marcin. *Komunizm, legitymizacja, nacjonalizm. Nacjonalistyczna legitymizacja władzy komunistycznej w Polsce*. Warszawa: Trio, 2005.

Zaremba, Marcin. *Wielka trwoga: Polska, 1944-1947: ludowa reakcja na kryzys*. Kraków: Wydawnictwo Znak, 2012.

Zarycki, Tomasz. *The Polish Elite and Language Sciences. A Perspective of Global Historical Sociology*. London: Palgrave Macmillan, 2022.

Zawadzki, Roman, ed. *Księga Sapieżyńska*. Vol. 2. Kraków: Polskie Towarzystwo Teologiczne, 1986.

Żdanow, Andrzej A. *Przemówienie wzgłoszone w dyskusje nad książką G. Aleksandrowa „Historia zachodnoewropejsrkiej filozofii" 24 czerwca 1947 r.* Warszawa: Książka i Wiedza, 1951.

Zhdanov, Andrej A. *Vystuplenie na diskussii po knige G.F. Aleksandrova "Istorija Zapadnoevropejskoj Filosofii" 24 ijulja 1947*. Moskva: Gospolitizdat, 1952.

Ziembiński, Zygmunt. "Prawo rodzinne polski Ludowej po dwudziestu latach." *Ruch Prawniczy, Ekonomiczny i Socjologiczny* 26, no. 4 (1964): 83–92.

Zinovyev, Aleksandr. *Homo sovieticus*. New York: Grove/Atlantic, 1986.

Żółkiewski, Stefan. "Sur l'exemple de l'hebdomadaire 'Kuźnica." *Acta Poloniae Historica* 31 (1975): 187–280.

Żółkiewski, Stefan. *Spór o Mickiewicza*. Wrocław: Zakład Narodowy im. Ossolińskich, 1952.

Żółkiewski, Stefan. *Stare i nowe literaturoznawstwo. Szkice krytyczno-naukowe*. Wrocław: Zakład Narodowy im. Ossolińskich, 1950.

Zolotarev, Oleg V. "Stalinskaja modernizacija i sovetskaja intelligencija." *Intelligencija i mir* 1 (2018): 18–29.

Zwierzchowski, Piotr. "Spór o wychowanie patriotyczne na podstawie "Nowej Szkoły" z lat 1948 -1953." *Biuletyn Studenckich Kół Naukowych* 3 (1995): 207–212.

Zysiak, Agata. "Modernizing Science: Between a Liberal, Social, and Socialistic University – The Case of Poland and the University of Łódź (1945–1953)." *Science in Context* 28, no. 2 (2015): 215–236.

Zysiak, Agata. "People Will Enter the Downtown – The Postwar Ruralization of the Proletarian City. Łódź 1945-1955." *Rural History* 30, no. 1 (2019) 30: 71–86.

Zysiak, Agata. *Punkty za pochodzenie: Powojenna modernizacja i uniwersytet w robotniczym mieście*. Kraków: Nomos, 2016.

Index

20th Congress of the Communist Party of the Soviet Union 197, 199, 200, 204, 209, 212, 221, 226

Ajdukiewicz, Kazimierz 156, 157, 161, 166, 175, 179–181, 185, 189, 194, 196, 224, 225
Akhmatova, Anna 56, 76, 90
Aleksandrov, Georgy 176, 182, 185, 193, 237, 251
Annas, Julia 14, 237
Apor, Balázs 10, 237
Aquinas, Thomas 184
Aragon, Louis 42
Aristotle 5, 6, 13, 121, 237
Arnold, Stanisław 111, 171, 192
Assorodobraj-Kula, Nina 44, 111, 191

Baczko, Bronisław 177–179, 182, 185, 186, 194
Bakunin, Mikhail 139
Bauman, Maurycy 168
Bauman, Zygmunt 11, 39, 168, 215, 220, 225, 226, 230, 233, 250
Benda, Julien 150, 164, 237
Benedict, Ruth 159
Berman, Jakub 42, 46, 164
Bierut, Bolesław 17, 153, 154, 165, 193, 200
Blok, Alexander 66
Bobińska, Celina 68, 89, 109, 170, 192
Bohomolec, Franciszek 100, 110
Borejsza, Jerzy 11, 22–25, 28, 30, 33, 36, 38, 41, 42, 44, 47, 49–52, 56, 63, 70, 71, 74, 76, 87, 90, 93, 108, 118, 131–133, 148–151, 153, 154, 164, 165, 240, 243
Borejsza, Jerzy W. xiii, 41, 44, 47, 236
Bourdieu, Pierre 12
Braun, Jerzy 127, 138, 238

Brentano, Franz 181
Broniewski, Władysław 66
Brystiger, Julia 36
Brzozowski, Stanisław 109, 112

Carnap, Rudolf 180
Catholicism 4, 9, 11, 33, 35, 37, 47, 62, 78, 81, 83, 84, 86, 87, 91, 92, 114, 126–131, 135, 138, 165, 185, 233, 243
Chałasiński, Józef 31, 32, 44, 45, 48, 67, 95–99, 101–103, 106, 107, 109–113, 118, 119, 136–138, 150, 152, 153, 156, 158–160, 165, 166, 171, 174, 175, 185, 187, 188, 191, 193, 195, 209–212, 217, 224–226, 238, 242, 244, 246, 251
Chałubiński, Mirosław 137, 238
Chekhov, Anton 182
Chopin, Frédéric 155
Choromański, Zygmunt 45
Churchill, Winston 17
Chwedeńczuk, Bohdan 141, 162, 238
Concordia 143, 154, 155, 158, 162, 163, 172, 175, 190, 231
Connelly, John xiii, 10, 11, 14, 167, 192, 193, 238, 239
Copernicus, Nicolaus 155
Cosmopolitanism 92, 175, 176
Courbet, Gustav 72
criticism and self-criticism (kritika and samokritika) 104, 142, 143, 153, 159, 162, 163, 171, 174–176, 179, 181, 185, 193, 194, 203
Crooked Circle Club 202, 203, 222, 242
Cult of personality 197, 200, 203, 208, 212–214
Cyrankiewicz, Józef 155
Czajkowski, Jacek 45, 239

254 *Index*

Czapski, Józef 89
Czarnowski, Stefan 44, 87, 101, 111, 153, 239
Czochralski, Jan 42

d'Arc, Jeanne 84
Daniélou, Jean 79, 91
Danton, Georges J. 70
Daston, Lorraine 5, 13–15, 239
Datner, Szymon 9, 235
Daumier, Honoré 72
Davies, Norman 38, 39, 239
Desanti, Dominique 151, 165, 239
Desmoulins, Camille 70
Diderot, Denis 72
Dilthey, Wilhelm 44
Dmowski, Roman 35, 69, 146–148, 164, 250
Duhem, Pierre 190
Dühring, Eugen 122, 138, 240
Duller, Matthias 11, 240
Durkheim, Émile 44, 115, 120
Dziś i Jutro (journal) 36, 47, 68, 83, 91, 139, 140, 236

Einstein, Albert 123, 149, 150
Eliots, Thomas S. 151
Engels, Friedrich 23, 59, 75, 119, 120–124, 128, 129, 137, 138, 147, 174, 212, 240, 244
Enlightenment 24, 29, 30, 33, 35, 43, 70, 72, 84, 100, 110, 127, 131, 155, 205, 229, 230
Erenburg, Ilja 148, 164
Erman, Lev 108, 240
Esprit (journal) 47, 78, 79, 83–86, 92, 245

Fadeyev, Alexander 151
Feuerbach, Ludwig 128
Fiedler, Franciszek 146–148, 163, 164
First Congress of Polish Science 155, 161, 168, 179
Flaubert, Gustave 72
Fleck, Christian xiii, 11, 240
Fleck, Ludwik 13, 196, 240
Foucault, Michel 14, 15, 240
French Revolution 24, 71
Fréville, Jean (Jacques Freville/ Eugène Schkaff) 75, 76, 89, 90
Fromm, Erich 233

Galilei, Galileo 121
Galison, Peter 5, 13, 15, 239
Garaudy, Roger 75, 89, 90, 240

Gawor, Krzysztof R. 140
Gentle revolution 8, 9, 17, 22, 24–26, 32, 38, 50, 53–56, 59, 62, 63, 65, 70–72, 74–78, 84–87, 90, 93, 102, 105, 107, 108, 114, 115, 125, 127, 131–135, 143, 144, 146, 148–151, 153, 154, 161, 203, 208, 211, 227–230
Giedroyc, Jerzy 72, 88, 89, 226
Gomułka, Władysław 47, 145, 153, 165, 193, 197, 198, 200, 201, 218, 220–223, 250
Gorky, Maxim 67, 75, 148, 149, 162, 164, 247
Górny, Maciej xiv, 12, 13, 42, 89, 167, 192, 241
Grekov, Boris 170
Griboyedov, Alexander 164

Habermas, Jürgen 15, 241
Haldane, John S. 16, 249
Hartwig, Julia 85, 92
Harvey, William H. 121
Hegel, Georg W. F. 128, 176
Herman, Paul 5, 13, 14, 246
Hertz, Paweł 78, 84, 90, 92
Hervé, Pierre 76, 90
Hessen, Sergei 27, 43, 249
Himmler, Heinrich 1
Hippocrates 121
Hirszfeld, Ludwik 42
Hirszowicz, Maria 10, 215, 225, 241
Historical Epistemology 5, 6, 13, 14, 239, 240
Hobbes, Thomas 183
Hochfeld, Julian 121–124, 137, 138, 157, 158, 191, 193, 238
Holland, Henryk 181, 182, 188, 194, 195, 241
Homer 29
Hübner, Piotr 11, 12, 162, 166, 167, 192, 241

Ingarden, Roman 181
Inglot, Mieczysław 44
Institute of the Formation of Academic Cadres (Instytut Kształcenia Kadr Naukowych) 172, 177, 183, 189, 193, 194, 214, 238
Intelligentsia 9, 29, 34, 93–113, 115, 118, 153, 163, 174, 178–180, 211, 242, 244, 250
Iwaszkiewicz, Jarosław 73, 74, 85, 89, 92, 247

Index 255

Jabłoński, Henryk 111
Jasienica, Paweł 61, 68
Jastrun, Mieczysław 28, 29, 43, 44
Jedlicz, Marian 133, 139
Jordan, Zbigniew 42, 111

Kaczyński, Zygmunt 33–35, 45, 61, 62, 69, 83, 86, 127, 133, 151, 152, 248
Kelles-Krauz, Kazimierz 120, 137, 248
Kersten, Krystyna 10, 39, 64, 242
Kętrzyński, Wojciech 83, 132, 139
Khrushchev, Nikita 108, 163, 196, 200, 201, 220–222, 250
Kieniewicz, Stefan 13, 99, 100, 101, 103, 110–112, 192, 246, 251
Kisielewski, Stefan 46, 45, 110
Kleeberg, Bernhard xiv, 14, 15, 238, 242
Kochanowski, Jan 29, 30, 98, 101, 103
Kołakowski, Leszek 43, 181, 189, 190, 194, 196, 206, 216–218, 220, 223, 224, 226, 227, 230, 233, 238, 242, 245, 247, 249
Kołłątaj, Hugo 29, 41, 43, 100, 110
Konarski, Stanisław 29, 43
Kormanowa, Żanna 170, 192
Korniłowicz, Władysław 91
Korniychuk, Oleksandr 18
Kosiewski, Piotr 233, 249
Kosminski, Evgenii 170, 171, 192
Kotarbiński, Tadeusz 26, 42, 58, 67, 87, 115, 150, 156, 159, 172, 175, 177, 185, 194–196, 208, 224, 243
Kott, Jan 28, 29, 43, 44, 74, 84, 89, 92, 166, 169, 191, 201, 202, 222, 243
Krasicki, Ignacy 100, 110
Krassowska-Jodłowska, Eugenia 167
Krasucki, Eryk xiv, 11, 41, 42, 47, 164, 165, 243
Kroński, Tadeusz 183, 184, 185, 195
Kruszewski, Zbigniew 43
Krzywicki, Ludwik 118, 138, 158
Kuciński, Julian 43, 243
Kuhn, Thomas 13, 243
Kula, Marcin 222, 243
Kula, Witold 87, 89, 116, 117, 136, 170, 192, 208, 224, 235
Kultura (Kultura Paryska, journal) xii, 72, 88, 89, 111, 208, 224, 226, 236, 245
Kutrzeba, Stanisław 60, 61, 68
Kuźnica (journal) 11, 28, 29, 30, 41, 43–45, 55, 56, 58, 65–68, 73, 85, 87–90, 92, 95, 109–111, 112, 114, 115, 120, 134, 136, 139, 150

Lange, Oskar 118
Le Roy, Édouard 189
Lebedev, Viktor 153, 165
Lelewel, Joachim 24
Lenin, Vladimir 62, 65, 75, 76, 88, 89, 90, 94, 98, 99, 108, 110, 119, 120, 129, 134, 137, 139, 147, 148, 163, 164, 172, 174–176, 178, 183, 192, 194, 195, 201, 211–213, 240, 244, 245
Leszczycki, Stanisław 158
Leszczyński, Kazimierz 9, 235
Litwin, Aleksander 98, 99, 101–103, 110
Łódź (city) 11, 12, 26–29, 31, 32, 35, 41–45, 74, 82, 89, 95, 97, 106, 109, 112, 114, 115, 118, 156, 160, 166, 171, 172, 187, 191, 192, 210, 222, 240, 241, 243, 245, 249–252
Lomonosov, Mikhail 183
Lossky, Nikolay 66, 244
Lukács, Georg 150, 164, 249
Lvov-Warsaw School 26, 42, 87, 175, 177, 179–183, 185, 186, 188, 189, 196, 238, 244
Lysenko, Trofim 166, 193, 242

MacIntyre, Alasdair C. 13, 15, 241, 244
Mandelstam, Nadezhda, 66, 244
Mandelstam, Osip 56, 244
Mann, Heinrich 149
Mannheim, Karl 13, 32, 118, 137, 237, 244
Manteuffel, Tadeusz 48, 63, 170, 192, 235
Mańkowski, Tadeusz 41, 244
Marat, Jean P. 70
Maritain, Jacques 79, 91, 139, 245
Marr, Nikolai 59, 68, 162, 237
Marx, Karl 23, 75, 79, 80, 116, 117, 119–123, 128, 129, 134, 135, 137, 139, 172, 174, 192, 211, 212, 244, 248
Marxism 4, 5, 8, 9, 11, 13, 23, 26–29, 31, 39, 43–45, 57, 59, 60, 66–68, 75–86, 88, 89, 91, 92, 94, 97–99, 102, 103, 107, 108, 110, 111, 114–139, 141–143, 147, 150, 152–160, 162, 163, 165–183, 185–187, 189, 190, 192, 195, 196, 204–206, 209, 211, 214–219, 225–230, 233, 241, 242, 245, 248
Masaryk, Tomáš 120, 137, 245
Maublanc, René 89
Maupassant, Guy de 72
Meyerson, Emil 136, 237
Micewski, Andrzej 126, 138, 222, 245
Michelet, Jules 77, 90, 245
Mickiewicz, Adam 23, 29, 30, 54, 55, 65

Mikołajczyk, Stanisław 20, 21, 33, 34, 40
Mikucki, Jerzy 43, 245
Miłosz, Czesław 22, 53, 65, 245
Mitzner, Zbigniew 88
Modzelewski, Karol 39, 245
Molotov, Vycheslav 17, 144, 147, 150, 161, 173, 200
Morgan, Lewis H. (Lewisa H. Morgana) 120, 124, 137, 244, 248, 251
Morris, Charles W. 180
Mounier, Emmanuel 79–86, 90–92, 245
Müller, Otto W. 111
Mussolini, Benito 36
Myśl Filozoficzna (journal) 173, 174, 193–196, 224, 226, 236
Myśl Współczesna (journal) 43, 112, 119, 136–138, 167, 236

Nałkowska, Zofia 28
Napoleon Bonaparte 123
Norwid, Cyprian 29, 30, 44
Nowa Kultura (journal) 154, 203–207, 216–218, 223–226, 236
Nowe Drogi (journal) 75, 85, 89, 92, 135, 146, 147, 163–166, 191, 194, 225, 236

October Revolution 52, 59–62, 66, 68, 75, 77, 147, 148, 164
Odrodzenie (journal) 11, 24, 28, 29, 41, 44, 55, 56, 65–67, 70, 73, 87, 92, 108, 118, 131, 137, 139, 154, 236, 237, 249
Ossowska, Maria 27, 48, 63, 112, 191, 246
Ossowski, Stanisław 23, 27, 41, 44, 45, 48, 49, 63, 87, 114, 119–124, 127, 136–138, 150, 158, 161, 191, 246

Pasternak, Boris 55, 66, 164, 240
Pavlov, Ivan 166
PAX 36, 37, 46, 47, 68, 91, 138, 152, 222, 245–247
Personalism 78–82, 86, 90, 91, 202, 244
Pettit, Philip 234, 246
Piasecki, Bolesław 35–38, 42, 46, 47, 60, 61, 68, 69, 81–83, 85, 86, 91, 92, 126, 132, 138, 152, 165, 202, 222, 233, 240, 242, 243, 246, 249
Picasso, Pablo 78, 151
Pierre-Quint, Léon 76, 90
Pigoń, Stanisław 170, 192, 251
Piłsudski, Józef 26, 28, 42, 51, 52, 64, 72, 110, 146, 148, 152, 164, 178, 212, 211, 217

Pius XI 45, 79
Piwowarczyk, Jan 34, 35, 45, 46, 62, 69, 128–131, 139
Plekhanov, Georgi 120, 124, 137
Po Prostu (journal) 47, 204, 205, 218, 222–224, 226, 236, 250
Poincaré, Henri 136, 189
Polish Academy of Sciences xii, 48, 63, 71, 88, 109, 154, 169, 170, 172, 191, 192, 196, 209, 210
Polish Sociological Institute 31, 32, 49, 70, 168, 210
Political Epistemology 6, 14
Pomian, Krzysztof xiii, 224–226, 230, 234, 236, 247
Poniatowski, Stanisław August 24, 98, 110
Popper, Karl 32, 45, 136, 226, 241, 247
Porshnev, Mikhail 162
Progressiveness 8, 9, 22, 23, 25, 27–30, 32, 34, 35, 37, 38, 43, 54–56, 58, 60, 63, 71, 74, 76, 78, 79, 84–87, 95–99, 101–105, 108, 114, 115, 120, 124, 125, 127, 129, 133, 135, 136, 172, 178, 208, 219, 220, 227–229, 231
Przegląd Filozoficzny (journal) 65, 173, 194, 236
Przegląd Socjologiczny (journal) 31, 32, 44, 45, 65, 110, 137, 152, 153, 165, 210, 224, 225, 236
Putrament, Jerzy 23, 198

quotology (cytatologia) 171, 192

Ranke, Leopold von 111
Robespierre, Maximilien 70
Russell, Bertrand 180

Sapieha, Adam 34, 45, 82, 239
Sartre, Jean-Paul 91, 151
Schaff, Adam 43, 59, 60, 67, 68, 89, 92, 117–119, 122–126, 128, 130, 131, 133, 136–139, 141, 160, 162, 166, 171–182, 186–194, 196, 206, 208, 210–216, 218, 219, 224, 225, 230, 233, 234, 243, 244, 247, 248
Schipachev, Stepan 66
Schlick, Moritz 180
Serov, Ivan A. 36, 163, 248
Shakespeare, William 164
Shaw, William H. 137, 248
Shore, Marci 11, 39, 43, 66, 88, 136, 165, 248
Siekierska, Jadwiga 95, 109

Sienkiewicz, Henryk 97, 109, 110, 248
Sikorski, Tomasz 165, 248
Simmel, Georg 44
Skłodowska-Curie, Maria 155
Słonimski, Antoni 22
Słowacki, Juliusz 29, 30
Snyder, Timothy 10, 38, 137, 248
Sokorski, Włodzimierz 94, 105, 106, 109, 112, 214
Sologub, Fyodor 66
Solovyov, Vladimir 66
Sovinformburo 55, 148
Spengler, Oswald 80
Spinoza, Baruch 183, 184
Stalin, Iosif 2, 7–13, 15–22, 25, 29, 37, 39–43, 46, 49, 50, 52–57, 59, 62, 64–68, 71, 76, 77, 87, 89, 90, 94, 108, 114, 123, 134, 138, 139, 141–145, 147, 148, 152–156, 160–165, 167–177, 182, 188, 190–194, 197–203, 205–221, 223–226, 229, 230, 234, 235, 237, 239–243, 245–251
Staszic, Stanisław 29, 43, 100, 110
Stern, Lina 231, 234, 250
Stobiecki, Rafał 12, 166, 192, 249
Stola, Dariusz 233, 249
Stomma, Stanisław 35, 46, 79, 80, 91, 133
Strachnik, Paweł 45
Struve, Peter 112
Studentowicz, Kazimierz 34, 45, 151
Szacki, Jerzy 227, 233, 249
Szczepański, Jan 45, 109, 249
Szklarska Poręba (town) 144, 147, 150, 151, 173
Szumski, Jan 13, 249
Szwagrzyk, Krzysztof 46, 163, 249
Szymanowski, Zygmunt 104, 105, 112
Śliwowska, Wiktoria 48, 63, 236, 248
Śliwowski, René 63, 248

Tatarkiewicz, Władysław 175, 181–185, 194–196, 249
Thomas, William I. 44
Tito, Josip B. 145
Tolstoy, Leo 55, 148
Torańska, Teresa 46, 250
Turowicz, Jerzy 35, 46, 79, 80, 83, 86, 91, 243
Tuwim, Julian 47, 65
Twardowski, Kazimierz 181, 182, 186, 188, 194–196, 241, 250

Tygodnik Powszechny (journal) 34, 35, 45, 46, 60, 68, 69, 83, 99, 110, 139, 222, 236
Tygodnik Warszawski (journal) 33, 45, 60, 69, 83, 111, 138, 139, 236, 238
Tynyanov, Yury 57, 148
Tyutchev, Fyodor 66

University of Łódź 12, 26, 27, 42, 43, 95, 97, 112, 115, 156, 172, 191, 210, 252

Vieweger, Teodore 26
Vinogradov, Sergej N. 57, 58, 67, 250
Voltaire 72

Wagner, Izabela 11, 39, 163, 191, 233, 250
Walicki, Andrzej 53, 65
Wasilewska, Wanda 18, 19, 22, 23, 29, 39, 250
Weber, Max 44, 250
Wells, Herbert G. 94, 109
Werfel, Roman 52, 64, 164, 223
Wierzbicki, Andrzej 41, 250
World Congress of Intellectuals in Defense of Peace (The Wrocław Congress) 149–151
Wyka, Kazimierz 85, 86, 92, 131, 132, 139, 169, 191

Yurchak, Alexei 234, 251

Żabicki, Zbigniew 11, 43, 251
Zaczkowska, Anna 137, 251
Zahorska, Marta 111
Zaremba, Marcin 39, 42, 64, 112, 251
Zarycki, Tomasz 12, 251
Zawodziński, Karol W. 98, 101, 103, 110
Żeromski, Stefan 25, 41, 46, 97, 101, 110
Zhdanov, Andrei 76, 90, 138, 144, 145, 147, 150, 161, 163, 173, 176, 182, 185, 193, 238, 243, 251
Zinovyev, Aleksandr 234, 251
Żółkiewski, Stefan 11, 28–30, 44, 56–58, 67, 115–117, 122, 136, 153, 165, 166, 169, 170, 191, 192, 201, 203, 204, 223, 238, 251
Znaniecki, Florian 31, 32, 44, 102, 118, 152, 174, 193, 210, 225, 241
Zysiak, Agata 12, 42, 43, 112, 113, 166, 246, 252